EXPERIENCING
the HEART *of*
JESUS

KNOWING HIS HEART,
FEELING HIS LOVE

MAX LUCADO

THOMAS NELSON
Since 1798

NASHVILLE DALLAS MEXICO CITY RIO DE JANEIRO BEIJING

Published by Thomas Nelson, Inc., P.O. Box 141000, Nashville, Tennessee, 37214.

Library of Congress Cataloging-in-Publication Data is available.

ISBN 0-7852-4991-5

27 - 14 13 12 11

EXPERIENCING
the HEART *of*
JESUS

Contents

INTRODUCTION

When I was young we used to take our family vacations in Colorado. We'd drive from Texas to Colorado every summer. It was what my Dad loved to do. It's a long drive though. We'd drive through west Texas and up through New Mexico, and then into eastern Colorado. The land along that whole route is relatively flat, but then about fifty miles east of Denver, you begin spotting the Rocky Mountains. They just dominate the whole landscape.

You know, we could have stopped right there, fifty miles from the Rockies and said, "Well, we've finished our vacation. We've seen the Rockies." We could have turned around and gone back home. Then when people would say, "Where'd you go on your vacation?" we could say, "Well, we went to the Rockies."

Max's Insights — **Nobody can tell us the story of Jesus like Max Lucado. So in order to explore the character of Jesus, insights have been drawn from several of Max's books. Each week, you will focus in on just one facet of Jesus' life, and you will find yourself experiencing his heart.**

LESSON 1

Experiencing the Care of Jesus

*W*hen I see a flock of sheep I see exactly that, a flock. A rabble of wool. A herd of hooves. I don't see a sheep. I see sheep. All alike. None different. That's what I see.

But not so with the shepherd. To him every sheep is different. Every face is special. Every face has a story. And every sheep has a name. The one with the sad eyes, that's Droopy. And the fellow with one ear up and the other down, I call him Oscar. And the small one with the black patch on his leg, he's an orphan with no brothers. I call him Joseph.

---

3. No one is good. No one is strong. No one is secure. Why are we incapable of consistently caring for ourselves?

_____

4. Which of the following statements are true, and which ones are false? Mark your answers True (T) or False (F). Use the Bible verses below to help you answer.

____ Jesus expects us to rely on ourselves. (Matthew 11:28)
____ Jesus expects us to rely on him through his Spirit. (Acts 2:38)
____ Jesus saved us, but it's up to us from here on out. (Galatians 3:3)
____ Jesus is too busy to care for our petty concerns. (Philippians 4:19)

Leading Questions — **Like a shepherd leading his flock, Max uses a series of questions to lead you through this workbook. Drawing deeply on the Bible's teaching, you will uncover exciting truths about your Savior.**

Scripture Quotations — **Many texts have been provided from the Scriptures to aid in your research. These passages represent a wide range of translations, allowing you to glean from the various versions of the Bible that are available.**

It's one thing to give intellectual assent to the idea of Jesus' care. It's quite another to rest in his promise, fully dependent on his provision. The Bible is full of God's promises—yet all of them point to the one promise of Jesus Christ. Through him, God kept his promise to care for us. "The yes to all of God's promises is in Christ, and through Christ we say yes to the glory of God"—2 Corinthians 1:20

GOD'S FAVORITE WORD

God is an inviting God. He invited Mary to birth his Son, the disciples to fish for men, the adulteress woman to start over, and Thomas to touch his wounds. God is the King who prepares the palace, sets the table, and invites his subjects to come in.

In fact, it seems his favorite word is *come.*

"*Come*, let us talk about these things. Though your sins are like scarlet, they can be as white as snow."

"All you who are thirsty, *come* and drink."

"*Come* to me all, all of you who are tired and have heavy loads, and I will give you rest."

God is a God who invites. God is a God who calls.

—*And the Angels Were Silent*

Quotations from Max's Books — **Max Lucado has put to words the richness of Jesus' life in several different books over the years. Many pages throughout *Experiencing the Heart of Jesus* carry selections from these works, giving us further glimpses into Jesus and the gospels.**

Well, yeah. I guess you could say we saw the Rockies. But who would do that? Who wants to view the Rockies from a distance?

We want to get into the Rocky Mountains. We want to smell the mountain air. We want to smell the evergreen and the pine trees. We want to hear the running brook and put a hand into the ice-cold water. We want to hook a speckled trout. That's the difference between seeing the Rockies, and experiencing the Rockies.

This workbook is intended to take you from the flatlands—from seeing Christ at a distance—to the experience of being surrounded by Christ. We can experience his encouragement, his love, his friendship, his presence. *Experiencing the Heart of Jesus* is dramatic, powerful, and life-changing.

Summary Statements – **Throughout each day's lesson, summary statements are drawn from the content and listed in the side columns. These allow you to focus in on the main idea of the lesson.**

> If you're not sure what to do, allow God to take the lead.

EXPERIENCING THE CARE OF JESUS THIS WEEK

Before you read any further, spend some time in prayer now.

Dear Father, my heart is filled with anticipation for the week ahead. I want to feel the gentle touch of Jesus. I want to understand his concern for me. I want to know that he will catch me if I stumble. I want him to sooth my aching heart. I am ready, Father. Let me experience the care of Jesus. Amen.

This week, memorize this reminder that God cares for you:

"The person who loves God is the one God knows and cares for." —*1 Corinthians 8:3 NLT*

Weekly Memory Verses – **Our lives are changed when we encounter Jesus, and our hearts are changed by what is kept there. Max gives us the opportunity to plant a portion of God's Word in our heart. Each week's lesson is accompanied by a Scripture verse to review, ponder, meditate upon, and commit to memory.**

The Heart of the Matter – **Each day's lesson closes with a summary of the main points in the study. These serve as reminders to the key points of Max's teaching, and a review at the close of your quiet time.**

THE HEART OF THE MATTER

- ❦ If you're not sure what to do, allow God to take the lead.
- ❦ God will fight for us. We just need to trust.
- ❦ God's power is very great for those who believe.

The Heart of Jesus – **Nobody experienced the fullness of our Savior like the men and women whose lives were touched by his in the gospels. In the section called "The Heart of Jesus," Max gives us a totally fresh, new glimpse into the lives of people who were touched by Jesus.**

The Heart of Jesus

Jesus was a teller of parables on this earth, and his stories reached into the very hearts of his listeners. Can you find yourself in the parable of the lost sheep? Are you one of the ninety-nine, safe in the fold of faith? Or are you the wanderer, the stray, the outsider?

This one lonely straggler, stumbling in the darkness with jumbled emotions and mounting fears. With wistful eyes and tearstained cheeks, you walk aimlessly. Uncertain of your path, you wish for the shepherd's guiding staff.

> *You gave me life and showed me kindness, and in your care you watched over my life.*
> —Job 10:12

Corner Verses – **Every page in this study has a Scripture quotation in the bottom corner. These passages are the key verses on each chapter's character quality. So when you are studying the grace of Jesus, these verses provide you with a biblical theology of grace.**

LESSON 1

Experiencing the Care of Jesus

When I see a flock of sheep I see exactly that, a flock. A rabble of wool. A herd of hooves. I don't see a sheep. I see sheep. All alike. None different. That's what I see.

But not so with the shepherd. To him every sheep is different. Every face is special. Every face has a story. And every sheep has a name. The one with the sad eyes, that's Droopy. And the fellow with one ear up and the other down, I call him Oscar. And the small one with the black patch on his leg, he's an orphan with no brothers. I call him Joseph.

The shepherd knows his sheep. He calls them by name.

When we see a crowd, we see exactly that, a crowd. Filling a stadium or flooding a mall. When we see a crowd, we see people, not persons, but people. A herd of humans. A flock of faces. That's what we see.

But not so with the Shepherd. To him every face is different. Every face is a story. Every face is a child. Every child has a name. The one with the sad eyes, that's Sally. The old fellow with one eyebrow up and the other down, Harry's his name. And the young one with the limp? He's an orphan with no brothers. I call him Joey.

The Shepherd knows his sheep. He knows each one by name. The Shepherd knows you. He knows your name. And he will never forget it. "I have written your name on my hand" (Isaiah 49:16).

Quite a thought, isn't it? Your name on God's hand. Your name on God's lips. Maybe you've seen your name in some special places. On an award or diploma or walnut door. Or maybe you've heard your name from some important people—a coach, a celebrity, a teacher. But to think that your name is on God's hand and on God's lips . . . my, could it be?

Or perhaps you've never seen your name honored. And you can't remember when you heard it spoken with kindness. If so, it may be more difficult for you to believe that God knows your name.

But he does. Written on his hand. Spoken by his mouth. Whispered by his lips. Your name. And not only the name you now have, but the name he has in store for you. A new name he will give you . . . but wait, I'm getting ahead of myself. I'll tell you about your new name in the last lesson that we'll share this week. This is just the introduction.

You've been on my mind as I've been writing. I've thought of you often. I honestly have. Over the years I've gotten to know some of you folks well. I've read your letters, shaken your hands, and watched your eyes. I think I know you.

You're busy. Time passes before your tasks are finished. And if you get a chance to read, it's a slim chance indeed.

You're anxious. Bad news outpaces the good. Problems outnumber solutions. And you are concerned. What future do your children have on this earth? What future do you have?

You're cautious. You don't trust as easily as you once did.

Politicians lied. The system failed. The minister compromised. Your spouse cheated. It's not easy to trust. It's not that you don't want to. It's just that you want to be careful.

There is one other thing. You've made some mistakes. I met one of you at a bookstore in Michigan. A businessman, you seldom came out of your office at all and never to meet an author. But then you did. You were regretting the many hours at work and the few hours at home and wanted to talk.

And the single mom in Chicago. One kid was tugging, the other crying, but juggling them both, you made your point. "I made mistakes," you explained, "but I really want to try again."

And there was that night in Fresno. The musician sang and I spoke and you came. You almost didn't. You almost stayed home. Just that day you'd found the note from your wife. She was leaving you. But you came anyway. Hoping I'd have something for the pain. Hoping I'd have an answer. Where is God at a time like this?

And so as I wrote, I thought about you. All of you. You aren't malicious. You aren't evil. You aren't hard-hearted (hardheaded occasionally, but not hard-hearted). You really want to do what is right. But sometimes life turns south. Occasionally you need a reminder.

Not a sermon.

A reminder.

A reminder that God knows your name.

EXPERIENCING THE CARE OF JESUS THIS WEEK

Before you read any further, spend some time in prayer now.

Dear Father, my heart is filled with anticipation for the week ahead. I want to feel the gentle touch of Jesus. I want to understand his concern for me. I want to know that he will catch me if I stumble. I want him to sooth my aching heart. I am ready, Father. Let me experience the care of Jesus. Amen.

This week, memorize this reminder that God cares for you:

"The person who loves God is the one God knows and cares for." —*1 Corinthians 8:3 NLT*

DAY ONE—THE GOD YOU CAN TRUST

TRIALS BRING DOUBTS

Here is a big question. What is God doing when you are in a bind? When the lifeboat springs a leak? When the ripcord snaps? When the last penny is gone before the last bill is paid? When the last hope left on the last train? What is God doing?

I know what we are doing. Nibbling on nails like corn on the cob. Pacing floors. Taking pills. I know what we do.

But what does God do? Big question. Real big. If God is sleeping, I'm duck soup. If he is laughing, I'm lost. If he is crossing his arms and shaking his head, then saw off the limb, Honey, it's time to crash.

What is God doing?

1. Does God even care? Whether we verbalize that question or not, it's something we wonder. When everything seems to be falling apart around us, we can be sure we are not the first to wonder—does God care? Read the following passages below and identify Paul's experiences.

   2 Corinthians 1:8 – "Brothers and sisters, we want you to know about the trouble we suffered in Asia. We had great burdens there that were beyond our own strength. We even gave up hope of living."

   _____

   _____

2 Corinthians 4:8–9 – "We have troubles all around us, but we are not defeated. We do not know what to do, but we do not give up the hope of living. We are persecuted, but God does not leave us. We are hurt sometimes, but we are not destroyed."

_____

_____

2 Corinthians 6:4–5 – "But in every way we show we are servants of God: in accepting many hard things, in troubles, in difficulties, and in great problems. We are beaten and thrown into prison. We meet those who become upset with us and start riots. We work hard, and sometimes we get no sleep or food."

_____

_____

2 Corinthians 12:10 – "For this reason I am happy when I have weaknesses, insults, hard times, sufferings, and all kinds of troubles for Christ. Because when I am weak, then I am truly strong."

_____

_____

DOES GOD CARE?

Well, I decided to research that question. Being the astute researcher that I am, I discovered some ancient writings that may answer this question. Few people are aware—in fact, no one is aware—that newspaper journalists roamed the lands of the Old Testament era.

Yes, it is true that in the days of Noah, Abraham, and Moses, reporters were fast on the scene recording the drama of their days. And now, for the first time, their articles are to be shared.

How did I come upon them? one might ask.

Well, I discovered them pressed between the pages of an in-flight magazine on a red-eye flight out of Sheboygan, Wisconsin. I can only surmise that a courageous archaeologist had hidden them to protect himself from imminent danger of evil spies. We'll never know if he survived. But we do know what he discovered—ancient newspaper interviews with Moses.

So with a salute to his courage and a hunger for the truth, I proudly share with you heretofore undiscovered conversations with a man who can answer the question: What does God do when we are in a bind?

This interview is between the Holy Land Press (HLP) and Moses.
HLP: Tell us about your conflict with the Egyptians.
MOSES: Oh, the Egyptians—big people. Strong fighters. Mean as snakes.
HLP: But you got away.
MOSES: Not before they got washed away.
HLP: You're talking about the Red Sea conflict.
MOSES: You're right. That was scary.
HLP: Tell us what happened.
MOSES: Well, the Red Sea was on one side, and the Egyptians were on the other.
HLP: So you attacked?
MOSES: Are you kidding? With a half-million rock stackers? No, my people were too afraid. They wanted to go back to Egypt.
HLP: So you told everyone to retreat?
MOSES: Where? Into the water? We didn't have a boat. We didn't have anywhere to go.
HLP: What did your leaders recommend?
MOSES: I didn't ask them. There wasn't time.
HLP: Then what did you do?

I sing to the Lord because he has taken care of me.
—Psalm 13:6

MOSES: I told the people to stand still.

HLP: You mean, with the enemy coming, you told them not to move?

MOSES: Yep. I told the people, "Stand still and you will see the Lord save you."

HLP: Why would you want the people to stand still?

MOSES: To get out of God's way. If you don't know what to do, it's best just to sit tight till he does his thing.

2. What do you think of Moses' strategy: "If you don't know what to do, it's best just to sit tight till he does his thing"?

_____

_____

GOD'S CONCERN IN MOTION

HLP: That's odd strategy, don't you think?

MOSES: It is if you are big enough for the battle. But when the battle is bigger than you are and you want God to take over, it's all you can do.

HLP: Can we talk about something else?

MOSES: It's your paper.

HLP: Soon after your escape . . .

MOSES: Our deliverance.

HLP: What's the difference?

MOSES: There is a big difference. When you escape, you do it. When you are delivered, someone else does it and you just follow.

3. Though it is best to get out of God's way when you are overwhelmed by your circumstances, it isn't always easy to take a seat on the sidelines. Which of the following statements do you find to be true in your life? Check your response(s).

❏ Letting God take over is easier said than done.

❏ There are many battles in life bigger than we are.

❏ My first reaction is to try to fix my troubles on my own.

❏ We must want God to take over and willingly surrender our control to him.

❏ Trying to handle things myself often makes the situation worse.

❏ God's offer of deliverance gives me a sense of relief and gratitude.

4. Which of the following statements are true concerning God's deliverance, and which ones are false? Mark your answers True (T) or False (F). Use the Bible verses below to help you answer.

___ God shows his love for us by delivering us through trials (Psalm 109:21)

___ Putting our trust in ourselves or others is often a good strategy (Psalm 146:3)

___ Some trials are too difficult for God to handle (Luke 1:37)

___ God will help us only if we first help ourselves (2 Corinthians 1:9–10)

ENTRUSTING OURSELVES TO HIS CARE

So, what do you think? What does God do when we are in a bind? That question can be answered with one word: fight. He fights for us. He steps into the ring and points us to our corner and takes over. "You need only to remain calm; the Lord will fight for you" (Ex. 14:14).

His job is to fight. Our job is to trust.

Just trust. Not direct. Or question. Or yank the steering wheel out of his hands. Our job is to pray and wait. Nothing more is necessary. Nothing more is needed.

"He is my defender; I will not be defeated" (Ps. 62:6).

If you're not sure what to do, allow God to take the lead.

But you, Lord God, be kind to me so others will know you are good. Because your love is good, save me.

—Psalm 109:21

God will fight for us. We just need to trust.

He takes care of his people like a shepherd. He gathers them like lambs in his arms and carries them close to him. He gently leads the mothers of the lambs.

—Isaiah 40:11

THE COMPASSIONATE CHRIST

When Jesus lands on the shore of Bethsaida, he leaves the Sea of Galilee and steps into a sea of humanity. Keep in mind, he has crossed the sea to get away from the crowds. He needs to grieve. He longs to relax with his followers. He needs anything but another crowd of thousands to teach and heal.

But his love for people overcomes his need for rest. . . .

Many of those he healed would never say "thank you," but he healed them anyway. Most would be more concerned with being healthy than being holy, but he healed them anyway. Some of those who asked for bread today would cry for his blood a few months later, but he healed them anyway . . . He had compassion on them.

—In the Eye of the Storm

5. There is no comparison when we consider our own abilities versus God's resources. Read the following verses and write down what you learn about God's power.

Exodus 15:11 – "Are there any gods like you, Lord? There are no gods like you. You are wonderfully holy, amazingly powerful, a worker of miracles."

_____

_____

1 Chronicles 29:12 – "Riches and honor come from you. You rule everything. You have the power and strength to make anyone great and strong."

_____

_____

Jeremiah 10:6 – "Lord, there is no one like you. You are great, and your name is great and powerful."

_____

_____

Jeremiah 27:5 – "I made the earth, its people, and all its animals with my great power and strength. I can give the earth to anyone I want."

_____

_____

2 Corinthians 13:4 – "It is true that he was weak when he was killed on the cross, but he lives now by God's power. It is true that we are weak in Christ, but for you we will be alive in Christ by God's power."

_____

_____

I stand six steps from the bed's edge. My arms extended. Hands open. On the bed, Sara—all four years of her—crouches, poised like a playful kitten. She's going to jump. But she's not ready. I'm too close.

"Back more, Daddy," she stands and dares.

I dramatically comply, confessing admiration for her courage. After two giant steps I stop. "More?" I ask.

"Yes!" Sara squeals, hopping on the bed.

With each step she laughs and claps and motions for more. When I'm on the other side of the canyon, when I'm beyond the reach of mortal man, when I am but a tiny figure on the horizon, she stops me. "There, stop there."

"Are you sure?"

"I'm sure," she shouts. I extend my arms. Once again she crouches, then springs. Superman without a cape. Skydiver without a chute. Only her heart flies higher than her body. In that airborne instant her only hope is her father. If he proves weak, she'll fall. If he proves cruel, she'll crash. If he proves forgetful, she'll tumble to the hard floor.

But such fear she does not know, for her father she does know. She trusts him. Four years under the same roof have convinced her he is reliable. He is not superhuman, but he is strong. He is not holy, but he is good. He's not brilliant, but he doesn't have to be to remember to catch his child when she jumps.

And so she flies.

And so she soars.

And so he catches her and the two rejoice at the wedding of her trust and his faithfulness.

No, the Lord is all I need. He takes care of me.
—Psalm 16:5

6. Our approach to life says a lot about how much we believe God cares for us. Little faith? Little amount of trust. Large faith? Large amount of trust. How do you see yourself in this illustration? Check any that apply.

❏ I prefer to be in control of my life at all times.

❏ In the big decisions of life, I am willing to take a leap of faith. God won't let me down.

❏ God doesn't care about the routine areas of my day. I save my faith for the big stuff.

❏ My faith is enough to encompass the seemingly small areas in life where it is tested.

❏ I believe what God has said, and that affects how I live out my day.

HIS CARE IS ENOUGH

How do I know this is true, that his care is enough? Nice prose, but give me the facts. How do I know these aren't just fanciful hopes?

Part of the answer can be found in Sara's little leaps of faith. Her older sister, Andrea, was in the room watching, and I asked Sara if she would jump to Andrea. Sara refused. I tried to convince her. She wouldn't budge. "Why not?" I asked.

"I only jump to big arms."

If we think the arms are weak, we won't jump.

For that reason, the Father flexed his muscles. "God's power is very great for those who believe," Paul taught. "That power is the same as the great strength God used to raise Christ from the dead" (Eph. 1:19–20).

Next time you wonder if God can catch you, read that verse. The very arms that defeated death are the arms awaiting you.

Next time you wonder if God can forgive you, read that verse. The very hands that were nailed to the cross are open for you.

And the next time you wonder if you will survive the jump, think of Sara and me. If a flesh-and-bone-headed dad like me can catch his child, don't you think your eternal Father can catch you?

7. Read the following verses. Then match the verse with what you learn about God's concern for you.

___ Psalm 10:14   a. He always helps in times of trouble.

___ Psalm 34:15   b. He will make us strong and support us.

___ Psalm 46:1   c. He listens to our prayers.

___ Isaiah 41:10   d. He helps us when we feel like orphans.

THE HEART OF THE MATTER

☙ **If you're not sure what to do, allow God to take the lead.**

☙ **God will fight for us. We just need to trust.**

☙ **God's power is very great for those who believe.**

Take a few moments and review your Bible memory verse for this month. Write out 1 Corinthians 8:3 here.

_____

_____

_____

The Heart of Jesus

Jesus was a teller of parables on this earth, and his stories reached into the very hearts of his listeners. Can you find yourself in the parable of the lost sheep? Are you one of the ninety-nine, safe in the fold of faith? Or are you the wanderer, the stray, the outsider?

This one lonely straggler, stumbling in the darkness with jumbled emotions and mounting fears. With wistful eyes and tearstained cheeks, you walk aimlessly. Uncertain of your path, you wish for the shepherd's guiding staff.

GOD CALLS YOUR NAME

He's waiting for you. God is standing on the porch of heaven, expectantly hoping, searching the horizon for a glimpse of his child. You're the one God is seeking.

God is the waiting Father, the caring Shepherd in search of his lamb. His legs are scratched, his feet are sore, and his eyes are burning. He scales the cliffs and traverses the fields. He explores the caves. He cups his hands to his mouth and calls into the canyon.

And the name he calls is yours . . .

The message is simple: God gave up his Son in order to rescue all his sons and daughters. To bring his children home. He's listening for your answer.

—*And the Angels Were Silent*

The helpless put their trust in you. You are the defender of orphans.

—Psalm 10:14 NLT

God's power is very great for those who believe.

—**Ephesians 1:19**

Give all your worries to him, because he cares about you.

—**1 Peter 5:7**

Limping, you long for the shepherd's gentle touch.

Then your ears turn at the sound of a voice, calling your name.

Relief floods your weary heart as the shepherd lifts you onto his shoulders. Tears of gratitude fill your eyes as he tends to your bumps and bruises. The Scripture says that we all, like sheep, have gone astray.

But Jesus calls to us, cares for us, and carries us home.

DAY TWO—GOD'S PROVISION

THE SECRET OF SUCCESS

You, me, and Dorothy of The Wizard of Oz—we have a lot in common.

We all know what it's like to find ourselves in a distant land surrounded by strange people.

Though our chosen path isn't paved with yellow bricks, we still hope it will lead us home.

The witches of the East want more than our ruby slippers.

And Dorothy is not the first person to find herself surrounded by brainless, heartless, and spineless people.

We can relate to Dorothy.

But when Dorothy gets to the Emerald City the comparison is uncanny. For what the Wizard said to her, some think God says to us.

You remember the plot. Each of the chief characters comes to the Wizard with a need. Dorothy seeks a way home. The scarecrow wants wisdom. The tin man desires a heart. The lion needs courage. The Wizard of Oz, they've heard, could grant all four. So they come. Trembling and reverent, they come. They shiver in his presence and gasp at his power. And with all the courage they can muster, they present their requests.

His response? He will help after they demonstrate their worthiness. He will help as soon as they overcome the source of evil. Bring me the witch's broom, he says, and I will help you.

So they do. They scale the castle walls and make wax of the witch, and in the process, they make some startling discoveries. They discover they can overcome evil. They discover that, with a little luck, a quick mind can handle the best the worst has to give. And they discover they can do it all without the wizard.

The movie ends with Dorothy discovering that her worst nightmare was in reality just a bad dream. That her somewhere-over-the-rainbow home was right where she'd always been. And that it's nice to have friends in high places, but in the end, it's up to you to find your own way home.

The moral of The Wizard of Oz? Everything you may need, you've already got.

The power you need is really a power you already have. Just look deep enough, long enough, and there's nothing you can't do.

LAY DOWN YOUR CARES

Perhaps the heaviest burden we try to carry is the burden of mistakes and failures. What do you do with your failures?

Even if you've fallen, even if you've failed, even if everyone else has rejected you, Christ will not turn away from you. He came first an foremost to those who have no hope. He goes to those no one else would go to and says, "I'll give you eternity."

Only you can surrender your concerns to the Father. No one else can take those away and give them to God. Only you can cast all your anxieties on the one who cares for you. What better way to start the day than by laying your cares at his feet?

—*Walking with the Savior*

You gave me life and showed me kindness, and in your care you watched over my life.
—**Job 10:12**

1. Which of the following phrases sound familiar to you in our society? Check your response(s).

   ❏ God helps those who help themselves.
   ❏ Pull yourself up by your own bootstraps.
   ❏ A self-made man or woman is the ideal.
   ❏ Success is yours for the taking.

2. The world tells us if we try hard enough, we can recreate ourselves into passionate, powerful, and purposeful human beings. All we need is to harness our own potential. However, Scripture stands in steep contrast to that mindset. Read

Zechariah 4:6 and summarize what this passage says about succeeding in on our own strength.

_____

_____

Then he told me, "This is the word of the Lord to Zerubbabel: 'You will not succeed by your own strength or power, but by my Spirit,'" says the Lord All-Powerful.
—Zechariah 4:6

GOD PROVIDES THE SPIRIT

I'm an offspring of sturdy stock. A product of a rugged, blue-collar culture that honored decency, loyalty, and hard work and loved Bible verses like "God helps those who help themselves." (No, it's not in there.)

"God started it and now we must finish it" was our motto. He's done his part; now we do ours. It's a fifty-fifty proposition. A do-it-yourself curriculum that majors in our part and minors in God's part.

"Blessed are the busy," this theology proclaims, "for they are the true Christians."

No need for the supernatural. No place for the extraordinary. No room for the transcendent. Prayer becomes a token. (The real strength is within you, not "up there.") Communion becomes a ritual. (The true hero is you, not him.) And the Holy Spirit? Well, the Holy Spirit becomes anything from a sweet disposition to a positive mental attitude.

It's a wind-the-world-up-and-walk-away view of God. And the philosophy works . . . as long as you work. Your faith is strong, as long as you are strong. Your position is secure, as long as you are secure. Your life is good, as long as you are good.

But, alas, therein lies the problem. As the Teacher said, "No one is good" (Matt. 19:17 NKJV). Nor is anyone always strong; nor is anyone always secure.

Do-it-yourself Christianity is not much encouragement to the done in and worn out.

Self-sanctification holds little hope for the addict.

"Try a little harder" is little encouragement for the abused.

You began your life in Christ by the Spirit. Now are you trying to make it complete by your own power? That is foolish.
—Galatians 3:3

3. No one is good. No on is strong. No one is secure. Why are we incapable of consistently caring for ourselves?

    _____

    _____

4. Which of the following statements are true, and which ones are false? Mark your answers True (T) or False (F). Use the Bible verses below to help you answer.

    ____ Jesus expects us to rely on ourselves. (Matthew 11:28)
    ____ Jesus expects us to rely on him through his Spirit. (Acts 2:38)
    ____ Jesus saved us, but it's up to us from here on out. (Galatians 3:3)
    ____ Jesus is too busy to care for our petty concerns. (Philippians 4:19)

5. Read the following verses. Then match the verse with what you learn about what Jesus said about the role of the Holy Spirit.

    ____ Matthew 10:19–20   a. The Spirit gives us life.
    ____ John 6:63   b. He leads us into truth.
    ____ John 14:26   c. He speaks through you.
    ____ John 16:13   d. He helps us remember Jesus' teachings.

Jesus promises us the Holy Spirit so he can care for us in our time of need.

Jesus promises us the Holy Spirit so he can care for us at every level of our need. Don't know what to do? He will guide us. Need an answer for life's questions? He will bring Scripture to mind. Suddenly speechless in a witnessing opportunity? He will give you the right words to say.

He is our God and we are the people he takes care of and the sheep that he tends.
—Psalm 95:7

FROM THE INSIDE OUT

I will ask the Father, and he will give you another Helper to be with you forever—the Spirit of truth. The world cannot accept him, because it does not see him or know him. But you know him, because he lives with you and will be in you.

—John 14:16–17

At some point we need more than good advice; we need help. Somewhere on this journey home we realize that a fifty-fifty proposition is too little. We need more—more than a pudgy wizard who thanks us for coming but tells us the trip was unnecessary.

We need help. Help from the inside out. The kind of help Jesus promised. "I will ask the Father, and he will give you another Helper to be with you forever—the Spirit of truth. The world cannot accept him, because it does not see him or know him. But you know him, because he lives with you and will be *in* you" (John 14:16–17, emphasis mine).

Other Christians can give us good advice, but only God can help us.

6. Fill in the blanks about Jesus' provision of the Holy Spirit.

   The Holy Spirit helps us from the _____ out.
   Jesus called the Holy Spirit the _____ and the Spirit of _____.
   Jesus said we would _____ the Spirit, and he would _____ in us and be _____ us.

7. Read the following verses and write down what you learn about how God helps us from the inside out.

"If God is able to place the stars in their sockets and suspend the sky like a curtain, do you think it is remotely possible that God is able to guide your life? If your God is mighty enough to ignite the sun, could it be that he is mighty enough to light your path? If he cares enough about the planet Saturn to give it rings or Venus to make it sparkle, is there an outside chance that he cares enough about you to meet your needs?"

—*The Great House of God*

Ezekiel 36:26–27 – "Also, I will teach you to respect me completely, and I will put a new way of thinking inside you. I will take out the stubborn hearts of stone from your bodies, and I will give you obedient hearts of flesh. I will put my Spirit inside you and help you live by my rules and carefully obey my laws."

_____

_____

Acts 15:9 – "To God, those people are not different from us. When they believed, he made their hearts pure."

_____

_____

Romans 5:5 – "And this hope will never disappoint us, because God has poured out his love to fill our hearts. He gave us his love through the Holy Spirit, whom God has given to us."

_____

_____

Jesus' gift of the Holy Spirit is a tangible expression of his care and concern.

Note the dwelling place of God—"in you." Not near us. Not above us. Not around us. But in us. In the part of us we don't even know. In the heart no one else has seen. In the hidden recesses of our being dwells, not an angel, not a philosophy, not a genie, but God.

Imagine that.

When my daughter Jenna was six years old, I came upon her standing in front of a full-length mirror. She was looking down her throat. I asked her what she was doing, and she answered, "I'm looking to see if God is in my heart."

I chuckled and turned and then overheard her ask him, "Are you in there?" When no answer came, she grew impatient and spoke on his behalf. With a voice deepened as much as a six-year-old can, she said, "Yes."

She's asking the right question. "Are you in there?" Could it be what they say is true? It wasn't enough for you to appear in a bush or dwell in the temple? It wasn't enough for you to become human flesh and walk on the earth? It wasn't enough to leave your word and the promise of your return? You had to go further? You had to take up residence in us?

Depend on the Lord; trust him, and he will take care of you.
—Psalm 37:5

8. Read the following verses. Then match the verse with what you learn about how the Spirit takes up residence in us and helps care for us. Use the Bible verses below to help you answer.

___ Romans 8:26   a. He produces Christ-like character in our lives.
___ Romans 8:27   b. His presence assures us God lives inside of us.
___ 2 Corinthians 5:5   c. He helps us whenever we don't know what to pray.
___ Galatians 5:22   d. He guarantees us new life.
___ 1 John 3:24   e. He speaks to God for us in the way God wants.

This is what God made us for, and he has given us the Spirit to be a guarantee for this new life.

—2 Corinthians 5:5

"Do you not know," Paul penned, "that your body is the temple of the Holy Spirit?"

Perhaps you didn't. Perhaps you didn't know God would go that far to make sure you got home. If not, thanks for letting me remind you.

The wizard says look inside yourself and find self. God says look inside yourself and find God. The first will get you to Kansas.

The latter will get you to heaven.

Take your pick.

The people who obey God's commands live in God, and God lives in them. We know that God lives in us because of the Spirit God gave us.

—1 John 3:24

9. Read 1 Corinthians 6:19–20. What can you learn about God's care from this passage? Check all that apply.

❏ We do not belong to ourselves—we are God's.
❏ God bought us with the price of Jesus' blood so he could care for us.
❏ He places his Holy Spirit inside of us.

The dwelling place of God is *in* us.

THE HEART OF THE MATTER

🐦 **Jesus promises us the Holy Spirit so he can care for us in our time of need.**
🐦 **Other Christians can give us good advice, but only God can help us.**
🐦 **Jesus' gift of the Holy Spirit is a tangible expression of his care and concern.**
🐦 **The dwelling place of God is *in* us.**

Your memory verse for the week is 1 Corinthians 8:3 in the New Living Translation. Review it by writing it out here.

_____

_____

_____

You should know that your body is a temple for the Holy Spirit who is in you. You have received the Holy Spirit from God. So you do not belong to yourselves, because you were bought by God for a price. So honor God with your bodies.

—1 Corinthians 6:19–20

The Heart of Jesus

A life without hope. Nothing to look forward to but a downward spiral of decay—and death. He was a leper—avoided, outcast, untouchable. A rough cloak and hood masked his withered body. A scrap of cloth covered his ghastly face. Coming into a town, he began to swing a clumsy bell and announce his approach, "Unclean, unclean." All around him, people looked the other way, edged in another direction, pretended not to see, and turned their backs in hasty retreat. Though disease ate away at his body, his soul was ravaged by loneliness. No one ever looked him in the eyes. No one ever reached out to him. He felt utterly alone. But he was on a mission. Word had reached him of a healer in the area—a man who could make a leper clean again. He found Jesus, approached him, and kneeled before him. "If you wanted to, you could make me clean." he said, with pleading eyes. Jesus did not recoil. He did not step back. He didn't turn away or ignore the man's plea. Jesus was moved with compassion. Jesus reached out to the kneeling man. Jesus touched him. "I am willing." And with a word and a touch, the leper was healed. He is a man who can testify that Jesus cares, even for the avoided, the outcasts, and the untouchables.

Do not worry about anything, but pray and ask God for everything you need, always giving thanks.

—Philippians 4:6

DAY THREE—JESUS—GOD'S GIFT TO THE WORLD

WHO CARES ABOUT OUR WORLD?

Late-night news is a poor sedative.

Last night it was for me. All I wanted was the allergen count and the basketball scores. But to get them, I had to endure the usual monologue of global misery. And last night the world seemed worse than usual.

Watching the news doesn't usually disturb me so. I'm not a gloom-and-doom sort of fellow. I feel I'm as good as the next guy in taking human tragedy with a spoon of faith. But last night . . . well, the world seemed dark.

Perhaps it was the two youngsters shot in a drive-by shooting—one was six, the other ten.

Perhaps it was the reassuring announcement that twenty-six thousand highway bridges in America are near collapse.

A billionaire rock star is accused of molesting children. One senator is accused of seducing associates, another of tampering with election procedures.

Pistol-packing drivers give rise to a new bumper sticker: "Keep honking. I'm reloading."

The national debt is deeper. Our taxes are higher, the pollen count is up, and the Dallas Mavericks lost their fifteenth game in a row.

"And that's the world tonight!" the well-dressed man announces. I wonder why he's smiling.

On the way to bed, I step into the rooms of my three sleeping daughters. At the bedside of each I pause and ponder the plight of their future. "What in the world awaits you?" I whisper as I brush back hair and straighten blankets.

Their greatest concerns today are math tests, presents, and birthday parties. Would that their world would always be so innocent. It won't. Forests shadow every trail, and cliffs edge every turn. Every life has its share of fear. My children are no exception.

Nor are yours. And as appealing as a desert island or a monastery might be, seclusion is simply not the answer for facing a scary tomorrow.

Then what is? Does someone have a hand on the throttle of this train, or has the engineer bailed out just as we come in sight of dead-man's curve?

One of the themes running through the entire Bible can be summarized in two words: Fear not. Angels spoke it as a greeting. God commanded it from his people. Jesus used it to comfort his fearful disciples. No matter how out-of-control things appear, we are not to be afraid. He is in control. He will take care of us.

1. God asks us to abandon our fears and trust him. Read the following verses and write down what you learn about this biblical theme.

   Joshua 1:9 – "Remember that I commanded you to be strong and brave. Don't be afraid, because the Lord your God will be with you everywhere you go."

   _____

   _____

   Isaiah 41:10 – "So don't worry, because I am with you. Don't be afraid, because I am your God. I will make you strong and will help you; I will support you with my right hand that saves you."

   _____

   _____

No matter how out-of-control things appear, we are not to be afraid.

And God can give you more blessings than you need. Then you will always have plenty of everything—enough to give to every good work.
—2 Corinthians 9:8

John 14:27 – "I leave you peace; my peace I give you. I do not give it to you as the world does. So don't let your hearts be troubled or afraid."

_____

_____

2. Which of the following statements are true and which are false? Mark your answers True (T) or False (F). Use the Bible verses below to help you answer.

____ God only cares about certain populations of the world. (Mark 16:15)

____ God created the world, but he is no longer intimately involved in it. (2 Corinthians 5:19)

____ Jesus said God even knows when a sparrow falls to the ground and the number of hairs on our head. (Matthew 10:29)

GOD'S PROMISE TO CARE FOR US

I may have found part of the answer in, of all places, the first chapter of the New Testament. I've often thought it strange that Matthew would begin his book with a genealogy. Certainly not good journalism. A list of who-sired-whom wouldn't get past most editors.

But then again, Matthew wasn't a journalist, and the Holy Spirit wasn't trying to get our attention. He was making a point. God had promised he would give a Messiah through the bloodline of Abraham (Gen. 12:3), and he did.

"Having doubts about the future?" Matthew asks. "Just take a look at the past." And with that he opens the cedar chest of Jesus' lineage and begins pulling out the dirty laundry.

Believe me, you and I would have kept some of these stories in the closet. Jesus' lineage is anything but a roll call at the Institute for Halos and Harps. Reads more like the Sunday morning occupancy at the county jail.

It begins with Abraham, the father of the nation, who more than once lied like Pinocchio just to save his neck (Gen. 12:10–20).

Abraham's grandson Jacob was slicker than a Las Vegas card shark. He cheated his brother, lied to his father, got swindled, and then swindled his uncle (Gen. 27, 29).

Jacob's son Judah was so blinded by testosterone that he engaged the services of a streetwalker, not knowing she was his daughter-in-law! When he learned her identity, he threatened to have her burned to death for solicitation (Gen. 38).

Special mention is made of Solomon's mother, Bathsheba (who bathed in questionable places), and Solomon's father, David, who watched the bath of Bathsheba (2 Sam. 11:2–3).

Rahab was a harlot (Josh. 2:1). Ruth was a foreigner (Ruth 1:4).

Manasseh made the list, even though he forced his children to walk through fire (2 Kin. 21:6). His son Amon is on the list, even though he rejected God (2 Kin. 21:22).

Seems that almost half the kings were crooks, half were embezzlers, and all but a handful worshiped an idol or two for good measure.

And so reads the list of Jesus' not-so-great grandparents. Seems like the only common bond between this lot was a promise. A promise from heaven that God would use them to send his son.

The promise held true—even during the darkest periods. When it seemed like God might have to scrap his plan—the promise held true. When it seemed like things were going from bad to worse—the promise held true.

3. How does Jesus' lineage illustrate the steadfastness of God's promise?

_____

_____

HIS BROKEN HEART

I can't understand it. I honestly cannot. Why did Jesus [die on the cross]? Oh, I know, I know. I have heard the official answers. "To gratify the old law." "To fulfill prophecy." And these answers are right. They are. But there is something more here. Something very compassionate. Something yearning. Something personal.

What is it?

Could it be that his heart was broken for all the people who cast despairing eyes toward the dark heavens and cry the same "Why?" Could it be that his heart was broken for the hurting? . . .

I imagine him, bending close to those who hurt. I imagine him listening. I picture his eyes misting and a pierced hand brushing away a tear . . . He who also was once alone, understands.

—*No Wonder They Call Him the Savior*

God was in Christ, making peace between the world and himself. In Christ, God did not hold the world guilty of its sins. And he gave us this message of peace.

—2 Corinthians 5:19

The Lord is my shepherd; I have everything I need.

—Psalm 23:1

> *It's one thing to give intellectual assent to the idea of Jesus' care. It's quite another to rest in his promise, fully dependent on his provision. The Bible is full of God's promises—yet all of them point to the one promise of Jesus Christ. Through him, God kept his promise to care for us. "The yes to all of God's promises is in Christ, and through Christ we say yes to the glory of God"*—2 Corinthians 1:20

God has kept all of his promises.

4. Summarize what you learn about Jesus' fulfillment of God's promise in 2 Corinthians 1:20 by filling in the blanks below.

   The answer to all of God's promises is _____. His promises are yes in _____.

5. The Bible is filled with urges to trust God. He never lies. He keeps his promises. He will never fail. Look up a couple of these verses now.

   Joshua proclaimed that God had never failed to do what in Joshua 23:15?

   _____

   _____

   Why can we continue to have hope, according to Hebrews 10:23?

   _____

   _____

GOD HEALS OUR HURTS

The Greek word for compassion is *splanchnizomai*, which won't mean much to you unless you are in the health professions and studied "splanchnology" in school. If so, you remember that "splanchnology" is the study of . . . the gut.

When Matthew writes that Jesus has compassion on the people, he is not saying that Jesus felt casual pity for them. No, the term is far more graphic. Matthew is saying that Jesus felt their hurt in his gut:

He felt the limp of the crippled.
He felt the hurt of the diseased.
He felt the loneliness of the leper.
He felt the embarrassment of the sinful.

And once he felt their hurts, he couldn't help but heal their hurts.

—*In the Eye of the Storm*

THE POWER OF A PROMISE

Why did God use these people? Didn't have to. Could have just laid the Savior on a doorstep. Would have been simpler that way. And why does God tell us their stories? Why does God give us an entire testament of blunders and stumbles of his people?

Simple. He knew what you and I watched on the news last night. He knew you would fret. He knew I would worry. And he wants us to know that when the world goes wild, he stays calm.

Want proof? Read the last name on the list. In spite of all the crooked halos and tasteless gambols of his people, the last name on the list is the first one promised—Jesus.

"Joseph was the husband of Mary, and Mary was the mother of Jesus. Jesus is called the Christ" (Matt. 1:16).

Period. No more names are listed. No more are needed. As if God is announcing to a doubting world, "See, I did it. Just like I said I would. The plan succeeded."

The famine couldn't starve it.
Four hundred years of Egyptian slavery couldn't oppress it.
Wilderness wanderings couldn't lose it.
Babylonian captivity couldn't stop it.
Clay-footed pilgrims couldn't spoil it.

The promise of the Messiah threads its way through forty-two generations of rough-cut stones, forming a necklace fit for the King who came. Just as promised.

6. What earthly circumstances threaten your belief in God's promise to care for his people? Check all that apply.

   ❏ Famine in the world
   ❏ Terrorist attacks on our country
   ❏ National and personal debt
   ❏ Disease
   ❏ Rampant crime
   ❏ Disintegration of the family

My God will use his wonderful riches in Christ Jesus to give you everything you need.
—**Philippians 4:19**

7. Read John 16:33. Underline the reason why Jesus says we can be confident of his concern for us. Then fill in the blanks about what this verse says regarding the world's worries.

We will have _____ in this world—no doubt. However, Jesus wants us to be _____ and realize he has _____ the world.

8. Read Matthew 24:6. Even when the evening news carries stories of imminent war, why don't we have to fear?

_____

_____

And the promise remains.

Those people who keep their faith until the end will be saved (Matt. 24:13), Joseph's child assures.

In this world you will have trouble, but be brave! I have defeated the world (John 16:33).

The engineer has not abandoned the train. Nuclear war is no threat to God. Yo-yo economies don't intimidate the heavens. Immoral leaders have never derailed the plan.

God keeps his promise.

See for yourself. In the manger. He's there.

See for yourself. In the tomb. He's gone.

In this world, you will have trouble, but be brave! I have defeated the world.

—John 16:33

THE HEART OF THE MATTER

- **No matter how out-of-control things appear, we are not to be afraid.**
- **God has kept all of his promises.**
- **Nothing and no one can thwart God's promise to save us.**

Take a few moments to review your memory verse. Fill in the blanks of 1 Corinthians 8:3.

The person who _____ God is the one God _____ and _____ for. (NLT)

You will hear about wars and stories of wars that are coming, but don't be afraid. These things must happen before the end comes.

—Matthew 24:6

The Heart of Jesus

Crowds milled in the street in front of the house, but the low roof of the stable in the back had presented a solution. Four men, with a determined set to their jaws, were easing a man strapped to a pallet up onto the roof. "Are you sure about this?" The man gave a quick gasp as his pallet was hefted from shoulders up to waiting hands. "It's the only way. Don't worry." Up the slant of the low roof, over the low wall, onto the flat rooftop. "Now what?" one man growled as he nudged the packed flooring with his toe in frustration. The muddy clay cracked and chipped beneath his sandal. "Roof needs replacing before the rains come," he mumbled to himself. Then he brightened. "Where's the Master from here? Which room is he in?" Leaning over the sides and listening carefully, they chose their spot and began to dig. The paralyzed man groaned inwardly. How would Jesus look at him when his friends were causing such a commotion? They were acting like vandals! Surely the Teacher would turn them away now. Doubt and fear mingled with desperate hope as his friends tied ropes to his pallet and began to lower him into the room below. The faces of his four friends above him were pleased—triumphant. They had found a way in. Would Jesus still be there? Would he be angry? What would he do? The pallet gently bumped the floor, and the room that had echoed with surprised exclamations and hushed whispers a moment ago fell quiet. The paralyzed man looked from one fact to another fearfully, but then one man stepped forward. He was not angry. He was not shocked. His eyes were filled with kindness—caring. Jesus reached out his hand, and helped the man on the pallet . . . to his feet.

Nothing and no one can thwart God's promise to save us.

He will cover you with his feathers, and under his wings you can hide. His truth will be your shield and protection.

—Psalm 91:4

DAY FOUR—THE GIFT OF UNHAPPINESS

THE SEARCH FOR SATISFACTION

There dwells inside you, deep within, a tiny whippoorwill. Listen. You will hear him sing. His aria mourns the dusk. His solo signals the dawn.

It is the song of the whippoorwill.

He will not be silent until the sun is seen.

We forget he is there, so easy is he to ignore. Other animals of the heart are larger, noisier, more demanding, more imposing.

But none is so constant.

Other creatures of the soul are more quickly fed. More simply satisfied. We feed the lion who growls for power. We stroke the tiger who demands affection. We bridle the stallion who bucks control.

But what do we do with the whippoorwill who yearns for eternity?

For that is his song. That is his task. Out of the gray he sings a golden song. Perched in time he chirps a timeless verse. Peering through pain's shroud, he sees a painless place. Of that place he sings.

And though we try to ignore him, we cannot. He is us, and his song is ours. Our heart song won't be silenced until we see the dawn.

"God has planted eternity in the hearts of men" (Eccl. 3:10 TLB), says the wise man. But it doesn't take a wise person to know that people long for more than earth. When we see pain, we yearn. When we see hunger, we question why. Senseless deaths. Endless tears. Needless loss. Where do they come from? Where will they lead?

Isn't there more to life than death? Will we never be satisfied this side of heaven?

The human search for satisfaction winds its way through history. Every man and woman has longed for it. Some seek it in relationships, some in possessions, still others in wealth. However, the Bible has much to say about this idea of satisfaction.

1. Look up the following verses and make a note of what Scripture says about satisfaction.

    Psalm 145:16 – "You open your hand, and you satisfy all living things."

    _____

    _____

    Ecclesiastes 5:10 – "Whoever loves money will never have enough money; Whoever loves wealth will not be satisfied with it. This is also useless."

    _____

    _____

    Isaiah 55:2 – "Why spend your money on something that is not real food? Why work for something that doesn't really satisfy you? Listen closely to me, and you will eat what is good; your soul will enjoy the rich food that satisfies."

    _____

    _____

    Luke 6:21 – "You people who are now hungry are happy, because you will be satisfied. You people who are now crying are happy, because you will laugh with joy."

    _____

No one has ever imagined what God has prepared for those who love him.
—1 Corinthians 2:9

Our heart longs for satisfaction.

Two sparrows cost only a penny, but not even one of them can die without your Father's knowing it.
—Matthew 10:29

2. Then why does discontent cause us to question if God is really all that concerned for us?

_____

_____

HUNGER FOR HEAVEN

The only ultimate disaster that can befall us, I have come to realize, is to feel ourselves to be home on earth. As long as we are aliens, we cannot forget our true homeland.[1i]

Unhappiness on earth cultivates a hunger for heaven. By gracing us with a deep dissatisfaction, God holds our attention. The only tragedy, then, is to be satisfied prematurely. To settle for earth. To be content in a strange land. To intermarry with the Babylonians and forget Jerusalem.

3. Read these verses and write what they say about how earthly pleasures are temporary at best.

Psalm 49:16–17 – "Don't be afraid of rich people because their houses are more beautiful. They don't take anything to the grave; their wealth won't go down with them."

_____

_____

Haggai 1:6 – "You have planted much, but you harvest little. You eat, but you do not become full. You drink, but you are still thirsty. You put on clothes, but you are not warm enough. You earn money, but then you lose it all as if you had put it into a purse full of holes."

_____

_____

2 Corinthians 4:18 – "We set our eyes not on what we see but on what we cannot see. What we see will last only a short time, but what we cannot see will last forever."

_____

_____

Matthew 6:19 – "Don't store treasures for yourselves here on earth where moths and rust will destroy them and thieves can break in and steal them."

_____

_____

4. Based on what you just read, why is earthly satisfaction premature?

_____

_____

NOT AT HOME

We are not happy here because we are not at home here. We are not happy here because we are not supposed to be happy here. We are "like foreigners and strangers in this world" (1 Pet. 2:11).

Take a fish and place him on the beach.[2] Watch his gills gasp and scales dry. Is he happy? No! How do you make him happy? Do you cover him with a mountain of cash? Do you get him a beach chair and sunglasses? Do you bring him a Playfish magazine and martini? Do you wardrobe him in double-breasted fins and people-skinned shoes?

When we are unhappy, it makes us look forward to heaven all the more.

People who do what is right may have many problems, but the Lord will solve them all.

—Psalm 34:19

SOLE PROVIDER, SOLE COMFORTER

As long as Jesus is one of many options, he is not an option.

As long as you can carry your burdens alone, you don't need a burden bearer. As long as your situation brings you no grief, you will receive no comfort. And as long as you can take him or leave him, you might as well leave him, because he won't be taken half-heartedly.

But when you mourn, when you get to the point of sorrow for your sins, when you admit that you have no other option but to cast all your cares on him, and when there is truly no other name that you can call, then cast all your cares on him, for he is waiting in the midst of the storm.

—*The Applause of Heaven*

Happiness on earth is always temporary.

My God will use his wonderful riches in Christ Jesus to give you everything you need.

—Philippians 4:19

All these great people died in faith. They did not get the things that God promised his people, but they saw them coming far in the future and were glad. They said they were like visitors and strangers on earth. When people say such things, they show they are looking for a country that will be their own. If they had been thinking about the country they had left, they could have gone back. But they were waiting for a better country—a heavenly country. So God is not ashamed to be called their God, because he has prepared a city for them.

—Hebrews 11:13–16

We will only be satisfied when we reach heaven.

God clothes the grass in the field, which is alive today but tomorrow is thrown into the fire. So you can be even more sure that God will clothe you. Don't have so little faith!

—Matthew 6:30

Of course not. Then how do you make him happy? You put him back in his element. You put him back in the water. He will never be happy on the beach simply because he was not made for the beach.

And you will never be completely happy on earth simply because you were not made for earth. Oh, you will have your moments of joy. You will catch glimpses of light. You will know moments or even days of peace. But they simply do not compare with the happiness that lies ahead.

Thou hast made us for thyself and our hearts are restless until they rest in thee.[3]

Strangely enough, even when we do happen upon earthly pleasures, the happiness is usually temporary at best. Soon, we are on the look-out again, our eyes peeled for the next perk in our existence.

5. Fill in the blanks below about our happiness on earth.

"And you will _____ be completely _____ on _____ simply because you were not _____ for _____."

Sometimes we doubt Jesus cares for us because we confuse our desires with our needs. When our desires go unmet, despite having all we really need, we are disappointed. Disappointed with what we perceive as a lapse in care. "If God really cared for me he would . . . " And we fill in the blank.

6. How do you sometimes fill in the blank above? If God really cared for me he would . . .

_____
_____

7. Read Philippians 4:19 and choose the statements that best describe God's strategy to meet your needs.

❏ He will meet some and miss some when it comes to meeting your needs.
❏ Two out of three ain't bad.
❏ He will give you all you need and all you want.
❏ He will meet your needs until the money runs out or he runs out of time—whichever comes first.
❏ He will use his riches in Christ Jesus to meet all of your needs.

8. Read Hebrews 11:13–16. What does this passage say to you about why Christians long for a better place?

_____
_____

UNTIL WE GET HOME

Only when we find him will we be satisfied. Moses can tell you.

He had as much of God as any man in the Bible. God spoke to him in a bush. God guided him with fire. God amazed Moses with the plagues. And when God grew angry with the Israelites and withdrew from them, he stayed close to Moses. He spoke to Moses "as a man speaks with his friend" (Ex. 33:11). Moses knew God like no other man.

But that wasn't enough. Moses yearned for more. Moses longed to see God. He even dared to ask, "Please show me your glory" (Ex. 33:18).

Isn't that why we long for heaven? We may speak about a place where there are no tears, no death, no fear, no night; but those are just the benefits of heaven. The beauty of heaven is seeing God.

Heaven is God's ultimate expression a continuum of care. He provides the promise of heaven one day to get us through the stuff of earth. Yet at the same time, he also promises to provide what we need most—a vision of himself.

9. Which one of the following statements is true, and which one is false? Mark your answer True (T) or False (F).

___ There is nothing on earth that can satisfy our deepest longing.
___ Some things on earth can fully satisfy our deepest longing.

Nothing on earth can satisfy our deepest longing—to see God.

GOD ALONE SATISFIES US

And our heart will only be at peace when we see him. "Because I have lived right, I will see your face. When I wake up, I will see your likeness and be satisfied" (Ps. 17:15).

Satisfied? That is one thing we are not. We are not satisfied.

We push back from the Thanksgiving table and pat our round bellies. "I'm satisfied," we declare. But look at us a few hours later, back in the kitchen picking the meat from the bone.

We wake up after a good night's rest and hop out of bed. We couldn't go back to sleep if someone paid us. We are satisfied—for a while. But look at us a dozen or so hours later, crawling back in the sheets.

We take the vacation of a lifetime. For years we planned. For years we saved. And off we go. We satiate ourselves with sun, fun, and good food. But we are not even on the way home before we dread the end of the trip and begin planning another.

We are not satisfied.

Why? Because there is nothing on earth that can satisfy our deepest longing. We long to see God. The leaves of life are rustling with the rumor that we will—and we won't be satisfied until we do.

THE HEART OF THE MATTER

- ❦ **Our heart longs for satisfaction.**
- ❦ **When we are unhappy, it makes us look forward to heaven all the more.**
- ❦ **Happiness on earth is only temporary.**
- ❦ **We will only be satisfied when we reach heaven.**
- ❦ **Nothing on earth can satisfy our deepest longing—to see God.**

Review your memory verse for the week. Write out 1 Corinthians 8:3 below.

_____

_____

_____

The Heart of Jesus

Jesus knows you intimately. He welcomes you to tell him your troubles. He has offered to carry your burdens for you. His caring touches your deepest places, giving you comfort, assurance, and peace. This same Jesus has gone ahead, and is preparing a place for you. He is the architect of your heavenly home—it's builder and interior decorator too. He who knows your secret woes also knows your heart's desires. He knows your favorite color, your favorite flower, your favorite views. Jesus knows what will delight you. He knows how to surprise you. He knows what you've always longed for. And in his infinite care for you, he prepares the perfect place for you. Jesus can't wait to show you your new home, made with heavenly TLC.

Jesus said, "Don't let your hearts be troubled. Trust in God, and trust in me.
—John 14:1

DAY FIVE—WHEN GOD WHISPERS YOUR NAME

DERAILED DREAMS

"I could have gone to college on a golf scholarship," a fellow told me just last week on the fourth tee box. "Had an offer right out of school. But I joined a rock-and-roll band. Ended up never going. Now I'm stuck fixing garage doors."

"Now I'm stuck." Epitaph of a derailed dream.

Pick up a high school yearbook and read the "What I want to do" sentence under each picture. You'll get dizzy breathing the thin air of mountaintop visions:

"Ivy-League school."

"Write books and live in Switzerland."

"Physician in a Third World country."

"Teach inner-city kids."

Yet, take the yearbook to a twentieth-year reunion and read the next chapter. Some dreams have come true, but many haven't. Not that all should, mind you. I hope the little guy who dreamed of being a sumo wrestler came to his senses. And I hope he didn't lose his passion in the process. Changing direction in life is not tragic. Losing passion in life is.

Something happens to us along the way. Convictions to change the world downgrade to commitments to pay the bills. Rather than make a difference, we make a salary. Rather than look forward, we look back. Rather than look outward, we look inward.

And we don't like what we see.

1. What is the difference between "changing direction" and "losing passion" in life?

   _____

   _____

2. Does God care about our dreams? Scripture seems to affirm he does. More importantly, he cares about us. He cares when we feel defeated. Deflated. And discouraged. Look up the following verses and write down what you learn about God's concern for those burdened with cares.

   Psalm 55:22 – "Give your worries to the Lord, and he will take care of you. He will never let good people down."

   Nahum 1:7 – "The Lord is good, giving protection in times of trouble. He knows who trusts in him."

   1 Peter 5:7 – "Give all your worries to him, because he cares about you."

   _____

   _____

GOD'S PLAN DEMONSTRATES HIS CARE

If anyone had reason to doubt God cared for his broken dreams, it was Moses.

You remember his story. Adopted nobility. An Israelite reared in an Egyptian palace. His countrymen were slaves, but Moses was privileged. Ate at the royal table. Educated in the finest schools.

But his most influential teacher had no degree. She was his mother. A Jewess who was hired to be his nanny. "Moses," you can almost hear her whisper to her young son, "God has put you here on purpose. Someday you will set your people free. Never forget, Moses. Never forget."

God began doing a good work in you, and I am sure he will continue it until it is finished when Jesus Christ comes again.

—Philippians 1:6

Depend on the Lord in whatever you do, and your plans will succeed.

—Proverbs 16:3

Moses didn't. The flame of justice grew hotter until it blazed. Moses saw an Egyptian beating a Hebrew slave. Something inside Moses snapped. He lashed out and killed the Egyptian guard.

The next day Moses saw the Hebrew. You'd think the slave would say thanks. He didn't. Rather than express gratitude, he expressed anger. "Will you kill me too?" he asked (Ex. 2:14).

Moses knew he was in trouble. He fled Egypt and hid in the wilderness. Call it a career shift. He went from dining with the heads of state to counting heads of sheep.

Hardly an upward move.

And so it happened that a bright, promising Hebrew began herding sheep in the hills. From the Ivy League to the cotton patch. From the Oval Office to a taxicab. From swinging a golf club to digging a ditch.

Moses thought the move was permanent. There is no indication he ever intended to go back to Egypt. In fact, there is every indication he wanted to stay with his sheep. Standing barefoot before the bush, he confessed, "I am not a great man! How can I go to the king and lead the Israelites out of Egypt?" (Ex. 3:11).

GOD'S NOT THROUGH YET

Why Moses? Or, more specifically, why eighty-year-old Moses?

The forty-year-old version was more appealing. The Moses we saw in Egypt was brash and confident. But the Moses we find four decades later is reluctant and weather-beaten.

Had you or I looked at Moses back in Egypt, we would have said, "This man is ready for battle." Educated in the finest system in the world. Trained by the ablest soldiers. Instant access to the inner circle of the Pharaoh. Moses spoke their language and knew their habits. He was the perfect man for the job.

Moses at forty we like. But Moses at eighty? No way. Too old. Too tired. Smells like a shepherd. Speaks like a foreigner. What impact would he have on Pharaoh? He's the wrong man for the job.

And Moses would have agreed. "Tried that once before," he would say. "Those people don't want to be helped. Just leave me here to tend my sheep. They're easier to lead."

Moses wouldn't have gone. You wouldn't have sent him. I wouldn't have sent him.

But God did.

God says Moses is ready.

And to convince him, God speaks through a bush. (Had to do something dramatic to get Moses' attention.)

"School's out," God tells him. "Now it's time to get to work." Poor Moses. He didn't even know he was enrolled.

God puts us back in service to remind us he cares for us. When we make mistakes, he does not banish us to a spiritual junkyard. No, he salvages our mistakes because he cares for us. He removes the rust and grime, buffs out the scratches, and hammers out the dents in our frame until we are in working condition again.

> **God demonstrates his care for us by using us in his service.**

3. Read the following verses. Then match the verse with what you learn about how God cares for and uses the weak in service to him.

   ___ Psalm 41:3   a. God chooses the weak to shame the strong.
   ___ 1 Corinthians 1:27 b. The sick are made strong.
   ___ 2 Corinthians 12:9 c. God gives the weak strength again.
   ___ Hebrews 11:34   d. God's power is made perfect in our weakness.

A GOOD WORK IN YOU

The voice from the bush is the voice that whispers to you. It reminds you that God is not finished with you yet. Oh, you may think he is. You may think you've peaked. You may think he's got someone else to do the job.

> *The Lord will always lead you. He will satisfy your needs in dry lands and give strength to your bones. You will be like a garden that has much water, like a spring that never runs dry.*
>
> —Isaiah 58:11

The Lord will give him strength when he is sick, and he will make him well again.

—Psalm 41:3

That is why we always pray for you, asking our God to help you live the kind of life he called you to live. We pray that with his power God will help you do the good things you want and perform the works that come from your faith.

—2 Thessalonians 1:11

God won't be finished with you until Jesus comes again.

THE BEST IS YET TO BE

Makes sense. Fathers are fond of giving their children special names. Princess. Tiger. Sweetheart. Bubba. Angel . . .

Isn't it incredible to think that God has saved a name just for you? One you don't even know? We've always assumed that the name we got is the name we will keep. Not so. . . . The road ahead is so bright a fresh name is needed. Your eternity is so special no common name will do.

So God has one reserved just for you. There is more to your life than you ever thought. There is more to your story than what you have read. . . .

And so I plead . . . Be there when God whispers your name.

—*When God Whispers Your Name*

God has a new name for you—a unique, one-of-a-kind name that only he knows.

I will be with you always, even until the end of this age.

—Matthew 28:20

If so, think again.

"God began doing a good work in you, and I am sure he will continue it until it is finished when Jesus Christ comes again" (Phil. 1:6).

Did you see what God is doing? A good work in you.

Did you see when he will be finished? When Jesus comes again.

May I spell out the message? God ain't finished with you yet.

Your Father wants you to know that.

4. Based on what you have learned so far about God's care, which of the following statements are true, and which ones are false? Mark your answers True (T) or False (F). Use the Bible verses below to help you answer.

___ God is not finished with us until Jesus comes again. (1 Peter 5:4)
___ God will help us live the kind of life he called us to live. (2 Thessalonians 1:11)
___ Our mistakes disqualify us for ever serving God again. (1 Peter 5:10)
___ God makes unholy people holy. (2 Timothy 1:9)

THE NAME ONLY GOD KNOWS

Can't say I've given a lot of thought to my given name. Never figured it made much difference. I do recall a kid in elementary school wondering if I were German. I said no. "Then why do you have a German name?" I didn't even know Max was German. He assured me it was. So I decided to find out.

"Why did you name me Max?" I asked Mom when I got home.

She looked up from the sink and replied, "You just looked like one."

Like I say, I haven't given much thought to my name. But there is one name that has caught my interest lately. A name only God knows. A name only God gives. A unique, one-of-a-kind, once-to-be-given name.

What am I talking about? Well, you may not have known it, but God has a new name for you. When you get home, he won't call you Alice or Bob or Juan or Geraldo. The name you've always heard won't be the one he uses. When God says he will make all things new, he means it. You will have a new home, a new body, a new life, and you guessed it, a new name.

"I will give some of the hidden manna to everyone who wins the victory. I will also give to each one who wins the victory a white stone with a new name written on it. No one knows this new name except the one who receives it" (Rev. 2:17).

5. Remember John 10:3—the Shepherd knows the sheep by name? With that in mind, how does God's reserved name further illustrate this same concern for individuals?

_____

_____

6. He knows our name—and all that goes with it. The highlights. The lowlights. And everything in-between. He cares so much for us that he does not want anyone to miss out on "winning the victory" at the finish line of heaven. Read 2 Peter 3:8–9. What do these verses teach you about God's care for each person on earth? Choose all that apply.

❏ God is patient with everyone.
❏ God wants to help each person to change his/her heart and life.
❏ God does not want anyone to be lost.

Isn't it incredible to think that God has saved a name just for you? One you don't even know? We've always assumed that the name we got is the name we will keep. Not so. Imagine what that implies. Apparently your future is so promising it warrants a new title. The road ahead is so bright a fresh name is needed. Your eternity is so special no common name will do.

So God has one reserved just for you. There is more to your life than you ever thought. There is more to your story than what you have read. There is more to your song than what you have sung. A good author saves the best for last. A great composer keeps his finest for the finish. And God, the author of life and composer of hope, has done the same for you.

The best is yet to be.
And so I urge you, don't give up.
And so I plead, finish the journey.
And so I exhort, be there.
Be there when God whispers your name.

The doorkeeper opens it for him, and the sheep hear his voice. He calls his own sheep by name and leads them out.

—John 10:3

THE HEART OF THE MATTER

- 🐑 **God demonstrates his care for us by using us in his service.**
- 🐑 **God won't be finished with you until Jesus comes again.**
- 🐑 **God has a new name for you—a unique, one-of-a-kind name that only he knows.**
- 🐑 **Our future in heaven is so promising it warrants a new home, a new body, a new life, and a new name.**

This is it. One last review of your memory verse for this week. Write out 1 Corinthians 8:3, your verse about God's care for you.

_____

_____

_____

Dear friends, don't let this one thing escape you: with the Lord one day is like 1,000 years, and 1,000 years like one day. The Lord does not delay His promise, as some understand delay, but is patient with you, not wanting any to perish, but all to come to repentance.

—2 Peter 3:8–9

The Heart of Jesus

Jesus washed his disciples' feet. Much is made of Peter's humorous outburst—first insisting that Jesus should not stoop to scrub his toes, then begging him to wash his head and hands too! But Peter wasn't the only one whose sandals were removed and whose feet were doused. Jesus gave this care to each one of the twelve, one at a time. He looked into the eyes of Thomas. He soothed the tired feet of Matthew. He poured the water over Judas' feet. Andrew felt the Lord's hands massage his soles. Bartholomew's feet were toweled by his Teacher. James met his Master's eyes over the basin. John returned Jesus' smile as the water splashed. One by one. Jesus tends to his people individually. He personally sees to our needs. We all receive Jesus' touch. We experience his care.

FOR FURTHER READING

Selections throughout this lesson were taken from *When God Whispers Your Name*.

[1] Augustine, Confessions I.i, quoted in Peter Kreeft, *Heaven: The Heart's Deepest Longing* (San Francisco: Ignatius Press, 1989), 49. The inspiration for this essay about the whippoorwill is drawn from Kreeft's description of "The Nightingale in the Heart," 51–54.
[2] With appreciation to Landon Saunders for this idea.
[3] Malcolm Muggeridge, *Jesus Rediscovered* (New York: Doubleday, 1979), 47–48, quoted in Peter Kreeft, *Heaven*, 63.

If my father and mother leave me, the Lord will take me in.

—Psalm 27:10

LESSON 2

Experiencing the Peace of Jesus

Maybe you can relate to the morning I just had.

It's Sunday. Sundays are always busy days for me. Sundays are always early days for me. Today promised to be no exception.

With a full slate of activities planned, I got up early and drove to church. There was not much traffic at 6:00 A.M. I had the roads to myself. The orange of dawn had yet to break the nighttime spell on the summer's black sky. The twilight sparkled. Cool air wafted.

I parked outside my church office and took a minute to enjoy the quietude. I set down my books, picked up my coffee, and leaned against the car.

It was calm. But calm has a way of becoming chaos.

With a briefcase in one hand and a coffee cup in the other, I walked and whistled across the parking lot to the office door. To enter my office, I had to get past the sleeping dog of the twentieth century: the alarm system. I set down my briefcase and unlocked the door. I picked up my briefcase and walked in.

The code box on the wall was flashing a red light.

The siren pounced on me like a mountain lion. I thought we were under nuclear attack. Floodlights flash flooded the hallway, and red strobes turned. I kept pushing buttons, and the alarm kept blaring. You'd have thought it was a breakout at Alcatraz.

My pulse raced, my forehead moistened, and my situation was desperate. I raced down the hall to my office, pulled open the lap drawer of my desk, and found the phone number of the alarm company.

The next twenty minutes were loud, demanding, confusing, and aggravating. I was speaking to technicians I couldn't see about equipment I didn't understand trying to understand words I couldn't hear.

Ever happened to you? When was the last time your life went from calm to chaos in half a minute? ("How many examples would you like?" you ask.) When was the last time you found yourself pushing buttons that didn't respond, struggling with instructions you couldn't hear, or operating a system you didn't understand?

If you've ever had your spouse call you at the office and say, "Just got a letter from the IRS. They are going to audit . . ."

If your boss has ever begun a conversation with these words: "You're a good worker, but with all this talk about a recession we have to cut back . . ."

If your teenager has ever walked in and asked, "Does our car insurance cover the other guy's car?"

Then you know that life can go from calm to chaos in a matter of moments. No warnings. No announcements. No preparation.

Little red lights blink, and you start pushing buttons. Sometimes you silence the alarm; sometimes it rips the air like a demon. The result can be peace or panic. The result can be calm or chaos.

It all depends on one factor: Do you know the code?

For me, this morning became chaos. Had I been prepared . . . had I known the code . . . had I known what to do when the warning flashed . . . calm would have triumphed.

Since we have been made right with God by our faith, we have peace with God. This happened through our Lord Jesus Christ.

—Romans 5:1

Throughout this week, you will be ushered into a day in Jesus' life when the calm could have become chaos. It has all the elements of anxiety: bad news and a death threat, followed by swarming demands, interruptions, inept disciples, and a blazing temptation to follow the crowd. In twenty-four pressure-packed hours, Jesus was carried from the summit of celebration to the valley of frustration.

It was the second most stressful day of his life. As soon as one alarm was disarmed, another began blinking. The rulers threatened. The crowds pressed. The followers doubted. The people demanded. When you see what he endured that day, you will wonder how he kept his cool.

Somehow, though, he did. Although the people pressed and the problems monsooned, Jesus didn't blow up or bail out. In fact, he did just the opposite. He served people, thanked God, and made cool-headed decisions.

I want to help you see how he did it. Through the studies this week, I'd like to share with you a few "internal codes" that you desperately need. Equip yourself with these internal codes, punch them in when the red lights of your world start to flash, and you will be amazed at how quickly the alarms will be disarmed.

EXPERIENCING THE PEACE OF JESUS THIS WEEK

Before you read any further, spend some time in prayer.

> *Dear Father, I need to hear your voice above the chaos in my life. Sometimes I am faced with hard decisions, and sometimes I am plagued with doubts. Teach me to trust you. I want to experience the peace of Jesus. Help me see his peaceful attitudes, decisions, and demeanor. Help me mirror him in my own life. Amen.*

This week, memorize John 14:27, Jesus' signature verse on peace.

"I leave you peace; my peace I give you. I do not give it to you as the world does. So don't let your hearts be troubled or afraid."

A HEART AT PEACE

The heart of Jesus was pure. The Savior was adored by thousands, yet content to live a simple life. He was cared for by women (Luke 8:1–3, yet never accused of lustful thoughts; scorned by his own creation, but willing to forgive them before they even requested his mercy. Peter, who traveled with Jesus for three and a half years, described him as a "lamb, unblemished and spotless" (1 Peter 1:19 NASB).

After spending the same amount of time with Jesus, John concluded, "And in him is no sin" (1 John 3:5 NIV).

Jesus' heart was peaceful. The disciples fretted over the need to feed the thousands, but not Jesus. He thanked God for the problem. The disciples shouted for fear in the storm, but not Jesus. He slept through it. Peter drew his sword to fight the soldiers, but not Jesus. He lifted his hand to heal. His heart was at peace.

—Just Like Jesus

DAY ONE—JESUS UNDER PRESSURE

MODELED BY THE MASTER

If you've ever had a day in which you've been blitzkrieged by demands, if you've ever ridden the roller coaster of sorrow and celebration, if you've ever wondered if God in heaven can relate to you on earth, then read and reread about this pressure-packed day in the life of Christ.

Take heart. Jesus knows how you feel.

Look up the following verses below and write down what you learn about God's ability to understand exactly what we are going through.

1. It is a comfort to know that you don't have to try to explain yourself to your Heavenly Father. He already knows how you tick. What does Paul say about God in 1 Corinthians 8:3?

   the man that love God is know by God.

2. According to Hebrews 2:17–18, why did Jesus have to experience bad days like this one?

   Knowing Jesus suffered pain and temptation Jesus trial understand are struggles. and that can trust Jesus to be with in my needed time

Jesus is able to understand our weaknesses.

For our high priest is able to understand our weaknesses. When he lived on earth, he was tempted in every way that we are, but he did not sin.

—Hebrews 4:15

I leave you peace; my peace I give you. I do not give it to you as the world does. So don't let your hearts be troubled or afraid.

—John 14:27

Therefore, it was necessary for Jesus to be in every respect like us, his brothers and sisters, so that he could be our merciful and faithful High Priest before God. He then could offer a sacrifice that would take away the sins of the people. Since he himself has gone through suffering and temptation, he is able to help us when we are being tempted.

—Hebrews 2:17–18 NLT

JESUS UNDERSTANDS

Jesus knows how you feel. You're under the gun at work? Jesus knows how you feel. You've got more to do than is humanly possible? So did he. People take more from you than they give? Jesus understands. Your teenagers won't listen? Your students won't try? Jesus knows how you feel.

You are precious to him. So precious that he became like you so that you would come to him.

When you struggle, he listens. When you yearn, he responds. When you question, he hears. He has been there.

—*In the Eye of the Storm*

And God's peace, which is so great we cannot understand it, will keep your hearts and minds in Christ Jesus.
—**Philippians 4:7**

UNEXPECTED NEWS

Jesus begins the morning by hearing about the death of John the Baptist: his cousin, his forerunner, his coworker, his friend (Matt. 14:1–13). The man who came closer to understanding Jesus than any other is dead.

Imagine losing the one person who knows you better than anyone else, and you will feel what Jesus is feeling. Reflect on the horror of being told that your dearest friend has just been murdered, and you will relate to Jesus' sorrow. Consider your reaction if you were told that your best friend had just been decapitated by a people-pleasing, incestuous monarch, and you'll see how the day begins for Christ. His world is beginning to turn upside down.

The emissaries brought more than news of sorrow, however; they brought a warning: "The same Herod who took John's head is interested in yours." Listen to how Luke presents the monarch's madness: "Herod said, 'I beheaded John. Who, then, is this I hear such things about?' *And he tried to see him*" (Luke 9:9 NIV, emphasis mine). Something tells me that Herod wanted more than a social visit.

So, with John's life taken and his own life threatened, Jesus chooses to get away for a while.

But before he can get away, his disciples arrive. The Gospel of Mark states that the "apostles gathered around Jesus and reported to him all they had done and taught" (Mark 6:30 NIV). They return exuberant. Jesus had commissioned them to proclaim the gospel and authenticate it with miracles. "They went out and preached that people should repent. They drove out many demons and anointed many sick people with oil and healed them" (Mark 6:12–13 NIV).

In a matter of moments, Jesus' heart goes from the pace of a funeral dirge to the triumphant march of a ticker-tape parade.

3. Why is the term "roller coaster" an appropriate description of our experience with human emotions?

   We all have more then we can handle we are so precious he became like us that we would come by him know what are need el Jesus know are every need.

4. While Jesus' emotions may have varied, his demeanor did not. In fact, the Bible reminds us we can count on Jesus' consistency at all times. Look up Hebrews 13:8, and fill in the blanks below.

   No matter the changes going on in our world, Jesus Christ remains the *same*. He is the same *yesterday*, *today* and *forever*.

UNEXPECTED DEMANDS

Look who follows the disciples to locate Jesus. About five thousand men plus women and children (Matt. 14:21)! Rivers of people cascade out of the hills and villages. Some scholars estimate the crowd to be as high as twenty-five thousand.[i] They swarm around Jesus, each with one desire: to meet the man who had empowered the disciples.

What had been a calm morning now buzzes with activity. "So many people were coming and going that they did not even have a chance to eat" (Mark 6:31 NIV).

I've had people demand my attention. I know what it's like to have a half-dozen kids wanting different things at the same time. I know the feeling of receiving one call with two other people waiting impatiently on other lines. I even know what it's like to be encircled by a dozen or so people, each making a separate request.

But twenty-five thousand? That's larger than many cities! No wonder the disciples couldn't eat. I'm surprised they could breathe!

5. What is your typical reaction to stressful environments of unexpected demands? Check your response.

   ❏ Panic-city—I stress myself out and worry those around me, too.
   ☒ Paralysis—I get so frazzled I can't make any decisions.

❏ Pack up—I am so overwhelmed that I just want to run away.
❏ Peace—I look to Jesus to see how he is going to work this out for me.

6. So, how can we find calm amid chaos? Look up the following Bible verses below and write down what you learn.

Isaiah 26:3 – To whom does God give peace?

He whose is steadfast because he trust in God is!

Philippians 4:6–7 – How can we find peace in the midst of our worries?

(prayer) is the work of the people of God God

A QUIET PLACE

The morning has been a jungle trail of the unexpected. First Jesus grieves over the death of a dear friend and relative. Then his life is threatened. Next he celebrates the triumphant return of his followers. Then he is nearly suffocated by a brouhaha of humanity. Bereavement . . . jeopardy . . . jubilation . . . bedlam.

Are you beginning to see why I call this the second most stressful day in the life of Christ? And it's far from over.

Jesus decides to take the disciples to a quiet place where they can rest and reflect. He shouts a command over the noise of the crowd. "Come with me by yourselves to a quiet place and get some rest" (Mark 6:31 NIV). The thirteen fight their way to the beach and climb into a boat.

Who would question his desire to get away from the people? He just needs a few hours alone. Just a respite. Just a retreat. Time to pray. Time to ponder. Time to weep. A time without crowds or demands. A campfire wreathed with friends. An evening with those he loves. The people can wait until tomorrow.

7. Jesus wants you to have peace. He knows the value of calm. Read the following verses. Then match each Scripture text with its corresponding statement about peace.

b Judges 6:24   a. God named his son, The Prince of Peace.
c Psalm 119:165   b. Gideon named an altar, The Lord is Peace.
a Isaiah 9:6   c. True peace is found in God's teachings.
e Matthew 5:9   d. God is a God of peace.
d 1 Corinthians 14:33   e. God calls those who work for peace his children.

8. Peace comes easily when we find ourselves in quiet places, alone with the Lord. But how can we experience peace when faced with interruption after interruption? What does Paul pray in 2 Thessalonians 3:16? *The Grace of our Lord be with us all*

The people, however, have other ideas. "The crowds learned about it and followed him" (Luke 9:11 NIV). It's a six-mile walk around the northeastern corner of the Sea of Galilee, so the crowd takes a hike. When Jesus got to Bethsaida, his desired retreat had become a roaring arena.

"Surprise!"

Add to the list of sorrow, peril, excitement, and bedlam, the word *interruption*. Jesus' plans are interrupted. What he has in mind for his day and what the people have in mind for his day are two different agendas. What Jesus seeks and what Jesus gets are not the same.

Sound familiar?

Remember when you sought a night's rest and got a colicky baby? Remember when you sought to catch up at the office and got even further behind? Remember when you sought to use your Saturday for leisure, but ended up fixing your neighbor's sink?

God gives peace to those who trust him.

You, Lord, give true peace to those who depend on you, because they trust you.
—Isaiah 26:3

Do not worry about anything, but pray and ask God for everything you need, always giving thanks. And God's peace, which is so great we cannot understand it, will keep your hearts and minds in Christ Jesus.
—Philippians 4:6–7

For God is not a God of confusion but of peace.
—1 Corinthians 14:33

May the Lord of peace himself always give you his peace no matter what happens.
—2 Thessalonians 3:16 NLT

May the Lord bless you and keep you. May the Lord show you his kindness and have mercy on you. May the Lord watch over you and give you peace.
—Numbers 6:24–26

Jesus knows how you feel.

Take comfort, friend. It happened to Jesus, too.

In fact, this would be a good time to pause and digest the central message of this chapter.

Jesus knows how you feel.

Ponder this and use it the next time your world goes from calm to chaos.

His pulse has raced. His eyes have grown weary. His heart has grown heavy. He has had to climb out of bed with a sore throat. He has been kept awake late and has gotten up early. He knows how you feel.

9. Fill in the blanks in the statement below that summarizes what we learn about Jesus in Hebrews 4:15.

Jesus is able to *sympathize* our weakness. He knows we sometimes sin when we are overwhelmed. However, when he lived on earth, he was *tempted in* to react the same way and yet he did not *Sin*. *every way*

OUR HIGH PRIEST

Read how J. B. Phillips translates Hebrews 4:15:

For we have no superhuman High Priest to whom our weaknesses are unintelligible—he himself has shared fully in all our experience of temptation, except that he never sinned.

It's as if he knows that we will say to God . . . "God, it's easy for you up there. You don't know how hard it is from down here." So he boldly proclaims Jesus' ability to understand. Look at the wording again.

He himself. Not an angel. Not an ambassador. Not an emissary, but Jesus himself.

Shared fully. Not partially. Not nearly. Not to a large degree. Entirely! Jesus shared fully.

In all our experience. Every hurt. Each ache. All the stresses and all the strains. No exceptions. No substitutes. Why? So he could sympathize with our weaknesses.

—*In the Eye of the Storm*

You may have trouble believing that. You probably believe that Jesus knows what it means to endure heavy-duty tragedies. You are no doubt convinced that Jesus is acquainted with sorrow and has wrestled with fear. Most people accept that. But can God relate to the hassles and headaches of my life? Of your life?

For some reason this is harder to believe.

Perhaps that's why portions of this day are recorded in all the Gospel accounts. No other event, other than the Crucifixion, is told by all four Gospel writers. Not Jesus' baptism. Not his temptation. Not even his birth. But all four writers chronicle this day. It's as if Matthew, Mark, Luke, and John knew that you would wonder if God understands. And they proclaim their response in four-part harmony:

Jesus knows how you feel.

10. Which of the following statements are true concerning Jesus' ability to understand how you feel, and which ones are false? Mark your answers True (T) or False (F). Use the Bible verses below to help you answer.

T Because Jesus was tempted and suffered, he can help us through our temptations and sufferings. (Hebrews 2:18)

F Jesus is frustrated by our weaknesses. (Hebrews 5:2)

T Jesus offers to carry our loads because he is humble and willing. (Matthew 11:28–30)

F Jesus is unmoved by our tears. (John 11:33, 35)

Since he himself is weak, he is able to be gentle with those who do not understand and who are doing wrong things.

—*Hebrews 5:2*

11. Was your heart stirred by one of the Scripture verses today? Did one statement in particular stand out and deepen your understanding of peace? Summarize what you learned here.

Over + over he telles me he unstands. I never felt so at peace that Im never alone.

Jesus can help us through our temptations and sufferings.

THE HEART OF THE MATTER

- **Jesus is able to understand our weaknesses.**
- **God gives peace to those who trust him.**
- **Jesus knows how we feel.**
- **Jesus can help us through our temptations and sufferings.**

Take a few moments here to write out your Bible memory verse. It is John 14:27.

Peace I leave with you. My peace I give you. I do not give to you as the world gives. Do not let your hearts be troubled and do not be afraid.

You, Lord, give true peace to those who depend on you, because they trust you.

—*Isaiah 26:3*

The Heart of Jesus

"I can't believe he's sleeping through this," muttered a disciple through clenched teeth. Straining at the oars as another swell lifted them high, the twelve clung to the sides for dear life. Water had washed over the sides, nearly swamping them. The fishermen—Peter and Andrew, James and John—were used to rough seas, but Matthew the tax collector was looking pretty green. The storm had come up suddenly, and they had been engulfed by its fury with almost no warning. Eyes narrowed against the wind and spray, feet spread to balance himself on the pitching deck, Peter finally called out the order. "Wake him." The disciple nearest Jesus crept forward and shook his shoulder. Panic tingeing his voice, "Teacher, don't you care that we are drowning?" Then Jesus stood up, and addressed the storm, "Be quiet!" The suddenness of the calm sent a few disciples sprawling. The wind they had been leaning into was simply . . . gone! Exchanging wondering glances for a moment, they turned their eyes as one to their Teacher. He had quieted the storm. He had given them peace.

DAY TWO—HEARING JESUS' VOICE

FENDING OFF THE VOICES

You've heard them. They tell you to swap your integrity for a new sale. To barter your convictions for an easy deal. To exchange your devotion for a quick thrill.

They whisper. They woo. They taunt. They tantalize. They flirt. They flatter. "Go ahead, it's OK." "Just wait until tomorrow." "Don't worry, no one will know." "How could anything that feels so right be so wrong?"

The voices of the crowd.

Our lives are Wall Streets of chaos, stock markets loud with demands. Grown men and women barking in a frenzied effort to get all they can before time runs out. "Buy. Sell. Trade. Swap. But whatever you do, do it fast—and loud."

A carnival of gray-flannel suits where no one smiles and everyone dashes.

An endless chorus of booming voices: some offering, some taking, and all screaming.

What do we do with the voices?

1. Read the following verses. Then match the verse with what you learn concerning "the voices of the crowd."

   E Proverbs 5:3   a. Wicked friends can lead the righteous astray.
   e Proverbs 7:21b   b. They are deceptive, and lead others into disaster.
   A Proverbs 12:26   c. They use clever and pleasing tactics.
   C Proverbs 16:29   d. They lead people astray, but fall into their own trap.
   d Proverbs 28:10   e. Their voices appear temptingly sweet.

FALSE PROMISES OF PEACE

Even the voices that Jesus heard promised something.

"After the people saw the miraculous sign that Jesus did, they began to say, 'Surely this is the Prophet who is to come into the world'" (John 6:14 NIV).

To the casual observer, these are the voices of victory. To the untrained ear, these are the sounds of triumph. What could be better? Five thousand men plus women and

And the sheep listen to the voice of the shepherd.

—John 10:3

The voices of the crowd are persuasive and clamor for attention.

God is not a God of confusion but a God of peace.

—1 Corinthians 14:33a

children proclaiming Christ to be the prophet. Thousands of voices swelling into a roar of revival, an ovation of adulation.

The people have everything they need for a revolution.

They have an enemy: Herod. They have a martyr: John the Baptist. They have leadership: the disciples. They have ample supplies: Jesus the bread maker. And they have a king: Jesus of Nazareth.

Why wait? The time has come. Israel will be restored. God's people have heard God's voice.

"King Jesus!" someone proclaims. And the crowd chimes in.

The righteous should choose his friends carefully, For the way of the wicked leads them astray.

—Proverbs 12:26 NKJV

2. The noise of the world will try to distract you and steal your peace in his presence. God warns us throughout Scripture concerning these peace-robbing false promises. Which of the following are true concerning God's teachings on these lying voices? Check all that apply. Use the Bible verses below to help you answer.

☑ Good people hate what is false. (Proverbs 13:5)
☑ Liars will never escape punishment. (Proverbs 19:5)
☑ Lying voices tell us to pay no attention to God. (Jeremiah 23:16)
☑ Jesus said to watch out for false prophets. (Matthew 7:15)
☐ There is nothing false about Jesus' promises. (John 1:47)

Violent people deceive their friends and lead them to disaster.

—Prov. 16:29 TEV

And don't think for a minute that Christ didn't hear their chant.

A chorus promising power intoxicates. No cross needed. No sacrifice required. An army of disciples at his fingertips. Power to change the world without having to die doing it.

Revenge would be sweet. The one who took the head of John the Baptist is only a few miles away. I wonder if he has ever felt a cold blade on his neck.

Yes, Jesus heard the voices. He heard the lurings. But he also heard someone else. And when Jesus heard him, he sought him.

"Jesus, knowing that they intended to come and make him king by force, withdrew again to a mountain by himself" (John 6:15 NIV).

Jesus preferred to be alone with the true God rather than in a crowd with the wrong people.

Logic didn't tell him to dismiss the crowds. Conventional wisdom didn't tell him to turn his back on a willing army. No, it wasn't a voice from without that Jesus heard. It was a voice from within.

My dear children, you belong to God and have defeated them; because God's Spirit, who is in you, is greater than the devil, who is in the world. And they belong to the world, so what they say is from the world, and the world listens to them. But we belong to God, and those who know God listen to us. But those who are not from God do not listen to us. That is how we know the Spirit that is true and the spirit that is false.

—1 John 4:4–6

3. Read 1 John 4:4–6 at the left. Fill in the blanks below about what you learn from this passage concerning listening to God's voice.

We belong to ___God___. God's Spirit, who is in ___us___, is greater than the ___world___, who is in the ___Spirit___. Worldly people speak the ___different___ language. That's why the rest of the ___world___ listens to them. However, we ___listen___ to God.

JESUS' VOICE

The mark of a sheep is its ability to hear the Shepherd's voice.

"And the sheep listen to the voice of the shepherd. He calls his own sheep by name and leads them out" (John 10:3).

The mark of a disciple is his or her ability to hear the Master's voice.

"Here I am! I stand at the door and knock. If anyone hears my voice and opens the door, I will come in and eat with him, and he with me" (Rev. 3:20 NIV).

The world rams at your door; Jesus taps at your door. The voices scream for your allegiance; Jesus softly and tenderly requests it. The world promises flashy pleasure; Jesus promises a quiet dinner . . . with God. "I will come in and eat."

Which voice do you hear?

Now may the Lord of peace give you peace at all times and in every way. The Lord be with all of you.

—2 Thessalonians 3:16

Let me state something important. There is never a time during which Jesus is not speaking. Never. There is never a place in which Jesus is not present. Never. There is never a room so dark . . . a lounge so sensual . . . an office so sophisticated . . . that the ever-present, ever-pursuing, relentlessly tender Friend is not there, tapping gently on the doors of our hearts—waiting to be invited in.

Few hear his voice. Fewer still open the door.

But never interpret our numbness as his absence. For amidst the fleeting promises of pleasure is the timeless promise of his presence.

"Surely I am with you always, to the very end of the age"(Matt. 28:20 NIV)

"Never will I leave you; never will I forsake you" (Heb. 13:5 NIV)

There is no chorus so loud that the voice of God cannot be heard . . . if we will but listen.

4. Based on what you have just read, what is true about listening to Jesus' voice? Check all that apply.

- ❏ Only Jesus' sheep recognize his voice.
- ❏ The world noisily clamors for our attention.
- ❏ Jesus speaks softly with his invitation of peace.
- ❏ Jesus is always speaking; we just have to listen.

> Jesus avoided the flattery of the crowd. He preferred to be alone with God.

JESUS' PEACE IN OUR DECISIONS

There is another side to the voices that rob our peace—those that attempt to confuse good with better, and better with best. When it comes to having peace in our decision-making process, we need to study the example of Jesus.

There is only so much sand in the hourglass. Who gets it?

You know what I'm talking about, don't you?

"The PTA needs a new treasurer. With your background and experience and talent and wisdom and love for kids and degree in accounting, YOU are the perfect one for the job!"

"There's going to be some shuffling in the ranks. With the retirement of the branch manager, somebody will move up. The company is looking for a bright, young sales-man—someone like you—who is willing to demonstrate his dedication to the orga-nization by taking on some extra projects . . . and working some late hours."

"I apologize that I have to ask you again, but you are such a good Sunday school teacher. If you could only take one more quarter . . ."

"I just lost my hygienist. Will you come back to work for me? I know you don't want to go back to work until your children start school. But it's only four hours a day and there's a day care center just a few blocks from my office now. Wouldn't the extra money be nice?"

"Would I be willing to serve as chapter president? Well, to be honest, I was going to sit out this term because our youngest goes to college next fall. Yes, I realize this is a critical year for the organization . . . Oh, no, I wouldn't want the club to falter . . . Yes, we have made great progress over the last few months. It's just that . . ."

It's tug-of-war, and you are the rope.

On one side are the requests for your time and energy. They call. They compliment. They are valid and good. Great opportunities to do good things. If they were evil, it'd be easy to say no. But they aren't, so it's easy to rationalize.

On the other side are the loved ones in your world. They don't write you letters. They don't ask you to consult your calendar. They don't offer to pay your expenses. They don't use terms like "appointment," "engagement," or "do lunch." They don't want you for what you can do for them; they want you for who you are.

> Sheep know the voice of their shepherd.

5. In what ways do you feel the strain of the "tug of war" concerning your decisions?

you have to stick to want feel what important
if you agree to say no stick with it, feel good
of yourself turn it over to God, it never makes the wrong answer

> *Christ himself is our peace.*
> —**Ephesians 2:14a**

If you go the wrong way—to the right or to the left—you will hear a voice behind you saying, "This is the right way. You should go this way."

—Isaiah 30:21

A CLEARED CALENDAR

Jesus often withdrew to lonely places and prayed.

—Luke 5:16 NIV

How long has it been since you let God have you?

I mean really *have* you? How long since you gave him a portion of undiluted, uninterrupted time listening for his voice? Apparently, Jesus did. He made a deliberate effort to spend time with God.

Spend much time reading about the listening life of Jesus and a distinct pattern emerges. He spent regular time with God, praying and listening. Mark says, "Very early in the morning, while it was still dark, Jesus got up, left the house and went off to a solitary place, where he prayed" (Mark 1:35 NIV) . . .

Let me ask the obvious. If Jesus, the Son of God, the sinless Savior of humankind, thought it worthwhile to clear his calendar to pray, wouldn't we be wise to do the same?

—*Just Like Jesus*

He sent the people home.

—Matt. 14:22, NLT

Sometimes peace comes from saying no to good things in order to choose what is better.

I told you these things so that you can have peace in me. In this world you will have trouble, but be brave! I have defeated the world.

—John 16:33

6. Read Isaiah 30:21 on the left. Sometimes we are in danger of wandering off of God's path. What should we be listening for during times of indecision?

God's voice

JESUS' DECISION

A world of insight is hidden in four words in Matthew 14:22: "He dismissed the crowd" (NIV). This wasn't just any crowd that Jesus dismissed.

These weren't casually curious.

These weren't coincidental bystanders.

This was a multitude with a mission. They had heard the disciples. They had left their homes. They had followed Jesus around the sea. They had heard him teach and had seen him heal. They had eaten the bread. And they were ready to make him king.

Surely Jesus will commandeer the crowd and focus their frenzy. Surely he will seize the chance to convert the thousands. Surely he will spend the night baptizing the willing followers. No one would turn down an opportunity to minister to thousands of people, right?

Jesus did.

"He dismissed the crowd." Why? Read verse 23: "After he had dismissed them, he went up on a mountainside by himself to pray" (NIV).

He said no to the important in order to say yes to the vital.

He said no to a good opportunity in order to say yes to a better opportunity. It wasn't a selfish decision. It was a deliberate choice to honor priorities. If Jesus thought it necessary to say no to the demands of the crowds in order to pray, don't you think you and I should, too?

7. Why did Jesus dismiss the crowd?

He liked to be alone to pray.

8. What does Jesus' example teach you about the priority of prayer when it comes to experiencing peace?

Pray & Pray, and listen for the answer

9. Based on what you have learned about Jesus' peace, which of the following are true, and which are false? Mark your answers True (T) or False (F).

T Jesus' example teaches us to put a priority on prayer during chaotic times.
T Sometimes peace comes from saying no to good things in order to choose what is better.
F We can never say "yes" to too many good things.
T We must choose our priorities—they don't just happen naturally.

THE HEART OF THE MATTER

- The voices of the crowd are persuasive and clamor for attention.
- Jesus avoided the flattery of the crowd. He preferred to be alone with God.
- Sheep know the voice of their shepherd.
- When Jesus heard God's voice, he sought him.
- If great opportunities were obviously evil, it'd be easy to say no.
- Sometimes peace comes from saying no to good things in order to choose what is better.

Review your Scripture memory verse for the week by writing it out here. Remember, it's John 14:27.

Peace I leave with you my peace I give you, I do not give to you as the world gives. Do not let your heart be troubled and don't be afraid.

The Heart of Jesus

Her world was turned upside down. How could this have happened? He had seemed so . . . *alive* just a couple of weeks ago. The house seemed too quiet now. Empty. Lonely. Mary wouldn't even leave her room. There was a tension in the air because of the question that neither of them dared to ask out loud. Why hadn't Jesus come? He could have healed Lazarus. They had sent a messenger. They had asked for him to come. The message had been delivered. But still Jesus had not come. Why not?

Just then word arrived—Jesus was coming. Martha gathered herself up and trudged down the road to meet him. Her feet beat a steady rhythm on the path, "Too late, too late, too late." When she drew up to the Master, the accusations that had plagued her for four days leapt to her lips. "If you had been here, my brother would not have died." Jesus' words gave her a glimmer of hope, "Your brother will rise and live again." Eyeing him cautiously, Martha retorted, "I know he will rise again . . . in the last day." Little good that did her grief now. But Jesus patiently replied, "I am the resurrection. I am the life. Those who believe in me will never die." Then fixing her with a steady gaze, "Martha, do you believe this?" With a trembling sigh and a lift of her chin, Martha stated with confidence, "Yes, Lord." It was enough. Jesus had reminded her of her faith. He renewed her assurance. He lent her confidence. He filled her with peace. Though her grief over Lazarus' death was acute, her faith was stronger. Whether now or later, Lazarus would live again. Turning towards home, Martha hurried to Mary. Martha had experienced the peace of Jesus.

DAY THREE—DOUBTSTORMS

Thursday

WINDOW OF THE HEART

There is a window in your heart through which you can see God. Once upon a time that window was clear. Your view of God was crisp. You could see God as vividly as you could see a gentle valley or hillside. The glass was clean, the pane unbroken.

You knew God. You knew how he worked. You knew what he wanted you to do. No surprises. Nothing unexpected. You knew that God had a will, and you continually discovered what it was.

Then, suddenly, the window cracked. A pebble broke the window. A pebble of pain.

Perhaps the stone struck when you were a child and a parent left home—forever. Maybe the rock hit in adolescence when your heart was broken. Maybe you made it into adulthood before the window was cracked. But then the pebble came.

Was it a phone call? "We have your daughter at the station. You'd better come down."

Was it a letter on the kitchen table? "I've left. Don't try to reach me. Don't try to call me. It's over. I just don't love you anymore."

Was it a diagnosis from the doctor? "I'm afraid our news is not very good."

Was it a telegram? "We regret to inform you that your son is missing in action."

But if any of you needs wisdom, you should ask God for it . . . But when you ask God, you must believe and not doubt. Anyone who doubts is like a wave in the sea, blown up and down by the wind. Such doubters are thinking two different things at the same time, and they cannot decide about anything they do.

—James 1:5–8

I will give peace to your country; you will lie down in peace, and no one will make you afraid.

—Leviticus 26:6a

It is hard to see God through our pain.

THE LORD IS PEACE

God's peace, which is so great we cannot understand it, will keep your hearts and minds in Christ Jesus.

—Philippians 4:7

The Lord came to Gideon and told him he was to lead his people in victory over the Midianites. That's like God telling a housewife to stand up to her abusive husband or a high school student to take on drug peddlers or a preacher to preach the truth to a congregation of Pharisees. "Y-y-you-b-b-better get somebody else," we stammer. But then God reminds us that he knows we can't, but he can, and to prove it he gives a wonderful gift. He brings a spirit of peace. A peace before the storm. A peace beyond logic . . . He gave it to David after he showed him Goliath; he gave it to Saul after he showed him the gospel; he gave it to Jesus after he showed him the cross. And he gave it to Gideon. So Gideon, in turn, gave the name to God. He built an altar and named it Jehovah-shalom, the Lord is peace (Judges 65:24).

—*The Great House of God*

And through Christ, God has brought all things back to himself again—things on earth and things in heaven. God made peace through the blood of Christ's death on the cross.

—**Colossians 1:20**

Whatever the pebble's form, the result was the same—a shattered window. The pebble shot into the pane and shattered it. The crash echoed down the halls of your heart. Cracks shot out from the point of impact, creating a spider web of fragmented pieces.

And suddenly God was not so easy to see. The view that had been so crisp had changed. You turned to see God, and his figure was distorted. It was hard to see him through the pain. It was hard to see him through the fragments of hurt.

1. Pain is no stranger to those who love God. We are not exempt from life's suffering. Read the following verses and write down what you learn about the heartache of these men.

   Job – "At least I can take comfort in this: Despite the pain, I have not denied the words of the Holy One." —Job 6:10 NLT

   To trust God in Good times is one thing But how hard ~~tool~~ shatters its the trust deep down of Jesus that brings you back.

   Jeremiah – "Oh, how I hurt! How I hurt! I am bent over in pain. Oh, the torture in my heart! My heart is pounding inside me. I cannot keep quiet, because I have heard the sound of the trumpet. I have heard the shouts of war." —Jeremiah 4:19

   God is not ~~deing~~ deceiving us hard times it makes us stronger and trust him more

   Jonah – "But this made Jonah very unhappy, and he became angry. 'I ask you, Lord, please kill me. It is better for me to die than to live.'" —Jonah 4:1, 3

   We do not tell the Lord when its are time even He is the one He knows when its are time

   Paul – "Brothers and sisters, we want you to know about the trouble we suffered in Asia. We had great burdens there that were beyond our own strength. We even gave up hope of living." —2 Corinthians 1:8

   Our burden are never so bad that when we live with Jesus we can make it through

   Jesus – "He was hated and rejected by people. He had much pain and suffering. People would not even look at him. He was hated, and we didn't even notice him." —Isaiah 53:3

   I love him with all my heart. I'm sure their are times hes not happy with me but he died on the cross for me and all how Beline

You were puzzled. God wouldn't allow something like this to happen, would he? Tragedy and travesty weren't on the agenda of the One you had seen, were they? Had you been fooled? Had you been blind?

The moment the pebble struck, the glass became a reference point for you. From then on, there was life before the pain and life after the pain. Before your pain, the view was clear; God seemed so near. After your pain, well, he was harder to see. He seemed a bit distant . . . harder to perceive. Your pain distorted the view—not eclipsed it, but distorted it.

Maybe these words don't describe your situation. There are some people who never have to redefine or refocus their view of God. Most of us do.

Most of us know what it means to feel disappointed by God.

We look for God, but can't find him. Fragmented glass hinders our vision. He is enlarged through this piece and reduced through that one. Lines jigsaw their way across his face. Large sections of shattered glass opaque the view.

And now you aren't quite sure what you see.

2. Pain disturbs our peace more easily and more often than any other event. Heartbreak can take our eyes off Jesus. We turn inward. To mourn. To grieve. Fill in the blanks about what you learn from the following verses about God's reaction to heartbreak.

Pain disturbs our peace more easily than anything else.

The Lord is _close_ to the brokenhearted. (Psalm 34:18)
He promises to _heals_ those who are brokenhearted. (Psalm 147:3) *binds their wounds.*
God sent Jesus to _bind up_ all the broken hearts. (Isaiah 61:1)

WHERE IS JESUS?

"Immediately Jesus told his followers to get into the boat and go ahead of him across the lake. He stayed there to send the people home. After he had sent them away, he went by himself up into the hills to pray. It was late, and Jesus was there alone. By this time, the boat was already far away from land. It was being hit by waves, because the wind was blowing against it. Between three and six o'clock in the morning, Jesus came to them, walking on the water. When his followers saw him walking on the water, they were afraid. They said, 'It's a ghost!' and cried out in fear. But Jesus quickly spoke to them, 'Have courage! It is I. Do not be afraid.'" —Matthew 14:22–27

3. Read Matthew 14:22–27 above and answer the following questions.

What were Jesus' instructions to the disciples?
Get in the boat and go ahead of him as Jesus wanted be alone to pray

What did Jesus do once he dismissed the crowd?
whnt on top of a mountain to pray by him self.

Meanwhile, what was happening to the disciples?
storm

How did Jesus respond to their fear and doubts?

The Lord is close to the brokenhearted, and he saves those whose spirits have been crushed.
—Psalm 34:18

Matthew is specific about the order of events. Jesus sent the disciples to the boat. Then he dismissed the crowd and ascended a mountainside. It was evening, probably around 6:00 P.M. The storm struck immediately. The sun had scarcely set before typhoon-like winds began to roar.

Note that Jesus sent the disciples out into the storm alone. Even as he was ascending the mountainside, he could feel and hear the gale's force. Jesus was not ignorant of the storm. He was aware that a torrent was coming that would carpet-bomb the sea's surface. But he didn't turn around. The disciples were left to face the storm . . . alone.

The greatest storm that night was not in the sky; it was in the disciples' hearts. The greatest fear was not from seeing the storm-driven waves; it came from seeing the back of their leader as he left them to face the night with only questions as companions.

4. How do the storms of life—painful trials and suffering— make us feel alone?
We fell were alone

Imagine the incredible strain of bouncing from wave to wave in a tiny fishing vessel. One hour would weary you. Two hours would exhaust you.

Surely Jesus will help us, they thought. They'd seen him still storms like this before. On this same sea, they had awakened him during a storm, and he had commanded the

The God who gives peace be with you all.
—Romans 15:33

When all we have are questions, we must cling to faith.

skies to be silent. They'd seen him quiet the wind and soothe the waves. Surely he will come off the mountain.

But he doesn't. Their arms begin to ache from rowing. Still no sign of Jesus. Three hours. Four hours. The winds rage. The boat bounces. Still no Jesus. Midnight comes. Their eyes search for God—in vain.

By now the disciples have been on the sea for as long as six hours.

All this time they have fought the storm and sought the Master. And, so far, the storm is winning. And the Master is nowhere to be found.

"Where is he?" cried one.

"Has he forgotten us?" yelled another.

"He feeds thousands of strangers and yet leaves us to die?" muttered a third.

5. We may feel like God has forgotten us at times. However, God's Word challenges our feelings and encourages us to exercise faith instead. Read Isaiah 49:14–15 and fill in the blanks below.

We may say to ourselves, "The ___Lord.___ has left ___Me___. The Lord has ___forgotten___ about me." That's like saying a mother could ___forget___ her nursing baby. Even if she could forget, God says he will ___not___ forget us.

DOUBTSTORMS

"The Lord has left me; the Lord has forgotten me." The Lord answers, "Can a woman forget the baby she nurses? Can she feel no kindness for the child to which she gave birth? Even if she could forget her children, I will not forget you."

—Isaiah 49:14–15

There are snowstorms. There are hailstorms. There are rainstorms. And there are doubtstorms.

"If God is so good, why do I sometimes feel so bad?"

"If his message is so clear, why do I get so confused?"

"If the Father is in control, why do good people have gut-wrenching problems?"

Tough questions. Throw-in-the-towel questions. Questions the disciples must have asked in the storm.

All they could see were black skies as they bounced in the battered boat. Swirling clouds. Wind-driven white caps. Pessimism that buried the coastline. Gloom that swamped the bow. What could have been a pleasant trip became a white-knuckled ride through a sea of fear.

Their question—What hope do we have of surviving a stormy night?

My question—Where is God when his world is stormy?

Doubtstorms: turbulent days when the enemy is too big, the task too great, the future too bleak, and the answers too few.

6. Which of the following are true concerning doubtstorms, and which ones are false? Mark your answers True (T) or False (F).

___F___ True Christians never experience doubtstorms.

___T___ Doubtstorms typically focus on one question: Where is God?

___T___ The disciples faced their doubtstorm when it seemed Jesus had abandoned them.

___T___ We feel alone in doubtstorms.

PEACE IN JESUS' PRESENCE

When you lie down, you won't be afraid; when you lie down, you will sleep in peace.
—Proverbs 3:24

It's 1:00 A.M., no Jesus.

It's 2:00 A.M., no Jesus.

Peter, Andrew, James, and John have seen storms like this. They are fishermen; the sea is their life. They know the havoc the gale-force winds can wreak. They've seen the splintered hulls float to shore. They've attended the funerals. They know, better than anyone, that this night could be their last. "Why doesn't he come?" they sputter.

Finally, he does. "During the fourth watch of the night [3:00 to 6:00 A.M.] Jesus went out to them, walking on the lake" (Matt. 14:25 NIV).

Jesus came. He finally came. But between verse 24—being buffeted by waves—and verse 25—when Jesus appeared—a thousand questions are asked.

Questions you have probably asked, too. Perhaps you know the angst of being suspended between verses 24 and 25. Maybe you're riding a storm, searching the coastline for a light, a glimmer of hope. You know that Jesus knows what you are going through. You know that he's aware of your storm. But as hard as you look to find him, you can't see him.

7. Read Matthew 14:25–27 and respond to the following. Which statements are true regarding Jesus' reaction to the disciples' fear? Check all that apply.

☑ He saw their fear and immediately reassured them.
☐ He scolded them and shook his head.
☑ He told them to have courage—he was here now.

Between three and six o'clock in the morning, Jesus came to them, walking on the water. When his followers saw him walking on the water, they were afraid. They said, "It's a ghost!" and cried out in fear. But Jesus quickly spoke to them, "Have courage! It is I. Do not be afraid."
—Matthew 14:25–27

Every so often a storm will come, and I'll look up into the blackening sky and say, "God, a little light, please?"

The light came for the disciples. A figure came to them walking on the water. It wasn't what they expected. Perhaps they were looking for angels to descend or heaven to open. Maybe they were listening for a divine proclamation to still the storm. We don't know what they were looking for. But one thing is for sure, they weren't looking for Jesus to come walking on the water.

"'It's a ghost,' they said and cried out in fear" (Matt. 14:26 NIV).

And since Jesus came in a way they didn't expect, they almost missed seeing the answer to their prayers.

The message? When you can't see him, trust him. The figure you see is not a ghost. The voice you hear is not the wind.

Jesus is closer than you've ever dreamed.

Even when we can't see Jesus, we must trust him.

8. How is experiencing Jesus' peace directly related to exercising our faith?

_____

_____

THE HEART OF THE MATTER

❦ **It is hard to see God through our pain.**
❦ **Pain disturbs our peace more than anything else.**
❦ **When all we have are questions, we must cling to faith.**
❦ **Even when we can't see Jesus, we must trust him.**
❦ **Jesus is closer than you've ever dreamed.**

Fill in the blanks here to review your memory verse for the week.

I leave you __peace__ ; my __peace__ I __give__ you. I do not __give__ it to you as the __world__ does. So don't let your __heart__ be __trouble__ or __afraid__." —John 14:27

The Heart of Jesus

His life was torment. Pure torment. Days were spent ranging in amidst the tombs of the dead. Nights found him wandering through the mountains, keening and wailing through the cold nights. He was lonely, but never alone, this demon-possessed man. Those who pitied him could not tame him. Those who feared him could not bind him. To the children in the nearby town, he was like the boogeyman—the stuff of nightmares. His arms and legs bore the scars of rope and chain. Rocks had cut into his flesh. He ran about naked, hair and beard unkempt and matted. A prisoner who had

This is what the Lord says: "I will give her peace that will flow to her like a river. The wealth of the nations will come to her like a river overflowing its banks. Like babies you will be nursed and held in my arms and bounced on my knees.

—Isaiah 66:12

Jesus is closer than you've ever dreamed.

abandoned hope. A slave to forces beyond his control. All he knew were madness and mayhem. Then, Jesus stepped onto his shore, and everything changed. The hand that touched him was gentle. The voice that reached him spoke peace. Jesus did not fear him—he freed him! Word spread, and by the time the townspeople arrived on the scene, they barely recognized the man. He was clothed and in his right mind. He was released from his torment. Jesus had made him whole again. The man now knew the peace of Jesus.

Friday

DAY FOUR—FEAR THAT BECOMES FAITH

FAITH—THE CHILD OF FEAR

Faith is often the child of fear.

Fear propelled Peter out of the boat. He'd ridden these waves before. He knew what these storms could do. He'd heard the stories. He'd seen the wreckage. He knew the widows. He knew the storm could kill. And he wanted out.

All night he wanted out. For nine hours he'd tugged on sails, wrestled with oars, and searched every shadow on the horizon for hope. He was soaked to the soul and bone weary of the wind's banshee wail.

Look into Peter's eyes and you won't see a man of conviction. Search his face and you won't find a gutsy grimace. Later on, you will. You'll see his courage in the garden. You'll witness his devotion at Pentecost. You'll behold his faith in his epistles.

But not tonight. Look into his eyes tonight and see fear—a suffocating, heart-racing fear of a man who has no way out.

But out of this fear would be born an act of faith, for faith is often the child of fear.

"The fear of the Lord is the beginning of wisdom," (Prov. 9:10 NIV) wrote the wise man.

1. Summarize the statement "faith is often the child of fear" in your own words.

   My Faith is when I want something badly that I waite as long as it pleases to come.

2. Experiencing Jesus' peace often comes at a great price to our idea of security— what we can control. We have to let go of what we know and step out in faith. Which of the following statements are true? Check all that apply. Use the Bible verses below to help you answer.

   ☑ Moses did not raise his staff on the bank of the Red Sea because it was the logical thing to do. He merely did as God commanded. (Exodus 14:15–16)

   ☐ David did not face Goliath on the battlefield because he had studied his opponent's fighting style and had uncovered a weakness. He trusted God. (1 Samuel 17:37)

   ☑ Naaman did not dip seven times in the Jordan river because of recent findings in medical research. It was faith. (2 Kings 5:13–14)

   ☑ Paul did not decide to abandon the Law and embrace grace because it was common sense. He met Christ, and it changed him forever. (Romans 3)

Come to me, all of you who are tired and have heavy loads, and I will give you rest.
—Matthew 11:28

The individuals in these stories were never stronger than the moment they let go of their own security in order to experience what only God could provide. Ultimate victory. Lasting peace.

THE PEACE OF GOD

Biographies of bold disciples begin with chapters of honest terror. Fear of death. Fear of failure. Fear of loneliness. Fear of a wasted life. Fear of failing to know God.

Faith begins when you see God on the mountain and you are in the valley and you know that you're too weak to make the climb. You see what you need . . . you see what you have . . . and what you have isn't enough to accomplish anything.

Peter had given it his best. But his best wasn't enough.

He is aware of two facts: He is going down, and Jesus is staying up. He knows where he would rather be. There's nothing wrong with this response. Faith that begins with fear will end up nearer the Father.

We must realize all we are doing to produce lasting peace in our own strength is not working. We work, but there is never enough money to go around. We try, but it seems relational harmony doesn't last long enough. Our households are in upheaval more times than not. Then we panic because we are running out of human strategies to "keep the peace." We need to experience the peace of God.

3. Read Isaiah 55:2 and fill in the blanks.

Why should we _Money_ our resources on something that is _not Bread but_ ~~offered~~ real food? Why should we _Pray_ for something if it's not really going to _satisfy_ us? God says if we will _call on God_ closely to him instead, we will enjoy what is _Good_ for us. Our soul will enjoy rich food. We will then be _delight in the Richest of fares,_

[margin handwritten notes: offered but to nourish our soul we must eat real]

I went to West Texas some time back to speak at the funeral of a godly, family friend. He had raised five children. One son, Paul, told a story about his earliest memory of his father.

It was spring in West Texas–tornado season. Paul was only three or four years old at the time, but he remembers vividly the day that a tornado hit their small town.

His father hustled the kids indoors and had them lie on the floor while he laid a mattress over them. But his father didn't climb under the protection. Paul remembers peeking out from under the mattress and seeing him standing by an open window, watching the funnel cloud twist and churn across the prairie.

When Paul saw his father, he knew where he wanted to be. He struggled out of his mother's arms, crawled out from under the mattress, and ran to wrap his arms around his dad's leg.

"Something told me," Paul said, "that the safest place to stand in a storm was next to my father."

Something told Peter the same thing.

4. Look up the following verses and write down what you learn about staying close to God in order to experience his peace and comfort.

Psalm 23:4

Even thought I walk through the valley of the Shadow of death I will fear no evil, for you are with me, your rod and staff they comfort me.

Jeremiah 31:13

I will turn their mourning into gladness. I will give them comfort and joy instead of sorrow

Hebrews 7:19

for the law made nothing perfect) and a better hope is introduced by which we draw near to God

James 4:8

Come near to God and he will come near to you.

Peter said, "Lord, if it is really you, then command me to come to you on the water." Jesus said, "Come."

—Matthew 14:29

We must let go of our own security to experience lasting peace.

Why spend your money on something that is not real food? Why work for something that doesn't really satisfy you? Listen closely to me, and you will eat what is good; your soul will enjoy the rich food that satisfies.

—Isaiah 55:2

Lasting peace comes only from God.

Even if I walk through a very dark valley, I will not be afraid, because you are with me. Your rod and your walking stick comfort me.

—Psalm 23:4

For I will turn their mourning to joy, Will comfort them, And make them rejoice rather than sorrow.

—Jeremiah 31:13 NKJV

5. When was a time you "stayed close" to Jesus during a period of potential chaos? What was the result?

was the last time I had to move my son to his home away from home, Made me feel that some time it was he instead of me.

EXPERIENCING PEACE WITH GOD

The peace **of** God is one thing—experiencing Jesus' presence in our lives has a calming effect. However, we cannot have the peace of God until, through Jesus, until and unless we have experienced peace **with** God. Faith comes first.

Draw close to God, and God will draw close to you.

—James 4:8 NLT

6. Read Romans 5:1, 10, then fill in the blanks.

Jesus Christ makes us right with ___God___ . As a result, we now have peace ___with___ God. While we were God's _____, he made ___+ the Holy Spirit___ with us through the death of ___Jesus___ ___on the cross___.

Stepping onto a stormy sea is not a move of logic; it is a move of desperation.

Peter grabs the edge of the boat. Throws out a leg . . . follows with the other. Several steps are taken. It's as if an invisible ridge of rocks runs beneath his feet. At the end of the ridge is the glowing face of a never-say-die friend.

We do the same, don't we? We come to Christ in an hour of deep need. We abandon the boat of good works. We realize, like Peter, that spanning the gap between us and Jesus is a feat too great for our feet. So we beg for help. Hear his voice. And step out in fear, hoping that our little faith will be enough.

Since we have been made right with God by our faith, we have peace with God. This happened through our Lord Jesus Christ. While we were God's enemies, he made friends with us through the death of his Son. Surely, now that we are his friends, he will save us through his Son's life.

—Romans 5:1, 10

7. Based on what you just read about Peter's example, what are the steps to experiencing God's peace? Read the following statements, and number the steps in order.

___6___ We realize spanning the gap between us and Jesus is a feat too great for our feet.

___2___ We come to Christ in our hour of deep need.

___3___ We abandon the boat of good works.

___5___ We then step out in fear, hoping that our little faith will be enough.

___4___ So we beg for help.

___1___ We hear his voice.

We cannot have the peace of God until we have peace with God.

HIS CALMING PRESENCE

Faith is not born at the negotiating table where we barter our gifts in exchange for God's goodness. Faith is not an award given to the most learned. It's not a prize given to the most disciplined. It's not a title bequeathed to the most religious.

Faith is a desperate dive out of the sinking boat of human effort and a prayer that God will be there to pull us out of the water. Paul wrote about this kind of faith in the letter to the Ephesians:

"For it is by grace you have been saved, through faith—and this not from yourselves, it is the gift of God—not by works, so that no one can boast." (Eph. 2:8–9 NIV)

Paul is clear. The supreme force in salvation is God's grace. Not our works. Not our talents. Not our feelings. Not our strength.

Salvation is God's sudden, calming presence during the stormy seas of our lives. We hear his voice; we take the step.

Then wolves will live in peace with lambs, and leopards will lie down to rest with goats. Calves, lions, and young bulls will eat together, and a little child will lead them.

—Isaiah 11:6

8. How is "peace" a good description for salvation?

Salvation is God's sudden calming presence during the stormy seas of our lives. we hear his voice we take the step.

REACHING FOR JESUS

We, like Paul, are aware of two things: We are great sinners and we need a great Savior.

We, like Peter, are aware of two facts: We are going down and God is standing up. So we scramble out. We leave behind the Titanic of self-righteousness and stand on the solid path of God's grace.

9. Read Psalm 62:5–8. What did David testify was the source of his peace? Check all that apply.

☑ He found rest in God alone.

☑ God was his rock, salvation, and defender.

☑ His salvation and honor depended on God, not his own ability.

And, surprisingly, we are able to walk on water. Death is disarmed. Failures are forgivable. Life has real purpose. And God is not only within sight, he is within reach.

With precious, wobbly steps, we draw closer to him. For a season of surprising strength, we stand upon his promises. It doesn't make sense that we are able to do this. We don't claim to be worthy of such an incredible gift. When people ask how in the world we can keep our balance during such stormy times, we don't boast. We don't brag. We point unabashedly to the One who makes it possible. Our eyes are on him.

Some of us, unlike Peter, never look back.

Others of us, like Peter, feel the wind and are afraid (Matt. 14:30).

10. Read Matthew 14:29–30 and respond to the following.

What did Peter do once he got out of the boat? (v. 29)

got out of the boat and started walking on the water.

What happened to cause him to sink? (v. 30)

He got scared of wind and when he began to sink he cried out LORD— SAVE ME

Maybe we face the wind of pride: "I'm not such a bad sinner after all. Look at what I can do."

Perhaps we face the wind of legalism: "I know that Jesus is doing part of this, but I have to do the rest."

Most of us, though, face the wind of doubt: "I'm too bad for God to treat me this well. I don't deserve such a rescue."

And downward we plunge. Weighted down by mortality's mortar, we sink. Gulping and thrashing, we fall into a dark, wet world. We open our eyes and see only blackness. We try to breathe, and no air comes. We kick and fight our way back to the surface.

With our heads barely above the water, we have to make a decision.

The prideful ask: "Do we 'save face' and drown in pride? Or do we scream for help and take God's hand?"

The legalists ask: "Do we sink under the lead-heavy weight of the Law? Or do we abandon the codes and beg for grace?"

The doubters ask: "Do we nurture doubt by mumbling, 'I've really let him down this time?' Or do we hope that the same Christ who called us out of the boat will call us out of the sea?"

We know Peter's choice.

"[As he was] beginning to sink, [he] cried out, 'Lord, save me!' Immediately Jesus reached out his hand and caught him" (Matt. 14:30–31 NIV).

FRIENDS WITH GOD

Through Christ's sacrifice, our past is pardoned and our future secure. And, "Since we have been made right with God by our faith, we have peace with God." (Romans 5:1)

Peace with God. What a happy consequence of faith! Not just peace between countries, peace between neighbors, or peace at home; salvation brings peace with God . . .

God is no longer a foe, but a friend. We are at peace with him.

—*In the Grip of Grace*

We are great sinners and we need a great Savior.

I find rest in God; only he gives me hope. He is my rock and my salvation. He is my defender; I will not be defeated. My honor and salvation come from God. He is my mighty rock and my protection. People, trust God all the time. Tell him all your problems, because God is our protection.

—Psalm 62:5–8

When we cry out, "Lord save me!" Jesus is there to catch us.

He will wipe away every tear from their eyes, and there will be no more death, sadness, crying, or pain, because all the old ways are gone.

—Revelation 21:4

THE HEART OF THE MATTER

- ❦ We must let go of our own security to experience lasting peace.
- ❦ Lasting peace comes only from God.
- ❦ We cannot have the peace *of* God until we have peace *with* God.
- ❦ We are great sinners and we need a great Savior.
- ❦ When we cry out, "Lord save me!" Jesus is there to catch us.

The Heart of Jesus

His heart was beating fast. His mouth had gone dry. He was nearly beside himself with impatience. The ever-present crowds were making it difficult to reach the Teacher, to get a word with him. Jairus' heart was wrenched, for his little daughter was dangerously ill. He had done all he could at home, and desperation had driven him from his child's side. Tears stung at his eyelids as he tried to swallow the lump rising in his throat. At last it was his turn before Jesus, and he gasped out his request. When Jesus agreed to accompany him to his home, Jairus had to fight back a sob of relief. Then, when they were nearly there, a servant came to tell him it was too late. The impact of those words left him numb. Too late. She was gone. Dead. Then the gentle voice of the Teacher was in his ear. Have faith. Believe. She's only sleeping. "Help me. Help my faith," Jairus pleaded. And so he was guided past the mourners and musicians, into the tiny room where his daughter lay so still. It was almost more than he could bear. But Jesus' next words whisked away every doubt and replaced it with joy. "Get up, little girl." She sat up. She blinked. She smiled. She reached out to her parents. In a home where there had been nothing but fear, desperation, and grief, there only remained joy and peace—perfect peace.

DAY FIVE—THE JOURNEY'S END

TIRED TRAVELERS

I drove the family to Grandma's last night for Thanksgiving. Three hours into the six-hour trip, I realized that I was in a theology lab. A day with a car full of kids will teach you a lot about God. Transporting a family from one city to another is closely akin to God transporting us from our home to his. And some of life's stormiest hours occur when the passenger and the Driver disagree on the destination.

A journey is a journey, whether the destination be the Thanksgiving table or the heavenly one. Both demand patience, a good sense of direction, and a driver who knows that the feast at the end of the trip is worth the hassles in the midst of the trip.

The fact that my pilgrims were all under the age of seven only enriched my learning experience.

As minutes rolled into hours and our car rolled through the hills, I began to realize that what I was saying to my kids had a familiar ring. I had heard it before—from God. All of a sudden, the car became a classroom. I realized that I was doing for a few hours what God has done for centuries: encouraging travelers who'd rather rest than ride.

1. Which of the following are true for both an earthly journey and a heavenly journey? Check all that apply.

   ☒ The travelers must have patience.
   ☒ The driver must have a good sense of direction.
   ☒ The driver must be convinced the destination is worth the journey.
   ❏ If the driver and passengers disagree on the destination, the journey is long.
   ❏ Long journeys bring the temptation to rest rather than ride.

Those who work to bring peace are happy, because God will call them his children.
—Matthew 5:9

2. The Bible speaks often of our spiritual journey. Look up the following verses below and fill in the blanks.

God keeps us from *handon tight* when the path grows steep. (Psalm 18:33)
God guides us in *your truth* (Psalm 25:5)
God's Word lights our *feet and high* along this journey. (Psalm 119:105)
God will guide us into the ___*shadow*___ of ___*death*___. (Luke 1:79)
path *Peace*

We have small troubles for a while now, but they are helping us gain an eternal glory that is much greater than the troubles. We set our eyes not on what we see but on what we cannot see. What we see will last only a short time, but what we cannot see will last forever.

—2 Corinthians 4:17–18

WHEN "NO" DISTURBS OUR PEACE

I shared the idea with my wife, Denalyn. We began to discover similarities between the two journeys. Here are a few we noted.

In order to reach the destination, we have to say no to some requests.

Can you imagine the outcome if a parent honored each request of each child during a trip? We'd inch our bloated bellies from one ice-cream store to the next. Our priority would be popcorn and our itinerary would read like a fast-food menu. "Go to the Cherry Malt and make a right. Head north until you find the Chili Cheeseburger. Stay north for 1,300 calories and bear left at the Giant Pizza. When you see the two-for-one Chili Dog Special, take the Pepto-Bismol Turnpike east for five convenience stores. At the sixth toilet . . ."

Can you imagine the chaos if a parent indulged every indulgence?

Can you imagine the chaos if God indulged each of ours?

No is a necessary word to take on a trip. Destination has to reign over Dairy Deluxe Ice Cream Sundae.

Some of us don't do "no" very well. We just don't like the sound of it. So final. So confounding.

The requests my children made last night on the road to Grandma's weren't evil. They weren't unfair. They weren't rebellious. In fact, we had a couple of cones and Cokes. But most of the requests were unnecessary.

My four-year-old daughter would argue that fact. From her viewpoint, another soft drink is indispensable to her happiness. I know otherwise, so I say no.

A forty-year-old adult would argue that fact. From his standpoint, a new boss is indispensable to his happiness. God knows otherwise and says no.

A thirty-year-old woman would argue that fact. From her standpoint, that man with that job and that name is exactly who she needs to be happy. Her Father, who is more concerned that she arrive at his City than at the altar, says, "Wait a few miles. There's a better option down the road."

Sometimes God has to say no to our requests.

3. How would you characterize your typical response when God's leadership style disturbs your sense of peace? Check all that apply.

❏ "If God really loved me he would give me what I want."
❏ "If God is in charge of this journey, let me off the ride."
❏ "I won't stop asking until I get my way."
✔ "I don't understand why God said no, but I trust he knows best."

WHEN WAITING DISTURBS OUR PEACE

Children have no concept of minutes or miles.

"We'll be there in three hours," I said.

"How long is three hours?" Jenna asked. (How do you explain time to a child who can't tell time?)

"Well, it's about as long as three Sesame Streets," I ventured.

The children groaned in unison. "Three Sesame Streets?! That's forever!"

And to them, it is.

And to us, it seems that way, too.

A child has been born to us; God has given a son to us. He will be responsible for leading the people. His name will be Wonderful Counselor, Powerful God, Father Who Lives Forever, Prince of Peace.

—Isaiah 9:6

He who "lives forever" (Is. 57:15) has placed himself at the head of a band of pilgrims who mutter, "How long, O Lord? How long?" (Ps. 74:10; 89:46)

"How long must I endure this sickness?"

"How long must I endure this spouse?"

"How long must I endure this paycheck?"

Do you really want God to answer? He could, you know. He could answer in terms of the here and now with time increments we know. "Two more years on the illness." "The rest of your life in the marriage." "Ten more years for the bills."

But he seldom does that. He usually opts to measure the here and now against the there and then. And when you compare this life to that life, this life ain't long.

God loves us too much to indulge our every whim.

4. Look up the following verses and fill in the blanks of these Scriptures about the fleeting nature of our lives.

   1 Chronicles 29:15 – Our _____ on earth is like a _____.

   Psalm 39:5 – Our lifetime is _____ from God's perspective.

   Psalm 103:15–16 – Human life is like _____. For a time, we grow like a _____ in the field. Then the _____ blows and our life is _____.

   James 4:14 – We are a _____ that appears for a _____ time and then it _____ away.

In light of God's Word, periods of unrest along the journey (that seem to stretch for miles to us) will seem like a mere matter of minutes in eternity.

Compared to eternity, this life is fleeting.

5. Look up the following verses and write down what you learn about "waiting" on God's timing.

   Isaiah 30:18 – "The Lord wants to show his mercy to you. He wants to rise and comfort you. The Lord is a fair God, and everyone who waits for his help will be happy."

   _____

   _____

   Psalm 27:14 – "Wait for the Lord's help. Be strong and brave, and wait for the Lord's help."

   _____

   _____

   Lamentations 3:26 – "It is good to wait quietly for the Lord to save."

   _____

   _____

WHEN WE LOSE SIGHT OF THE REWARD

Children can't envision the reward.

For me, six hours on the road is a small price to pay for my mom's strawberry cake. I don't mind the drive because I know the reward. I have three decades of Thanksgivings under my belt, literally. As I drive, I can taste the turkey. Hear the dinner-table laughter. Smell the smoke from the fireplace.

I can endure the journey because I know the destiny.

My daughters have forgotten the destiny. After all, they are young. Children easily forget. Besides, the road is strange, and the dark night has come. They can't see where we're going. It's my job, as their father, to guide them.

I try to help them see what they can't see.

Perhaps that's how the apostle Paul stayed motivated. He had a clear vision of the reward.

Stop doing evil and do good. Look for peace and work for it.
—Psalm 34:14

6. Read 2 Corinthians 4:16–18 on the right. Then match the word with the truth you learned from this passage.

    ____ Physical body   a. Help us gain an eternal glory
    ____ Spirit inside   b. Made new every day
    ____ Small troubles   c. Will last forever.
    ____ What we cannot see   d. Growing older and weaker
    ____ What we see   e. Will last only a short time

So we do not give up. Our physical body is becoming older and weaker, but our spirit inside us is made new every day. We have small troubles for a while now, but they are helping us gain an eternal glory that is much greater than the troubles. We set our eyes not on what we see but on what we cannot see. What we see will last only a short time, but what we cannot see will last forever.
    —2 Corinthians 4:16–18

It's not easy to get three girls under the age of seven to see a city they can't see. But it's necessary.

It's not easy for us to see a City we've never seen, either, especially when the road is bumpy . . . the hour is late . . . and companions are wanting to cancel the trip and take up residence in a motel. It's not easy to fix our eyes on what is unseen. But it's necessary.

It's not easy to fix our eyes on what is unseen. But it's necessary.

7. Read 2 Corinthians 11:23–27. Choose the correct troubles that Paul experienced, which he referred to in 2 Corinthians 4:17 as "small troubles." Check all that apply.

❏ Imprisoned.
❏ Beaten with a whip five times.
❏ Faced death.
❏ Beaten with rods three times.
❏ Stoned once.
❏ Shipwrecked three times.
❏ Stranded in the open sea.
❏ Left homeless.
❏ In constant danger.
❏ Hungry and thirsty.

DO SOMETHING
Faith that does nothing is dead!
    —James 2:26

Long and trying ordeals, perhaps. Arduous and deadly afflictions, OK. But small troubles? How could Paul describe endless trials like that?

He tells us. He could see "an eternal glory that far outweighs them all" (2 Cor. 17 NIV).

Can I speak candidly for a few lines?

For some of you, the journey has been long. Very long and stormy. In no way do I wish to minimize the difficulties that you have had to face along the way. Some of you have shouldered burdens that few of us could ever carry. You have bid farewell to lifelong partners. You have been robbed of lifelong dreams. You have been given bodies that can't sustain your spirit. You have spouses who can't tolerate your faith. You have bills that outnumber the paychecks and challenges that outweigh the strength.

And you are tired.

It's hard for you to see the City in the midst of the storms. The desire to pull over to the side of the road and get out entices you. You want to go on, but some days the road seems so long.

God never said that the journey would be easy, but he did say that the arrival would be worthwhile.

Remember this: God may not do what you want, but he will do what is right . . . and best. He's the Father of forward motion. Trust him. He will get you home. And the trials of the trip will be lost in the joys of the feast.

Faith is not the belief that God will do what you want. Faith is the belief that God will do what is right. God is always near and always available. Just waiting for your touch. So let him know. Demonstrate your devotion:
    Write a letter.
    Ask forgiveness.
    Be baptized.
    Feed a hungry person.
    Pray.
    Teach.
    Go.
    Do something that demonstrates faith. For faith with no effort is no faith at all. *God will respond.* He has never rejected a genuine gesture of faith. Never.

    —*He Still Moves Stones*

8. How has Jesus given you peace on your long journey?

_____

_____

So let us try to do what makes peace and helps one another.
    —**Romans 14:19**

THE HEART OF THE MATTER

- ❧ **Sometimes God has to say no to our requests.**
- ❧ **God loves us too much to indulge our every whim.**
- ❧ **Compared to eternity, this life is fleeting.**
- ❧ **It's not easy to fix our eyes on what is unseen. But it's necessary.**
- ❧ **God never said that the journey would be easy, but he did say that the arrival would be worthwhile.**

This is it! Can you say your memory verse by heart now? Write it out one last time below.

_____

_____

_____

The Heart of Jesus

God never said that the journey would be easy, but he did say that the arrival would be worthwhile.

Jesus spends some time preparing his disciples for what is ahead. He begins early with the difficult task of saying goodbye. He says, "I am going away, but don't be troubled." "Trust God, and trust me." They have questions for him, and they do not fully understand him. Though they know him so well, Jesus seems to be talking in riddles. "I will not leave you alone like orphans, I will come back to you." "Don't worry if you forget what I have said today, for I will send you a Helper, and he will remind you of everything I have said." But the last words he gave them that day must have rung clearly in their ears. "I leave you peace; my peace I give you. I do not give it to you as the world does. So don't let your hearts be troubled or afraid." Like a final bequest, Jesus promised that they would experience his peace, even when he returned to his Father. "I leave you my peace." Peace that passes understanding. Perfect peace.

FOR FURTHER READING

Selections throughout this lesson were taken from *In the Eye of the Storm.*

People who work for peace in a peaceful way plant a good crop of right-living.
—**James 3:18**

i John MacArthur, *The MacArthur Commentary: Matthew 8—15* (Chicago, Ill.: Moody Press, 1987), 427.

LESSON 3

Experiencing the Grace of Jesus

THE GREATEST DISCOVERY OF MY LIFE

CLOTHES OF SALVATION

This body that dies must clothe itself with something that can never die.

—1 Corinthians 15:53

[Does] Jesus care what clothes we wear?

Apparently so. In fact, the Bible tells us exactly the wardrobe God desires.

"But clothe yourselves with the Lord Jesus Christ and forget about satisfying your sinful self" (Rom. 13:14).

"You were all baptized into Christ, and so you were all clothed with Christ. This means that you are all children of God through faith in Christ Jesus" (Gal. 3:26–27).

This clothing has nothing to do with dresses and jeans and suits. God's concern is with our spiritual garment. He offers a heavenly robe that only heaven can see and only heaven can give. Listen to the words of Isaiah: "The Lord makes me very happy; all that I am rejoices in my God. He has covered me with clothes of salvation and wrapped me with a coat of goodness" (Is. 61:10).

—*When Christ Comes*

For years I owned an elegant suit complete with coat, trousers, even a hat. I considered myself quite dapper in the outfit and was confident others agreed. The pants were cut from the cloth of my good works, sturdy fabric of deeds done, and projects completed. Some studies here, some sermons there. Many people complimented my trousers, and I confess, I tended to hitch them up in public so people would notice them. The coat was equally impressive. It was woven together from my convictions. Each day I dressed myself in deep feelings of religious fervor. My emotions were quite strong. So strong, in fact, that I was often asked to model my cloak of zeal in public gatherings to inspire others. Of course, I was happy to comply. While there I'd also display my hat, a feathered cap of knowledge. Formed with my own hands from the fabric of personal opinion, I wore it proudly.

Surely God is impressed with my garments, I often thought. Occasionally I strutted into his presence so he could compliment the self-tailored wear. He never spoke. *His silence must mean admiration,* I convinced myself. But then my wardrobe began to suffer. The fabric of my trousers grew thin. My best works started coming unstitched. I began leaving more undone than done, and what little I did was nothing to boast about. *No problem,* I thought. *I'll work harder.*

But working harder *was* a problem. There was a hole in my coat of convictions. My resolve was threadbare. A cold wind cut into my chest. I reached up to pull my hat down firmly, and the brim ripped off in my hands. Over a period of a few months, my wardrobe of self-righteousness completely unraveled. I went from tailored gentlemen's apparel to beggars' rags. Fearful that God might be angry at my tattered suit, I did my best to stitch it together and cover my mistakes. But the cloth was so worn. And the wind was so icy. I gave up. I went back to God. (Where else could I go?)

On a wintry Thursday afternoon, I stepped into his presence, not for applause, but for warmth. My prayer was feeble. "I feel naked."

"You are. And you have been for a long time."

What he did next I'll never forget. "I have something to give you," he said. He gently removed the remaining threads and then picked up a robe, the clothing of his own goodness. He wrapped it around my shoulders. His words to me were tender. *"My son, you are now clothed with Christ"* (Gal. 3:27). I have a hunch that some of you know what I'm talking about. You're wearing a handmade wardrobe yourself. You've sewn your garments, and you're sporting your religious deeds . . . and, already, you've noticed a tear in the fabric. Before you start stitching yourself together I'd like to share some thoughts with you on the greatest discovery of my life: the grace of God.

EXPERIENCING THE GRACE OF JESUS THIS WEEK

Before we move ahead, into the remarkable experience of God's grace, let's spend some time in prayer.

> *Dear Father, forgive me for trying to impress you with garments of my own making. You have shown me grace, and clothed me with Christ instead. I know that it is only through your grace that I have been saved. Guide my studies this week. Teach me more about You. Show me how amazing grace really is. And help me experience the grace of Jesus. Amen.*

The law came to make sin worse. But when sin grew worse, God's grace increased.

—**Romans 5:20**

This week, take the time to memorize Ephesians 2:8–9, one of the Bible's clearest passages on God's grace:

"For by grace you have been saved through faith, and that not of yourselves; it is the gift of God, not of works, lest anyone should boast." —*Ephesians 2:8–9* NKJV

Tuesday DAY ONE—WE NEED GRACE

FIRST, THE BAD NEWS

I might as well prepare you: The first chapters of Romans are not exactly upbeat. An epistle for the self-sufficient, Romans contrasts the plight of people who choose to dress in self-made garments with those who gladly accept the robes of grace. Paul gives us the bad news before he gives us the good news. He will eventually tell us that we are all equal candidates for grace but not before he proves that we are all desperately sinful. We have to see the mess we are in before we can appreciate the God we have. Before presenting the grace of God, we must understand the wrath of God.

God is a just judge, And God is angry with the wicked every day.
—Psalm 7:11 NKJV

It is easy to accept grace from a loving, forgiving God. But when it comes to the "wrath of God," we cringe. An angry God makes us uneasy. Have you ever turned to the Bible to find out why God gets stirred up? Let's look up some passages that deal with God's wrath.

1. Read Psalm 78:24–32. What have the Israelites done that stirred up God's wrath?

_____

_____

2. What is the heart attitude of someone who will eventually have to face the wrath of God? Find it in Romans 2:5.

_____

_____

3. What kinds of disobedience will bring down the wrath of God according to Colossians 3:5–6?

_____

_____

> God's anger is shown from heaven against all the evil and wrong things people do. By their own evil lives they hide the truth. God shows his anger because some knowledge of him has been made clear to them. Yes, God has shown himself to them. There are things about him that people cannot see—his eternal power and all the things that make him God. But since the beginning of the world those things have been easy to understand by what God has made. So people have no excuse for the bad things they do. —Romans 1:18–20

God is jealous, and the Lord avenges; The Lord avenges and is furious. The Lord will take vengeance on His adversaries, And He reserves wrath for His enemies; The Lord is slow to anger and great in power, And will not at all acquit the wicked.
—Nahum 1:2–3 NKJV

God is angry at evil.

For many, this is a revelation. Some assume God is a harried high-school principal, too busy monitoring the planets to notice us.

He's not.

Others assume he is a doting parent, blind to the evil of his children.

Wrong.

Still others insist he loves us so much he cannot be angry at our evil.

They don't understand that love is always angry at evil.

I don't care about my own life. The most important thing is that I complete my mission, the work that the Lord Jesus gave me—to tell people the Good News about God's grace.
—Acts 20:24

God is a holy God.

4. Read the following verses. Then match the verse with what you learn about why a loving God is always angry at evil:

___ Job 34:10	a. God wants us to be perfect like him.
___ Psalm 18:30	b. God does not want his name to be dishonored.
___ Psalm 33:4–5	c. There is no darkness in God.
___ Ezekiel 39:7	d. God is without fault.
___ Matthew 5:48	e. God loves what is right and fair.
___ 1 John 1:5	f. It's impossible for God to do evil.

Many don't understand God's anger because they confuse the wrath of God with the wrath of man. The two have little in common. Human anger is typically self-driven and prone to explosions of temper and violent deeds. We get ticked off because we've been overlooked, neglected, or cheated. This is the anger of man. It is not, however, the anger of God.

God doesn't get angry because he doesn't get his way. He gets angry because disobedience always results in self-destruction. What kind of father sits by and watches his child hurt himself?

What kind of God would do the same? Do we think he giggles at adultery or snickers at murder? Do you think he looks the other way when we produce television talk shows based on perverse pleasures? Does he shake his head and say, "Humans will be humans"? I don't think so. Mark it down and underline it in red. God is rightfully angry. God is a holy God. Our sins are an affront to his holiness. His eyes "are too good to look at evil; [he] cannot stand to see those who do wrong" (Hab. 1:13).

God is angry at the evil that ruins his children. "As long as God is God, he cannot behold with indifference that his creation is destroyed and his holy will trodden underfoot."[i]

5. Based on what you have read so far, what does it mean that God is "rightfully angry" concerning our sin?

_____

_____

OUR CONDITION

In the first three chapters of Romans, you also will get a stark glimpse into the human condition—the condition of everyone who ever walked this earth. What separates us from God is sin. We aren't strong enough to remove it, and we aren't good enough to erase it. For all of our differences, there is one problem we all share. We are separated from God.

What separates us from God is sin.

Paul describes three kinds of people in the world: the **hedonist** (i.e., the person who lives solely for pleasure, 1:21–25); the **judgmentalist** (i.e., the person who sees himself/herself as basically good through comparisons to "worse" people, 2:1–6); and the **legalist** (i.e., the person who attempts to earn God's favor through religious effort, 2:17–24). Let's look at what we can learn about each one and see if anything sounds familiar.

The hedonist opts to live as if there is no creator at all. The hedonist says, "Who cares? I may be bad, but so what? What I do is my business." He's more concerned about satisfying his pleasures than in knowing the Father. His life is so desperate for pleasure that he has no time or room for God.

6. Underline the words above used to describe the "hedonist." Then read Romans 1:21–25 below and fill in the blanks about what this passage says about the "hedonist." *They knew God, but they did not give glory to God or thank him. Their thinking became useless. Their foolish minds were filled with darkness. They said they were wise, but they became fools. They traded the glory of God who lives forever for the worship of idols made to look like earthly people, birds, animals, and snakes. Because they did these things, God left them and let them go their sinful way, wanting only to do evil. As a result, they became full of sexual sin, using their bodies*

Sin will not be your master, because you are not under law but under God's grace.
—Romans 6:14

wrongly with each other. They traded the truth of God for a lie. They worshiped and served what had been created instead of the God who created those things, who should be praised forever. Amen. —Romans 1:21–25

They did not give _____ to God. They traded God's truth for a _____ and worshiped what was _____. Their _____ minds became filled with _____.

The second type of person says, "Why deal with my mistakes when I can focus on the mistakes of others? He is a judgmentalist. I may be bad, but as long as I can find someone worse, I am safe. He fuels his goodness with the failures of others. He is the self-appointed teacher's pet in elementary school. He tattles on the sloppy work of others, oblivious to the F on his own paper. He's the neighborhood watchdog, passing out citations for people to clean up their act, never noticing the garbage on his own front lawn.

7. Underline the words above used to describe the "judgmentalist." Then read Romans 2:1–6 below and fill in the blanks on what this passage says about the "judgmentalists."

If you think you can judge others, you are wrong. When you judge them, you are really judging yourself guilty, because you do the same things they do. God judges those who do wrong things, and we know that his judging is right. You judge those who do wrong, but you do wrong yourselves. Do you think you will be able to escape the judgment of God? He has been very kind and patient, waiting for you to change, but you think nothing of his kindness. Perhaps you do not understand that God is kind to you so you will change your hearts and lives. But you are stubborn and refuse to change, so you are making your own punishment even greater on the day he shows his anger. On that day everyone will see God's right judgments. God will reward or punish every person for what that person has done. —Romans 2:1–6

When they judge others, they are _____ because they do _____ themselves. They don't think anything of God's _____ and patience. They are _____ and refuse to _____.

Then there is the legalist. Ahh, now here is a person we can respect. Hardworking. Industrious. Zealous. Intense. Here is a fellow who sees his sin and sets out to resolve it by himself. Surely he is worthy of our applause. Surely he is worthy of our emulation.

The legalist thinks: If I do this God will accept me. The problem? We can never earn our salvation based on our own efforts. We can never teach enough Sunday school classes, give enough money to mission work, do enough Bible studies, spend enough time in church—we can never do enough to save ourselves.

8. Underline the words above used to describe the "legalist." Then read Romans 2:17–24 below. Check all the following phrases below that apply to what the passage has to say about the "legalist."

What about you? You call yourself a Jew. You trust in the law of Moses and brag that you are close to God. You know what he wants you to do and what is important, because you have learned the law. You think you are a guide for the blind and a light for those who are in darkness. You think you can show foolish people what is right and teach those who know nothing. You have the law; so you think you know everything and have all truth. You teach others, so why don't you teach yourself? You tell others not to steal, but you steal. You say that others must not take part in adultery, but you are guilty of that sin. You hate idols, but you steal from temples. You brag about having God's law, but you bring shame to God by breaking his law, just as the Scriptures say: "Those who are not Jews speak against God's name because of you." —Romans 2:17–24

❏ Teaches foolish people truth
❏ Brags about being close to God
❏ Willing to teach themselves

Judge not, that you be not judged. For with what judgment you judge, you will be judged; and with the measure you use, it will be measured back to you. And why do you look at the speck in your brother's eye, but do not consider the plank in your own eye? Or how can you say to your brother, 'Let me remove the speck from your eye'; and look, a plank is in your own eye? Hypocrite! First remove the plank from your own eye, and then you will see clearly to remove the speck from your brother's eye.

—Matthew 7:1–5 NKJV

THE STANDARD

We are made holy through the sacrifice Christ made in his body once and for all time.

—Hebrews 10:10

Only the holy will see God. Holiness is a prerequisite to heaven. Perfection is a requirement for eternity. We wish it weren't so. We act like it isn't so. We act like those who are "decent" will see God. We suggest that those who try hard will see God. We act as if we're good if we never do anything too bad. And that goodness is enough to qualify us for heaven.

Sounds right to us, but it doesn't sound right to God. And he sets the standard. And the standard is high. "You must be perfect, just as your Father in heaven is perfect (Matt. 5:48).

You see, in God's plan, God is the standard for perfection. We don't compare ourselves to others; they are just as fouled up as we are. The goal is to be like him; anything less is inadequate.

—*He Still Moves Stones*

May our Lord Jesus Christ himself and God our Father encourage you and strengthen you in every good thing you do and say. God loved us, and through his grace he gave us a good hope and encouragement that continues forever.

—2 Thessalonians 2:16

❏ Guide for the blind
❏ Obeys all God's laws
❏ Brings shame to God

Every person on God's green earth has blown it. The hedonists blew it because they were pleasure-centered and not God-centered. The judgmentalists blew it because they were high-minded and not God-minded. The legalists blew it because they were work-driven and not grace-driven. Assess yourself honestly against what Paul says are the three types of people in the world.

9. Into which category might you tend to fall? Check your response.

❏ I'd rather live in sin than try to live for God.
❏ I compare myself to others who are worse than me.
❏ I try to make it up to God whenever I sin.

10. Which of the following statements are true about sin? Check all that apply.

❏ Sin is rebellion against God—disregarding his plans and purposes and substituting our own ideas and wills.
❏ It is refusing to give God the glory and honor he deserves.
❏ It is a declaration of independence from our Creator—a willful rejection of his rule in our lives.
❏ It is falling short of God's standard of perfection.
❏ It is attempting to find life apart from him.

LIFE MINUS GOD

The wrath of God is being revealed from heaven against all the godlessness and wickedness of men who suppress the truth by their wickedness.

—Romans 1:18 NIV

Though the three types of individuals you just looked at may appear different, they are very much alike. All are separated from the Father. And none is asking for help. The first indulges his passions, the second monitors his neighbor, and the third measures his merits. Self-satisfaction. Self-justification. Self-salvation. The operative word is *self.* Self-sufficient. "They never give God the time of day" (Rom. 3:18 MSG).

Paul's word to describe all three is *godlessness* (Rom. 1:18 NIV). *Godlessness.* The word defines itself. A life minus God. Worse than a disdain for God, this is a disregard for God. A disdain at least acknowledges his presence. Godlessness doesn't. Whereas disdain will lead people to act with irreverence, disregard causes them to act as if God were irrelevant, as if he is not a factor in the journey.

Our efforts to save ourselves will only fail.

GOD'S RESPONSE

So now that you've considered God's rightful wrath and your own condition, as well as humanity's universal problem, the question remains: how does God respond to godless living? Not flippantly. Again we read, "The wrath of God is being revealed from heaven against all godlessness and wickedness" (Rom. 1:18 NIV). Paul's main point is not a light one. God is justly angered over the actions of his children.

11. What would happen if Paul's letter to the Romans ended right at Romans 3:20? Would there be a flicker of hope for the sinner standing before a righteous and holy God?

_____

_____

Let us, then, feel very sure that we can come before God's throne where there is grace. There we can receive mercy and grace to help us when we need it.

—Hebrews 4:16

We would stand "guilty as charged," rightly condemned before a holy God. We would be on a kind of spiritual "death row." We would have no hope. The Good News isn't good until we first wrestle with the unspeakably bad news of our lostness. We can't rush on to grace until we have felt the awful weight of human sin and its consequences.

We can summarize the first three and one-half chapters of Romans with three words: *We have failed.*

We have attempted to reach the moon but scarcely made it off the ground. We tried to swim the Atlantic, but couldn't get beyond the reef. We have attempted to scale the Everest of salvation, but we have yet to leave the base camp, much less ascend the slope. The quest is simply too great; we don't need more supplies or muscle or technique; we need a helicopter.

Can you hear it hovering?

12. Which of the following statements are true concerning our sinful condition, and which ones are false? Mark your answers True (T) or False (F). Look up and read the Scriptures listed if you do not already know the answer.

____ If we try hard enough we can deal with sin through our own efforts. (Ephesians 4:18)

____ It is possible to be somewhat righteous in and of oneself. (Romans 3:11–12)

____ Apart from God's grace, our sins can never be forgiven. (Ephesians 2:8–9)

____ God alone can provide a way for us to be saved. (Romans 3:22)

THE GOOD NEWS

"God has a way to *make people right with him*" (Rom. 3:21, italics mine). How vital that we embrace this truth. God's highest dream is not to make us rich, not to make us successful or popular or famous. God's dream is to make us right with him.

13. Read Acts 13:39 and Romans 3:25 on the left. What does it mean to be "right" with God?

_____

_____

14. Read 2 Corinthians 5:16–21. Fill in the blanks below about what you learn from this passage concerning being made right with God.

If anyone belongs to _____, there is a new _____. Everything _____ is gone; everything is now _____. Through Christ, God made _____ between us and himself., so now he does not hold the world _____ of its sins. God made him who had no _____ to become _____ so that in _____ we could become _____ with God.

15. What do Romans 5:9 and 1 Thessalonians 5:9 (on the left) tell us that Jesus' grace has saved us from?

_____

_____

THE HEART OF THE MATTER

- ❧ **God is a holy God.**
- ❧ **What separates us from God is sin.**
- ❧ **Our efforts to save ourselves will only fail.**
- ❧ **Jesus has rescued us from wrath.**

Your salvation is indeed a gift from God! Write your scripture memory verse for this week on the following lines—Ephesians 2:8–9.

_____

_____

_____

CALL IT GRACE

Being made right with God by his grace, we could have the hope of receiving the life that never ends.

—Titus 3:7

You may be decent. You may pay taxes and kiss your kids and sleep with a clean conscience. But apart from Christ you aren't holy. So how can you go to heaven?

Only believe. Accept the work already done, the work of Jesus on the cross.

Accept the goodness of Jesus Christ. Abandon your own works and accept his. Abandon your own decency and accept his. Stand before God in his name, not yours.

It's that easy? There was nothing easy about it at all. The cross was heavy, the blood was real, and the price was extravagant. It would have bankrupted you or me, so he paid it for us. Call it simple. Call it a gift. But don't call it easy.

Call it what it is. Call it grace.

—*A Gentle Thunder*

Jesus has rescued us from wrath.

Everyone who believes in him is freed from all guilt and declared right with God—something the Jewish law couold never do.

—Acts 13:39 NLT

For God sent Jesus to take the punishment for our sins and to satisfy God's anger against us. We are made right with God when we believe that Jesus shed his blood, sacrificing his life for us.

—Romans 3:25 NLT

Much more then, having now been justified by His blood, we shall be saved from wrath through Him.

—Romans 5:9 NKJV

For God did not appoint us to wrath, but to obtain salvation through our Lord Jesus Christ.

—1 Thessalonians 5:9 NKJV

The Heart of Jesus

No one wants to spend a lot of time dwelling on sin and the wrath of God. But experiencing God's grace becomes all the more precious to us when we realize what we have been rescued from. Remember the woman caught in adultery?

Caught in sin.

Dragged before a holy judge.

No defense for her actions.

No hope.

According to the letter of the law, all she deserved now was death. The men ringed about her were clamoring for the Teacher to give the word. Then she would be stoned.

But Jesus did not call the wrath of the crowd down on her head.

Instead, the woman who had been caught experienced the grace of Jesus.

He dismissed the accusers. His next words were a gift: "Neither do I condemn you." A new lease on life. Forgiveness.

Grace.

DAY TWO—GOD TO THE RESCUE

GOOD FOR EVIL?

I'm glad the letter wasn't sent from heaven.

It came from my automobile insurance company, my former automobile insurance company. I didn't drop them; they dropped me. Not because I didn't pay my premiums; I was on time and caught up. Not because I failed to do the paperwork; every document was signed and delivered.

I was dropped for making too many mistakes.

Wait a minute. Let me see if I get this right. I bought the insurance to cover my mistakes. But then I get dropped for making mistakes. Hello. Did I miss something? Did I fail to see a footnote? Did I skip over some fine print in the contract?

Isn't that like a doctor treating healthy patients only? Or a dentist hanging a sign in the window, "No cavities, please." Or a teacher penalizing you for asking too many questions? Isn't that like qualifying for a loan by proving you don't need one? What if the fire department said it would protect you until you had a fire?

Or what if, perish the thought, heaven had limitations to its coverage? What if you got a letter from the Pearly Gate Underwriting Division that read:

> Dear Mrs. Smith,
> I'm writing in response to this morning's request for forgiveness. I'm sorry to inform you that you have reached your quota of sins. Our records show that, since employing our services, you have erred seven times in the area of greed, and your prayer life is substandard when compared to others of like age and circumstances.
>
> Further review reveals that your understanding of doctrine is in the lower 20 percentile and you have excessive tendencies to gossip. Because of your sins you are a high-risk candidate for heaven. You understand that grace has its limits. Jesus sends his regrets and kindest regards and hopes that you will find some other form of coverage.

Many fear receiving such a letter. Some worry they already have! If an insurance company can't cover my honest mistakes, can I expect God to cover my intentional rebellion?

Paul answers that question with what John Stott calls "the most startling statement in Romans." God "makes even evil people right in his sight" (Rom. 4:5). What an incredible claim!

God makes us right in his sight.

The law was given through Moses, but grace and truth came through Jesus Christ.
—John 1:17

1. Fill in the blanks below about what you learn from this passage concerning becoming right with God.

"But God has a way to make people right with him without the law, and he has now shown us that way which the law and the prophets told us about. God makes people right with himself through their faith in Jesus Christ. This is true for all who believe in Christ, because all people are the same: All have sinned and are not good enough for God's glory, and all need to be made right with God by his grace, which is a free gift. They need to be made free from sin through Jesus Christ. God gave him as a way to forgive sin through faith in the blood of Jesus' death. This showed that God always does what is right and fair, as in the past when he was patient and did not punish people for their sins. And God gave Jesus to show today that he does what is right. God did this so he could judge rightly and so he could make right any person who has faith in Jesus." (Romans 3:21–26)

God has a _____ to make people _____ with him. God makes people right with himself through their _____ in Jesus Christ. All of us have _____. Yet God sets us _____ from sin through the sacrifice of Jesus Christ.

2. Read the following verses. Then match the verse with what you learn about how God made a way for sinful people to be right with him.

____ John 8:24
____ 1 John 2:2
____ Galatians 1:4
____ Hebrews 7:27
____ 2 Corinthians 5:19
____ Matthew 9:6

a. Jesus satisfied the penalty of sin through his sacrifice.
b. Without God's provision, we would die in our sins.
c. Jesus sacrificed for our sins once and for all.
d. Jesus has the authority to forgive our sins.
e. Jesus gave himself to rescue us from evil.
f. God does not count our sins against us.

Think about it. It's one thing to make good people right, but those who are evil? We can expect God to justify the decent, but the dirty? Surely coverage is provided for the driver with the clean record, but the speeder? The ticketed? The high-risk client? How in the world can justification come for the evil?

GOD HAS A WAY

Up until this point in Paul's letter, all efforts at salvation have been from earth upward. Man has inflated his balloon with his own hot air and not been able to leave the atmosphere. The conclusion is unavoidable: self-salvation simply does not work. Man has no way to save himself.

But Paul announces that *God has a way*. Where man fails God excels. Salvation comes from heaven downward, not earth upward. "A new day *from* heaven will dawn upon us" (Luke 1:78). "Every good action and every perfect gift is *from* God" (James 1:17). Please note: Salvation is God-given, God-driven, God-empowered, and God-originated. The gift is not from man to God. It is from God to man.

3. Read Ephesians 2:8–9 on the left. Based upon what you just read, which of the following statements are true concerning God's gift of salvation and which ones are false? Mark your answers True (T) or False (F). Use the Bible verses below to help you answer.

____ God's gift of grace comes to us through Jesus Christ.
____ Some people have to work harder at being saved than others.
____ God freely gives us his grace—no strings attached.
____ No one can take the credit for God's gift of salvation.

I realize that there's a sense in which we're imperfect. We still err. We still stumble. We still do exactly what we don't want to do. And that part of us is, according to Hebrews 10:14, "being made holy." But when it comes to our position before God, we're perfect. When he sees each of us, he sees one who has been made perfect through the One who is perfect—Jesus Christ.

—*In the Eye of the Storm*

VOICE OF GRACE

I tell you the truth, today you will be with me in paradise.

—Luke 23:43

Tell me, what has [the thief on the cross] done to warrant help? He has wasted his life. Who is he to beg for forgiveness? He publicly scoffed at Jesus. What right does he have to pray . . . , "Jesus remember me when you come into your kingdom"?

Do you really want to know? The same right you have to pray . . .

You see, that is you and me on the cross. Naked, desolate, hopeless, and estranged. That is us. That is us asking . . .

We don't boast. We don't produce our list. Any sacrifice appears silly when placed before God on a cross . . .

We, like the thief, have one more prayer. And we, like the thief, pray.

And we, like the thief, hear the voice of grace.

—*He Still Moves Stones*

I mean that you have been saved by grace through believing. You did not save yourselves; it was a gift from God. It was not the result of your own efforts, so you cannot brag about it.

—Ephesians 2:8–9

We are all equally guilty before a holy God.

At this point, you may be tempted to put conditions on grace. *We can be forgiven for certain sins, but not for others,* or, *Yes, I can see where so-and-so might make it into heaven, but her?* Such attitudes fly in the face of God's infinite grace. Moreover, they ignore the Bible truths that, apart from Christ, we are *all* equally guilty before a holy God. We all need Jesus, because we've all sinned and fallen short of God's standard of perfection (Rom. 3:23). In heaven's economy, nobody is better off than anybody else. We all have a massive sin debt that only Jesus has the ability to pay.

> *God makes people right with himself through their faith in Jesus Christ. This is true for all who believe in Christ, because all people are the same: All have sinned and are not good enough for God's glory, and all need to be made right with God by his grace, which is a free gift. They need to be made free from sin through Jesus Christ.* —Romans 3:22–24

Go and learn what this means: "I want kindness more than I want animal sacrifices." I did not come to invite good people but to invite sinners.

—Matthew 9:13

4. Choose the correct answer for each of the following questions. Base your answers on Romans 3:22–24 above. Check all that apply.

   Who does God make right with himself?
   ❏ Only a few good individuals
   ❏ Only those who try to be good
   ❏ Every individual who has faith in Jesus Christ

   How do we receive salvation?
   ❏ We must earn it by being good enough.
   ❏ We must pay God back for it someday.
   ❏ It is a free gift of his grace.

5. Why is it hard to accept something we didn't earn or work for?

   _____

   _____

And if he chose them by grace, it is not for the things they have done. If they could be made God's people by what they did, God's gift of grace would not really be a gift.

—Romans 11:6

THE DECISION OF GRACE

For "God was in Christ, making peace between the world and himself . . . Christ had no sin, but God made him become sin so that in Christ we could become right with God" (2 Cor. 5:19, 21). The perfect record of Jesus was given to you, and your imperfect record was given to Christ. Jesus was "not guilty, but he suffered for those who are guilty to bring you to God" (1 Pet. 3:18). As a result, God's holiness is honored and his children are forgiven. By his perfect life Jesus fulfilled the commands of the law. By his death he satisfied the demands of sin. Jesus suffered not like a sinner, but as a sinner. Why else would he cry, "My GOD, My GOD, why have you forsaken Me?" (Matt. 27:46 NKJV). When God sent Jesus as a sacrifice or substitute for our sins, he put grace in motion. Simply put, the cost of our sins is infinitely more than we can pay. Grace must come to our rescue—in the person of Jesus Christ.

The cost of our sins is so much more than we could ever pay.

6. Based upon what you have learned about God's plan for salvation, how did the sacrifice of Jesus Christ honor God's standard for holiness?

   _____

   _____

TOO GOOD TO BE TRUE?

But he said to me, "My grace is enough for you. When you are weak, my power is made perfect in you." So I am very happy to brag about my weaknesses. Then Christ's power can live in me.

—2 Corinthians 12:9

This may very well be the most difficult spiritual truth for us to embrace. For some reason, people accept Jesus as Lord before they accept him as Savior. It's easier to comprehend his power than his mercy. We'll celebrate the empty tomb long before we'll kneel at the cross.

Deep down, we often believe what Jesus has done for us may be "too good to be true." This is by far the most common objection to grace. Take the young woman who spent two university years saying yes to the flesh and no to God. Or the young husband who wonders if God could forgive an abortion he funded a decade ago. Then there was the father who's just realized he'd devoted his life to work and neglected his kids.

All are wondering if they've overextended their credit line with God. They aren't alone. The vast majority of people simply state, "God may give grace to you, but not to me. You see, I've charted the waters of failure. I've pushed the envelope too many times. I'm not your typical sinner, I'm guilty of _____." And they fill in the blank.

7. No matter what sin may be lurking in your past, Jesus has made a way for you to experience true grace. Read the promise in 1 John 1:9. Fill in the blanks below from this passage about forgiveness of sin.

If we _____ our sins, God is _____ and _____ to forgive us from every sin. Not only that, he will also _____ us from _____ unrighteousness.

If we confess our sins, He is faithful and just to forgive us our sins and cleanse us from all unrighteousness

—1 John 1:9 NKJV

INTO GOD'S PRESENCE

"Since we have been made right with God by our faith, we have peace with God. This happened through our Lord Jesus Christ, who has brought us into that blessing of God's grace that we now enjoy. And we are happy because of the hope we have of sharing God's glory. We also have joy with our troubles, because we know that these troubles produce patience. And patience produces character, and character produces hope. And this hope will never disappoint us, because God has poured out his love to fill our hearts. He gave us his love through the Holy Spirit, whom God has given to us." —Romans 5:1–5

Jesus has made a way for you to experience forgiveness.

8. Underline the words in the passage above that describe many of the positive results of receiving God's salvation. Now, check all the statements below that describe the blessings that result from salvation.

❑ We have peace with God.
❑ We enjoy God's grace.
❑ We are happy because we have hope.
❑ We will share God's glory.
❑ We are joyful in trouble.
❑ We have God's love in our hearts.
❑ We receive the gift of the Holy Spirit.

Let's look at the phrase, "brought us into." The Greek word means "to usher into the presence of royalty." Christ meets you outside the throne room, takes you by the hand, and walks you into the presence of God. Upon entrance we find grace, not condemnation; mercy, not punishment. Where we would never be granted an audience with the king, we are now welcomed into his presence.

Let us therefore come boldly to the throne of grace, that we may obtain mercy and find grace to help in time of need

—Hebrews 4:16, NKJV

9. Sometimes we feel so unlovable. We can't imagine God wants our company at all. We would blush with shame in the presence of his perfect holiness. But what does Hebrews 4:16 urge us to do?

_____

_____

And all need to be made right with God by his grace, which is a free gift. They need to be made free from sin through Jesus Christ.

—Romans 3:24

If a child you don't know appears on your doorstep and asks to spend the night, what would you do? Likely you would ask his name, where he lives, find out why he is roaming the streets, and contact his parents. On the other hand, if a youngster enters your house escorted by your child, that child is welcomed. The same is true with God. By becoming friends with the Son, we have entrance to the throne room. He ushers us into that "blessing of God's grace that we now enjoy" (Rom. 5:2).

10. How would you describe the "blessings of God's grace" that you now enjoy? Check all that apply.

   ❏ Grace means God accepts me as I am.
   ❏ Grace means my past is forgiven and forgotten.
   ❏ Grace means I am welcome in God's presence anytime.

Ponder the achievement of God. He doesn't condone our sin, nor does he compromise his standard. He doesn't ignore our rebellion, nor does he relax his demands. Rather than dismiss our sin, he assumes our sin and, incredibly, sentences himself. God's holiness is honored. Our sin is punished . . . and we are redeemed. God is still God. The wages of sin is still death. And we are made perfect . . . God does what we cannot do so we can be what we dare not dream: perfect before God.

Grace means my past is forgiven and forgotten.

11. Many people are familiar with stories invented about "arriving at the gates of heaven." But suppose there was such an experience. What would you say if God met you on the threshold and asked, "Why should I let you in?"

   _____

   _____

THE HEART OF THE MATTER

- **The cost of our sins is so much more than we could ever pay.**
- **We are all equally guilty before a holy God.**
- **Jesus has made a way for you to experience forgiveness.**
- **God makes us right in his sight.**
- **Grace means my past is forgiven and forgotten.**

Spend a few moments reviewing your memory verse for the week—Ephesians 2:8–9. Write it out below for a little extra practice.

   _____

   _____

   _____

The Heart of Jesus

Levi was not a popular man, at least not among those of good society. Those folks distrusted him, avoided him, cast suspicious glances his way. They were afraid of the power he held, and they hated him for it. Such was the life of a tax collector. Levi was not alone, though. He had his own circle of friends—other tax collectors, thugs, prostitutes, outcasts, and others the Jews had branded as "sinners." One day, at the office, Jesus popped his head in through the door and simply said, "Follow me." For a moment, Levi stopped breathing. Had he heard rightly? Everyone knew Jesus was a righteous man, not the sort to have anything to do with tax collectors.

But the invitation had been extended!

He would follow.

In return, Levi extended an invitation of his own, "Come over for dinner, and I'll introduce you to all my friends." All good society was scandalized, but Jesus was unconcerned. "This is why I came." Not for good society. Not for decent folks.

Jesus came so that sinners could experience grace.

Though we were spiritually dead because of the things we did against God, he gave us new life with Christ. You have been saved by God's grace.
—Ephesians 2:5

(handwritten margin note: Bradley Thursday glory)

DAY THREE—THE ROYAL PAUPERS

THE PRIVILEGE OF PAUPERS

One of the more incredible realizations we can make about God's gift of grace is his timing. It wasn't after we changed that he loved us. It wasn't after we had been in church for ten years that he decided to love us. It wasn't after we had filled out all the applications, submitted three recommendations, and passed an extensive interview that he loved us. God loved us *while we were still sinners.* Incredible. He loved us without provocation. He treated us like royalty at a time when we were mere paupers.

God loved us while we were still sinners.

> *When we were unable to help ourselves, at the moment of our need, Christ died for us, although we were living against God. Very few people will die to save the life of someone else. Although perhaps for a good person someone might possibly die. But God shows his great love for us in this way: Christ died for us while we were still sinners.* —Romans 5:6–8

1. Based on what you just read in Romans 5:6–8, fill in the blanks for the following statements concerning when God stepped in to save us.

   When we were _____ to help _____
   When we were _____ against _____
   At the moment of our greatest _____
   While we were still _____

My first ministry position was in Miami, Florida. In our congregation we had more than our share of Southern ladies who loved to cook. I fit in well because I was a single guy who loved to eat. The church was fond of having Sunday evening potluck dinners, and about once a quarter they feasted.

My, it was good, a veritable cornucopia of CorningWare. Juicy ham bathed in pineapple, baked beans, pickled relish, pecan pie . . . (Oops, I just drooled on my computer keyboard.) Ever wondered why there are so many hefty preachers? You enter the ministry for meals like those.

As a bachelor I counted on potluck dinners for my survival strategy. While others were planning what to cook, I was studying the storage techniques of camels. Knowing I should bring something, I'd make it a point to raid my kitchen shelves on Sunday afternoon. The result was pitiful: One time I took a half-empty jar of Planters Peanuts; another time I made a half-dozen jelly sandwiches. One of my better offerings was an unopened sack of chips; a more meager gift was a can of tomato soup, also unopened.

Wasn't much, but no one ever complained. In fact, the way those ladies acted, you would've thought I brought the Thanksgiving turkey. They'd take my jar of peanuts and set it on the long table with the rest of the food and hand me a plate. "Go ahead, Max, don't be bashful. Fill up your plate." And I would! Mashed potatoes and gravy. Roast beef. Fried chicken. I took a little bit of everything, except the peanuts.

I came like a pauper and ate like a king!

2. We understand physical hunger pangs. However, what can we learn from the following verses about what it means to be "hungry" in a spiritual sense?

   Psalm 73:25 – "I have no one in heaven but you; I want nothing on earth besides you."

   _____

   _____

ALL GOD'S CHILDREN
To whom does God offer his gift? To the brightest? The most beautiful or the most charming? No. His gift is for us all—beggars and bankers, clergy and clerks, judges and janitors. All God's children.

And he wants us so badly, he'll take us in any condition—"as is" reads the tag on our collars. He's not about to wait for us to reach perfection (he knows we'll never get there!). Do you think he's waiting for us to overcome all temptations? Hardly. When we master the Christian walk? Far from it. Remember, Christ died for us when we were still sinners. His sacrifice, then, was not dependent on our performance.

He wants us *now.*
—*No Wonder They Call Him the Savior*

The Word became a human and lived among us. We saw his glory—the glory that belongs to the only Son of the Father—and he was full of grace and truth.

—John 1:14

Psalm 119:20 – "I am overwhelmed continually with a desire for your laws." NLT

_____

_____

Isaiah 26:8–9 – "Lord, we love to obey your laws; our heart's desire is to glorify your name. All night long I search for you; earnestly I seek for God." NLT

_____

_____

John 6:35 – "Jesus said to them, 'I am the bread of life. He who comes to Me shall never hunger, and he who believes in Me shall never thirst.'" NKJV

_____

_____

Matthew 5:6 – "Blessed are those who hunger and thirst for righteousness, for they shall be filled." NKJV

_____

_____

Go to Jesus. He will satisfy your spiritual hunger.

SPIRITUAL HUNGER

Though Paul never attended a potluck, he would have loved the symbolism. He would say that Christ does for us precisely what those women did for me. He welcomes us to his table by virtue of his love and our request. It is not our offerings that grant us a place at the feast; indeed, anything we bring appears puny at his table. Our admission of hunger is the only demand, for "Blessed are those who hunger and thirst for righteousness, for they shall be filled" (Matt. 5:6).

Our hunger, then, is not a yearning to be avoided but rather a God-given desire to be heeded. Our weakness is not to be dismissed but to be confessed.

3. According to Matthew 5:6, which of the following statements are true concerning the result of spiritual hunger and which ones are false? Mark your answers True (T) or False (F).

___ We will be filled and find satisfaction.
___ We will continue longing to be filled.
___ We will be somewhat satisfied from time to time.

He satisfies me with good things and makes me young again, like the eagle.

—Psalm 103:5

Sometimes we realize our spiritual hunger when we have experienced a long absence from fellowship with God. We may recognize our emptiness after going through a "dry" time spiritually, where we seemed to be just going through the motions of a relationship with God. Or it may be that we have had our fill of disobedience and now we are yearning to be with Jesus once again. Spiritual hunger leads us to hear our hearts rumble with emptiness and realize anew how much we miss him.

4. What statement best describes your current level of spiritual "hunger"? Check your response.

❑ I am completely satisfied with myself, and do not hunger for anything more spiritually.
❑ I can go for days without realizing how hungry I am.
❑ I have a nagging hunger for spiritual things, but I have no time to prepare a meal.
❑ I get the spiritual "munchies" and satisfy my cravings with a few quick verses.
❑ I cannot get through my day without at least one solid spiritual meal.

And it brings praise to God because of his wonderful grace. God gave that grace to us freely, in Christ, the One he loves.

—Ephesians 1:6

PORTRAIT OF A PAUPER

It's not pretty. That's the portrait Paul paints when he describes us in Romans 5. Think about it. We were "unable to help ourselves," "living against God," "sinners," and "God's enemies" (Rom. 5:6, 8, 10). How pitiful and pathetic, really. Yet, these are the very people for whom Jesus Christ died. You see, we come to Christ as is—or we cannot come at all. He alone can change us into the people we were meant to be. We are wasting time when we try to "clean up our act" before we come to him.

Family therapist Paul Faulkner tells of the man who set out to adopt a troubled teenage girl. One would question the father's logic. The girl was destructive, disobedient, and dishonest. One day she came home from school and ransacked the house looking for money. By the time he arrived, she was gone and the house was in shambles.

Upon hearing of her actions, friends urged him not to finalize the adoption. "Let her go," they said. "After all, she's not really your daughter." His response was simply. "Yes, I know. But I told her she was."[ii]

God, too, has made a covenant to adopt his people. His covenant is not invalidated by our rebellion. It's one thing to love us when we are strong, obedient, and willing. But when we ransack his house and steal what is his? This is the test of love.

And God passes the test. "God shows his great love for us in this way: Christ died for us while we were still sinners" (Rom. 5:8).

The ladies at our church didn't see me and my peanuts and say, "Come back when you've learned to cook."

The father didn't look at the wrecked house and say, "Come back when you've learned respect."

God didn't look at our frazzled lives and say, "I'll die for you when you deserve it."

5. Read the following verses. Then fill in the blanks according to what you learn about how God expresses his great love for us.

He is _____ to anger and abounds in _____. (Joel 2:13)
God pours his _____ into our hearts. (Romans 5:5)
Nothing can _____ from God's love. (Romans 8:38)
I pray that you will understand the greatness of God's love—how _____ and how _____ and how _____ and how _____ that love is. (Ephesians 3:18)

THE PAIN OF OUR PAST

Many of you know what it's like to carry a stigma. Each time your name is mentioned, your calamity follows.

"Have you heard from John lately? You know, the fellow who got divorced?"

"We got a letter from Jerry. Remember him, the alcoholic?"

"Sharon is in town. What a shame that she has to raise those kids alone."

"I saw Melissa today. I don't know why she can't keep a job."

Like a pesky sibling, your past follows you wherever you go. Isn't there anyone who sees you for who you are and not what you did? Yes. There is One who does. Your King. When God speaks of you, he doesn't mention your plight, pain, or problem; he lets you share his glory. He calls you his child.

He will not always accuse us, and he will not be angry forever. He has not punished us as our sins should be punished; he has not repaid us for the evil we have done. As high as the sky is above the earth, so great is his love for those who respect him. He has taken our sins away from us as far as the east is from west. The Lord has mercy on those who respect him, as a father has mercy on his children. He knows how we were made; he remembers that we are dust. —Psalm 103:9–14

GOD MAKES US RIGHT AGAIN

We are thirsty.

Not thirsty for fame, possessions, passion, or romance. We've drunk from those pools. They are salt water in the desert. They don't quench—they kill.

"Blessed are those who hunger and thirst for righteousness. . . ."

Righteousness. That's it. That's what we are thirsty for. We're thirsty for a clean conscience. We crave a clean slate. We yearn for a fresh start. We pray for a hand that will enter the dark cavern of our world and do for us the one thing we can't do for ourselves—make us right again.

—*The Applause of Heaven*

Only Jesus can make us into the people we were meant to be.

And after you suffer for a short time, God, who gives all grace, will make everything right. He will make you strong and support you and keep you from falling. He called you to share in his glory in Christ, a glory that will continue forever.

—1 Peter 5:10

Come back to the Lord your God, because He is kind and shows mercy. He doesn't become angry quickly, and he has great love.

—Joel 2:13

And I pray that you and all God's holy people will have the power to understand the greatness of God's love—how wide and how long and how high and how deep that love is.

—Ephesians 3:18

Jesus has taken our sins away from us as far as the east is from the west.

He has delivered us from the power of darkness and conveyed us into the kingdom of the Son of His love.

—Colossians 1:13 NKJV

But now in Christ Jesus, you who were far away from God are brought near through the blood of Christ's death.

—Ephesians 2:13

You are a chosen generation, a royal priesthood, a holy nation, His own special people, that you may proclaim the praises of Him who called you out of darkness into His marvelous light.

—1 Peter 2:9 NKJV

God calls you his child

One man sinned, and so death ruled all people because of that one man. But now those people who accept God's full grace and the great gift of being made right with him will surely have true life and rule through the one man, Jesus Christ.

—Romans 5:17

6. It's human nature to slip up. Make a mistake. Rebel. Disobey. Yet based on what you read in Psalm 103:9–14, how does our continued stumbling affect God's promise of grace?

_____

_____

7. Some days you may feel more like a pauper, than a privileged child of God. For those times, turn to the Scriptures to remind yourself of who you are. Look up and read aloud the verses below regarding your identity. Then match the truth with its text.

____ Romans 8:1　　　　a. You have been adopted.
____ Ephesians 2:13　　 b. You are perfect.
____ Colossians 1:13　　 c. You are justified.
____ Romans 5:1　　　　d. You are delivered from the power of evil.
____ Hebrews 10:14　　 e. You are near God.
____ Hebrews 13:5　　　f. You have access to God at any moment.
____ Romans 8:15　　　 g. You are beyond condemnation.
____ Ephesians 2:18　　 h. You will never be abandoned.
____ 1 Peter 1:4　　　　i. You have an imperishable inheritance.

8. When you experience the grace of Jesus, you are given a privileged place. Match these verses with what they proclaim about your position in Christ.

You are a . . .

____ John 15:5　　　　　a. dwelling place of the Spirit
____ 1 Corinthians 6:19　b. stone in the building
____ 1 Corinthians 12:13 c. branch in the vine
____ Ephesians 2:19–22　d. bride for the groom
____ Ephesians 5:25–27　e. priest in the new generation
____ 1 Peter 2:9　　　　f. member of his body

9. We were paupers, with nothing to recommend ourselves to Jesus. Perhaps, in His mercy, he might toss a few coins our way—we could expect no more. But He did the unexpected. He gathered us up in His arms and brought us to his Father. The pauper is adopted into the royal family, and made a prince! Now that you have learned about who you have become in Christ, and the place He has made for you, write a prayer of response to God:

_____

_____

THE HEART OF THE MATTER

- **God loved us while we were still sinners.**
- **Go to Jesus. He will satisfy your spiritual hunger.**
- **Only Jesus can make us into the people we were meant to be.**
- **Jesus has taken our sins away as far as the east is from the west.**
- **God calls you his child.**

Fill in the blanks below for a little memory verse practice:

For by _____ you have been _____ through _____, and that not of _____; it is the _____ of God, not of _____, lest anyone should _____. —Ephesians 2:8–9 NKJV

The Heart of Jesus

She didn't belong in the home of that Pharisee. Simon was an upstanding Jew. His home, the setting for a fine banquet. He was playing host to a virtual celebrity, and Simon wanted everything to go smoothly.

Then, a woman slipped in.

She interrupted the dinner conversation. She made heads turn. She caused whispers to relay around the room. "She was once inhabited by demons." "They say she has played the harlot." "Look at her! She hasn't even worn a veil."

Simon was scandalized.

This woman, tearfully anointing the feet of his guest with perfume, was a sinner. How had she gotten in here! Jesus was not scandalized. He wasn't shocked by her reputation. He wasn't put off by her emotional display—even when she began to kiss his feet and bathe them with her tears.

Jesus reached out to that repentant sinner, "Your sins are forgiven."

The woman left Simon's house with peace in her heart, having experienced the grace of Jesus.

Luke 7:36–50

ADOPTED BY GOD

The Spirit himself bears witness with our spirit that we are children of God.

—Romans 8:16 NASB

When we come to Christ, God not only forgives us, he also adopts us. Through a dramatic series of events, we go from condemned orphans with no hope to adopted children with no fear. Here is how it happens. You come before the judgment seat of God full of rebellion and mistakes. Because of his justice he cannot dismiss your sin, but because of his love he cannot dismiss you. So, in an act which stunned the heavens, he punished himself on the cross for your sins. God's justice and love are equally honored. And you, God's creation, are forgiven. But the story doesn't end with God's forgiveness . . .

It would be enough if God just cleansed your name, but he does more. He gives you his name.

—*The Great House of God*

DAY FOUR—HOW GRACE WORKS

FREELY GIVEN

Sometimes I give away money at the end of a sermon. Not to pay the listeners (though some may feel they've earned it) but to make a point. I offer a dollar to anyone who will accept it. Free money. A gift. I invite anyone who wants the cash to come and take it.

The response is predictable. A pause. Some shuffling of feet. A wife elbows her husband, and he shakes his head. A teen starts to stand and then remembers her reputation. A five-year-old starts walking down the aisle, and his mother pulls him back. Finally some courageous (or impoverished) soul stands up and says, "I'll take it!" The dollar is given, and the application begins.

"Why didn't you take my offer?" I ask the rest. Some say they were too embarrassed. The pain wasn't worth the gain. Others feared a catch, a trick. And then there are those whose wallets are fat. What's a buck to someone who has hundreds?

Then the obvious follow-up question. "Why don't people accept Christ's free gift?" The answers are similar. Some are too embarrassed. To accept forgiveness is to admit sin, a step we are slow to take. Others fear a trick, a catch. Surely there is some fine print in the Bible. Others think, who needs forgiveness when you're as good as I am?

The point makes itself. Though grace is available to all, it's accepted by few. Many choose to sit and wait, while only a few choose to stand and trust.

1. Why don't some people accept God's free gift of grace? Check all that apply.

   ❑ Some are embarrassed to admit their needs.
   ❑ Some are oblivious to their needs.
   ❑ Some fear it's too good to be true.

GRACE WORKS

In Romans 6 Paul asks a crucial question: "How can we who died to sin still live in it?" (v. 2 RSV). How can we who have been made right not live righteous lives? How can

I mean that you have been saved by grace through believing. You did not save yourselves; it was a gift from God.

—Ephesians 2:8

we who have been loved not love? How can we who have been blessed not bless? How can we who have been given grace not live graciously?

Paul seems stunned that an alternative would even exist! How could grace result in anything but gracious living? "So do you think we should continue sinning so that God will give us even more grace? No!" (Rom. 6:1).

We'd scoff at such hypocrisy. We wouldn't tolerate it, and we wouldn't do it.

Or would we? Let's answer that one slowly. Perhaps we don't sin so God can give grace, but do we ever sin knowing God will give grace? Do we ever compromise tonight, knowing we'll confess tomorrow?

Grace is available to all.

2. Some people have learned to twist grace to suit their own selfishness. We easily rationalize away our behavior. Do any of these phrases sound familiar to you?

   ❑ "Sometimes it's easier to ask for forgiveness than to ask for permission."
   ❑ "I like knowing grace is there in case I need it."
   ❑ "If God will forgive me tomorrow, why not do what I want today?"

3. In contrast to these human arguments, fill in the blanks about Paul's approach to sin and grace as expressed in Romans 6:15–18.

   Should we _____ because we are under _____ and not under _____? No! In the past you were _____ to sin. It _____ you. Now you are _____ from sin and slaves to _____.

So what should we do? Should we sin because we are under grace and not under law? No! Surely you know that when you give yourselves like slaves to obey someone, then you are really slaves of that person. The person you obey is your master. You can follow sin, which brings spiritual death, or you can obey God, which makes you right with him. In the past you were slaves to sin—sin controlled you. But thank God, you fully obeyed the things that you were taught. You were made free from sin, and now you are slaves to goodness.

—Romans 6:15–18

It's easy to be like the fellow visiting Las Vegas who called the preacher, wanting to know the hours of the Sunday service. The preacher was impressed. "Most people who come to Las Vegas don't do so to go to church."

"Oh, I'm not coming for the church. I'm coming for the gambling and parties and wild women. If I have half as much fun as I intend to, I'll need a church come Sunday morning."

Is that the intent of grace? Is God's goal to promote disobedience? Hardly. "Grace . . . teaches us not to live against God nor to do the evil things the world wants us to do. Instead, that grace teaches us to live now in a wise and right way and in a way that shows we serve God" (Titus 2:11–12). God's grace has released us from selfishness. Why return?

For the grace of God has been revealed, bringing salvation to all people. And we are instructed to turn from godless living and sinful pleasures. We should live in this evil world with self-control, right conduct, and devotion to God.

—Titus 2:11-12 NLT

4. Read Titus 2:11–12 at the right. Fill in the blanks below about what you learn from this passage concerning how grace works.

   The grace of God has been _____. We are instructed to _____ from _____ living and _____. We should live in this evil world with _____, _____, and _____ to God.

THE PENALTY HAS BEEN PAID

Think of it this way. Sin put you in prison. Sin locked you behind the bars of guilt and shame and deception and fear. Sin did nothing but shackle you to the wall of misery. Then Jesus came and paid your bail. He served your time; he satisfied the penalty and set you free. Christ died, and when you cast your lot with him, your old self died too.

The only way to be set free from the prison of sin is to serve its penalty. In this case the penalty is death. Someone has to die, either you or a heaven-sent substitute. You cannot leave prison unless there is a death. But that death has occurred at Calvary. And when Jesus died, you died to sin's claim on your life. You are free.

Sometimes we feel so caught up in our failures and repeated attempts to live the way we know we should. Nagging bad habits. Persistent personality flaws. We feel trapped in the presumption that we can't change. Experiencing the grace of Jesus means we feel his strong hand on our shoulder as we hear the words, "My child, you are free."

Grace to all of you who love our Lord Jesus Christ with love that never ends.
—Ephesians 6:24

5. What is your typical reaction when, despite repeated efforts, you seem unable to change a troubling area of your life? Check all that apply.

❏ Give up trying—what's the use?
❏ Berate myself for not having more self-control.
❏ Try harder.
❏ Ask God for his grace—again.

No matter what charge is laid up against you, realize this:

Christ has taken your place. There is no need for you to remain in the cell. Ever heard of a discharged prisoner who wanted to stay? Nor have I. When the doors open, prisoners leave. The thought of a person preferring jail over freedom doesn't compute. Once the penalty is paid, why live under bondage? You are discharged from the penitentiary of sin. Why, in heaven's name, would you ever want to set foot in that prison again?

Paul reminds us: "Our old life died with Christ on the cross so that our sinful selves would have no power over us and we would not be slaves to sin. Anyone who has died is made free from sin's control" (Rom. 6:6–7).

He is not saying that it is impossible for believers to sin; he's saying it is stupid for believers to sin.

What does the prison have that you desire? Do you miss the guilt? Are you homesick for dishonesty? Do you have fond memories of being lied to and forgotten? Was life better when you were dejected and rejected? Do you have a longing to once again see a sinner in the mirror?

It makes no sense to go back to prison.

6. Mark each statement True (T) or False (F). Use the Bible verses below to help you answer.

___ Our old life died with Christ on the cross. (Galatians 2:20)
___ Our sinful self has no power over us. (Romans 6:6)
___ We should not be slaves to sin. (2 Peter 2:19)
___ If we have died to sin, we are free from its control. (Romans 8:9)

Grace has set you free from your failures.

Since sin has no power over us any more, we don't *have* to sin anymore. We are no longer slaves. So when we sin, it is because we have chosen to sin!

THE VOW HAS BEEN MADE

Not only has a price been paid, but a vow has been made. "Did you forget that all of us became part of Christ when we were baptized?" (Rom. 6:3).

Baptism was no casual custom, no ho-hum ritual. Baptism was, and is, "a pledge made to God from a good conscience" (1 Pet. 3:21 TJB).

What form of amnesia is this? Like a bride horrified to see her new husband flirting with women at the wedding reception, Paul asks, "Did you forget your vows?"

Indeed, baptism is a vow, a sacred vow of the believer to follow Christ. Just as a wedding celebrates the fusion of two hearts, baptism celebrates the union of sinner with Savior. We "became part of Christ when we were baptized" (Rom. 6:3).

Similarly God asks, "Does our union mean nothing to you? Is our covenant so fragile that you would choose the arms of a harlot over mine?"

Who, in their right mind, would want to abandon these vows? Who will care for you more than Christ? Have we forgotten what life was like before our baptism? Have we forgotten the mess we were in before we were united with him?

So do you think we should continue sinning so that God will give us even more grace? No! We died to our old sinful lives, so how can we continue living with sin? Did you forget that all of us became part of Christ when we were baptized? We shared his death in our baptism. When we were baptized, we were buried with

In Christ we are set free by the blood of his death, and so we have forgiveness of sins. How rich is God's grace, which he has given to us so fully and freely.
—**Ephesians 1:7–8**

> *Christ and shared his death. So, just as Christ was raised from the dead by the wonderful power of the Father, we also can live a new life. Christ died, and we have been joined with him by dying too. So we will also be joined with him by rising from the dead as he did. We know that our old life died with Christ on the cross so that our sinful selves would have no power over us and we would not be slaves to sin. Anyone who has died is made free from sin's control.* —Romans 6:1–7

I was put to death on the cross with Christ, and I do not live anymore—it is Christ who lives in me. I still live in my body, but I live by faith in the Son of God who loved me and gave himself to save me.
—Galatians 2:20

But you are not ruled by your sinful selves. You are ruled by the Spirit, if that Spirit of God really lives in you. But the person who does not have the Spirit of Christ does not belong to Christ.
—Romans 8:9

Believers have made a sacred vow to follow Jesus Christ.

You then, Timothy, my child, be strong in the grace we have in Christ Jesus.
—2 Timothy 2:1

7. Read Romans 6:1–7. Fill in the blanks below in this passage concerning our union with Christ.

We _____ to our old sinful selves. All of us became _____ of _____. We shared his _____. We can live a _____. Our sinful selves have no _____ over us and we are not _____ to sin. We are free from sin's _____.

8. Many young couples today favor writing their own vows over the more traditional ones. It's a creative expression of their love and commitment to one another. Imagine writing your vows describing your union with Christ. What would you want to say to express your love and commitment to him?

_____
_____

A HIGHER STANDARD

Most of my life I've been a closet slob. I was slow to see the logic of neatness.

Then I got married.

Denalyn was so patient. She said she didn't mind my habits . . . if I didn't mind sleeping outside. Since I did, I began to change.

I enrolled in a twelve-step program for slobs. ("My name is Max, I hate to vacuum.") A physical therapist helped me rediscover the muscles used for hanging shirts and placing toilet paper on the holder. My nose was reintroduced to the fragrance of Pine Sol. By the time Denalyn's parents came to visit, I was a new man. I could go three days without throwing a sock behind the couch.

But then came the moment of truth. Denalyn went out of town for a week. Initially I reverted to the old man. I figured I'd be a slob for six days and clean on the seventh. But something strange happened, a curious discomfort. I couldn't relax with dirty dishes in the sink. When I saw an empty potato-chip sack on the floor I—hang on to your hat—bent over and picked it up! I actually put my bath towel back on the rack. What had happened to me?

Simple. I'd been exposed to a higher standard.

Isn't that what has happened with us? Isn't that the heart of Paul's argument? How could we who have been freed from sin return to it? Before Christ our lives were out of control, sloppy, and indulgent. We didn't even know we were slobs until we met him.

Then he moved in. Things began to change. What we threw around we began putting away. What we neglected we cleaned up. What had been clutter became order. Oh, there were and still are occasional lapses of thought and deed, but by and large he got our house in order.

Suddenly we find ourselves wanting to do good. Go back to the old mess? Are you kidding? "In the past you were slaves to sin—sin controlled you. But thank God, you fully obeyed the things that you were taught. You were made free from sin, and now you are slaves to goodness" (Romans 6:17–18).

9. What happens to our spiritual "slobbiness" when Christ comes into our lives? Check all that apply.

❏ We continue to live just as we did before Christ.
❏ We desire to do good and please Christ.
❏ We are no longer slaves to the old way of doing things.

10. God is at work in our hearts, changing us. What are two of the things he is doing, according to Philippians 2:13?

_____

_____

THE CALL OF GRACE

Can a discharged prisoner return to confinement? Yes. But let him remember the gray walls and the long nights. Can a newlywed forget his vows? Yes. But let him remember his holy vow and his beautiful bride. Can a converted slob once again be messy? Yes. But let him consider the difference between the filth of yesterday and the purity of today.

Can one who has been given a free gift not share that gift with others? I suppose. But let him remember that all of life is a gift of grace. And let him remember that the call of grace is to live a gracious life.

For that is how grace works.

THE HEART OF THE MATTER

- Grace is available to all.
- Grace has set you free from your failures.
- Sin has no power over you any more.
- Believers have made a sacred vow to follow Jesus Christ.
- God gives you the desire to do what pleases him.

For God is working in you, giving you the desire to obey him and the power to do what pleases him.

—Philippians 2:13

Review your memory verse for this week again by writing Ephesians 2:8–9 on the lines below.

_____

_____

The Heart of Jesus

The afternoon sun was getting lower in the sky, and the workmen studied its slow descent with a sinking feeling. They had been sitting in the square all day, shifting their weight from foot to foot, scuffing their sandals in the dust, waiting.

Unless someone came along soon with even the smallest request for work, they would have no money—and no food—to bring home to hungry families.

When a prosperous farmer came into view, spirits lifted.

He would put the lot of them to work for the rest of the day. They couldn't hope to earn much in these last few hours—a few sheckles at best—but it was better than nothing. Gratefully, they joined the other workers in the fields.

At day's end, they filed out of the fields past the owner with his money purse. It was then that each man experienced an astonishing kindness.

A *full day's* wage was placed in each hand.

Though they had arrived late and accomplished little, they experienced the fullness of grace.

God gives you the desire to do what pleases him.

The Lord laughs at those who laugh at him, but he gives grace to those who are not proud.

—**Proverbs 3:34**

DAY FIVE—SUFFICIENT GRACE

5th day
Friday

ONLY ONE THING IS NECESSARY

Here is the scene: You and I and a half-dozen other folks are flying across the country in a chartered plane. All of a sudden the engine bursts into flames, and the pilot rushes out of the cockpit.

"We're going to crash!" he yells. "We've got to bail out!"

Good thing he knows where the parachutes are because we don't. He passes them out, gives us a few pointers, and we stand in line as he throws open the door. The first passenger steps up to the door and shouts over the wind, "Could I make a request?"

"Sure, what is it?"

"Any way I could get a pink parachute?"

The pilot shakes his head in disbelief. "Isn't it enough that I gave you a parachute at all?" And so the first passenger jumps.

The second steps to the door. "I'm wondering if there is any way you could ensure that I won't get nauseated during the fall?"

"No, but I can ensure that you will have a parachute for the fall."

Each of us comes with a request and receives a parachute.

"Please, captain," says one, "I am afraid of heights. Would you remove my fear?"

"No," he replies, "but I'll give you a parachute."

Another pleads for a different strategy, "Couldn't you change the plans? Let's crash with the plane. We might survive."

The pilot smiles and says, "You don't know what you are asking" and gently shoves the fellow out the door. One passenger wants some goggles, another wants boots, another wants to wait until the plane is closer to the ground.

"You people don't understand," the pilot shouts as he "helps" us, one by one. "I've given you a parachute; that is enough."

Only one item is necessary for the jump, and he provides it. He places the strategic tool in our hands. The gift is adequate. But are we content? No. We are restless, anxious, even demanding.

Too crazy to be possible? Maybe in a plane with pilots and parachutes, but on earth with people and grace? God hears thousands of appeals per second. Some are legitimate. We, too, ask God to remove the fear or change the plans. He usually answers with a gentle shove that leaves us airborne and suspended by his grace.

Truth be known, some of us discover we have a fear of heights when we are dangling above precarious circumstances—suspended by his grace alone. We'd rather have our feet firmly planted on the ground. We want certainty and facts. We feel a need to know all is going to work out the way we planned. In fact, if we can't be sure of the outcome of our problems, we'd rather not have them at all. Like Paul, we ask God to please make them disappear.

To keep me from becoming conceited because of these surpassingly great revelations, there was given me a thorn in my flesh, a messenger of Satan, to torment me. Three times I pleaded with the Lord to take it away from me. But he said to me, "My grace is sufficient for you, for my power is made perfect in weakness."

—2 Corinthians 12:7–9

1. What does the illustration about the pilot and the parachutes tell you about the sufficiency of God's grace during trials?

   _____

   _____

2. Read 2 Corinthians 9:8 on the right. Fill in the blanks of the verse about the sufficiency of Jesus' grace.

   God is able to make _____ grace about toward you, that you, _____ having _____ sufficiency in _____ things, may have an abundance of _____ good work.

And God is able to make all grace abound toward you, that you, always having all sufficiency in all things, may have an abundance for every good work.

—2 Corinthians 9:8 NKJV

WHEN GOD SAYS NO

There are times when the one thing you want is the one thing you never get. You're not being picky or demanding; you're only obeying his command to "ask God for everything you need" (Phil. 4:6). All you want is an open door or an extra day or an answered prayer, for which you will be thankful.

And so you pray and wait.

No answer.

You pray and wait.

No answer.

You pray and wait.

May I ask a very important question? What if God says no?

What if the request is delayed or even denied? When God says no to you, how will you respond? If God says, "I've given you my grace, and that is enough," will you be content?

3. Think of a time when God did say no to a specific prayer request. How did you react at the time?

_____

_____

4. Looking back, do you have a better understanding now why God may have answered you the way he did?

_____

_____

God does not always take away our troubles.

CONTENT IN CHRIST

Content. That's the word. A state of heart in which you would be at peace if God gave you nothing more than he already has. Test yourself with this question: What if God's only gift to you were his grace to save you? Would you be content? You beg him to save the life of your child. You plead with him to keep your business afloat. You implore him to remove the cancer from your body. What if his answer is, "My grace is enough." Would you be content?

5. Paul knew what his answer to that question would be. Read Philippians 4:12–13 and choose the statements that describe Paul's attitude. Check all that apply.

❏ I can trust God to take care of my needs.
❏ I can live victoriously in every situation.
❏ I have to have my needs met before I can be happy.

6. Describe the "contentment quotient" in your life right now. Are you completely satisfied? Where is your greatest area of discontent?

_____

_____

We are not satisfied. Contentment is a difficult virtue. Why? Because there is nothing on earth that can satisfy our deepest longing. We long to see God. The leaves of life are rustling with the rumor that we will—and we won't be satisfied until we do.
—*When God Whispers Your Name*

You see, from heaven's perspective, grace is enough. If God did nothing more than save us from hell, could anyone complain? If God saved our souls and then left us to spend our lives leprosy-struck on a deserted island, would he be unjust? Having been given eternal life, dare we grumble at an aching body? Having been given heavenly riches, dare we bemoan earthly poverty?

Let me be quick to add, God has not left you with "just salvation." If you have eyes to read these words, hands to hold this book, the means to own this volume, he has already given you grace upon grace. The vast majority of us have been saved and then blessed even more!

Each of you has received a gift to use to serve others. Be good servants of God's various gifts of grace.
—*1 Peter 4:10*

But there are those times when God, having given us his grace, hears our appeals and says, "My grace is sufficient for you." Is he being unfair?

In *God Came Near* I've told how our oldest daughter fell into a swimming pool when she was two years old. A friend saw her and pulled her to safety. What I didn't tell was what happened the next morning in my prayer time. I made a special effort to record my gratitude in my journal. I told God how wonderful he was for saving her. As clearly as if God himself were speaking, this question came to mind: Would I be less wonderful had I let her drown? Would I be any less a good God for calling her home? Would I still be receiving your praise this morning had I not saved her?

I know how to live when I am poor, and I know how to live when I have plenty. I have learned the secret of being happy at any time in everything that happens, when I have enough to eat and when I go hungry, when I have more than I need and when I do not have enough. I can do all things through Christ, because he gives me strength.

—Philippians 4:12–13

7. It's a question that races through everyone's mind at one time or another. Is God still a good God when he says no? Our answer boils down to one of two responses. Choose yours.

❏ God is a good all the time.
❏ God is good some of the time.

REMOVE THE THORN

Paul wrestled with that one. He knew the angst of unanswered prayer. At the top of his prayer list was an unidentified request that dominated his thoughts. He gave the appeal a code name: "a thorn in my flesh" (2 Cor. 12:7 NIV). Perhaps the pain was too intimate to put on paper. Maybe the request was made so often he reverted to shorthand. "I'm here to talk about the thorn again, Father." Or could it be that by leaving the appeal generic, Paul's prayer could be our prayer? For don't we all have a thorn in the flesh?

8. What is the "thorn" in your flesh? What concern have you been praying about for some time?

_____

_____

From heaven's perspective, grace is enough.

Somewhere on life's path our flesh is pierced by a person or a problem. Our stride becomes a limp, our pace is slowed to a halt, we try to walk again only to wince at each effort. Finally we plead with God for help.

Such was the case with Paul. (By the way, don't you find it encouraging that even Paul had a thorn in the flesh? There is comfort in learning that one of the writers of the Bible wasn't always on the same page with God.)

This was no casual request, no P.S. in a letter. It was the first plea of the first sentence. "Dear God, I need some help!"

Nor was this a superficial prickle. It was a "stabbing pain" (PHILLIPS). Every step he took sent a shudder up his leg. Three different times he limped over to the side of the trail and prayed. His request was clear, and so was God's response, "My grace is sufficient" (2 Cor. 12:9 NIV).

Experiencing Jesus is not a nirvana-like experience—oblivious or exempt from personal pain. In fact, pain is an essential to experiencing the fullness of Jesus—his strength, his faithfulness, his comfort. The Bible teaches we are to share in the "fellowship of his sufferings" (Phil. 3:10 NKJV). Pain was a central feature of Jesus' life—betrayal, heartache, suffering, and even death. It is one thing to go through pain alone. Jesus promises his fellowship—he's been down that road before you. Those who have yet to go through the yaw and pitch of life have not tasted the sweet fellowship that results from experiencing these trying times with him.

9. What can we understand more fully when we suffer, according to Philippians 3:10?

_____

_____

He has not punished us as our sins should be punished; he has not repaid us for the evil we have done.

—Psalm 103:10

10. James 1:2–4 tells us that the trials we face actually do us some good. How does God use them to work in our lives?

_____

_____

Pain is an essential to experiencing the fullness of Jesus.

GRACE IS ENOUGH

Had God removed temptation, Paul might never have embraced God's grace. Only the hungry value a feast, and Paul was starving. The self-given title on his office door read, "Paul, Chief of Sinners." No pen ever articulated grace like Paul's. That may be because no person ever appreciated grace like Paul.

You wonder why God doesn't remove temptation from your life? If he did, you might lean on your strength instead of his grace. A few stumbles might be what you need to convince you: His grace is sufficient for your sin.

You wonder why God doesn't remove the enemies in your life? Perhaps because he wants you to love like he loves. Anyone can love a friend, but only a few can love an enemy. So what if you aren't everyone's hero? His grace is sufficient for your self-image.

You wonder why God doesn't alter your personality? You, like Paul, are a bit rough around the edges? Say things you later regret or do things you later question? Why doesn't God make you more like him? He is. He's just not finished yet. Until he is, his grace is sufficient to overcome your flaws.

You wonder why God doesn't heal you? He has healed you. If you are in Christ, you have a perfected soul and a perfected body. His plan is to give you the soul now and the body when you get home. He may choose to heal parts of your body before heaven. But if he doesn't, don't you still have reason for gratitude? If he never gave you more than eternal life, could you ask for more than that? His grace is sufficient for gratitude.

Wonder why God won't give you a skill? If only God had made you a singer or a runner or a writer or a missionary. But there you are, tone-deaf, slow of foot and mind. Don't despair. God's grace is still sufficient to finish what he began. And until he's finished, let Paul remind you that the power is in the message, not the messenger. His grace is sufficient to speak clearly even when you don't.

For all we don't know about thorns, we can be sure of this: God would prefer we have an occasional limp than a perpetual strut. And if it takes a thorn for him to make his point, he loves us enough not to pluck it out.

God has every right to say no to us. We have every reason to say thanks to him. The parachute is strong, and the landing will be safe. His grace is sufficient.

When we are hurting, it doesn't matter how much we know about doctrine or theology. What we really need to know is Jesus. To walk with him. Talk to him. Crawl into his lap and let him hold us for a while. Perhaps we'll never say, "Jesus is all I need" until he is all we have. At that moment, he will prove to be all we need and more.

11. God sometimes allows seasons of pain to strengthen your dependence upon Jesus' grace to take you through it. According to 2 Corinthians 1:9, why did God allow Paul to undergo trials? Fill in the blanks below.

    Truly we believed we would _____. But this happened so we would not _____ in _____ but in _____.

12. When we are faced with trials, it is easy to muster up our own strength, grit our teeth, and trust in our ability to endure. What adjustments need to be made in order to put our faith in the grace of Jesus alone?

_____

_____

HE KEPT THE FAITH

Continue to have faith and do what you know is right. Some people have rejected this, and their faith has been shipwrecked.

—1 Timothy 1:19

I sit a few feet from a man on death row. Jewish by birth. Tentmaker by trade. Apostle by calling. His days are marked. I'm curious about what bolsters this man as he nears his execution. So I ask some questions.

Do you have family, Paul? *I have none.*

What about your health? *My body is beaten and tired . . .*

Any rewards? *Not on earth.*

Then what do you have, Paul? No belongings. No family . . . What do you have that matters?

I have my faith. It's all I have. But it's all I need. I have kept the faith.

Paul leans back against the wall of his cell and smiles.

—*When God Whispers Your Name*

As a result, I can really know Christ and experience the mighty power that raised him from the dead. I can learn what it means to suffer with him, sharing in his death.

—Philippians 3:10 NLT

My brethren, count it all joy when you fall into various trials, knowing that the testing of your faith produces patience. But let patience have its perfect work, that you may be perfect and complete, lacking nothing.

—James 1:2–4 NKJV

My friends, do not be surprised at the terrible trouble which now comes to test you. Do not think that something strange is happening to you. But be happy that you are sharing in Christ's sufferings so that you will be happy and full of joy when Christ comes again in glory.

—1 Peter 4:12–13

THE HEART OF THE MATTER

- ❦ **God does not always take away our troubles.**
- ❦ **From heaven's perspective, grace is enough.**
- ❦ **Pain is an essential to experiencing the fullness of Jesus.**
- ❦ **Jesus really is all you need.**

Jesus really is all you need.

You've been practicing all week. Have you hidden Ephesians 2:8–9 in your heart? Write out your memory verse here one last time.

_____

_____

_____

The Heart of Jesus

He didn't deserve any special favors. He'd walked with Jesus—knew his teachings. He knew better. But he'd blown it.

He'd wanted to protect Jesus. When the crowd of soldiers had come with their swords and their torches, they were so outnumbered. He'd managed to swing a sword around, but Jesus had gently rebuked him, then healed the soldier who'd been struck.

From there it had all gone downhill.

He'd trembled as he'd followed them. Then swore and denied he even knew Jesus. He'd watched his master beaten, scourged, and executed without lifting a hand to stop it. There must have been something he could have done.

But no.

He had blown it.

In Peter's darkest hour, when he deserved nothing from the Master he had denied, Jesus extended grace to him.

In the new dawn light of that Resurrection morning, Jesus went to find Peter. Pouring out his failings and finding forgiveness, Peter's joy overflowed.

His relationship with his Savoir was restored as Peter experienced the grace of Jesus.

Truly, in our own hearts we believed we would die. But this happened so we would not trust in ourselves but in God, who raises people from the dead.
—2 Corinthians 1:9

FOR FURTHER READING

Selections throughout this lesson were taken from *In the Grip of Grace*.

He saved us because of his mercy. It was not because of good deeds we did to be right with him.
—Titus 3:5

[i] Anders Nygren, *Commentary on Romans*, (Philadelphia: Fortress Press, 1949), 98.
[ii] Dr. Paul Faulkner, *Achieving Success without Failing Your Family* (W. Monroe LA.: Howard Publishing, 1994), 14–15.

LESSON 4

Experiencing the Freedom of Jesus

I've never been one to travel light.

I've tried. Believe me, I've tried. But ever since I stuck three fingers in the air and took the Boy Scout pledge to be prepared, I've been determined to be exactly that—prepared.

Prepared for a bar mitzvah, baby dedication, or costume party. Prepared to parachute behind enemy lines or enter a cricket tournament. And if, perchance, the Dalai Lama might be on my flight and invite me to dine in Tibet, I carry snowshoes. One has to be prepared.

I don't know how to travel light.

Fact is, there's a lot about travel I don't know. I don't know how to interpret the restrictions of a supersaver seat—half price if you leave on Wednesdays during duck-hunting season and return when the moon is full in a non-election year. I don't know why they don't build the whole plane out of the same metal they use to build the little black box. I don't know how to escape the airplane toilet without sacrificing one of my extremities to the jaws of the folding door. And I don't know what to say to guys like the taxi driver in Rio who learned I was an American and asked me if I knew his cousin Eddie who lives in the U.S.

There's a lot about traveling I don't know.

I don't know why we men would rather floss a crocodile than ask for directions. I don't know why vacation slides aren't used to treat insomnia, and I don't know when I'll learn not to eat food whose names I can't pronounce.

But most of all, I don't know how to travel light.

I don't know how to travel light. But I need to learn. Denalyn refuses to give birth to any more children even though the airlines allow each passenger three checked bags and two carry-ons.

I need to learn to travel light.

You're wondering why I can't. Loosen up! you're thinking. You can't enjoy a journey carrying so much stuff. Why don't you just drop all that luggage?

Funny you should ask. I'd like to inquire the same of you. Haven't you been known to pick up a few bags?

Odds are, you did this morning. Somewhere between the first step on the floor and the last step out the door, you grabbed some luggage. You stepped over to the baggage carousel and loaded up. Don't remember doing so? That's because you did it without thinking. Don't remember seeing a baggage terminal? That's because the carousel is not the one in the airport; it's the one in the mind. And the bags we grab are not made of leather; they're made of burdens.

The suitcase of guilt. A sack of discontent. You drape a duffel bag of weariness on one shoulder and a hanging bag of grief on the other. Add on a backpack of doubt, an overnight bag of loneliness, and a trunk of fear. Pretty soon you're pulling more stuff than a skycap. No wonder you're so tired at the end of the day. Lugging luggage is exhausting.

What you were saying to me, God is saying to you, "Set that stuff down! You're carrying burdens you don't need to bear."

"Come to me," he invites, "all of you who are weary and carry heavy burdens, and I will give you rest" (Matthew 11:28 NLT).

NO FEARS AT ALL

Could you use some courage? Are you backing down more than you are standing up? Jesus scattered the butterflies out of the stomachs of his nervous disciples . . .

We need to remember that the disciples were common men given a compelling task. Before they were the stain-glassed saints in the windows of cathedrals, they were somebody's next-door-neighbors trying to make a living and raise a family. They weren't cut from theological cloth or raised on supernatural milk. But they were an ounce more devoted than they were afraid and, as a result, did some extraordinary things.

Earthly fears are no fears at all. Answer the big question of eternity, and the little questions of life fall into perspective.

—*The Applause of Heaven*

In Christ we can come before God with freedom and without fear. We can do this through faith in Christ.
—**Ephesians 3:12**

EXPERIENCING THE FREEDOM OF JESUS THIS WEEK

Before you read any further, spend some time in prayer.

Dear Father, I don't know how to travel light. I go through my days, burdened by doubts, fears, loneliness, and grief. Show me how to be free from these earthly cares. Throughout this week, teach me, Lord, to come to you. Teach me to unburden myself. Teach me to seek your rest. Amen.

This week, memorize John 8:36—Jesus' promise of freedom.

So if the Son sets you free, you will indeed be free. —*John 8:36 NLT*

DAY ONE—THE LUGGAGE OF LIFE

LIGHTENING OUR LOADS

Jesus invites us to drop all the baggage we try to carry through life.

To get an idea of the freedom found in Jesus Christ, first imagine yourself donning the literal pieces of luggage (all over-packed) that were just described. Which of these can you relate to most? Check all that apply.

- ❏ Carrying a suitcase of guilt.
- ❏ Holding a sack of discontent.
- ❏ A duffel bag of weariness on one shoulder.
- ❏ A hanging bag of grief on the other.
- ❏ A backpack of doubt strapped on back.
- ❏ Shouldering an overnight bag of loneliness.
- ❏ Pushing a trunk of fear.

Now, let those mental pictures linger for a moment. The exhaustion. The stretched muscles. The strain on your cramped fingers. Hold it. Hold it. OK, now, drop it. Each piece. Let each one slide off your body and onto the floor in a heap. Feel the release. Escape the tension. A deep breath—finally! You are free. Jesus summons release from the emotional luggage pieces we often carry through life. With his permission and blessing, we can let each piece slide off onto the floor in a heap. We are free.

"Come to me, all of you who are tired and have heavy loads, and I will give you rest. Accept my teachings and learn from me, because I am gentle and humble in spirit, and you will find rest for your lives. The teaching that I ask you to accept is easy; the load I give you to carry is light."

—Matthew 11:28–30

1. Read Matthew 11:28–30. Based on what you just read, which of the following statements apply to Jesus' teachings on traveling light? Check all that apply.

   - ☒ We should come to Jesus when we are tired.
   - ❏ Jesus makes more demands of us when we are tired.
   - ☒ Jesus realizes we are prone to carry heavy loads.
   - ☒ He promises rest.
   - ☒ His teaching is hard to accept.
   - ☒ The load he asks us to carry is light.

2. Why is traveling light is a good metaphor for experiencing freedom in Christ?

   Crist wants us to enjoy are time of every day problems. Jesus wants us to our problem thurs as he died on the cross for us.

If we let him, God will lighten our loads, but how do we let him? May I invite an old friend to show us? The Twenty-third Psalm.

The Lord is my shepherd;
I shall not want.
He makes me to lie down in green pastures;
He leads me beside the still waters.

Christ entered the Most Holy Place only once—and for all time. He did not take with him the blood of goats and calves. His sacrifice was his own blood, and by it he set us free from sin forever.

—Hebrews 9:12

He restores my soul;

He leads me in the paths of righteousness

For His name's sake.

Yea, though I walk through the valley of the shadow of death,

I will fear no evil;

For You are with me;

Your rod and Your staff, they comfort me.

You prepare a table before me in the presence of my enemies;

You anoint my head with oil.

My cup runs over.

Surely goodness and mercy shall follow me

All the days of my life;

And I will dwell in the house of the Lord

Forever. (NKJV)

Do more beloved words exist? Framed and hung in hospital halls, scratched on prison walls, quoted by the young, and whispered by the dying. In these lines sailors have found a harbor, the frightened have found a father, and strugglers have found a friend.

And because the passage is so deeply loved, it is widely known. Can you find ears on which these words have never fallen? Set to music in a hundred songs, translated into a thousand tongues, domiciled in a million hearts.

One of those hearts might be yours. What kinship do you feel with these words? Where do the verses transport you? To a fireside? Bedside? Graveside?

This passage is to the minister what balm is to the physician. I recently applied them to the heart of a dear friend. Summoned to his house with the words "The doctors aren't giving him more than a few days," I looked at him and understood. Face pale. Lips stretched and parched. Skin draping between bones like old umbrella cloth between spokes. The cancer had taken so much: his appetite, his strength, his days. But the cancer hadn't touched his faith. Pulling a chair to his bed and squeezing his hand, I whispered, "Bill, 'The Lord is my shepherd; I shall not want.'" He rolled his head toward me as if to welcome the words.

"He makes me to lie down in green pastures; He leads me beside the still waters. He restores my soul; He leads me in the paths of righteousness for His name's sake."

Reaching the fourth verse, fearful that he might not hear, I leaned forward until I was a couple of inches from his ear and said, "Though I walk through the valley of the shadow of death, I will fear no evil; for You are with me; Your rod and Your staff, they comfort me."

He didn't open his eyes, but he arched his brows. He didn't speak, but his thin fingers curled around mine, and I wondered if the Lord was helping him set down some luggage, the fear of dying.

Do you have some luggage of your own? Do you think God might use David's psalm to lighten your load? Traveling light means trusting God with the burdens you were never intended to bear.

3. Look up the following verses below and write down what you learn about what the Bible says concerning our burdens.

Psalm 38:4 – "My guilt has overwhelmed me; like a load it weighs me down."

I think Jesus wants us to know he is with us always and through Jesus does not burden who died on the cross to relieve our pour

Psalm 68:19 – "Praise the Lord, God our Savior, who helps us every day."

Jesus wants us to learn to part our burdens to him. He wants us no know (He died for us). Its so simple it hard to realize he can love me that much. (Never forget.

We try to carry burdens that we were never intended to bear.

THE CHOICE IS OURS

For all its peculiarities and unevenness, the Bible has a simple story. God made man. Man rejected God. God won't give up until he wins him back.

God will whisper. He will shout. He will touch and tug. He will take away our burdens; he'll even take away our blessings. If there are a thousand steps between us and him, he will take all but one. But he will leave the final one to us. The choice is ours.

Please understand. His goal is not to make you happy. His goal is to make you his. His goal is not to get you what you want; it is to get you what you need.

—*A Gentle Thunder*

We have freedom now, because Christ made us free. So stand strong. Do not change and go back into the slavery of the law.

—Galatians 5:1

2 Corinthians 5:4 – "While we live in this body, we have burdens, and we groan. We do not want to be naked, but we want to be clothed with our heavenly home. Then this body that dies will be fully covered with life."

God creates all we call. He will never not ans. are problem
I burden. He with, is always! listen & be patine he does hearyou.

1 Peter 5:7 – "Give all your worries to him, because he cares about you."

he will take care of all your worries
because he loves us so much

FOR THE SAKE OF THE GOD WE SERVE

He wants to use you, you know. But how can he if you are exhausted? Preparing for a jog, I couldn't decide what to wear. The sun was out, but the wind was chilly. The sky was clear, but the forecast said rain. Jacket or sweatshirt? The Boy Scout within me prevailed. I wore both.

I grabbed my Walkman but couldn't decide which tape to bring. A sermon or music? You guessed it, I took both. Needing to stay in touch with my kids, I carried a cell phone. So no one would steal my car, I pocketed my keys. As a precaution against thirst, I brought along some drink money in a pouch. I looked more like a pack mule than a runner! Within half a mile I was peeling off the jacket and hiding it in a bush. That kind of weight will slow you down.

What's true in jogging is true in faith. God has a great race for you to run. Under his care you will go where you've never been and serve in ways you've never dreamed. But you have to drop some stuff. How can you share grace if you are full of guilt? How can you offer comfort if you are disheartened? How can you lift someone else's load if your arms are full with your own?

> *We cannot reach out to others if our hands are full.*

4. Burdens hinder us from fulfilling what the Bible describes as our responsibility to care for others. Read the following verses. Then match the verse with what you learn about this responsibility.

   d Romans 15:1   a. Show mercy, kindness, gentleness to others.
   c 2 Corinthians 1:4   b. Help the weak.
   e Galatians 6:2   c. Comfort as we have been comforted.
   d Philippians 2:4   d. Care for the interests of others.
   b Colossians 3:12–13   e. Help with others' troubles.

FOR THE SAKE OF THOSE WE LOVE

When we are preoccupied with our own troubles, we are not free to help others. We grow frustrated with loved ones who persistently preoccupy themselves with their own problems—we can't access their attention or affection when we need them. Likewise, others may feel the same way about us at times when we similarly burden ourselves with worries to the exclusion of others' needs.

> *He comforts us every time we have trouble, so when others have trouble, we can comfort them with the same comfort God gives us.*
>
> —2 Corinthians 1:4

5. Why does persistent preoccupation with our own problems makes us ineffective Christians?

   sometimes we fell more for are own Problem
   then How were how we are to helping others

6. Jesus reminds us not to get entangled with the stuff of life—especially when it makes us take our eyes off eternal life. Read Luke 21:34–35 and fill in the blanks regarding what Jesus taught about worldly preoccupation.

   Be _____ not to spend your __time__ feasting, drinking, or ____ about __life__ things. If you do, Jesus' return will come on you __unexpted__ like a __trap__.

> *But the truly happy people are those who carefully study God's perfect law that makes people free, and they continue to study it. They do not forget what they heard, but they obey what God's teaching says. Those who do this will be made happy.*
>
> —James 1:25

Be careful not to spend your time feasting, drinking, or worrying about worldly things. If you do, that day might come on you suddenly, like a trap on all people on earth.

—Luke 21:34–35

Prior to this week's study, have you ever considered the impact that excess baggage has on relationships? We've made this point at our church by virtue of a drama. A wedding is reenacted in which we hear the thoughts of the bride and groom. The groom enters, laden with luggage. A bag dangles from every appendage. And each bag is labeled: guilt, anger, arrogance, insecurities. This fellow is loaded. As he stands at the altar, the audience hears him thinking, *Finally, a woman who will help me carry all my burdens. She's so strong, so stable, so . . .*

As his thoughts continue, hers begin. She enters, wearing a wedding gown but, like her fiancé, covered with luggage. Pulling a hanging bag, shouldering a carry-on, hauling a makeup kit, paper sack—everything you could imagine and everything labeled. She has her own bags: prejudice, loneliness, disappointments. And her expectations? Listen to what she is thinking: *Just a few more minutes and I've got me a man. No more counselors. No more group sessions. So long, discouragement and worry. I won't be seeing you anymore. He's going to fix me.*

Finally they stand at the altar, lost in a mountain of luggage. They smile their way through the ceremony, but when given the invitation to kiss each other, they can't. How do you embrace someone if your arms are full of bags?

Worrying over our own troubles interferes with our ability to help others with theirs.

7. It's a human tendency to expect others to carry our baggage for us. Jesus reminds us although we must care for each other's burdens, the only way we can experience true freedom is to let him shoulder the full weight of our problems. Why is Jesus perfectly suited to bear our burdens?

He died on the cross for us.

FOR THE SAKE OF OUR OWN JOY

For the sake of the God you serve, travel light.

For the sake of those you love, travel light.

For the sake of your own joy, travel light.

There are certain weights in life you simply cannot carry. Your Lord is asking you to set them down and trust him. He is the father at the baggage claim. When a dad sees his five-year-old son trying to drag the family trunk off the carousel, what does he say? The father will say to his son what God is saying to you.

The Lord's loved ones will lie down in safety, because he protects them all day long. The ones he loves rest with him.

—Deuteronomy 33:12

"Set it down, child. I'll carry that one."

What do you say we take God up on his offer? We just might find ourselves traveling a little lighter.

By the way, earlier in this lesson, I may have overstated my packing problems. (I don't usually take snowshoes.) But I can't overstate God's promise: "Unload all your worries onto him, since he is looking after you" (1 Peter 5:7 JB).

8. Read Deuteronomy 33:12. Which of the following is true concerning resting in God? Check all that apply.

❑ We can lie down in safety.
☑ God protects us while we rest in him.
❑ The ones God loves rest with him.

THE HEART OF THE MATTER

❧ Jesus invites us to drop all the baggage we try to carry through life.
❧ We try to carry burdens that we were never intended to bear.
❧ We cannot reach out to others if our hands are full.
❧ Worrying over our own troubles interferes with our ability to help others with theirs.

My brothers and sisters, God called you to be free, but do not use your freedom as an excuse to do what pleases your sinful self. Serve each other with love.
—Galatians 5:13

Your memory verse for this week is John 8:36. Take a few moments to review it by writing the passage out here.

*John 8-36 So if the Son sets you free you
~~will~~ you will be ~~feel~~ free in deed.*
John 8:36

The Heart of Jesus

Mary, like the rest, stood amazed at the appearance of Jesus in the room. She had been weeping since Friday, when news of his capture and trial had reached her. Her heart had been pierced at the sight of him, beaten almost beyond recognition. But a mother always knew her son. She had longed to run to his side, to clean the blood from his face and sooth his tattered back. She had wanted to stand between him and the Roman soldiers, protect him from his executioners. When the nails had pierced his hands, she'd turned her eyes from the scene, but she'd stood her ground. She'd not abandon this precious son, her gift from God. And though it had broken her heart, she'd stayed nearby until he was gone. She had seen him dead. And yet here he was, alive! And in his resurrection, she found freedom. She was free from the disapproval of the temple leaders, free from all her little motherly worries about him, free from the tensions and sibling rivalries within her family, and free from the sorrow that had pierced her heart like a sword (Luke 2:35).

DAY TWO—FREEDOM FROM WANT

THE BURDEN OF DISCONTENT

Come with me to the most populated prison in the world. The facility has more inmates than bunks. More prisoners than plates. More residents than resources.

Come with me to the world's most oppressive prison. Just ask the inmates; they will tell you. They are overworked and underfed. Their walls are bare and bunks are hard.

No prison is so populated, no prison so oppressive, and, what's more, no prison is so permanent. Most inmates never leave. They never escape. They never get released. They serve a life sentence in this overcrowded, underprovisioned facility.

The name of the prison? You'll see it over the entrance. Rainbowed over the gate are four cast-iron letters that spell out its name:

W-A-N-T

The prison of want. You've seen her prisoners. They are "in want." They want something. They want something bigger. Nicer. Faster. Thinner. They want.

They don't want much, mind you. They want just one thing. One new job. One new car. One new house. One new spouse. They don't want much. They want just one.

And when they have "one," they will be happy. And they are right—they will be happy. When they have "one," they will leave the prison. But then it happens. The new-car smell passes. The new job gets old. The neighbors buy a larger television set. The new spouse has bad habits. The sizzle fizzles, and before you know it, another ex-con breaks parole and returns to jail.

The Lord is my shepherd; I shall not want.
—Psalm 23:1 NKJV

Discontentment is a kind of prison.

That everything God made would be set free from ruin to have the freedom and glory that belong to God's children.
—Romans 8:21

1. Read the following verses. Then match the verse with what you learn about our desires.

C Psalm 37:4   a. Evil desires don't result in anything profitable.
P Psalm 73:25   b. God longs to give us what we want.
d Proverbs 11:18   c. We should desire nothing more than God.
A James 1:14   d. Evil desires lead us to sin.

Are you in prison? You are if you feel better when you have more and worse when you have less. You are if joy is one delivery away, one transfer away, one award away, or one makeover away. If your happiness comes from something you deposit, drive, drink, or digest, then face it—you are in prison, the prison of want.

In the end, they will be destroyed. They do whatever their bodies want, they are proud of their shameful acts, and they think only about earthly things.
—Philippians 3:19

2. Read Philippians 3:19. Which of the following statements are true, and which ones are false concerning worldly desires? Mark your answers True (T) or False (F).

F Doing whatever we want is the definition of true freedom.
T Doing whatever we want ends in personal destruction.
F We can trust our fleshly desires.
T Thinking only about earthly things is dangerous.

CONTENTMENT REDEFINED

That's the bad news. The good news is, you have a visitor. And your visitor has a message that can get you paroled. Make your way to the receiving room. Take your seat in the chair, and look across the table at the psalmist David. He motions for you to lean forward. "I have a secret to tell you," he whispers, "the secret of satisfaction. 'The Lord is my shepherd; I shall not want'" (Ps. 23:1 NKJV).

David has found the pasture where discontent goes to die. It's as if he is saying, "What I have in God is greater than what I don't have in life." You think you and I could learn to say the same?

3. When God is our greatest desire, we experience freedom. We don't "want" for anything because nothing compares with knowing and loving him—and we trust him to meet our needs. Look up the following verses and write down what you learn about desiring God.

Psalm 40:8 – "My God, I want to do what you want. Your teachings are in my heart."
all desire to do your will

Psalm 42:2 – "I thirst for the living God. When can I go to meet with him?"
We have to be patient

Except God and choice his way.

Proverbs 10:24 – "Evil people will get what they fear most, but good people will get what they want most."
you make your choice you can't have both. to always choice

Philippians 1:22–24 – "If I continue living in my body, I will be able to work for the Lord. I do not know what to choose—living or dying. It is hard to choose between the two. I want to leave this life and be with Christ, which is much better, but you need me here in my body."
I just have to choice the right to life here with Jesus who ready ell be weighting for him

Live as free people, but do not use your freedom as an excuse to do evil. Live as servants of God.
—1 Peter 2:16

Think for just a moment about the things you own. Think about the house you have, the car you drive, the money you've saved. Think about the jewelry you've inherited and the stocks you've traded and the clothes you've purchased. Envision all your stuff, and let me remind you of two biblical truths.

Your stuff isn't yours. Ask any coroner. Ask any embalmer. Ask any funeral-home director. No one takes anything with him. When one of the wealthiest men in history, John D. Rockefeller, died, his accountant was asked, "How much did John D. leave?" The accountant's reply? "All of it."[1]

4. Read Ecclesiastes 5:15 and fill in the blanks concerning our possessions.

People come into this ___*world*___ with ___*nothing*___, and when they ___*leave*___ they leave with ___*nothing*___. In spite of all their ___*labor*___ work, they leave just as they came.

5. What would you say is a healthy balance between acquiring necessary or useful stuff and allowing it to consume you?

___*I don't like stuff*___
___*Live Gods Way.*___

All that stuff—it's not yours. And you know what else about all that stuff? It's not you. Who you are has nothing to do with the clothes you wear or the car you drive. Jesus said, "Life is not defined by what you have, even when you have a lot" (Luke 12:15 MSG). Heaven does not know you as the fellow with the nice suit or the woman with the big house or the kid with the new bike. Heaven knows your heart. "The Lord does not look at the things man looks at. Man looks at the outward appearance, but the Lord looks at the heart" (1 Sam. 16:7 NIV). When God thinks of you, he may see your compassion, your devotion, your tenderness or quick mind, but he doesn't think of your things.

And when you think of you, you shouldn't either. Define yourself by your stuff, and you'll feel good when you have a lot and bad when you don't.

6. What is the Bible's definition of contentment? Read Philippians 4:11–13. Which of the following statements are true concerning Paul's definition of contentment. Check all that apply.

- ☒ Being satisfied came naturally to Paul—he was super-spiritual.
- ☒ Paul had to learn to be content with what he had.
- ☐ Paul threw a fit when his wants went unmet.
- ☒ Paul knew how to live when he had little and plenty.
- ☒ Paul could be content in any situation because of Christ.

TRUE SATISFACTION

Like Paul, Doug McKnight found the secret to true satisfaction. At the age of thirty-two he was diagnosed with multiple sclerosis. Over the next sixteen years it would cost him his career, his mobility, and eventually his life. Because of MS, he couldn't feed himself or walk; he battled depression and fear. But through it all, Doug never lost his sense of gratitude. Evidence of this was seen in his prayer list. Friends in his congregation asked him to compile a list of requests so they could intercede for him. His response included eighteen blessings for which to be grateful and six concerns for which to be prayerful. His blessings outweighed his needs by three times. Doug McKnight had learned to be content.[2]

So had the leper on the island of Tobago. A short-term missionary met her on a mission trip. On the final day, he was leading worship in a leper colony. He asked if anyone had a favorite song. When he did, a woman turned around, and he saw the most disfigured face he'd ever seen. She had no ears and no nose. Her lips were gone. But she raised a fingerless hand and asked, "Could we sing 'Count Your Many Blessings'?"

People come into this world with nothing, and when they die they leave with nothing. In spite of all their hard work, they leave just as they came.

—Ecclesiastes 5:15

We do not really own all the stuff we possess on earth.

I am not telling you this because I need anything. I have learned to be satisfied with the things I have and with everything that happens. I know how to live when I am poor, and I know how to live when I have plenty. I have learned the secret of being happy at any time in everything that happens, when I have enough to eat and when I go hungry, when I have more than I need and when I do not have enough. I can do all things through Christ, because he gives me strength.

—Philippians 4:11–13

A LIFE FREE OF CLUTTER

The most powerful life is the most simple life. The most powerful life is the life that knows where it is going, that knows where the source of strength is, and the life that stays free of clutter and happenstance and hurriedness.

Being busy is not a sin. Jesus was busy. Paul was busy. Peter was busy. Nothing of significance is achieved without effort and hard work and weariness. Being busy, in and of itself, is not a sin. But being busy in an endless pursuit of *things* that leave us empty and hollow and broken inside—that cannot be pleasing to God.

One source of man's weariness is the pursuit of things that never satisfy; but which one of us has not been caught up in that pursuit at some time in our life? Our passions, possessions, and pride—these are all *dead* things. When we try to get life out of dead things, the result is only weariness and dissatisfaction.

—*Walking with the Savior*

Do not wait for a change in circumstances to change your attitude.

The missionary started the song but couldn't finish. Someone later commented, "I suppose you'll never be able to sing the song again." He answered, "No, I'll sing it again. Just never in the same way."[3]

Are you hoping that a change in circumstances will bring a change in your attitude? If so, you are in prison, and you need to learn a secret of traveling light. *What you have in your Shepherd is greater than what you don't have in life.*

WAITING FOR CHANGE

So, what is the one thing separating you from joy? How do you fill in this blank: "I will be happy when *I'm with Jesus*." When I am healed. When I am promoted. When I am married. When I am single. When I am rich. How would you finish that statement?

If your ship never comes in, if your dream never comes true, if the situation never changes, can you be happy? If not, then you are sleeping in the cold cell of discontent. You are in prison. And you need to know what you have in your Shepherd.

7. Look up the following verses and write down what you learn about our incomparable Shepherd.

   Psalm 89:6 – "Who in heaven is equal to the Lord? None of the angels is like the Lord."
   Nobody

   Isaiah 40:18 – "Can you compare God to anything? Can you compare him to an image of anything?"
   No, by picture.

   Isaiah 40:25 – "God, the Holy One, says, "Can you compare me to anyone? Is anyone equal to me?"
   No. No.

EVERYTHING TO GAIN

Gratitude is a sure sign of someone's freedom from want and contentment in Christ.

Paul says that "godliness with contentment is great gain" (1 Tim. 6:6 NIV). When we surrender to God the cumbersome sack of discontent, we don't just give up something; we gain something. God replaces it with a lightweight, tailor-made, sorrow-resistant attaché of gratitude.

8. Gratitude is a sure-sign of someone's freedom from want and contentment in Christ. Which of the following statements are true when it comes to gratitude? Check all that apply. Use the Bible verses below to help you answer.

   ☑ We ought to always be thankful. (Colossians 2:7)
   ☑ We can be thankful because what we have in God is unshakable. (Hebrews 12:28)
   ☑ We ought to thank God even when we present him with our needs. (Philippians 4:6)

What will you gain with contentment? You may gain your marriage. You may gain precious hours with your children. You may gain your self-respect. You may gain joy. You may gain the faith to say, "The Lord is my shepherd; I shall not want."

Try saying it slowly. "The Lord is my shepherd; I shall not want."

Again, "The Lord is my shepherd; I shall not want."

Again, "The Lord is my shepherd; I shall not want."

Shhhhhhh. Did you hear something? I think I did. I'm not sure . . . but I think I heard the opening of a jail door.

You were made free from sin, and now you are slaves to goodness.
—Romans 6:18

THE HEART OF THE MATTER

❧ Discontentment is a kind of poison.
❧ We do not really own all the stuff we possess on earth.
❧ Do not wait for a change in circumstances to change your attitude.
❧ Gratitude is a sure-sign of someone's freedom from want and contentment in Christ.

John 8:36 is your Bible memorization verse for the week. Write it out now for a quick review.

So if the Son sets you free, you will be free indeed.

The Heart of Jesus

He had it made. His family was well off, well-connected, and well-to-do. His home was a showplace—cool marble floors, columned porches, airy upper rooms for entertaining, splashing fountains in the courtyard, and a staff of servants to wait upon him. He was bright, educated, well-liked, and respected. Many of his neighbors admired him for his devotion to the Law and his righteous lifestyle. His behavior was beyond reproach. The community counted him as an upstanding citizen—courteous, dependable, and benevolent. What more could a young man want? So when the rich young ruler came before Jesus, his friends expected the Teacher to acknowledge the man's goodness, perhaps setting him up as an example to the rest of them. But instead, Jesus looked into the eyes of the young man, and saw his discontentment. Jesus held out to the man an offer of freedom. There was just one change that needed to happen first. He had but one thing to do. Give it all away. The house, the staff, the status, the money—it would all have to go. And with astonishment, the rich young ruler was confronted with his own lack of faith. Though it pained him, he turned and walked away, ashamed by his need to cling to earthly possessions.

—Luke 18:22–24

DAY THREE—FREEDOM FROM HOPELESSNESS

IT'S A JUNGLE OUT THERE

I wonder if you could imagine yourself in a jungle. A dense jungle. A dark jungle. Your friends convinced you it was time for a once-in-a-lifetime trip, and here you are. You paid the fare. You crossed the ocean. You hired the guide and joined the group. And you ventured where you had never ventured before—into the thick, strange world of the jungle.

Sound interesting? Let's take it a step farther. Imagine that you were in the jungle, lost and alone. You paused to lace your boot, and when you looked up, no one was near. You took a chance and went to the right; now you're wondering if the others went to the left. (Or did you go left and they go right?)

You have a problem. First, you were not made for this place. Drop you in the center of avenues and buildings, and you could sniff your way home. But here in sky-blocking foliage? Here in trail-hiding thickets? You are out of your element. You weren't made for this jungle.

So Jesus said to the Jews who believed in him, "If you continue to obey my teaching, you are truly my followers. Then you will know the truth, and the truth will make you free."

—John 8:31–32

For many people, life is a jungle.

He restores my soul.

—Psalm 23:3 NKJV

Remember that in the past you were without Christ. You were not citizens of Israel, and you had no part in the agreements with the promise that God made to his people. You had no hope, and you did not know God.

—Ephesians 2:12

The Lord God has put his Spirit in me, because the Lord has appointed me to tell the good news to the poor. He has sent me to comfort those whose hearts are broken, to tell the captives they are free, and to tell the prisoners they are released.

—Isaiah 61:1

Who could blame you for sitting on a log (better check for snakes first), burying your face in your hands, and thinking, *I'll never get out of here.* You have no direction, no equipment, no hope.

Can you freeze-frame that emotion for a moment? Can you sense, for just a second, how it feels to be out of your element? Out of solutions? Out of ideas and energy? Can you imagine, just for a moment, how it feels to be out of hope?

1. Look up the following verses below and write down what you learn about the importance of hope.

   Psalm 33:18 – "The Lord looks after those who fear him, those who put their hope in his love."

   unfailing love, emotional

   Psalm 42:5 – "Why am I so sad? Why am I so upset? I should put my hope in God and keep praising him."

   Depression is one of the most common emot ailments

   Psalm 62:5 – "I find rest in God; only he gives me hope."

   peace

   Romans 8:24–25 – "We were saved, and we have this hope. If we see what we are waiting for, that is not really hope. People do not hope for something they already have. But we are hoping for something we do not have yet, and we are waiting for it patiently."

   God often uses a setback to move us forward.

For many people, life is—well, life is a jungle. Not a jungle of trees and beasts. Would that it were so simple. Would that our jungles could be cut with a machete or our adversaries trapped in a cage. But our jungles are comprised of the thicker thickets of failing health, broken hearts, and empty wallets. Our forests are framed with hospital walls and divorce courts. We don't hear the screeching of birds or the roaring of lions, but we do hear the complaints of neighbors and the demands of bosses. Our predators are our creditors, and the brush that surrounds us is the rush that exhausts us.

It's a jungle out there.

And for some, even for many, hope is in short supply. Hopelessness is an odd bag. Unlike the others, it isn't full. It is empty, and its emptiness creates the burden. Unzip the top and examine all the pockets. Turn it upside down and shake it hard. The bag of hopelessness is painfully empty.

2. Read Ephesians 2:12. Fill in the blanks about the utter hopelessness of those who do not know Christ.

   Those who are without Christ are not citizens of *Israel* ; they have no part in the promise that God made to his *people* . They have no *hope* because they do not know *God in the world*

3. What key areas in life often seem to be jungle-like—confusing, difficult to maneuver, and often scary? Check all that apply.

   ☑ Relationships
   ❑ Job situations
   ❑ Finances
   ☑ Health

TO THE RESCUE

What would it take to restore your hope? What would you need to reenergize your journey?

Though the answers are abundant, three come quickly to mind.

The first would be a person. Not just any person. You don't need someone equally confused. You need someone who knows the way out.

4. Read the following verses. Then match the verse with what you learn about how God's presence helps us wrestle free of hopelessness.

_c_ Psalm 23:4   a. His presence is light in our darkness.
_d_ Psalm 89:15   b. Hoping in him makes us happy.
_a_ Psalm 31:20   _c._ When he is with us we are not afraid.
_b_ Psalm 146:5   _d._ His presence protects us.

And from him you need some vision. You need someone to lift your spirits. You need someone to look you in the face and say, "This isn't the end. Don't give up. There is a better place than this. And I'll lead you there."

And, perhaps most important, you need direction. If you have only a person but no renewed vision, all you have is company. If he has a vision but no direction, you have a dreamer for company. But if you have a person with direction—who can take you from this place to the right place—ah, then you have one who can restore your hope.

5. God's leadership releases us from the fear of not knowing what to do. We simply follow him. Which of the following statements are true concerning his leadership? Check all that apply. Use the Bible verses below to help you answer.

❏ His guidance is unpredictable and unreliable. (Exodus 15:13)
☒ He leads those with whom he is pleased. (Numbers 14:8)
☒ He leads us on level ground. (Psalm 143:10)
☒ His leadership style is that of a taskmaster. (Isaiah 40:11)

Have you ever met someone like the type of person we just described? David has. And in his words, this person "restores my soul." David, of course, is talking about his Shepherd. Our Shepherd.

He majors in restoring hope to the soul. Whether you are a lamb lost on a craggy ledge or a city slicker alone in a deep jungle, everything changes when your rescuer appears.

Your loneliness diminishes, because you have fellowship.

Your despair decreases, because you have vision.

Your confusion begins to lift, because you have direction.

6. How does Jesus exemplify the three qualities needed to rescue you from a hopeless situation? Complete the following phrases. Use the Bible verses below to help you answer.

I know Jesus knows the way I need to go because _____. (John 14:6)
the way the truth
and the light

I know Jesus has the best plan or vision for me because _know well (Luke 12:7) hairs on my head._
We don't fear Jesus he loves us so
much he died for my forgiveness

Jesus has the direction to lead me because _____. (John 12:26)
Whoever serves me will follow me.
My father will ~~don't~~ honor the one who serves
_me._

Happy are the people who know how to praise you. Lord, let them live in the light of your presence.

—Psalm 89:15

He takes care of his people like a shepherd. He gathers them like lambs in his arms and carries them close to him. He gently leads the mothers of the lambs.

—Isaiah 40:11

Jesus gives us hope because he keeps us company, has a vision, and knows the way we should go.

God has freed us from the power of darkness, and he brought us into the kingdom of his dear Son.

—Colossians 1:13

WHAT FREEDOM MEANS

You still haven't left the jungle. The trees still eclipse the sky, and the thorns still cut the skin. Animals lurk and rodents scurry. The jungle is still a jungle. It hasn't changed, but you have. You have changed because you have hope. And you have hope because you have met someone who can lead you out.

Your Shepherd knows that you were not made for this place. He knows you are not equipped for this place. So he has come to guide you out.

He has come to restore your soul. He is the perfect one to do so.

7. Why is it important that Jesus does not necessarily free us from the jungle itself—only from the hopelessness we feel in the midst of the jungle?

We have to make some ~~choices~~ choices for our self but he will be their father

The story is told of a man on an African safari deep in the jungle. The guide before him had a machete and was whacking away the tall weeds and thick underbrush. The traveler, wearied and hot, asked in frustration, "Where are we? Do you know where you are taking me? Where is the path?!" The seasoned guide stopped and looked back at the man and replied, "I am the path."

We ask the same questions, don't we? We ask God, "Where are you taking me? Where is the path?" And he, like the guide, doesn't tell us. Oh, he may give us a hint or two, but that's all. If he did, would we understand? Would we comprehend our location? No, like the traveler, we are unacquainted with this jungle. So rather than give us an answer, Jesus gives us a far greater gift. He gives us himself.

We often think freedom in the midst of a trial translates as having all the answers we need. Instead, God offers all the Jesus we will need to get through the trial.

8. How would you describe your prayer life during the midst of trials: Asking for answers? Or asking for Jesus?

Asking for Jesus & asking for his help in prayer

9. Read James 5:13. Fill in the blanks regarding God's prescription for peril.

Is anyone who is having *trouble* should *pray*.

Does he remove the jungle? No, the vegetation is still thick.

Does he purge the predators? No, danger still lurks.

Jesus doesn't give hope by changing the jungle; he restores our hope by giving us himself. And he has promised to stay until the very end. "I am with you always, to the very end of the age" (Matt. 28:20 NIV).

10. Freedom is not something we learn *about* Jesus. Freedom *is* Jesus. In him, freedom flourishes. Which of the following statements are true about spiritual freedom, and which are false? Mark your answers True (T) or False (F). Use the Bible verses below to help you answer.

T Jesus frees us from being slaves to anything or anyone else. (Psalm 116:16)
F God hears our cry and ignores us. (Psalm 118:5)
___ Following God's orders stifles us. (Psalm 119:45)
T Where God's Spirit is, there is freedom. (2 Corinthians 3:17)

11. Read Lamentations 3:19–25—a testimony of hope from the prophet Jeremiah. What phrase in this passage speaks the most to your heart today?

Because of Lord's great We are not consumed for his compassions never fail.

Sidebar

Jesus answered, "I am the way, and the truth, and the life. The only way to the Father is through me."
—John 14:6

But God even knows how many hairs you have on your head. Don't be afraid. You are worth much more than many sparrows.
—Luke 12:7

Whoever serves me must follow me. Then my servant will be with me everywhere I am. My Father will honor anyone who serves me.
—John 12:26

Jesus is the Shepherd, and he wants to guide you through life.

GOVERNED BY LOVE
Jesus spoke of freedom, but he spoke of a different kind of freedom: the type of freedom that comes not through power but through submission. Not through control but through surrender. Not through possessions but through open hands.

God wants to emancipate his people; he wants to set them free. He wants his people to be not slaves but sons. He wants them governed not by law but by love.

We have been liberated from our own guilt and our own legalism. We have the freedom to pray and the freedom to love the God of our heart. And we have been forgiven by the only one who could condemn us. We are truly free!
—*Walking with the Savior*

Those who were slaves when the Lord called them are free persons who belong to the Lord. In the same way, those who were free when they were called are now Christ's slaves.
—1 Corinthians 7:22

HOPE FOR TOMORROW

All of us need hope at some point in our lives.

Some of you don't need it right now. Your jungle has become a meadow and your journey a delight. If such is the case, congratulations. But remember—we do not know what tomorrow holds. We do not know where this road will lead. You may be one turn from a cemetery, from a hospital bed, from an empty house. You may be a bend in the road from a jungle.

And though you don't need your hope restored today, you may tomorrow. And you need to know to whom to turn.

Or perhaps you do need hope today. You know you were not made for this place. You know you are not equipped. You want someone to lead you out.

If so, call out for your Shepherd. He knows your voice. And he's just waiting for your request.

THE HEART OF THE MATTER

- ❦ For many people, life is a jungle.
- ❦ Jesus gives us hope because he keeps us company, has a vision, and knows the way we should go.
- ❦ Jesus is the Shepherd, and he wants to guide you through life.
- ❦ Jesus doesn't give hope by changing the jungle; he restores our hope by giving us himself.

Today's memory verse review will be fill-in-the-blank.

So if the ___*Son set*___ you ___*free*___, you will ___*indeed*___ be ~~*free God*~~ John 8:36 NLT

The Heart of Jesus

Peter faced the growing crowds, waiting for the milling mob to settle down enough so that he would be heard. He should be fighting butterflies in his stomach and nervous doubts. Here he was, an uneducated fisherman, ready to address this great assembly. He was no orator. No scholar. No learned man. He had no training. No qualifications. No prior experience. His hands were used to pulling at oars and hefting nets. He could gut a fish, hoist an anchor, and trim a sail—but this? Even so, Peter stood calmly. He was no slave to the doubts that tried to plague his mind. He was free in Christ, and nothing could turn him away from telling these people the truth—the wonderful good news. So Peter cleared his throat and lifted his voice. The crowds fell into rapt silence as the words poured out over them. Words of life. Words of hope. Words of salvation. An invitation to freedom.

—Acts 2:14

DAY FOUR—FREEDOM FROM FEAR

FROM PANIC TO PEACE

It's the expression of Jesus that puzzles us. We've never seen his face like this.

Jesus smiling, yes.

Jesus weeping, absolutely.

Jesus stern, even that.

But Jesus anguished? Cheeks streaked with tears? Face flooded in sweat? Rivulets of blood dripping from his chin? You remember the night.

Anyone who is having troubles should pray. Anyone who is happy should sing praises.

—James 5:13

Jesus doesn't give hope by changing the jungle; he restores our hope by giving us himself.

Lord, remember my suffering and my misery, my sorrow and trouble. Please remember me and think about me. But I have hope when I think of this: The Lord's love never ends; his mercies never stop. They are new every morning; Lord, your loyalty is great. I say to myself, "The Lord is mine, so I hope in him." The Lord is good to those who hope in him, to those who seek him.

—Lamentations 3:19–25

It is the same for us. We were once like children, slaves to the useless rules of this world. But when the right time came, God sent his Son who was born of a woman and lived under the law. God did this so he could buy freedom for those who were under the law and so we could become his children.

—Galatians 4:3–5

I will fear no evil.

—Psalm 23:4 NKJV

Jesus experienced fear.

Since we have a great high priest, Jesus the Son of God, who has gone into heaven, let us hold on to the faith we have. For our high priest is able to understand our weaknesses. When he lived on earth, he was tempted in every way that we are, but he did not sin. Let us, then, feel very sure that we can come before God's throne where there is grace. There we can receive mercy and grace to help us when we need it.

—Hebrews 4:14–16

We have freedom now, because Christ made us free. So stand strong. Do not change and go back into the slavery of the law.

—Galatians 5:1

1. Read Luke 22:39–44 and answer the following:

   What did Jesus do at the Mount of Olives? (vv. 39–41)

   He prayed
   ~~anguish~~

   What does the Bible indicate were his emotions? (v. 44)

   in anguish

The Bible I carried as a child contained a picture of Jesus in the Garden of Gethsemane. His face was soft, hands calmly folded as he knelt beside a rock and prayed. Jesus seemed peaceful. One reading of the Gospels disrupts that image. Mark says, "Jesus fell to the ground" (Mark 14:35). Matthew tells us Jesus was "very sad and troubled . . . to the point of death" (Matt. 26:37–38). According to Luke, Jesus was "full of pain" (Luke 22:44).

2. Equipped with those passages, how would you paint this scene? Check all that apply.

   ☑ Jesus flat on the ground?
   ☑ Face in the dirt?
   ❑ Extended hands gripping grass?
   ☑ Body rising and falling with sobs?
   ❑ Face as twisted as the olive trees that surround him?

What do we do with this image of Jesus?

Simple. We turn to it when we look the same. We read it when we feel the same; we read it when we feel afraid. For isn't it likely that fear is one of the emotions Jesus felt? One might even argue that fear was the primary emotion. He saw something in the future so fierce, so foreboding that he begged for a change of plans. "Father, if you are willing, take away this cup of suffering" (Luke 22:42).

What causes you to pray the same prayer? Boarding an airplane? Facing a crowd? Public speaking? Taking a job? Taking a spouse? Driving on a highway? The source of your fear may seem small to others. But to you, it freezes your feet, makes your heart pound, and brings blood to your face. That's what happened to Jesus.

3. Read Hebrews 4:14–16. Based on what you just read, which of the following statements are true about Jesus? Check all that apply.

   ❑ He was perfect; he can't relate to our fears.
   ☑ He was perfect; yet he can still relate to our fears.
   ☑ He sympathizes with our weaknesses.
   ☑ He is able to help us because he knows how we feel.

He was so afraid that he bled. Doctors describe this condition as hematidrosis. Severe anxiety causes the release of chemicals that break down the capillaries in the sweat glands. When this occurs, sweat comes out tinged with blood.

Jesus was more than anxious; he was afraid. Fear is worry's big brother. If worry is a burlap bag, fear is a trunk of concrete. It wouldn't budge.

4. Look up the following verses and write down what you learn about fear.

   Psalm 27:1 – "The Lord is my light and the one who saves me. I fear no one. The Lord protects my life; I am afraid of no one."

   And, He is the one we should not be afraid. He will be closer to us in time trouble & fear.

Psalm 46:1–2 – "God is our protection and our strength. He always helps in times of trouble. So we will not be afraid even if the earth shakes, or the mountains fall into the sea."

He will be with us through all are troubles give us strength guiding us our choices

Isaiah 35:4 – "Say to people who are frightened, 'Be strong. Don't be afraid. Look, your God will come, and he will punish your enemies. He will make them pay for the wrongs they did, but he will save you.'"

He loves us sooo much he died on the cross to save us from sin.

FOCUS ON THE FATHER

Isn't it remarkable to discover that Jesus felt such fear? But how kind that he told us about it. We tend to do the opposite. Gloss over our fears. Cover them up. Keep our sweaty palms in our pockets, our nausea and dry mouths a secret. Not so with Jesus. We see no mask of strength. But we do hear a request for strength.

"Father, if you are willing, take away this cup of suffering." The first one to hear his fear is his Father. He could have gone to his mother. He could have confided in his disciples. He could have assembled a prayer meeting. All would have been appropriate, but none were his priority. He went first to his Father.

Oh, how we tend to go everywhere else. First to the bar, to the counselor, to the self-help book or the friend next door. Not Jesus. The first one to hear his fear was his Father in heaven.

5. What is your usual course of action when fear seizes you? Check all that apply.

   ☑ Talk about it with a friend.
   ☐ Discuss it with a family member.
   ☐ Clam up.
   ☐ Gloss over it.
   ☑ Go to the Father.

6. Read Isaiah 41:10 and respond to the following.

   Why shouldn't we worry?

   For God is with us 100% of time

   Why shouldn't we be afraid?

   Because God is are strength and he will help us and loves us so often

   What will God do for us when we are afraid?

   Be beside me always ~~and the air~~ He will strengthen you + help you uphold you with my righteous right hand.

"I will fear no evil." How could David make such a claim? Because he knew where to look. "You are with me; Your rod and Your staff, they comfort me."

Rather than turn to the other sheep, David turned to the Shepherd. Rather than stare at the problems, he stared at the rod and staff. Because he knew where to look, David was able to say, "I will fear no evil."

I know a fellow who has a fear of crowds. When encircled by large groups, his breath grows short, panic surfaces, and he begins to sweat like a sumo wrestler in a sauna. He received some help, curiously, from a golfing buddy.

The two were at a movie theatre, waiting their turn to enter, when fear struck again. The crowd closed in like a forest. He wanted out and out fast. His buddy told him to

---

THE CLOAK OF HUMANITY
"During the days of Jesus' life on earth, he offered up prayers and petitions with loud cries and tears to the one who could save him from death" (Heb. 5:7).

My, what a portrait! Jesus is in pain! Jesus is on the stage of fear. Jesus is cloaked, not in sainthood, but in humanity.

The next time the fog finds you, you might do well to remember Jesus in the garden. The next time you think that no one understands, reread the fourteenth chapter of Mark. The next time your self-pity convinces you that no one cares, pay a visit to Gethsemane. And the next time you wonder if God really perceives the pain that prevails on this dusty planet, listen to him pleading among the twisted trees.
—*No Wonder They Call Him the Savior*

In the face of his greatest fear, Jesus asked God for strength.

So don't worry, because I am with you. Don't be afraid, because I am your God. I will make you strong and will help you; I will support you with my right hand that saves you.

—Isaiah 41:10

The Spirit we received does not make us slaves again to fear; it makes us children of God. With that Spirit we cry out, "Father."

—**Romans 8:15**

I look up to the hills, but where does my help come from? My help comes from the Lord, who made heaven and earth.

—Psalm 121:1–2

Keep your eyes focused on what is right, and look straight ahead to what is good . . . Don't turn off the road of goodness; keep away from evil paths.

—Proverbs 4:25, 27

When fears surround us, we are urged to fix our eyes on Jesus.

ONE WORD FROM HIS LIPS

Many players appear on the stage of Gethsemane. Judas and his betrayal. Peter and his sword . . . The soldiers and their weapons. And though these are crucial, they aren't instrumental. The encounter is not between Jesus and the soldiers; it is between God and Satan. Satan dares to enter yet another garden, but God stands and Satan hasn't a prayer . . .

Satan falls in the presence of Christ. One word from his lips, and the finest army in the world collapsed.

Satan is silent in the proclamation of Christ. Not once did the enemy speak without Jesus' invitation. Before Christ, Satan had nothing to say.

Satan is powerless against the protection of Christ . . .

When Jesus says he will keep you safe, he means it. Hell will have to get through him to get to you. Jesus is able to protect you. When he says he will get you home, he will get you home.

—*A Gentle Thunder*

The Lord is the Spirit, and where the Spirit of the Lord is, there is freedom.
—**2 Corinthians 3:17**

take a few deep breaths. Then he helped manage the crisis by reminding him of the golf course.

"When you are hitting your ball out of the rough, and you are surrounded by trees, what do you do?"

"I look for an opening."

"You don't stare at the trees?"

"Of course not. I find an opening and focus on hitting the ball through it."

"Do the same in the crowd. When you feel the panic, don't focus on the people; focus on the opening."

Good counsel in golf. Good counsel in life. Rather than focus on the fear, focus on the solution.

That's what Jesus did.

That's what David did.

7. Read Psalm 121:1–2 and fill in the blanks about what you learn concerning our focus during fear.

I *my eyes . Look* up to the hills, but *where* does my *help* come from? My help comes from the *Lord* who *made* heaven and earth.

And that's what the writer of Hebrews urges us to do. "Let us run with endurance the race that is set before us, looking unto Jesus, the author and finisher of our faith" (Heb. 12:1–2 NKJV).

8. Based on Proverbs 4:25, 27, how is distraction an effective tool Satan uses to compound our fear?

keep your eyes fixed on your goals and don't get sidetracked on detours that lead to sin

LOOK TO JESUS

The writer of Hebrews was not a golfer, but he could have been a jogger, for he speaks of a runner and a forerunner. The forerunner is Jesus, the "author and finisher of our faith." He is the author—that is to say he wrote the book on salvation. And he is the finisher—he not only charted the map, he blazed the trail. He is the forerunner, and we are the runners. And we runners are urged to keep our eyes on Jesus.

9. Yet who is free to run if we are encumbered by fear? We will only take hesitating steps here and there if we are afraid. Read the following verses. Then match the verse with what you learn about how Scripture often compares our spiritual life to a race.

d Isaiah 40:31   a. We should run to win the prize.
A 1 Corinthians 9:24   b. We'll be happy if we run the race and win.
C Philippians 2:16   c. We shouldn't give up running.
b Hebrews 12:1   d. Trusting God helps us run without needing a rest.

Since heart disease runs in our family, I run in our neighborhood. As the sun is rising, I am running. And as I am running, my body is groaning. It doesn't want to cooperate. My knee hurts. My hip is stiff. My ankles complain. Sometimes a passerby laughs at my legs, and my ego hurts.

Things hurt. And as things hurt, I've learned that I have three options. Go home. (Denalyn would laugh at me.) Meditate on my hurts until I start imagining I'm having chest pains. (Pleasant thought.) Or I can keep running and watch the sun come up. My trail has just enough easterly bend to give me a front-row seat for God's morning miracle. If I watch God's world go from dark to golden, guess what? The same happens to my attitude. The pain passes and the joints loosen, and before I know it, the run is half over and life ain't half bad. Everything improves as I fix my eyes on the sun.

Wasn't that the counsel of the Hebrew epistle—"looking unto Jesus"? What was the focus of David? "You are with me; Your rod and Your staff, they comfort me."

We are never alone—God is with us.

THE FEAR OF LONELINESS

The discovery of David is indeed the message of Scripture—the Lord is with us. And, since the Lord is near, everything is different. Everything!

You may be facing death, but you aren't facing death alone; the Lord is with you. You may be facing unemployment, but you aren't facing unemployment alone; the Lord is with you. You may be facing marital struggles, but you aren't facing them alone; the Lord is with you. You may be facing debt, but you aren't facing debt alone; the Lord is with you.

Underline these words: You are not alone.

Your family may turn against you, but God won't. Your friends may betray you, but God won't. You may feel alone in the wilderness, but you are not. He is with you. And because he is, everything is different. You are different.

10. Loneliness is at the top of many people's lists when it comes to tallying our fears. What is the difference between being alone and being lonely?

alone you have nobody
belonely Jesus whato to be with you.

Don't avoid life's Gardens of Gethsemane. Enter them. Just don't enter them alone. And while there, be honest. Pounding the ground is permitted. Tears are allowed. And if you sweat blood, you won't be the first. Do what Jesus did; open your heart.

And be specific. Jesus was. "Take this cup," he prayed. Give God the number of the flight. Tell him the length of the speech. Share the details of the job transfer. He has plenty of time. He also has plenty of compassion.

He doesn't think your fears are foolish or silly. He won't tell you to "buck up" or "get tough." He's been where you are. He knows how you feel.

And he knows what you need. That's why we punctuate our prayers as Jesus did. "If you are willing . . ."

Was God willing? Yes and no. He didn't take away the Cross, but he took the fear. God didn't still the storm, but he calmed the sailor.

Who's to say he won't do the same for you?

Don't avoid your fears, just don't face them alone.

11. Read Philippians 4:6 and fill in the blanks concerning our strategy for wrestling free from fear.

Do not _worry_ about anything, but _pray_ and _ask_ _God_ for everything you need, always giving _thanks_.

Don't measure the size of the mountain; talk to the One who can move it. Instead of carrying the world on your shoulders, talk to the One who holds the universe on his.

Hope is a look away.

Now, what were you looking at?

Do not worry about anything, but pray and ask God for everything you need, always giving thanks.

—Philippians 4:6

THE HEART OF THE MATTER

❦ **Jesus experienced fear.**
❦ **In the face of his greatest fear, Jesus asked God for strength.**
❦ **When fears surround us, we are urged to fix our eyes on Jesus.**
❦ **We are never alone—God is with us.**
❦ **Don't avoid your fears, just don't face them alone.**

So if the Son makes you free, you will be truly free.

—John 8:36

So if the Son set you free, indeed you will be free John 8:36

In order to review your memory verse for the week, write it out on the lines below. Remember, it's John 8:36.

For if the Son set you free, indeed you will be free.
John 8:36

The Heart of Jesus

Paul's past was nothing to be proud of. He'd tried to root the "heresy" of Christianity out of the land. He'd badgered men and frightened women into confessions. He'd separated families. He'd burned down homes. He'd infiltrated underground churches. He'd brought charges against countless men. He'd turned whole households over to the authorities. He'd seen Christians fined, persecuted, imprisoned, and even killed. He was a Pharisaical bounty hunter, obsessed with bringing down his prey. Christians spoke of him in whispers, and feared the very sound of his name. Yet Paul was no longer the "Saul" that sought to destroy the church. He was Paul, tender Christian father to dozens of newly planted churches throughout the known world. Jesus had forgiven Paul, and Paul was able to do the work of the ministry, unburdened by his past and the load of guilt and shame that it held. He had left those cares at Jesus' feet and kept his eyes firmly on the goal, the prize that lies ahead. Paul had experienced the freedom of Jesus.

DAY FIVE—FREEDOM FROM SHAME

BURDENED WITH GUILT

See the fellow in the shadows? That's Peter. Peter the apostle. Peter the impetuous. Peter the passionate. He once walked on water. Stepped right out of the boat onto the lake. He'll soon preach to thousands. Fearless before friends and foes alike. But tonight the one who stepped on the water has hurried into hiding. The one who will speak with power is weeping in pain.

Not sniffling or whimpering, but weeping. Bawling. Bearded face buried in thick hands. His howl echoing in the Jerusalem night. What hurts more? The fact that he did it? Or the fact that he swore he never would?

You prepare a table before me in the presence of my enemies.
—Psalm 23:5 NKJV

1. *But Peter said to Jesus, "Lord, I am ready to go with you to prison and even to die with you!" But Jesus said, "Peter, before the rooster crows this day, you will say three times that you don't know me."* —Luke 22:33–34

   What did Peter pledge to Jesus?
   To prison and to Death

   What was Jesus' response?
   before the rooster crows today, you will deny three time that you know me.

Since these children are people with physical bodies, Jesus himself became like them. He did this so that, by dying, he could destroy the one who has the power of death—the devil—and free those who were like slaves all their lives because of their fear of death.
—Hebrews 2:14–15

Denying Christ on the night of his betrayal was bad enough, but did he have to boast that he wouldn't? And one denial was pitiful, but three? Three denials were horrific, but did he have to curse? "Peter began to place a curse on himself and swear, 'I don't know the man'" (Matt. 26:74).

And now, awash in a whirlpool of sorrow, Peter is hiding. Peter is weeping.

2. Look up the following verses and write down what you learn about guilt.

Psalm 32:5 – "Then I confessed my sins to you and didn't hide my guilt. I said, 'I will confess my sins to the Lord,' and you forgave my guilt."

sometime are guilt seems so terrible but never so bad that. we turn to Jesus and he will always come to me with forgiveness

Jeremiah 2:22 – "Although you wash yourself with cleanser and use much soap, I can still see the stain of your guilt," says the Lord God."

The stain of sin is only more than skin-deep. Your skin has caused a great stain that God can will remove.

Hebrews 10:22 – "Let us come near to God with a sincere heart and a sure faith, because we have been made free from a guilty conscience, and our bodies have been washed with pure water."

draw nearer to God.

Our failures leave us mired down in guilt and shame.

One of the next times we see Peter interact with Jesus is back on the shores of Lake Galilee. Peter is back in the fishing boat, and we wonder why he goes fishing. We know why he goes to Galilee. He had been told that the risen Christ would meet the disciples there. The arranged meeting place is not the sea, however, but a mountain (Matt. 28:16). If the followers were to meet Jesus on a mountain, what are they doing in a boat? No one told them to fish, but that's what they did. "Simon Peter said, 'I am going out to fish.' The others said, 'We will go with you'" (John 21:3). Besides, didn't Peter quit fishing? Two years earlier, when Jesus called him to fish for men, didn't he drop his net and follow? We haven't seen him fish since. We never see him fish again. Why is he fishing now? Especially now! Jesus has risen from the dead. Peter has seen the empty tomb. Who could fish at a time like this?

Were they hungry? Perhaps that's the sum of it. Maybe the expedition was born out of growling stomachs.

Or then again, maybe it was born out of a broken heart.

You see, Peter could not deny his denial. The empty tomb did not erase the crowing rooster. Christ had returned, but Peter wondered, he must have wondered, "After what I did, would he return for someone like me?"

We've wondered the same. Is Peter the only person to do the very thing he swore he'd never do?

"Infidelity is behind me!"

"From now on, I'm going to bridle my tongue."

"No more shady deals. I've learned my lesson."

Oh, the volume of our boasting. And, oh, the heartbreak of our shame.

Rather than resist the flirting, we return it.

Rather than ignore the gossip, we share it.

Rather than stick to the truth, we shade it.

And the rooster crows, and conviction pierces, and Peter has a partner in the shadows.

3. Which of the following statements are true when it comes to comparing Jesus' offer to free us from shame and life on the run? Check all that apply. Use the Bible verses below to help you answer.

☑ If we try to hide our sins we will not succeed. (Proverbs 28:13)

☑ Once our sins are forgiven, we are happy. (Romans 4:7–8)

☑ When we confess our sins, he forgives us. (1 John 1:9)

TAKE JESUS AT HIS WORD

When it comes to healing our spiritual condition, we don't have a chance. We might as well be told to pole-vault the moon. We don't have what it takes to be healed. Our only hope is that God will do for us what he did for the man at Bethesda—that he will step out of the temple and step into our ward of hurt and helplessness.

Which is exactly what he has done . . .

I wish we would take Jesus at his word . . .

When he says we're forgiven, let's unload the guilt.

When he says we're valuable, let's believe him . . .

When he says we're provided for, let's stop worrying.

God's efforts are strongest when our efforts are useless.

—*He Still Moves Stones*

In the past, the law held us like prisoners, but our old selves died, and we were made free from the law. So now we serve God in a new way with the Spirit, and not in the old way with written rules.

—*Romans 7:6*

If you hide your sins, you will not succeed. If you confess and reject them, you will receive mercy.

—Proverbs 28:13

4. Read Proverbs 10:12 and fill in the blanks—a short and sweet reminder concerning God's ability to free us from shame by forgiving our sins.

Love <u>cover over</u> all <u>wrongs</u>.

BACK TO THE HEART OF JESUS

We weep as Peter wept, and we do what Peter did. We go fishing. We go back to our old lives. We return to our pre-Jesus practices. We do what comes naturally, rather than what comes spiritually. And we question whether Jesus has a place for folks like us.

Jesus answers that question. He answers it for you and me and all who tend to "Peter out" on Christ. His answer came on the shore of the sea in a gift to Peter. You know what Jesus did? Split the waters? Turn the boat to gold and the nets to silver? No, Jesus did something much more meaningful. He invited Peter to breakfast. Jesus prepared a meal.

Of course, the breakfast was one special moment among several that morning. There was the great catch of fish and the recognition of Jesus. The plunge of Peter and the paddling of the disciples. And there was the moment they reached the shore and found Jesus next to a fire of coals. The fish were sizzling, the bread was waiting, and the Defeater of hell and the Ruler of heaven invited his friends to sit down and have a bite to eat.

Hatred stirs up trouble, but love forgives all wrongs.

—Proverbs 10:12

5. Read the account of Jesus, Peter, and some followers in John 21:4–19 and respond to the following.

What did Peter do to show his eagerness for Jesus to set him free from shame and restore their fellowship? (v. 7)

<u>He wrapped garment around him and jumped into the water</u>

What did Jesus do to show his love for Peter and the followers? (v. 10, 13)

<u>He feed them to brekfast</u>

Who received Jesus' focus and attention after the meal? (v. 15)

<u>Simon Peter</u>

Jesus calls you to come, not for a scolding, but to welcome you back.

If you find yourself awash in the whirlpool of sorrow, hiding in the shadows of shame, continually reliving your failures, Jesus' invitation is for you. He wants face-time with you—not to scold you, but to hold you. He wants you to come back to his heart. Let him set you free.

No one could have been more grateful than Peter. The one Satan had sifted like wheat was eating bread at the hand of God. Peter was welcomed to the meal of Christ. Right there for the devil and his tempters to see, Jesus "prepared a table in the presence of his enemies."

OK, so maybe Peter didn't say it that way. But David did. "You prepare a table before me in the presence of my enemies" (Ps. 23:5 NKJV). What the shepherd did for the sheep sounds a lot like what Jesus did for Peter.

6. Jesus has a special heart for those who blow it. Read Luke 5:30–32. Which of the statements are true concerning Jesus' care for sinners? Mark your answers True (T) or False (F).

_____ Jesus is not interested in those who make mistakes.
_____ God sent Jesus to invite only good people to be with him.
__T__ Jesus had an affinity for sinners.
__T__ Jesus invites sinners to change their hearts and lives.

Through Christ Jesus the law of the Spirit that brings life made me free from the law that brings sin and death.
—Romans 8:2

At this point in the psalm, David's mind seems to be lingering in the high country with the sheep. Having guided the flock through the valley to the alp lands for greener grass, he remembers the shepherd's added responsibility. He must prepare the pasture.

This is new land, so the shepherd must be careful. Ideally, the grazing area will be flat, a mesa or tableland. The shepherd searches for poisonous plants and ample water. He looks for signs of wolves, coyotes, and bears.

Of special concern to the shepherd is the adder, a small brown snake that lives underground. Adders are known to pop out of their holes and nip the sheep on the nose. The bite often infects and can even kill. As defense against the snake, the shepherd pours a circle of oil at the top of each adder's hole. He also applies the oil to the noses of the animals. The oil on the snake's hole lubricates the exit, preventing the snake from climbing out. The smell of the oil on the sheep's nose drives the serpent away. The shepherd, in a very real sense, has prepared the table.[4]

What if your Shepherd did for you what the shepherd did for his flock? Suppose he dealt with your enemy, the devil, and prepared for you a safe place of nourishment? What if Jesus did for you what he did for Peter? Suppose he, in the hour of your failure, invited you to a meal?

> But the Pharisees and the men who taught the law for the Pharisees began to complain to Jesus' followers, "Why do you eat and drink with tax collectors and sinners?" Jesus answered them, "It is not the healthy people who need a doctor, but the sick. I have not come to invite good people but sinners to change their hearts and lives."
>
> —Luke 5:30–32

7. Isn't this the message of Jeremiah 31:18? Read this verse and fill in the blanks below about what you learn concerning God's willingness to help us make our way back to him after we fail.

   Lord, you *punished* me, and I have *learned* my lesson. Take me *Take me back* so that I may *come* back.

> Lord, you punished me, and I have learned my lesson. I was like a calf that had never been trained. Take me back so that I may come back. You truly are the Lord my God.
>
> —Jeremiah 31:18

8. What is your immediate reaction to the idea of welcoming you in spite of your failure?

   a. There must be some kind of catch.
   b. I am too embarrassed to look Jesus in the face ever again.
   c. Just say the word, and I will run to his arms.

COME TO THE TABLE

On the night before his death, Jesus prepared a table for his followers.

> It was now the first day of the Feast of Unleavened Bread when the Passover lamb was sacrificed. Jesus' followers said to him, "Where do you want us to go and prepare for you to eat the Passover meal?" Jesus sent two of his followers and said to them, "Go into the city and a man carrying a jar of water will meet you. Follow him. When he goes into a house, tell the owner of the house, 'The Teacher says: Where is my guest room in which I can eat the Passover meal with my followers?' The owner will show you a large room upstairs that is furnished and ready. Prepare the food for us there." —Mark 14:12–15

Look who did the "preparing" here. Jesus reserved a large room and arranged for the guide to lead the disciples. Jesus made certain the room was furnished and the food set out. What did the disciples do? They faithfully complied and were fed.

The Shepherd prepared the table.

Not only that, he dealt with the snakes. You'll remember that only one of the disciples didn't complete the meal that night. "The devil had already persuaded Judas Iscariot, the son of Simon, to turn against Jesus" (John 13:2). Judas started to eat, but Jesus didn't let him finish. On the command of Jesus, Judas left the room. "'The thing that you will do—do it quickly' . . . Judas took the bread Jesus gave him and immediately went out. It was night" (John 13:27, 30).

There is something dynamic in this dismissal. Jesus prepared a table in the presence of the enemy. Judas was allowed to see the supper, but he wasn't allowed to stay there.

> I am free and belong to no one. But I make myself a slave to all people to win as many as I can.
>
> —1 Corinthians 9:19

Jesus has prepared a place for you.

You are not welcome here. This table is for my children. You may tempt them. You may trip them. But you will never sit with them. This is how much he loves us.

And if any doubt remains, lest there be any "Peters" who wonder if there is a place at the table for them, Jesus issues a tender reminder as he passes the cup.

"Every one of you drink this." Those who feel unworthy, drink this. Those who feel ashamed, drink this. Those who feel embarrassed, drink this.

9. Read Matthew 26:27–28. Based on what you just read, which of the following statements are true concerning Jesus' reminder to free us from shame?

   ❏ He wanted each person to drink from the cup.
   ❏ He poured out his blood only for some people.
   ☑ He poured out his blood for many and forgave their sins.

10. How might this study of Jesus' freedom from shame affect your next experience of the Lord's Supper?

   _____

   _____

THE HEART OF THE MATTER

- **Our failures leave us mired down in guilt and shame.**
- **Jesus calls you to come, not for a scolding, but to welcome you back.**
- **Jesus has prepared a place for you.**

Here is one last chance for a little review. Have you hidden it in your heart? Write out John 8:36 below.

So if the Sons have sit Free, In deed you are free, so John 8:36

The Heart of Jesus

They expected him to perform wonders for their entertainment. They expected him to tell fascinating stories. They expected him to thrill them with impossible feats. They expected him to put the uppity Pharisees in their place. They expected him listen to all their troubles. They expected him to accomplish the miraculous. They expected him to have all the answers. They expected him to give them bread when they were hungry. They expected him to heal their sick. They expected him to come when called. They expected him to obey their Sabbath traditions. They expected him to overthrow the Roman Empire. They expected him to bring them peace. They expected him to become their king here on earth. But Jesus didn't worry about those things. He never attempted to live up to everybody else's agenda. Jesus was free from the expectations of others. He kept his ear tuned to heaven, and remained true to his Father's calling.

FOR FURTHER READING

Selections throughout this lesson were taken from *Traveling Light*.

Then Jesus took a cup and thanked God for it and gave it to the followers. He said, "Every one of you drink this. This is my blood which is the new agreement that God makes with his people. This blood is poured out for many to forgive their sins.
—Matthew 26:27–28

So I will live in freedom, because I want to follow your orders.
—Psalm 119:45

[1] Randy C. Alcorn, *Money, Possessions, and Eternity* (Wheaton, Ill,: Tyndale Publishers, 1989), 55.

[2] Chris Seidman, *Little Buddy* (Orange, Calif.: New Leaf Books, 2001), 138. Used with permission.

[3] Rick Athcley, "I Have Learned the Secret," audiotape 7 of the 1997 Pepperdine Lectures (Malibu, Calif., 1997). Used with permission.

[4] Charles W. Slemming, *He Leadeth Me: The Shepherd's Life in Palestine* (Fort Washington, Pa.: Christian Literature Crusade, 1964), quoted in Charles R. Swindoll, *Living Beyond the Daily Grind, Book 1: Reflections on the Songs and Sayings in Scripture* (Dallas: Word Publishing, 1988), 77–78.

Experiencing the Joy of Jesus

A LETTER OF JOY

Go with me back in history a couple of thousand years. Let's go to Rome . . . to a rather drab little room, surrounded by high walls . . . Inside we see a man seated on the floor. He's an older fellow, shoulders stooped and balding. Chains are on his hands and feet . . .

It is the apostle Paul . . . The apostle who was bound only by the will of God is now in chains—stuck in a dingy house—attached to a Roman officer. . . .

He is writing a letter. No doubt it is a complaint letter to God. No doubt it is a list of grievances . . . He has every reason to be bitter and complain. But he doesn't. Instead he writes a letter that two thousand years later is still known as the treatise on joy—Philippians . . .

Why don't you spend some time with it?

—*The Inspirational Study Bible*

He was joyful. He was joyful when he was poor. He was joyful when he was abandoned. He was joyful when he was betrayed. He was even joyful as he hung on a tool of torture, his hands pierced with six-inch Roman spikes.

Jesus embodied a stubborn joy. A joy that refused to bend in the wind of hard times. A joy that held its ground against pain. A joy whose roots extended deep into the bedrock of eternity.

What type of joy is this? What is this cheerfulness that dares to wink at adversity? What is this bird that sings while it is still dark? What is the source of this peace that defies pain?

I call it sacred delight.

It is sacred because it is not of the earth. What is sacred is God's. And this joy is God's.

It is delight because delight can both satisfy and surprise.

Sacred delight is good news coming through the back door of your heart. It's what you'd always dreamed but never expected. It's the too-good-to-be-true coming true. It's having God as your pinch-hitter, your lawyer, your dad, your biggest fan, and your best friend. God on your side, in your heart, out in front, and protecting your back. It's hope where you least expected it: a flower in life's sidewalk.

It's no accident that the same word used by Jesus to promise sacred delight is the word used by Paul to describe God: "The blessed God . . ." (1 Tim. 1:11 NIV); "God, the blessed and only Ruler . . ." (1 Tim. 6:15 NIV).

Think about God's joy. What can cloud it? What can quench it? What can kill it? Is God ever in a bad mood because of bad weather? Does God get ruffled over long lines or traffic jams? Does God ever refuse to rotate the earth because his feelings are hurt?

No. His is a joy which consequences cannot quench. His is a peace which circumstances cannot steal.

There is a delicious gladness that comes from God. A holy joy. A sacred delight.

And it is within your reach. You are one decision away from Joy.

EXPERIENCING THE JOY OF JESUS THIS WEEK

Before you read any further, spend some time in prayer.

Dear Father, Help me to know the joy that is at the heart of Jesus. I know that the joy you give cannot be affected by circumstances, other people, or my own emotions. Show me how I can experience this same joy in my own life. Amen.

This week, memorize Matthew 5:12—the hallmark of great joy.

Rejoice and be glad, for you have a great reward waiting for you in heaven. —*Matthew 5:12*

The hallmark of great joy Rejoice and be glad, for you have a great reward waiting for you in heaven. matthew 5:12

The angel said to them, "Do not be afraid. I am bringing you good news that will be a great joy to all the people."
—Luke 2:10

DAY ONE—SACRED DELIGHT

UNSPEAKABLE JOY

No man had more reason to be miserable than this one—yet no man was more joyful.

His first home was a palace. Servants were at his fingertips. The snap of his fingers changed the course of history. His name was known and loved. He had everything—wealth, power, respect.

And then he had nothing.

Students of the event still ponder it. Historians stumble as they attempt to explain it. How could a king lose everything in one instant?

One moment he was royalty; the next he was in poverty.

His bed became, at best, a borrowed pallet—and usually the hard earth. He never owned even the most basic mode of transportation and was dependent upon handouts for his income. He was sometimes so hungry he would eat raw grain or pick fruit off a tree. He knew what it was like to be rained on, to be cold. He knew what it meant to have no home.

His palace grounds had been spotless; now he was exposed to filth. He had never known disease, but was now surrounded by illness.

In his kingdom he had been revered; now he was ridiculed. His neighbors tried to lynch him. Some called him a lunatic. His family tried to confine him to their house.

Those who didn't ridicule him tried to use him. They wanted favors. They wanted tricks. He was a novelty. They wanted to be seen with him—that is, until being with him was out of fashion. Then they wanted to kill him.

He was accused of a crime he never committed. Witnesses were hired to lie. The jury was rigged. No lawyer was assigned to his defense. A judge swayed by politics handed down the death penalty.

They killed him. He left as he came—penniless. He was buried in a borrowed grave, his funeral financed by compassionate friends. Though he once had everything, he died with nothing.

He should have been miserable. He should have been bitter. He had every right to be a pot of boiling anger. But he wasn't.

He was joyful.

In spite of all Jesus had to endure, he was joyful.

1. Read Isaiah 53:1–12. Then match the verse with what you learn about Jesus' outward circumstances as described in Isaiah's prophecy.

   c. 53:2   a. He was wounded and crushed for sin.
   f. 53:3   b. He died among wicked men—though he was innocent.
   a. 53:5   c. As a man, Jesus lacked his heavenly beauty and majesty.
   d. 53:7   d. He was beaten down and punished—yet he didn't retaliate.
   e/a. 53:8   e. He was treated like a criminal.
   b/e. 53:9   f. People hated and rejected him.
   g. 53:12   g. Jesus never had children of his own.

Before we begin our study of joy, we must clearly identify the source of joy. We are not talking about happiness built on the shaky foundations of circumstances. We are talking about a life built on a different thing—an inner exuberance that comes from God. More than from him, it is in him. *En theos*—in God. Those who are enthusiastic about Jesus and serving him—not just focused on how we can benefit from the Christian life—radiate with true joy. Jesus showed us by example how to do it. If we feel we have reason to be bitter in life, he had more. Do we feel our cynicism is justified? How much more he could have said likewise! Yet he didn't. He wouldn't. Circumstances couldn't affect Jesus' joy—it was untouchable.

But be happy that you are sharing in Christ's sufferings so that you will be happy and full of joy when Christ comes again in glory.

—1 Peter 4:13

DEFINING SACRED DELIGHT

Delight is the Bethlehem shepherds dancing a jig outside a cave. Delight is Mary watching God sleep in a feed trough. Delight is white-haired Simeon praising God, who is about to be circumcised. Delight is Joseph teaching the Creator of the world how to hold a hammer.

Delight is the look on Andrew's face at the lunch pail that never came up empty. Delight is the dozing wedding guests who drank the wine that had been water. Delight is Jesus walking through waves as casually as you walk through curtains. Delight is a leper seeing a finger where there had been only a nub . . . a widow hosting a party with food made for a funeral . . . a paraplegic doing somersaults. Delight is Jesus doing impossible things in crazy ways: healing the blind with spit, paying taxes with a coin found in a fish's mouth, and coming back from the dead disguised as a gardener.

What is sacred delight? It is God doing what gods would be doing only in your wildest dreams—wearing diapers, riding donkeys, washing feet, dozing in storms. Delight is the day they accused God of having too much fun, attending too many parties, and spending too much time with the Happy Hour crowd.

Delight is the day's wage paid to workers who had worked only one hour . . . the father scrubbing the pig smell off his son's back . . . the shepherd throwing a party because the sheep was found. Delight is a discovered pearl, a multiplied talent, a heaven-bound beggar, a criminal in the kingdom. Delight is the surprise on the faces of street folks who have been invited to a king's banquet.

Delight is the Samaritan woman big-eyed and speechless, the adulteress walking out of the stone-cluttered courtyard, and a skivvy-clad Peter plunging into cold waters to get close to the One he'd cursed.

Sacred delight is an inner exuberance that comes from God.

2. Look up the following verses and write down what you learn about joy—God's sacred delight.

Psalm 4:7 – "You have given me greater joy than those who have abundant harvests of grain and wine." NLT

In angers search your hearts and be silent

Psalm 47:5 – "God has risen with a shout of joy; the Lord has risen as the trumpets sounded."

Total obedance and heartfelt praises, this will as long I have Jesus + God in my heart I will always have joy

Psalm 126:3 – "Yes, the Lord has done amazing things for us! What joy!" NLT

When Jesus come again their will be Joy beon our imagion.

Isaiah 61:7 – "Instead of shame and dishonor, you will inherit a double portion of prosperity and everlasting joy." NLT

their be know shame Joy & Everlasting Joy will be in are hearts forever

THE MESSAGE WE NEED TO HEAR

Certain things about God are easy to imagine. I can imagine him creating the world and suspending the stars. I can envision him as almighty, all-powerful, and in control. I can fathom a God who knows me, who made me, and I can even fathom a God who hears me. But a God who is in love with me? A God who is crazy for me? A God who cheers for me?

But that is the message of the Bible. Our Father is relentlessly in pursuit of his children. He has called us home with his word, paved the path with his blood, and is longing for our arrival.

God's love for his children is the message of the Bible.

I have told you these things so that you can have the same joy I have and so that your joy will be the fullest possible joy.
—**John 15:11**

3. Which of the following statements are true? Check all that apply.

❏ "When it comes to the way he feels about me, God could take me or leave me."

☒ "God is in love with me."

❏ "God is indifferent towards me."

☒ "God cheers for me."

4. Read Psalm 59:16–17 and fill in the blanks regarding a love worth singing.

In the morning, we can __sing__ about God's __love__. He is our defender and place of __refuge__ in times of __trouble__. We can sing __praises__ about him. He is the God who __loves__ us.

But as for me, I will sing about your power. I will shout with joy each morning because of your unfailing love. For you have been my refuge, a place of safety in the day of distress. O my Strength, to you I sing praises, for you, O God, are my refuge, the God who shows me unfailing love.

—Psalm 59:16–17

JOY IN JESUS' PRESENCE

We may know *about* God without *knowing him* at all. In fact, unless we experience him and what it means to be in his presence, it's likely we will never know him. Experiencing the heart of Jesus will radically change what you think you know about him. All it takes is hearing that first beat of his heart—knowing it's really him, and knowing he is so near.

The quietness will slow my pulse, the silence will open my ears, and something sacred will happen. The soft slap of sandaled feet will break the stillness, a pierced hand will extend a quiet invitation, and I will follow.

I wish I could say it happens every night; it doesn't. Some nights he asks and I don't listen. Other nights he asks and I just don't go. But some nights I hear his poetic whisper, "Come to me, all you who are weary and burdened . . ." and I follow. I leave behind the budgets, bills, and deadlines and walk the narrow trail up the mountain with him.

You've been there. You've escaped the sandy foundations of the valley and ascended his grand outcropping of granite. You've turned your back on the noise and sought his voice. You've stepped away from the masses and followed the Master as he led you up the winding path to the summit.

His summit. Clean air. Clear view. Crisp breeze. The roar of the marketplace is down there, and the perspective of the peak is up here.

Gently your guide invites you to sit on the rock above the tree line and look out with him at the ancient peaks that will never erode. "What is necessary is still what is sure," he confides. "just remember: 'You'll go nowhere tomorrow that I haven't already been. Truth will still triumph. Death will still die. The victory is yours. And delight is one decision away—seize it.'"

The sacred summit. A place of permanence in a world of transition.

INTIMACY WITH THE ALMIGHTY

Jesus didn't act unless he saw his father act. He didn't judge until he heard his father judge. No act or deed occurred without his father's guidance . . .

Because Jesus could hear what others couldn't, he acted differently than they did. Remember when everyone was troubled about the man born blind? Jesus wasn't. He knew that the blindness would reveal God's power (John 9:3). Remember when everyone was distraught about Lazarus's illness? Jesus wasn't . . . It was as if Jesus could hear what no one else could . . . Jesus had unbroken communion with his father.

Do you suppose the Father desires the same for us? Absolutely! . . . God desires the same abiding intimacy with you that he had with his son.

—Just Like Jesus

5. We must make the decision to pursue joy in Jesus' presence in spite of a busy schedule and many distractions. Which of the following verses are true concerning joy in Jesus' presence, and which ones are false? Mark your answers True (T) or False (F). Use the Bible verses below to help you answer.

__T__ Being with Jesus brings blessings. (Psalm 21:6)

__F__ Jesus only wants to be with us for a short time. (Psalm 41:12)

__F__ We are bored with Jesus at our side. (Acts 2:25–26)

__T__ Being with Jesus fills us with joy. (Acts 2:28)

In order to know Jesus, we must spend time in his presence.

Think about the people in your world. Can't you tell the ones who have been to his mountain? Oh, their problems aren't any different. And their challenges are just as severe. But there is a stubborn peace that enshrines them. A confidence that life isn't toppled by unmet budgets or re-routed airplanes. A serenity that softens the corners of their lips. A contagious delight sparkling in their eyes.

The people the Lord has freed will return there. They will enter Jerusalem with joy, and their happiness will last forever. Their gladness and joy will fill them completely, and sorrow and sadness will go far away.

—Isaiah 35:10

Those who share the joy of Jesus have a stubborn, unshakeable peace.

And in their hearts reigns a fortresslike confidence that the valley can be endured, even enjoyed, because the mountain is only a decision away.

6. Why does the joy in Jesus' presence have a physical effect on our countenance, stress level, attitude, and demeanor?

Jesus is the God of peace, joy an Love, and the greatest thes is Love

Then young women of Israel will be happy and dance, the young men and old men also. I will change their sadness into happiness; I will give them comfort and joy instead of sadness.

—Jeremiah 31:13

7. Read Jeremiah 31:13 and fill in the blanks about what you learn concerning this transformation of joy.

Those who were once sad will be happy and _Dance_. God will turn mourning our sadness into _gladness_. He will give us _Comfort_ and joy instead of _sorrow_.

I read recently about a man who had breathed the summit air. His trips up the trail began early in his life and sustained him to the end. A few days before he died, a priest went to visit him in the hospital. As the priest entered the room, he noticed an empty chair beside the man's bed. The priest asked him if someone had been by to visit. The old man smiled, "I place Jesus on that chair, and I talk to him."

The priest was puzzled, so the man explained. "Years ago a friend told me that prayer was as simple as talking to a good friend. So every day I pull up a chair, invite Jesus to sit, and we have a good talk."

Some days later, the daughter of this man came to the parish house to inform the priest that her father had just died. "Because he seemed so content," she said, "I left him in his room alone for a couple of hours. When I got back to the room, I found him dead. I noticed a strange thing, though: His head was resting, not on the pillow, but on an empty chair that was beside his bed."[1]

Learn a lesson from the man with the chair. Take a trip with the King to the mountain peak. It's pristine, uncrowded, and on top of the world. Stubborn joy begins by breathing deep up there before you go crazy down here.

THE HEART OF THE MATTER

- ❦ **In spite of all Jesus had to endure, he was joyful.**
- ❦ **Sacred delight is an inner exuberance that comes from God.**
- ❦ **In order to know Jesus, we must spend time in his presence.**
- ❦ **Those who share the joy of Jesus have a stubborn, unshakeable peace.**

Your new memory verse for the week is Matthew 5:12. Take a couple of minutes to review it, then write it out here.

Great Rejouce And be glad, for you have a Gift waiting for you in heaven. Reward

The Heart of Jesus

Cold. Gray. Blank. Numb. With plodding steps the woman followed the men who carried her son's body. Mourners keened and wailed all around her, filling the air with the mournful shrieks she couldn't quite bring herself to make. The shock of her only son's death was too fresh, too unthinkable to acknowledge with tears. She was alone now—completely bereft. Sure, the arms of friends steadied her. Yes, all her neighbors had come to sit with her, to mourn with her. But once things settled down again, she would be alone. Her husband had died years ago, and she had no other children. Her son had not yet married, and had no children of his own to look after her. She had no near relatives to take her in. How would she buy food? How would she buy oil? What

The Lord has filled my heart with joy; I feel very strong in the Lord.
—1 Samuel 2:1a

would she do when winter came? All these thoughts tumbled around in her head so that she didn't notice that the procession had halted. Startled, she looked around. They were still within the walls of the city, not yet at the cemetery. What was going on? Then she saw the cause of the interruption—a man was gently making his way through the crowd of mourners towards her son. Was he going to pay his respects? She didn't think she knew him—not a neighbor or an acquaintance. But then he spoke, and touched her son. She gasped and held her breath as she watched her dear son take a new breath. Her numbness left her as she watched her sweet boy sit up. And her feet ran to him as the men lifted him down from the pallet—then danced for sheer joy.

—Luke 7:11–15

DAY TWO—GOD'S GLADNESS

THE BLESSING OF GOD

1. Read Matthew 5:1–10. Match the following recipients of joy found in the above passage with the attitude/action of joy that they exhibit.

_b_	The poor in spirit	_a._	Famished orphans who know the difference between a TV dinner and a Thanksgiving feast.
_h_	Those who mourn		
_x_	The meek	_b._	Those who manage to keep an eye on heaven while walking through hell on earth.
_A_	Those who hunger and thirst		
_g_	The merciful	_c._	Architects who build bridges with wood from a Roman cross.
_d_	The pure in heart	_d._	Winners of the million-dollar lottery who share the prize with their enemies.
_e_	The peacemakers		
_c_	The persecuted	_e._	Pawnshop pianos played by Van Cliburn. (He's so good no one notices the missing keys.)
		f.	Beggars in God's soup kitchen.
		g.	Sinners Anonymous bound together by the truth of their introduction: "Hi, I am me. I'm a sinner."
		_h._	Physicians who love lepers and escape infection.

It is to this band of pilgrims that God promises a special blessing. A heavenly joy. A sacred delight.

2. Jesus shared his Father's affinity for the weak. Read Psalm 35:10 and fill in the blanks concerning God's gift to the weak.

God saves the ___poor___ from the ___too strong___ and rescues the ___poor___ and ___needy___.

RADICAL RECONSTRUCTION

But this joy is not cheap. What Jesus promises is not a gimmick to give you goose bumps nor a mental attitude that has to be pumped up at pep rallies. No, Matthew 5 describes God's radical reconstruction of the heart.

Observe the sequence. First, we recognize we are in need (we're poor in spirit). Next, we repent of our self-sufficiency (we mourn).

We quit calling the shots and surrender control to God (we're meek).

So grateful are we for his presence that we yearn for more of him (we hunger and thirst).

We recognize God alone will fill our cavernous needs, and we trust God to do it. The result? We rejoice!

Now when he saw the crowds, he went up on a mountainside and sat down. His disciples came to him, and he began to teach them, saying:
Blessed are the poor in spirit,
for theirs is the kingdom of heaven.
Blessed are those who mourn,
for they will be comforted.
Blessed are the meek,
for they will inherit the earth.
Blessed are those who hunger and thirst for righteousness,
for they will be filled.
Blessed are the merciful,
for they will be shown mercy.
Blessed are the pure in heart,
for they will see God.
Blessed are the peacemakers,
for they will be called sons of God.
Blessed are those who are persecuted because of righteousness,
for theirs is the kingdom of heaven.

—Matthew 5:1–10 NIV

Always be joyful.
—1 Thessalonians 5:16

I will praise him from the bottom of my heart: "Lord, who can compare with you? Who else rescues the weak and helpless from the strong? Who else protects the poor and needy from those who want to rob them?"

—Psalm 35:10 NLT

Joy is the result of an extensive reconstruction of our hearts.

Get rid of all the sins you have done, and get for yourselves a new heart and a new way of thinking.

—Ezekiel 18:31

Our faces, then, are not covered. We all show the Lord's glory, and we are being changed to be like him. This change in us brings ever greater glory, which comes from the Lord, who is the Spirit.

—2 Corinthians 3:18

Oh, what joy for those whose rebellion is forgiven, whose sin is put out of sight! Yes, what joy for those whose record the Lord has cleared of sin, whose lives are lived in complete honesty! When I refused to confess my sin, I was weak and miserable, and I groaned all day long. Day and night your hand of discipline was heavy on me. My strength evaporated like water in the summer heat. Interlude Finally, I confessed all my sins to you and stopped trying to hide them. I said to myself, "I will confess my rebellion to the Lord." And you forgave me! All my guilt is gone.

—Psalm 32:1–5 NLT

The more we allow God to change us, the greater our joy will be.

You have not seen Christ, but still you love him. You cannot see him now, but you believe in him. So you are filled with a joy that cannot be explained, a joy full of glory.
—1 Peter 1:8

3. Look up the following verses and write down what you learn about God's promise to satisfy us.

Psalm 22:26 – "The poor will eat and be satisfied. All who seek the Lord will praise him. Their hearts will rejoice with everlasting joy." NLT

may are hearts live forever

Psalm 81:10 – "For it was I, the Lord your God, who rescued you from the land of Egypt. Open your mouth wide, and I will fill it with good things." NLT

Lord always filling us with Goodness

4. Read the following verses. Then match the verse with what you learn about the first step toward joy—recognizing our inability to meet our needs apart from God.

_d_ Romans 6:23   a. Joy begins with a new heart and a new way of thinking.
_A_ Ezekiel 18:31   b. God's help is not a result of our own efforts.
_C_ Jeremiah 15:19   c. God's help is a free gift.
_b_ Ephesians 2:9   d. We must change our hearts and return to God to have joy.

As we grow closer to him, we become more like him. We forgive others (we're merciful). We change our outlook (we're pure in heart). We love others (we're peacemakers). We endure injustice (we're persecuted).

5. Read about this joyful process of transformation in 2 Corinthians 3:18 and fill in the blanks.

We are being ___*unveiled Faces*___ to be like ___*Lords glory*___. This change in us brings ever ___*Lords*___ glory, which comes from the ___*Lord Spirit*___.

It's no casual shift of attitude. It is a demolition of the old structure and a creation of the new. The more radical the change, the greater the joy. And it's worth every effort, for this is the joy of God.

6. The joy of salvation is incomparable. Read Psalm 32:1–5. Which of the following statements are true concerning the joy of repenting from sin and accepting Christ? Check all that apply.

☑ When we keep our sin to ourselves, we grow unhappy.
☑ God is willing to forgive us, consider us innocent, and pardon our wrongs.
☑ When God forgives our sins, we are happy.
❏ We are happy when our sins are hidden from God.

Remember, Matthew 5 is not a list of proverbs nor a compilation of independent sayings, but rather a step-by-step description of how God rebuilds the believer's heart.

The first step is to ask for help—to become "poor in spirit" and admit our need for a Savior. The next step is sorrow: "Blessed are those who mourn . . . " Those who mourn are those who know they are wrong and say they are sorry. No excuses. No justification. Just tears.

The first two steps are admittance of inadequacy and repentance for pride. The next step is the one of renewal: "Blessed are the meek . . . " Realization of weakness leads to the source of strength—God. And renewal comes when we become meek— when we give our lives to God to be his tool.

The first two beatitudes pass us through the fire of purification; the third places us in the hands of the Master.

The result of this process? Courage: " . . . they shall inherit the earth." No longer shall the earth and its fears dominate us, for we follow the one who dominates the earth.

THE BANDIT OF JOY

He was a professional thief. His name stirred fear as the desert wind stirs tumbleweeds. He terrorized the Wells Fargo stage line for thirteen years, roaring like a tornado in and out of the Sierra Nevadas, spooking the most rugged frontiersmen. In journals from San Francisco to New York, his name became synonymous with the danger of the frontier.

During his reign of terror between 1875 and 1883, he is credited with stealing the bags and the breath away from twenty-nine different stagecoach crews. And he did it all without firing a shot. His weapon was his reputation. His ammunition was intimidation.

A hood hid his face. No victim ever saw him. No artist ever sketched his features. No sheriff could ever track his trail. He never fired a shot or took a hostage.

He didn't have to. His presence was enough to paralyze.

Black Bart. A hooded bandit armed with a deadly weapon.

He reminds me of another thief—one who's still around. You know him. Oh you've never seen his face, either. You couldn't describe his voice or sketch his profile. But when he's near, you know it in a heartbeat.

If you've ever been in the hospital, you've felt the leathery brush of his hand against yours.

If you've ever sensed someone was following you, you've felt his cold breath down your neck.

If you've awakened late at night in a strange room, it was his husky whisper that stole your slumber.

You know him.

It was this thief who left your palms sweaty as you went for the job interview.

It was this con man who convinced you to swap your integrity for popularity.

And it was this scoundrel who whispered in your ear as you left the cemetery, "You may be next."

He's the Black Bart of the soul. He doesn't want your money. He doesn't want your diamonds. He won't go after your car. He wants something far more precious. He wants your peace of mind—your joy.

His name?

Fear.

His task is to take your courage and leave you timid and trembling. His modus operandi is to manipulate you with the mysterious, to taunt you with the unknown. Fear of death, fear of failure, fear of God, fear of tomorrow—his arsenal is vast. His goal? To create cowardly, joyless souls.

A thief comes to steal and kill and destroy, but I came to give life—life in all its fullness.

—John 10:10

7. The Bible identifies this thief who holds up Christians and makes us surrender our joy. Read John 10:10 and check all that apply.

A thief comes to . . .
- ☑ Steal
- ☑ Kill
- ☑ Destroy

But Jesus comes to . . .
- ☑ Give us life
- ☑ Give us life in all its fullness

Serve the Lord with joy; come before him with singing.

—Psalm 100:2

JESUS' PROMISE OF JOY

Joy begins with having the courage to believe that you are forgiven.

CHARACTER CREATES COURAGE

A legend from India tells about a mouse who was terrified of cats until a magician agreed to transform him into a cat. That resolved his fear . . . until he met a dog, so the magician changed him into a dog. Then mouse-turned-cat-turned-dog was content until he met a tiger—so, once again, the magician changed him into what he feared. But when the tiger came complaining that he had met a hunter, the magician refused to help. "I will make you into a mouse again, for though you have the body of a tiger, you still have the heart of a mouse."

Sound familiar? How many people do you know who have built a formidable exterior, only to tremble inside with fear? . . . We face our fears with force . . . or . . . we stockpile wealth. We seek security in things. We cultivate fame and seek status.

But do these approaches work?

Courage is an outgrowth of who we are. Exterior supports may temporarily sustain, but only inward character creates courage.

—*The Applause of Heaven*

8. Jesus' many promises are a source of joy to us. Read the following verses of promise. Why do we have reason to rejoice?

Acts 3:19 – "So you must change your hearts and lives! Come back to God, and he will forgive your sins. Then the Lord will send the time of rest."

repent and be blessed Baptized

Romans 3:26 – "And God gave Jesus to show today that he does what is right. God did this so he could judge rightly and so he could make right any person who has faith in Jesus."

by opening our hearts to Jesus and right choices

Romans 8:1 – "So now, those who are in Christ Jesus are not judged guilty."

praise God

Colossians 3:3 – "Your old sinful self has died, and your new life is kept with Christ in God."

my life is now hidden in christ in God. Praise the Lord!

Hebrews 8:12 – "I will forgive them for the wicked things they did, and I will not remember their sins anymore."

We're clean God by Christ in God.

If you are in Christ, these promises are not only a source of joy. They are also the foundations of true courage. You are guaranteed that your sins will be filtered through, hidden in, and screened out by the sacrifice of Jesus. When God looks at you, he doesn't see you; he sees the One who surrounds you. That means that failure is not a concern for you. Your victory is secure. How could you not be courageous?

Here is where the journey of joy begins to take shape: having the courage to believe God has forgiven you and wants to bestow joy on your life. Receiving his sacred delight begins with accepting his complete and total salvation.

9. What fears are keeping you from receiving God's forgiveness and beginning your journey of real joy?

by now with study my heart is jumping with joy with the The Holy Spirit with in

THE HEART OF THE MATTER

- Joy is the result of an extensive reconstruction of our hearts.
- The more we allow God to change us, the greater our joy will be.
- Fear tries to steal our joy away.
- Joy begins with having the courage to believe that you are forgiven.

Let's review your Bible memory verse for this week—it's Matthew 5:12. You can practice it by writing it out here.

rejoice and be glad as you have a reward waiting in heaven for you

Don't be sad, because the joy of the Lord will make you strong.
—Nehemiah 8:10b

The Heart of Jesus

Though they had set a quick pace, the two travelers were too glum for much conversation. They just wanted to get out of Jerusalem and get home as quickly as possible, putting all the recent events well behind them. When a third fell in with them, joining them on the road, they were a little annoyed when he'd tried to strike up some conversation. However courtesy required a certain degree of politeness, and they'd begun with the usual small talk. When the conversation turned to the Passover feast in Jerusalem, though, the men were depressed and almost sullen. They communicated their disappointment over Rome's execution of Jesus, and the downfall of all their hopes that the Messiah had finally come. The man questioned them about their understanding of Jesus' teaching and his subsequent death. Surprisingly, their fellow traveler was well acquainted with the Scriptures, and began to draw fascinating comparisons between the requirements of Messiah and the life of Jesus. By the time they reached Emmaus, the two travelers begged their companion to join them for a meal and finish their day's discussion. Their hearts were being stirred with something akin to hope, and they wanted to follow this study through to see where it brought them. Suddenly, the two from Emmaus felt a stirring of understanding—of recognition—this stranger was Jesus himself! And with this sudden illumination, all their previous glumness evaporated into shining joy.

—Luke 24:13–35

DAY THREE—THE STATE OF THE HEART

THE WELLSPRING OF LIFE

We tend to think of the heart as the seat of emotion. We speak of "heartthrobs," "heartaches," and "broken hearts."

But when Jesus said, "Blessed are the pure in heart," he was speaking in a different context. To Jesus' listeners, the heart was the totality of the inner person—the control tower, the cockpit. The heart was thought of as the seat of the character—the origin of desires, affections, perceptions, thoughts, reasoning, imagination, conscience, intentions, purpose, will, and faith.

Thus a proverb admonished, "Above all else, guard your heart, for it is the wellspring of life" (Prov. 4:23 NIV).

To the Hebrew mind, the heart is a freeway cloverleaf where all emotions and prejudices and wisdom converge. It is a switch house that receives freight cars loaded with moods, ideas, emotions, and convictions and puts them on the right track.

Our heart is like our control tower, where our thoughts and desires and faith are found.

1. Read what Jesus states in Matthew 15:18–19 and check all that apply concerning his descriptions of what originates from our hearts.

   - ☑ Evil thoughts
   - ☑ Murder
   - ☑ Adultery
   - ☐ Sexual sins
   - ☑ Stealing
   - ☑ Lying
   - ☑ Speaking evil of others

God will yet fill your mouth with laughter and your lips with shouts of joy.
—Job 8:21

But what people say with their mouths comes from the way they think; these are the things that make people unclean. Out of the mind come evil thoughts, murder, adultery, sexual sins, stealing, lying, and speaking evil of others.

—Matthew 15:18–19

2. Look up the following verses and write down what you learn about what Jesus says about the heart.

Matthew 6:21 – "Your heart will be where your treasure is."

With Jesus Christ son of God.
It hard to imagine we love and joy begives us all

Matthew 12:34–35 – "You snakes! You are evil people, so how can you say anything good? The mouth speaks the things that are in the heart. Good people have good things in their hearts, and so they say good things. But evil people have evil in their hearts, so they say evil things."

I say different then what I believe

THE HEART OF THE PROBLEM

The heart is the center of the spiritual life. If the fruit of a tree is bad, you don't try to fix the fruit; you treat the roots. And if a person's actions are evil, it's not enough to change habits; you have to go deeper. You have to go to the heart of the problem, which is the problem of the heart.

That is why the state of the heart is so critical. What's the state of yours?

When someone barks at you, do you <u>bark back</u> or bite your tongue? That depends on the state of your heart.

When your schedule is too tight or your to-do list too long, do you lose your cool or keep it? That depends on the state of your heart.

When you are offered a morsel of gossip marinated in slander, do you <u>turn it down</u> or pass it on? That depends on the state of your heart.

Do you see the bag lady on the street as a burden on society or as an <u>opportunity</u> for God? That, too, depends on the state of your heart.

The state of your heart dictates whether you harbor a grudge or give grace, seek self-pity or <u>seek Christ</u>, drink human misery or <u>taste God's mercy.</u>

THE GREENHOUSE OF THE HEART

Think for a moment of your heart as a greenhouse. . . . And you heart, like a greenhouse, has to be managed.

Consider for a moment your thoughts as seed. Some thoughts become flowers. Others become weeds. Sow seeds of hope and enjoy optimism. Sow seeds of doubt and expect insecurity . . .

The proof is everywhere you look. Ever wonder why some people have the Teflon capacity to resist negativism and remain patient, optimistic, and forgiving? Could it be that they have diligently sown seeds of goodness and are enjoying the harvest?

Ever wonder why others have such a sour outlook? Such a gloomy attitude? You would, too, if your heart were a greenhouse of weeds and thorns.

—*Just Like Jesus*

3. What are some good barometers of the condition of our hearts? Check all that apply.

- ☑ Temper
- ❑ Gossip
- ❑ Charity
- ❑ Mercy

4. Read the following verses. Then match the verse with what you learn about the importance of the heart.

A. Luke 16:15 — a. Our heart prompts us to give in God's service.
C. Acts 8:21–22 — b. We understand truth with our heart.
D. 2 Corinthians 9:7 — c. We can't serve God when our heart is not right.
a. Ephesians 1:18 — d. God knows what's really in our hearts.

Jesus' statement rings true: "Blessed are the pure in heart, for they shall see God" (NIV).

Note the order of this beatitude: first, purify the heart, then you will see God. We usually reverse the order. We try to change the inside by altering the outside.

5. The Bible reminds us purity is an inside job. God must change us from the inside out. Fill in the blanks concerning David's prayer in Psalm 51:10.

<u>Create</u> in me a <u>pure</u> <u>heart</u>, God, and make my <u>spirit</u> right again.

God is strong and can help you not to fall. He can bring you before his glory without any wrong in you and can give you great joy.
—**Jude 24**

Who would concentrate on the outside when the problem is on the inside?

Do you really want to know? A homemaker battles with depression. What is the solution suggested by some well-meaning friend? Buy a new dress. A husband is involved in an affair that brings him as much guilt as it does adventure. The solution? Change peer groups. Hang out with people who don't make you feel guilty! A young professional is plagued with loneliness. His obsession with success has left him with no friends. His boss gives him an idea: Change your style. Get a new haircut. Flash some cash.

Case after case of treating the outside while ignoring the inside—polishing the case while ignoring the interior. And what is the result? The homemaker gets a new dress, and the depression disappears . . . for a day, maybe. Then the shadow returns. The husband finds a bunch of buddies who sanction his adultery. The result? Peace . . . until the crowd is gone. Then the guilt is back. The young professional gets a new look and the people notice . . . until the styles change. Then he has to scurry out and buy more stuff so he won't appear outdated.

The exterior polished; the interior corroding. The outside altered; the inside faltering. One thing is clear: Cosmetic changes are only skin deep.

By now you could write the message of the beatitude. It's a clear one: You change your life by changing your heart.

6. Read Matthew 7:13–14 and respond to the following:

How does Jesus describe the two roads?

Enter, through narrow gate
The wide in the road leads to destruction

Many people long to be happy in life by pursuing their own way—which road does Jesus say they are traveling? (v. 13)

the wide

Few people learn the secret to being joyful in Christ—which road does Jesus say they are traveling? (v. 14)

narrow gate.

MAKE A CHANGE

How do you change your heart? Jesus gave the plan on the mountain. Back away from the Beatitudes once more and view them in sequence.

The first step is an admission of poverty: "Blessed are the poor in spirit . . . " God's gladness is not received by those who earn it, but by those who admit they don't deserve it.

The second step is sorrow: "Blessed are those who mourn . . . " Joy comes to those who are sincerely sorry for their sin. We discover gladness when we leave the prison of pride and repent of our rebellion.

Sorrow is followed by meekness. The meek are those who are willing to be used by God. Amazed that God would save them, they are just as surprised that God could use them. They are a junior-high-school clarinet section playing with the Boston Pops. They don't tell the maestro how to conduct; they're just thrilled to be part of the concert.

Create in me a pure heart, God, and make my spirit right again.

—Psalm 51:10

You cannot fix the root of any problem by making external changes.

You can change your life by having a changed heart.

"Enter through the narrow gate. The gate is wide and the road is wide that leads to hell, and many people enter through that gate. But the gate is small and the road is narrow that leads to true life. Only a few people find that road."

—Matthew 7:13–14

The important things are living right with God, peace, and joy in the Holy Spirit.

—Romans 14:17b

7. God wants us to experience euphoria when he uses us to make a difference in someone else's life. Read the following verses and write down what you learn concerning the joy Paul and the disciples felt as they influenced others for Christ.

1 Thessalonians 2:19 – "You are our hope, our joy, and the crown we will take pride in when our Lord Jesus Christ comes."

3 John 4 – "Nothing gives me greater joy than to hear that my children are following the way of truth."

truth

8. Why does serving God through serving others make us feel so good?

Gods feeling in us want to do good for others

The result of the first three steps? Hunger. Never have you seen anything like what is happening! You admit sin—you get saved. You confess weakness—you receive strength. You say you are sorry—you find forgiveness. It's a zany, unpredictable path full of pleasant encounters. For once in your life you're addicted to something positive—something that gives life instead of draining it. And you want more. Then comes mercy. The more you receive, the more you give. You find it easier to give grace because you realize you have been given so much. What has been done to you is nothing compared to what you did to God.

For the first time in your life, you have found a permanent joy, a joy that is not dependent upon your whims and actions. It's a joy from God, a joy no one can take away from you.

A sacred delight is placed in your heart.

It is sacred because only God can grant it.

It is a delight because you would never expect it.

And though your heart isn't perfect, it isn't rotten. And though you aren't invincible, at least you're plugged in. And you can bet that he who made you knows just how to purify you—from the inside out.

9. Although many experiences and relationships make us considerably happy, God alone can grant true joy. Which of statements below are true concerning joy, and which ones are false? Mark your answers True (T) or False (F). Use the Bible verses below to help you answer.

T Jesus is worth getting excited about. (Matthew 13:44–46)
F The announcement of Jesus' birth brought forth mild anticipation. (Luke 2:10)
T Jesus' teachings should bring joy. (John 15:11)
F Jesus wants to share only part of his joy with his followers. (John 17:13)

THE HEART OF THE MATTER

- Our heart is like our control tower, where our thoughts and desires and faith are found.
- You cannot fix the root of any problem by making external changes.
- You can change your life by having a changed heart.
- Real joy is not dependant on your actions or emotions.

In order to review your memory verse for the week, fill in the blanks:

" _rejoice_ and be _Glad_ , for you have a _reward in heaven_ waiting for you in _heaven_ ." —Matthew 5:12

The master answered, "You did well. You are a good and loyal servant. Because you were loyal with small things, I will let you care for much greater things. Come and share my joy with me."
—Matthew 25:21

The Heart of Jesus

He had followed every rule, every tradition. He had met every requirement. His clothes fit every standard of stylish righteousness, right down to the long blue tasseled fringe that dusted the ground as he walked. He attended morning and evening prayers faithfully. He had memorized great portions of the Scriptures. He engaged in rousing discussions of the Law of Moses with his colleagues. He had been elected to the ruling leaders of the faith. People nodded respectfully whenever he passed by, and he was used to being given preference wherever he went Yet the words of Jesus had stung Nicodemas deeply. He and his associates had been reprimanded, called a brood of vipers and whitewashed tombs. How had Jesus known of his own emptiness? His restlessness? His dissatisfaction? Though he kept up appearance, Nicodemas knew no joy. So he had arranged to meet this traveling Teacher discreetly. Under cover of darkness, he plied Jesus with all of his questions. And Nicodemas was astonished to discover that not only did Jesus hold all the answers he sought, he also promised him joy.

—John 3:1–3

DAY FOUR—THE KINGDOM OF THE ABSURD

THE WONDER OF JOY

Let's now consider the case of Sarai. She is in her golden years, but God promises her a son. She gets excited. She visits the maternity shop and buys a few dresses. She plans her shower and remodels her tent . . . but no son. She eats a few birthday cakes and blows out a lot of candles . . . still no son. She goes through a decade of wall calendars . . . still no son.

Finally, fourteen years later, when Abram is pushing a century of years and Sarai ninety . . . when the wallpaper in the nursery is faded and the baby furniture is several seasons out of date . . . when the topic of the promised child brings sighs and tears and long looks into a silent sky . . . God pays them a visit and tells them they had better select a name for their new son.

Abram and Sarai have the same response: laughter. They laugh partly because it is too good to happen and partly because it might. They laugh because they have given up hope, and hope born anew is always funny before it is real.

They laugh at the lunacy of it all.

Abram looks over at Sarai—toothless and snoring in her rocker, head back and mouth wide open, as fruitful as a pitted prune and just as wrinkled. And he cracks up. He tries to contain it, but he can't. He has always been a sucker for a good joke.

Sarai is just as amused. When she hears the news, a cackle escapes before she can contain it. She mumbles something about her husband's needing a lot more than what he's got and then laughs again.

They laugh because that is what you do when someone says he can do the impossible. They laugh a little at God, and a lot with God—for God is laughing, too. Then, with the smile still on his face, he gets busy doing what he does best—the unbelievable.

He changes a few things—beginning with their names. Abram, the father of one, will now be Abraham, the father of a multitude. Sarai, the barren one, will now be Sarah, the mother.

But I will still be glad in the Lord; I will rejoice in God my Savior.
—Habakkuk 3:18

God is not stopped by the impossible.

The Lord cared for Sarah as he had said and did for her what he had promised. Sarah became pregnant and gave birth to a son for Abraham in his old age. Everything happened at the time God had said it would.

—Genesis 21:1–2

We know that in everything God works for the good of those who love him. They are the people he called, because that was his plan.

—Romans 8:28

You can decide to be joyful, even if the odds are against you.

You changed my sorrow into dancing. You took away my clothes of sadness, and clothed me in happiness.

—Psalm 30:11

1. Read Genesis 21:1–2. How does this story end on a joyful note?

   Sarah had her baby a Boy Isaac.

2. Some situations make it seem difficult, if not impossible, for us to find joy. Yet, Scripture reminds us that God majors in the impossible. Look up the following verses and write down what you learn about the impossible.

   Mark 9:23 – "Jesus said to the father, 'You said, "If you can!" All things are possible for the one who believes.'"

   Luke 1:37 – "God can do anything!" *nothing impossible with God.*

   Luke 18:27 – "Jesus answered, 'God can do things that are not possible for people to do.'"

   impossible with men is possible with God.

   Sometimes we have to see it to believe it. We need to see people who've been through the stuff of life and come out joyful, rejoicing in the wonder of God. These flesh-and-blood examples inspire us. Motivate us. Convince us. We realize it is possible to make the decision for joy despite the odds against us.

3. Read Romans 8:28 and fill in the blanks of this verse about our confident anticipation to see God move despite our seemingly absurd situations.

   We know that in *all things* God works for the *good* of those who *love* him.

BITTER OR BETTER?

She has every reason to be bitter.

Though talented, she went unrecognized for years. Prestigious opera circles closed their ranks when she tried to enter. American critics ignored her compelling voice. She was repeatedly rejected for parts for which she easily qualified. It was only after she went to Europe and won the hearts of tough-to-please European audiences that stateside opinion leaders acknowledged her talent.

Not only has her professional life been a battle, her personal life also has been marked by challenge. She is the mother of two handicapped children, one of whom is severely retarded. Years ago, in order to escape the pace of New York City, she purchased a home on Martha's Vineyard.

It burned to the ground two days before she was to move in.

Professional rejection. Personal setbacks. Perfect soil for the seeds of bitterness. A receptive field for the roots of resentment. But in this case, anger found no home.

Her friends don't call her bitter; they call her "Bubbles."

Beverly Sills. Internationally acclaimed opera singer. Retired director of the New York City Opera.

Her phrases are sugared with laughter. Her face is softened with serenity. Upon interviewing her, Mike Wallace stated that "she is one of the most impressive—if not the most impressive—ladies I've ever interviewed."

How can a person handle such professional rejection and personal trauma and still be known as Bubbles? "I choose to be cheerful," she says. "Years ago I knew I had little or no choice about success, circumstances, or even happiness; but I knew I could choose to be cheerful."

4. Read Ephesians 4:26–32. What does this passage say about combating the "seeds of bitterness" and the "roots of resentment"? Fill in the blanks below.

Be sure to stop being _angry_ before the end of the day.
Don't give the devil a _foot hold_ to _____ you.
Don't say _unwholesome_ things.
Don't be _____ or angry or _____.
Never _____ angrily or _____ things to _____ others.
Be kind and _compassionate_ each other.
forgiving each other.

5. Circumstances often affect our joy—but Scripture tells us that doesn't have to be the case. Which of the following statements are true concerning our ability to have joy amid trouble, and which ones are false? Mark your answers True (T) or False (F). Use the Bible verses below to help you answer.

_T_ We can have joy in our troubles because other Christians comfort us. (2 Corinthians 7:4)
_F_ God doesn't expect us to always be joyful. (1 Thessalonians 5:16)
_T_ We should be filled with joy when we have troubles. (James 1:2)
_T_ Good things can come out of our times of testing. (James 1:3)

FOR BETTER OR WORSE

"We have prayed for healing. God has not given it. But he has blessed us."

Glyn spoke slowly. Partly because of her conviction. Partly because of her disease. Her husband, Don, sat in the chair next to her. The three of us had come together to plan a funeral—hers. And now, with that task done, with the hymns selected and the directions given, Glyn spoke.

"He has given us strength we did not know. He gave it when we needed it and not before." Her words were slurred, but clear. Her eyes were moist, but confident.

I wondered what it would be like to have my life taken from me at age forty-five. I wondered what it would be like to say good-bye to my children and spouse. I wondered what it would be like to be a witness to my own death.

"God has given us peace in our pain. He covers us all the time. Even when we are out of control, he is still there."

6. Read Romans 8:38–39. Based on what you just read, what will separate us from God's presence?

nothing

_____

It had been a year since Glyn and Don had learned of Glyn's condition—amyotrophic lateral sclerosis (Lou Gehrig's disease). The cause and the cure remain a mystery. But the result doesn't. Muscle strength and mobility steadily deteriorate, leaving only the mind and the faith.

And it was the coming together of Glyn's mind and faith that caused me to realize I was doing more than planning a funeral. I was beholding holy jewels she had quarried out of the mine of despair.

"We can use any tragedy as a stumbling block or a stepping stone. I hope this will not cause my family to be bitter. I hope I can be an example that God is wanting us to trust in the good times and the bad. For if we don't trust when times are tough, we don't trust at all," she said.

Don held her hand. He wiped her tears. He wiped his own.

"Who are these two?" I asked myself as I watched him touch a tissue to her cheek. "Who are these, who, on the edge of life's river, can look across with such faith?"

The moment was solemn and sweet. I said little. One is not bold in the presence of the sacred.

GUARD YOUR ATTITUDE
"Lord, don't you care that my sister has left me alone to do all the work?" (Luke 11:40 . . .

Martha's life is cluttered. She needed a break. "Martha, Martha, you are worried and upset about many things," the Master explained to her. "Only one thing is important. Mary has chosen [it]" (Luke 11:41–42).

What had Mary chosen? She had chosen to sit at the feet of Christ. God is more pleased with the quiet attention of a sincere servant than the noisy service of a sour one . . .

What matters more than the type of service is the heart behind the service. A bad attitude spoils the gift we leave on the altar for God.

—*He Still Moves Stones*

When you are angry, do not sin, and be sure to stop being angry before the end of the day. Do not give the devil a way to defeat you. Those who are stealing must stop stealing and start working. They should earn an honest living for themselves. Then they will have something to share with those who are poor. When you talk, do not say harmful things, but say what people need—words that will help others become stronger. Then what you say will do good to those who listen to you. And do not make the Holy Spirit sad. The Spirit is God's proof that you belong to him. God gave you the Spirit to show that God will make you free when the final day comes. Do not be bitter or angry or mad. Never shout angrily or say things to hurt others. Never do anything evil. Be kind and loving to each other, and forgive each other just as God forgave you in Christ.

—*Ephesians 4:26–32*

So you will go out with joy and be led out in peace. The mountains and hills will burst into song before you, and all the trees in the fields will clap their hands.

—*Isaiah 55:12*

Yes, I am sure that neither death, nor life, nor angels, nor ruling spirits, nothing now, nothing in the future, no powers, nothing above us, nothing below us, nor anything else in the whole world will ever be able to separate us from the love of God that is in Christ Jesus our Lord.

—Romans 8:38–39

My friends, do not be surprised at the terrible trouble which now comes to test you. Do not think that something strange is happening to you. But be happy that you are sharing in Christ's sufferings so that you will be happy and full of joy when Christ comes again in glory.

—1 Peter 4:12–13

God's gift of delight is always given to those who know they are needy.

Be full of joy in the Lord always. I will say again, be full of joy.
—Philippians 4:4

7. Joy often buries itself deep within despair. Consequently, we must make joy a willful decision and not rely on it as an emotion. Based on 1 Peter 4:12–13, which of the following statements are true concerning suffering? Check all that apply.

- ☐ Trouble comes to test us.
- ☑ We ought to be surprised when Christians have trials.
- ☐ Trials help us grow closer to Jesus by sharing in his sufferings.
- ☐ When Christ comes, we will once again be happy and full of joy.

HELD TOGETHER BY JOY

"I have everything I need for joy!" Robert Reed said. "Amazing!" I thought.

His hands are twisted and his feet are useless. He can't bathe himself. He can't feed himself. He can't brush his teeth, comb his hair, or put on his underwear. His shirts are held together by strips of Velcro. His speech drags like a worn-out audiocassette.

Robert has cerebral palsy.

The disease keeps him from driving a car, riding a bike, and going for a walk. But it didn't keep him from graduating from high school or attending Abilene Christian University, from which he graduated with a degree in Latin. Having cerebral palsy didn't keep him from teaching at a St. Louis junior college or from venturing overseas on five mission trips.

And Robert's disease didn't prevent him from becoming a missionary in Portugal.

He moved to Lisbon, alone, in 1972. There he rented a hotel room and began studying Portuguese. He found a restaurant owner who would feed him after the rush hour and a tutor who would instruct him in the language.

Then he stationed himself daily in a park, where he distributed brochures about Christ. Within six years he led seventy people to the Lord, one of whom became his wife, Rosa.

I heard Robert speak recently. I watched other men carry him in his wheelchair onto the platform. I watched them lay a Bible in his lap. I watched his stiff fingers force open the pages. And I watched people in the audience wipe away tears of admiration from their faces. Robert could have asked for sympathy or pity, but he did just the opposite. He held his bent hand up in the air and boasted, "I have everything I need for joy."

His shirts are held together by Velcro, but his life is held together by joy.

8. Although our own personal trials may vary—emotionally, physically, financially, relationally—we all need to be "held together by joy" at those times we fear we are falling apart. Joy should be enough, but what do we often convince ourselves we need in order to be happy? Check all that apply.

- ☑ Material possessions
- ☑ Relational harmony
- ☐ Career fulfillment
- ☑ Good health
- ☐ Popularity
- ☐ Financial stability

The jewel of joy is given to the impoverished spirits, not the affluent. God's delight is received upon surrender, not awarded upon conquest. Those who taste God's presence have declared spiritual bankruptcy and are aware of their spiritual crisis. Their cupboards are bare. Their pockets are empty. Their options are gone.

Oh, the irony of God's delight—born in the parched soil of destitution rather than the fertile ground of achievement.

9. Personal trials and problems actually put us in a good position to receive God's greatest blessing. Read Psalm 126:5–6 and match the statements below with the correct answer.

b "Those who cry as they plant crops . . ."
   a. will still be crying at harvest.
   b. will sing at harvest time.
   c. will be sorry they ever trusted God.

A "Those who cry as they carry out the seeds . . ."
   a. will return singing and carrying bundles of grain.
   b. will never be happy again.
   c. will never see the end of their problems.

> *Those who cry as they plant crops will sing at harvest time. Those who cry as they carry out the seeds will return singing and carrying bundles of grain.*
>
> —Psalm 126:5–6

THE HEART OF THE MATTER

- **God is not stopped by the impossible.**
- **You can decide to be joyful, even if the odds are against you.**
- **God's gift of delight is always given to those who know they are needy.**

This week's Bible memorization verse has been Matthew 5:12. Take a few moments to review it again here by writing it out on the lines provided.

rejoice and be Glad for you have a reward waiting for you in heaven.

The Heart of Jesus

Peter's feet pounded the dust of the path. When he and John had started out, they had speculated out loud together over the strange news that the women had brought. The body gone. Could the Roman soldiers have taken their Lord away? An angel's announcement. Could Jesus really be alive again? What if it was true! At that sudden thought, John had picked up his pace. Peter's enthusiasm equaled John's but he couldn't match the younger man's speed. He caught up to John, puffing outside the entrance to the tomb. The stone certainly had been rolled away. Peter barreled through the door, and slid to a stop before the stone shelf. The wrappings were there, undisturbed, but they were empty! Soldiers wouldn't have taken such care, if they had stolen Jesus' body. Maybe the women were right! Then a heavenly light struck their eyes, and they too received angelic confirmation. Jesus was alive! Though he had just run all the way to the tomb, joy gave Peter's feet wings for the return trip.

—John 20:3–10

DAY FIVE—THE APPLAUSE OF HEAVEN

ALMOST HOME

I'm almost home. After five days, four hotel beds, eleven restaurants, and twenty-two cups of coffee, I'm almost home. After eight airplane seats, five airports, two delays, one book, and 513 packages of peanuts, I'm almost home.

The plane resonates under me. A baby cries behind me. Businessmen converse around me. Cool air blows from a hole above me. But all that matters is what is before me—home.

> *You will teach me how to live a holy life. Being with you will fill me with joy; at your right hand I will find pleasure forever.*
>
> —Psalm 16:11

Heaven is our reward.

Home. It was my first thought when I awoke this morning. It was my first thought when I stepped down from the last podium. It was my first thought when I said good-bye to my last host at the last airport.

There is a leap of the heart as I exit the plane. I almost get nervous as I walk up the ramp. I step past people. I grip my satchel. My stomach tightens. My palms sweat. I walk into the lobby like an actor walking onto a stage. The curtain is lifted, and the audience stands in a half-moon. Most of the people see that I'm not the one they want and look past me.

But from the side I hear the familiar shriek of two little girls. "Daddy!" I turn and see them—faces scrubbed, standing on chairs, bouncing up and down in joy as the man in their life walks toward them. Jenna stops bouncing just long enough to clap. She applauds! I don't know who told her to do that, but you can bet I'm not going to tell her to stop . . . faces of home.

That is what makes the promise at the end of the Beatitudes so compelling: "Rejoice and be glad, because great is your reward in heaven." What is our reward? Home.

1. Jesus reminds us if we obey what he says to do in Matthew 5, then we will rejoice and enjoy great reward in heaven. Look up the following verses and write down what you learn about how knowing and obeying God's word as it relates to joy.

    I take joy in doing your will, my God, for your law is written on my heart.
    —Psalm 40:8 NLT

    Psalm 19:8 – "The commandments of the Lord are right, bringing joy to the heart. The commands of the Lord are clear, giving insight to life." NLT

    _____

    _____

    Psalm 119:111 – "I will follow your rules forever, because they make me happy."

    _____

    _____

    Psalm 119:162 – "I rejoice in your word like one who finds a great treasure." NLT

    _____

    _____

The most miserable person on earth is a disobedient Christian. Experiencing Jesus becomes bittersweet for that person—longing to enjoy fellowship with Christ, yet still lingering outside his door because of sin. What a difference it makes to know there is a heavenly reward for obedience to Christ!

You love right and hate evil, so God has chosen you from among your friends; he has set you apart with much joy.
—Hebrews 1:9

2. Read Psalm 40:8 and Hebrews 1:9. Fill in the blanks about what you learn concerning the joy of obedience.

    I _____ _____ in doing _____ _____, my God, for your _____ is _____ on my _____. (Psalm 40:8)

    You _____ right and _____ evil, so God has _____ you and has set you apart with much _____. (Hebrews 1:9)

THE BEST IS YET TO COME

The Book of Revelation could be entitled the Book of Homecoming, for in it we are given a picture of our heavenly home.

So God brought his people out with joy, his chosen ones with singing.
—Psalm 105:43

> *Then I saw a new heaven and a new earth, for the first heaven and the first earth had passed away, and there was no longer any sea. I saw the Holy City, the new Jerusalem, coming down out of heaven from God, prepared as a bride beautifully dressed for her husband. And I heard a loud voice from the throne saying, "Now the dwelling of God is with men, and he will live with them. They will be his people, and God himself will be with them and be their God. He will wipe every tear from their eyes. There will be no more death or mourning or crying or pain, for the old order of things has passed away. He who was seated on the throne said, "I am making everything new!"* –Revelation 21:1–5 NIV

The promise of heaven brings us hope today.

3. As you read this passage above, underline each time you see the word or idea of "new."

_____

_____

4. What particular image in this description of heaven's home brings a smile to your face?

_____

_____

All these great people died in faith. They did not get the things that God promised his people, but they saw them coming far in the future and were glad. They said they were like visitors and strangers on earth. When people say such things, they show they are looking for a country that will be their own. If they had been thinking about the country they had left, they could have gone back. But they were waiting for a better country—a heavenly country. So God is not ashamed to be called their God, because he has prepared a city for them.

—Hebrews 11:13–16

In this final mountaintop encounter, God pulls back the curtain and allows the warrior to peek into the homeland. When given the task of writing down what he sees, John chooses the most beautiful comparison earth has to offer. The Holy City, John says, is like "a bride beautifully dressed for her husband."

A bride. A commitment robed in elegance. "I'll be with you forever." Tomorrow bringing hope to today. Promised purity faithfully delivered. When you read that our heavenly home is similar to a bride, tell me, doesn't it make you want to go home?

Because the Lamb at the center of the throne will be their shepherd. He will lead them to springs of water that give life. And God will wipe away every tear from their eyes.

—Revelation 7:17

5. It's no coincidence that the Bible concludes with the Book of Revelation. The hope of a better future has kept joy alive for centuries. Now read Hebrews 11:13–16. Check all the following statements that apply to what the passage says concerning our future hope.

❏ We are glad when we keep our eyes on what is coming far in the future.
❏ Christians feel "right at home" on earth.
❏ Christians are more like visitors in a strange country.
❏ Heaven will be our own home—a better home.
❏ God has prepared a city for us.

6. According to Revelation 7:17, what will God do for us in heaven?

_____

_____

When I was a young man, I had plenty of people to wipe away my tears. I had two big sisters who put me under their wings. I had a dozen or so aunts and uncles. I had a mother who worked nights as a nurse and days as a mother—exercising both professions with tenderness. I even had a brother three years my elder who felt sorry for me occasionally.

But when I think about someone wiping away my tears, I think about Dad. His hands were callused and tough, his fingers short and stubby. And when my father wiped away a tear, he seemed to wipe it away forever. There was something in his touch that took away more than the drop of hurt from my cheek. It also took away my fear.

John says that someday God will wipe away your tears. The same hands that stretched the heavens will touch your cheeks. The same hands that formed the mountains will caress your face. The same hands that curled in agony as the Roman spike cut through will someday cup your face and brush away your tears. Forever.

You will receive your salvation with joy as you would draw water from a well.

—Isaiah 12:3

Heaven will be a place of rejoicing forever.

And you will be given a very great welcome into the eternal kingdom of our Lord and Savior Jesus Christ.

—2 Peter 1:11

This is what God told us: God has given us eternal life, and this life is in his Son.

—1 John 5:11

Brothers and sisters, we want you to know about those Christians who have died so you will not be sad, as others who have no hope. We believe that Jesus died and that he rose again. So, because of him, God will raise with Jesus those who have died.

—1 Thessalonians 4:13–14

Be full of joy at that time, because you have a great reward waiting for you in heaven.

—Luke 6:23a

When you think of a world where there will be no reason to cry, ever, doesn't it make you want to go home?

Jesus understands that we are human. Imperfect. Some days we can't seem to make the choice to be joyful. We may be overwhelmed. Grieving. Confused. Hurting. However, in heaven, there will be no such thing as "good days" and "bad days." We will rejoice forever.

7. Read the following verses. Then match the verse with what you learn about joy in heaven.

___ Psalm 92:8   a. We will be with the Lord forever.
___ Isaiah 6:2–3   b. We will honor God forever.
___ 1 Thessalonians 4:17   c. We will receive a great welcome into heaven.
___ 2 Peter 1:11   d. Our life is eternal in heaven because of Jesus.
___ 1 John 5:11   e. Creatures in heaven will cry out, "Holy!"

ETERNAL JOY

"There will be no more death . . ." John declares. Can you imagine it? A world with no hearses or morgues or cemeteries or tombstones? Can you imagine a world with no spades of dirt thrown on caskets? No names chiseled into marble? No funerals? No black dresses? No black wreaths?

In the next world, John says, "good-bye" will never be spoken.

Tell me, doesn't that make you want to go home?

8. Read 1 Thessalonians 4:13–14. Which of the following statements are true regarding our joy despite the reality of death, and which ones are false? Mark your answers True (T) or False (F).

___ Hopelessness is out of place at a Christian's funeral.
___ Jesus is proof God will also raise us from the dead.
___ We can't be sure God will raise Christians from the dead.
___ God promises to raise Christians from the dead.

The most hopeful words of that passage from Revelation are those of God's resolve: "I am making everything new."

It's hard to see things grow old. The town in which I grew up is growing old. I was there recently. Some of the buildings are boarded up. Some of the houses are torn down. Some of my teachers are retired; some are buried.

I wish I could make it all new again. I wish I could blow the dust off the streets. I wish I could walk through the familiar neighborhood, and wave at the familiar faces, and pet the familiar dogs, and hit one more home run in the Little League park. I wish I could walk down Main Street and call out the merchants that have retired and open the doors that have been boarded up. I wish I could make everything new . . . but I can't.

But God can. "He restores my soul," (Ps. 23:3). He doesn't reform; he restores. He doesn't camouflage the old; he restores the new. The Master Builder will pull out the original plan and restore it. He will restore the vigor. He will restore the energy. He will restore the hope. He will restore the soul.

When you see how this world grows stooped and weary and then read of a home where everything is made new, tell me, doesn't that make you want to go home?

9. How does having confidence in God's promise of heaven shore up your joy in this life?

_____

_____

10. For Jesus, the joy of returning to his Father and glorifying him was enough to get him through the Cross. Read Hebrews 12:2 and fill in the blanks.

    Jesus accepted the _____ of the Cross as if it were _____ because of the _____ that God put before him. And now he is _____ at the right side of _____ throne.

THE INCOMPARABLE VALUE OF JOY

What would you give in exchange for a home like the one mentioned above? Would you really rather have a few possessions on earth than eternal possessions in heaven? Would you really choose a life of slavery to passion over a life of freedom? Would you honestly give up all of your heavenly mansions for a second-rate sleazy motel on earth?

"Great," Jesus said, "is your reward in heaven." He must have smiled when he said that line. His eyes must have danced, and his hand must have pointed skyward.

For he should know. It was his idea. It was his home.

11. Earthly rewards and honors—diplomas, bonuses, promotions and the like—fail to compare to the value of Jesus' reward. Read Revelation 22:12 and fill in the blanks regarding Jesus' heavenly reward.

    Listen! I am coming _____! I will bring my _____ with me, and I will _____ each of you for what you have _____.

Experiencing the joy of Jesus makes us different. It affects us. Knowing what we know, seeing what we've seen, it just doesn't make sense to choose fleeting moments of earthly pleasures over eternal joy. It no longer seems appealing to grow bitter over our hurts instead of better. We find ourselves exactly where the Beatitudes said we would be—hungry for more of Jesus.

12. Words can be very persuasive. However, as we've studied this week, those who walk the talk are convincing. Based on Habakkuk 3:17–18, what might need to change in your attitude (not your circumstances) to make an even more convincing case for joy?

    _____

    _____

You may not have noticed it, but you are closer to home than ever before. Each moment is a step taken. Each breath is a page turned. Each day is a mile marked, a mountain climbed. You are closer to home than you've ever been. Before you know it, your appointed arrival time will come; you'll descend the ramp and enter the City. You'll see faces that are waiting for you. You'll hear your name spoken by those who love you. And, maybe, just maybe—in the back, behind the crowds—the One who would rather die than live without you will remove his pierced hands from his heavenly robe and applaud.

THE HEART OF THE MATTER

- ❦ **Heaven is our reward.**
- ❦ **The promise of heaven brings us hope today.**
- ❦ **Heaven will be a place of rejoicing forever.**
- ❦ **Heaven will be our home.**

THE WINNER'S CIRCLE

For all we don't know about the next life, this much is certain. The day Christ comes will be a day of reward. Those who went unknown on earth will be known in heaven. Those who never heard the cheers of men will hear the cheers of angels. Those who missed the blessing of a father will hear the blessing of their heavenly Father. The small will be great. The forgotten will be remembered. The unnoticed will be crowned and the faithful will be honored.

The winner's circle isn't reserved for a handful of the elite, but for a heaven full of God's children who "will receive the crown of life that God has promised to those who love him" (James 1:12 NIV).

—*When Christ Comes*

Let us look only to Jesus, the One who began our faith and who makes it perfect. He suffered death on the cross. But he accepted the shame as if it were nothing because of the joy that God put before him. And now he is sitting at the right side of God's throne.

—Hebrews 12:2

Heaven will be our home.

Listen! I am coming soon! I will bring my reward with me, and I will repay each one of you for what you have done.

—Revelation 22:12

Fig trees may not grow figs, and there may be no grapes on the vines. There may be no olives growing and no food growing in the fields. There may be no sheep in the pens and no cattle in the barns. But I will still be glad in the Lord; I will rejoice in God my Savior.

—Habakkuk 3:17–18

I pray that the God who gives hope will fill you with much joy and peace while you trust in him. Then your hope will overflow by the power of the Holy Spirit.

—Romans 15:13

One more chance to review your memory verse for this week. Write out Matthew 5:12 below.

_____

_____

_____

The Heart of Jesus

The cell was unpleasant—dank, musty, and infested. The soldiers who had shackled Paul and Silas had not been especially gentle, and the heavy chains prevented a body from finding a comfortable position in which to rest. The evening's chill was seeping through the walls. With aching muscles and weary heads, the two men faced a long night of darkness. But Paul was not a man to wallow in his circumstances. He was not beaten down and hopeless. In the midst of the prison cell in Philippi, he and Silas lift up prayers to their Savior. And when God meets them there in the cell, they experience such joy that their surroundings fade away. Ushered into worship, two rusty voices take up a tune, and soon the whole prison is filled with songs of praises to Jesus. Paul and Silas sing for the joy of their salvation.

—Acts 16:25

FOR FURTHER READING

Selections throughout this lesson were taken from *The Applause of Heaven.*

I am coming to you now. But I pray these things while I am still in the world so that these followers can have all of my joy in them.
—**John 17:13**

[1] Walter Burkhardt, *Tell the Next Generation* (Ramsey, NJ: Paulist, 1982), 80, quoted in Brennan Manning, *Lion and Lamb* (Old Tappan, NJ: Chosen, Revell, 1986), 129.

Experiencing the Love of Jesus

*C*ould two people be more different?

He is looked up to. She is looked down on.

He is a church leader. She is a streetwalker.

He makes a living promoting standards. She's made a living breaking them.

He's hosting the party. She's crashing it.

Ask the other residents of Capernaum to point out the more pious of the two, and they'll pick Simon. Why, after all, he's a student of theology, a man of the cloth. Anyone would pick him. Anyone, that is, except Jesus. Jesus knew them both. And Jesus would pick the woman. Jesus does pick the woman. And, what's more, he tells Simon why.

Not that Simon wants to know. His mind is elsewhere. *How did this whore get in my house?* He doesn't know whom to yell at first, the woman or the servant who let her in. After all, this dinner is a formal affair. Invitation only. Upper crust. Crème de la crème. Who let the riffraff in?

"Simon," he said to the Pharisee, "I have something to say to you."

"All right, Teacher," Simon replied, "go ahead."

Then Jesus told him this story: "A man loaned money to two people—five hundred pieces of silver to one and fifty pieces to the other. But neither of them could repay him, so he kindly forgave them both, canceling their debts. Who do you suppose loved him more after that?" Simon answered, "I suppose the one for whom he canceled the larger debt."

"That's right," Jesus said. Then he turned to the woman and said to Simon, "Look at this woman kneeling here. When I entered your home, you didn't offer me water to wash the dust from my feet, but she has washed them with her tears and wiped them with her hair. You didn't give me a kiss of greeting, but she has kissed my feet again and again from the time I first came in. You neglected the courtesy of olive oil to anoint my head, but she has anointed my feet with rare perfume. I tell you, her sins—and they are many—have been forgiven, so she has shown me much love. But a person who is forgiven little shows only little love" (Luke 7:40–47 NLT).

Simon invites Jesus to his house but treats him like an unwanted step-uncle. No customary courtesies. No kiss of greeting. No washing his feet. No oil for his head.

You'd think Simon of all people would show such love. Is he not the reverend of the church, the student of Scripture? But he is harsh, distant. You'd think the woman would avoid Jesus. Is she not the woman of the night, the town hussy? But she can't resist him. Simon's "love" is calibrated and stingy. Her love, on the other hand, is extravagant and risky.

How do we explain the difference between the two? Training? Education? Money? No, for Simon has outdistanced her in all three.

But there is one area in which the woman leaves him eating dust. Think about it. What one discovery has she made that Simon hasn't? What one treasure does she cherish that Simon doesn't? Simple. God's love. We don't know when she received it. We aren't told how she heard about it.

Could it be that the secret to loving is receiving? You give love by first receiving it. "We love, because he first loved us" (1 John 4:19 NASB).

Long to be more loving? Begin by accepting your place as a dearly loved child. "Be imitators of God, therefore, as dearly loved children and live a life of love, just as Christ loved us" (Eph. 5:1–2 NIV).

Yes, I am sure that neither death, nor life, nor angels, nor ruling spirits, nothing now, nothing in the future, no powers, nothing above us, nothing below us, nor anything else in the whole world will ever be able to separate us from the love of God that is in Christ Jesus our Lord.

—Romans 8:38–39

EXPERIENCING THE LOVE OF JESUS THIS WEEK

Before you read any further, spend some time in prayer now.

Dear Jesus, through this week I pray that your love—its depth, its steadfastness, and its cost—will be made evident to me. Help me to understand how I am able to pass your love on to others. Cause me to rest in the assurance that nothing can separate me from your love. Amen.

This week, memorize Ephesians 3:18–19—a testimony to Jesus' love for us.

And may you have the power to understand, as all God's people should, how wide, how long, how high, and how deep his love really is. May you experience the love of Christ, though it is so great you will never fully understand it. Then you will be filled with the fullness of life and power that comes from God. NLT

JUST THE WAY YOU ARE

It's dangerous to sum up grand truths in one statement, but I'm going to try. If a sentence or two could capture God's desire for each of us, it might read like this:

God loves you just the way you are, but he refuses to leave you that way. He wants you to be just like Jesus.

God loves you just the way you are. If you think his love for you would be stronger if your faith were, you are wrong. If you think his love would be deeper if your thoughts were, wrong again. Don't confuse God's love with the love of people. The love of people often increases with performance and decreases with mistakes. Not so with God's love. He loves you right where you are.

—Just Like Jesus

DAY ONE—WHERE LOVE AND JUSTICE MEET

GOD'S GIFT FROM HEAVEN

How in the world can justification come for the evil? It can't. It can't come from the world. It must come from heaven.

While Jesus' grace teaches us about his role as heaven's way for salvation, his love teaches us about why he was willing to save us. Understanding God gives us grace is one thing—but realizing *why* he is such a gracious God is something altogether mind-boggling. It's this simple: He gives us grace because he loves us. When we realize the magnitude of the love required for Jesus to go to the Cross, we will begin to live in the overflow of God's love. As we'll learn this week, we soon discover this love-gift is too good to keep to ourselves.

God gives us grace because he loves us.

This is what real love is: It is not our love for God; it is God's love for us in sending his Son to be the way to take away our sins.

—1 John 4:10

1. Read John 3:16–17 and fill in the blanks about what this passage says about God's love.

God **so loved** the world so much that he **gave** his one and only **Son** so that whoever **believes** in him may not be **perish** but have eternal life. God did not **send** his Son into the world to **condemn** the world guilty, but to save the world **through** him.

How can God punish the sin and love the sinner? Paul has made it clear, "The wrath of God is being revealed from heaven against all godlessness and wickedness" (Rom. 1:18 NIV). Is God going to lower his standard so we can be forgiven? Is God going to look away and pretend I've never sinned? Would we want a God who altered the rules and made exceptions? No. We want a God who "does not change like . . . shifting shadows" (James 1:17) and who "judges all people in the same way" (Rom. 2:11).

Besides, to ignore my sin is to endorse my sin. If my sin has no price, then sin on! If my sin brings no pain, then sin on! In fact, "We should do evil so that good will come" (Rom. 3:8). Is this the aim of God? To compromise his holiness and enable our evil?

Of course not. Then what is he to do? How can he be just and love the sinner? How can he be loving and punish the sin? How can he satisfy his standard and forgive my mistakes? Is there any way God could honor the integrity of heaven without turning his back on me?

But the Lord's love for those who respect him continues forever and ever, and his goodness continues to their grandchildren.

—Psalm 103:17

TIPPED SCALES

Christ's love is greater than anyone can ever know, but I pray that you will be able to know that love (Eph. 3:19).

It wasn't right that spikes pierced the hands that formed the earth. And it wasn't right that the Son of God was forced to hear the silence of God.

It wasn't right, but it happened.

For while Jesus was on the cross, God sat on his hands. He turned his back. He ignored the screams of the innocent.

He sat in silence while the sins of the world were placed upon his Son. And he did nothing while a cry a million times bloodier than John's echoed in the black sky: "My God, my God, why have you forsaken me?"

Was it right? No.

Was it fair? No.

Was it love? Yes.

—*The Applause of Heaven*

The Lord does what is right, and he loves justice, so honest people will see his face.

—Psalm 11:7

God's grace is where love and justice meet to provide our salvation.

God gave him as a way to forgive sin through faith in the blood of Jesus' death. This showed that God always does what is right and fair, as in the past when he was patient and did not punish people for their sins. And God gave Jesus to show today that he does what is right. God did this so he could judge rightly and so he could make right any person who has faith in Jesus.

—Romans 3:25–26

God loved the world so much that he gave his one and only Son so that whoever believes in him may not be lost, but have eternal life.

—**John 3:16**

God is motivated to save us both because of his love for us and his responsibility to deal with sin. His grace is where love and justice meet to provide our salvation.

2. Which of the following statements are true concerning God's justice? Use the Bible verses below to help you answer. Check all that apply.

   ☑ God must judge wickedness. (Psalm 7:11)
   ☒ God loves justice. (Psalm 11:7)
   ☐ God judges only his people. (Psalm 58:11)
   ☑ God does what is right and fair. (Psalm 99:4)

3. If you were to draw a pie chart of the required percentages of God's love and God's justice necessary to save us, how would you divide it? Why?

   With his love in me and mine in him their is no %. its all!! My God is an awsome God, his love is forever

THE DECISION

Holiness demands that sin be punished. Mercy compels that the sinner be loved. How can God do both?

A simple illustration might help shed some light on this dilemma. Imagine being arrested and brought before a judge for a speeding violation—your third in two years. You admit it. You were speeding—each and every time. However, imagine entering into his chambers, palms sweating, as you hear the judge render his decision:

"I have found a way to deal with your mistakes. I can't overlook them; to do so would be unjust. I can't pretend you didn't commit them; to do so would be a lie. But here is what I can do. In our records we have found a person with a spotless past. He has never broken a law. Not one violation, not one trespass, not even a parking ticket. He has volunteered to trade records with you. We will take your name and put it on his record. We will take his name and put it on yours. We will punish him for what you did. You, who did wrong, will be made right. He, who did right, will be made wrong."

Who is this person? What fool would do such a thing?

For the sake of illustration, imagine if it were the judge himself. He was the one willing to substitute his spotless record for yours.

In the same way, Jesus loves us so much he was willing to give us his own "perfect driving record" (a sinless life) so that he could take on the punishment for our imperfect one. The judge in this illustration had no reason to do us a favor. He didn't know us. He certainly wasn't indebted to us—we were guilty, remember? So it is with God.

4. Read Romans 3:25–26. Based on what you just read, why did God give Jesus? Check all that apply.

   ☒ God gave Jesus as a way to forgive sin through faith in the blood of Jesus' death.
   ☑ God gave Jesus to show God always does what is right and fair.
   ☐ God gave Jesus so he could judge rightly.
   ☑ God gave Jesus so he could make right any person who has faith in Jesus.

The love of God is born from within him, not from what he finds in us. His love is uncaused and spontaneous. As Charles Wesley said, "He hath loved us. He hath loved us. Because he would love."

Does he love us because of our goodness? Because of our kindness? Because of our great faith? No, he loves us because of *his* goodness, kindness, and great faith. John says it like this: "This is love: not that we loved God, but that he loved us" (1 John 4:10 NIV).

Doesn't this thought comfort you? God's love does not hinge on yours. The abundance of your love does not increase his. The lack of your love does not diminish his.

Your goodness does not enhance his love, nor does your weakness dilute it. What Moses said to Israel is what God says to us: "The LORD did not choose you and lavish his love on you because you were larger or greater than other nations, for you were the smallest of all nations! It was simply because the LORD loves you" (Deuteronomy 7:7–8 NLT).

God loves you simply because he has chosen to do so.

He loves you when you don't feel lovely.

He loves you when no one else loves you. Others may abandon you, divorce you, and ignore you, but God will love you. Always. No matter what.

This is his sentiment: "I'll call nobodies and make them somebodies; I'll call the unloved and make them beloved" (Romans 9:25 MSG).

This is his promise. "I have loved you, my people, with an everlasting love. With unfailing love I have drawn you to myself" (Jeremiah 31:3 NLT).

While we may theologically and intellectually understand the transaction, motivated by love, that took place at Calvary, the reality must reach our hearts in order to complete its course. We are loved. Let the words linger in our ears. We are loved.

> **God loves you because he has chosen to do so.**

5. Read the following verses. Then match the verse with what you learn about God's love.

_c_	Isaiah 54:10	a.	His love is great.
_a_	Joel 2:13	b.	He loves us like children.
_d_	Ephesians 3:19	c.	His love will never disappear.
_b_	1 John 3:1	d.	His love is more than we can ever know.

> *Come back to the Lord your God, because he is kind and shows mercy. He doesn't become angry quickly, and he has great love.*
>
> —Joel 2:13

Love goes the distance, and Christ traveled from limitless eternity to be confined by time in order to become one of us. He didn't have to. He could have given up. At any step along the way he could have called it quits.

When he saw the size of the womb, he could have stopped.

When he saw how tiny his hand would be, how soft his voice would be, how hungry his tummy would be, he could have stopped. At the first whiff of the stinky stable, at the first gust of cold air. The first time he scraped his knee or blew his nose or tasted burnt bagels, he could have turned and walked out.

When he saw the dirt floor of his Nazareth house. When Joseph gave him a chore to do. When his fellow students were dozing off during the reading of the Torah, his Torah. When the neighbor took his name in vain. When the lazy farmer blamed his poor crop on God. At any point Jesus could have said, "That's it! That's enough! I'm going home." But he didn't.

He didn't, because he is love. And "love . . . endures all things" (1 Cor. 13:4–7). He endured the distance.

> *The Father has loved us so much that we are called children of God. And we really are his children.*
>
> —1 John 3:1

> **Because he loved us, Jesus endured all things.**

6. What makes you want to stop, give up, get away? Why do you come back? Why do you stay?

When I feel I'm not wanted Because learning about my Lord and his love that I should have loved long ago I try very hard not to give up.

Some of us can pinpoint defining moments when we knew completely that God loved us. It may have been a camp, a revival, a beautiful sunset on the beach, or even a strange warming amid an unexpected heartbreak that brings us this revelation. His love meets us in the course of our lives, wherever we are, as a refreshing reminder on a gentle breeze.

7. Have you ever experienced a time where you truly understood that Jesus loved you? Try to describe this intimacy and familiarity with Jesus' love.

The rainbow

> *This is how God showed his love to us: He sent his one and only Son into the world so that we could have life through him.*
>
> —1 John 4:9

Where God's love is, there is no fear, because God's perfect love drives out fear. It is punishment that makes a person fear, so love is not made perfect in the person who fears.

—1 John 4:18

GOD IS CRAZY ABOUT YOU

There are many reasons God saves you: to bring glory to himself, to appease his justice, to demonstrate his sovereignty. But one of the sweetest reasons God saved you is because he is fond of you. He likes having you around. He thinks you are the best thing to come down the pike in quite a while . . .

If God had a refrigerator, your picture would be on it. If he had a wallet, your photo would be in it. He sends you flowers every spring and a sunrise every morning. Whenever you want to talk, he'll listen. He can live anywhere in the universe, and he chose your heart . . .

Face it, friend. He's crazy about you.

—*A Gentle Thunder*

God proved his love for us by sacrificing his Son.

Yes, I am sure that neither death, nor life, nor angels, nor ruling spirits, nothing now, nothing in the future, no powers, nothing above us, nothing below us, nor anything else in the whole world will ever be able to separate us from the love of God that is in Christ Jesus our Lord.

—Romans 8:38–39

Nothing will ever be able to separate us from the love of God.

Praise be to the God and Father of our Lord Jesus Christ. In Christ, God has given us every spiritual blessing in the heavenly world.
—Ephesians 1:3

OUR RESPONSE

Knowing we didn't do anything to earn God's love reminds us not to live in fear of losing it either. If you did nothing to gain it, how could your performance (or lack thereof) lose it? Many people live in fear of God's justice because they have never reckoned his justice with his love. Grace is where the two meet together, forming an insoluble bond.

8. Read 1 John 4:18 at the left and fill in the following blanks.

"Where God's *love* is, there is no *fear*, because God's perfect *love* drives out fear. It is *punishment* that makes a person *fear*, so *love* is not made perfect in the person who *fears*."

Are you aware that the most repeated command from the lips of Jesus was, "Fear not"? Are you aware that the command from heaven not to be afraid appears in every book of the Bible?

The apostle points to the Cross as our guarantee of God's love. "God shows his great love for us in this way: Christ died for us while we were still sinners" (Rom. 5:8). God proved his love for us by sacrificing his Son.

9. Based on what you have read so far, which of the following statements are true concerning Jesus' sacrifice? Mark your answers True (T) or False (F).

F Jesus was willing to sacrifice himself for us after we cleaned up our act.
T Jesus was willing to die "while we were yet sinners."
F Jesus could not be sacrificed for us until after we professed our faith in him.

10. What is significant about this timing of Jesus' sacrifice?
As we are still sinners christ Die for us,

Formerly God had sent prophets to preach: Now he has sent his son to die. Earlier God commissioned angels to aid, now he has offered his son to redeem. When we tremble he points us to the splattered blood on the splintered beams and says, "Don't be afraid."

11. Will Jesus love us forever? Scripture says so. Read Romans 8:38–39 on the left. Based on what you just read, check which of the following statements are true about the bond between us and God's love through Jesus.

☑ Death cannot separate us.
☑ Life cannot separate us.
☐ Present events cannot separate us.
☐ Future events cannot separate us.
☑ The powers-that-be cannot separate us.
☑ Nothing in the world can separate us.

THE HEART OF THE MATTER

- **God gives us grace because he loves us.**
- **God's grace is where love and justice meet to provide our salvation.**
- **God loves you because he has chosen to do so.**
- **Because he loved us, Jesus endured all things.**
- **God proved his love by sacrificing his Son for us.**
- **Nothing will ever be able to separate us from the love of God.**

Time to get familiar with your new Bible memory verse for the week. Take a couple of moments to write out Ephesians 3:18–19 on the lines provided here.

...May have power, together with all the saints, to grasp how wide and long and high and deep in the love of christ. and to know that this love that surpasses knowlege that you may be filled to the measure of all the fullness of God.

The Heart of Jesus

He had places to go, things to do, people to see. He was on a road trip, speaking in local synagogues, seaside venues, and country hillsides throughout the region. He had a message to communicate, questions to answer, parables to compose. And when he wasn't talking, he was listening. His chosen disciples, his closest friends, and even the religious rulers were vying for his time and attention. Jesus was a busy man. How could he possibly take on one more responsibility? Where would he find the time to commit to one more ministry opportunity? Didn't he deserve some down-time, some time off, some me-time? In the same situation, the last thing we would want to face is a crowd of needy people. Yet there he is, listening to stories of stiff joints and dimming sight. Holding the hand of the depressed and weary. Touching the faces of the desperate and dying. And did Jesus grit his teeth and smile through these interruptions to his schedule? Was he bored by hearing the same sorts of stories over and over again? Did it bother him that nobody seemed to care about his feelings, his problems, his needs? No. Those things never entered his mind. Though confronted with a sea of faces, Jesus saw every individual heart, every precious life, every eternal soul through the eyes of love.

DAY TWO—HONEST HEARTS

TURNING YOURSELF IN

When we consider love on a human level, we may fear others may not love us if they knew the person we really are deep inside. That is bondage—we can neither feel completely loved nor freely love others. Once we experience Jesus' love, however, we know what it is like to live in freedom. Jesus knows everything about us, the good and the bad, yet he loves us entirely. We are free to be honest with him about who we are—and who we are not. His love for us will not change.

But from the beginning God has called for honesty. He's never demanded perfection, but he has expected truthfulness. As far back as the days of Moses, God said: "But if they will confess their sins and the sins of their fathers—their treachery against me and their hostility toward me, which made me hostile toward them so that I sent them into the land of their enemies—then . . . I will remember my covenant with Jacob and my covenant with Isaac and my covenant with Abraham, and I will remember the land" (Lev. 26:40–42 NIV).

1. Look up the following verses and write down what you learn about God's priority on confessing our sins.

   Psalm 32:5 – "Then I confessed my sins to you and didn't hide my guilt. I said, 'I will confess my sins to the Lord,' and you forgave my guilt."

   We Bleive and God will be by our side forever he will not leave our side.

God has said, "I will never leave you; I will never forget you."
—Hebrews 13:5b

Psalm 38:18 – "I confess my guilt; I am troubled by my sin."

It is hard to believe Gods cares for us (me) the way He does.

1 John 1:9 – "If we confess our sins, he will forgive our sins, because we can trust God to do what is right. He will cleanse us from all the wrongs we have done."

I just say I feel sow clean to be able have my sins being freed by God his so Jesus Christ.

Charles Robertson should have turned himself in. Not that he would've been acquitted; he robbed a bank. But at least he wouldn't have been the laughingstock of Virginia Beach.

Cash-strapped Robertson, nineteen, went to Jefferson State Bank on a Wednesday afternoon, filled out a loan application, and left. Apparently he changed his mind about the loan and opted for a quicker plan. He returned within a couple of hours with a pistol, a bag, and a note demanding money. The teller complied, and all of a sudden Robertson was holding a sack of loot.

Figuring the police were fast on their way, he dashed out the front door. He was halfway to the car when he realized he'd left the note. Fearing it could be used as evidence against him, he ran back into the bank and snatched it from the teller. Now holding the note and the money, he ran a block to his parked car. That's when he realized he'd left his keys on the counter when he'd returned for the note.

"At this point," one detective chuckled, "total panic set in."

Robertson ducked into the restroom of a fast-food restaurant. He dislodged a ceiling tile and hid the money and the .25 caliber handgun. Scampering through alleys and creeping behind cars, he finally reached his apartment where his roommate, who knew nothing of the robbery, greeted him with the words, "I need my car."

You see, Robertson's getaway vehicle was a loaner. Rather than confess to the crime and admit the bungle, Robertson shoveled yet another spade of dirt deeper into the hole. "Uh, uh, your car was stolen," he lied.

While Robertson watched in panic, the roommate called the police to inform them of the stolen vehicle. About twenty minutes later an officer spotted the "stolen" car a block from the recently robbed bank. Word was already on the police radio that the robber had forgotten his keys. The officer put two and two together and tried the keys on the car. They worked.

Detectives went to the address of the person who'd reported the missing car. There they found Robertson. He confessed, was charged with robbery, and put in jail. No bail. No loan. No kidding.

Some days it's hard to do anything right. It's even harder to do anything wrong right. Robertson's not alone. We've done the same. Perhaps we didn't take money but we've taken advantage or taken control or taken leave of our senses and then, like the thief, we've taken off. Dashing down alleys of deceit. Hiding behind buildings of work to be done or deadlines to be met. Though we try to act normal, anyone who looks closely at us can see we are on the lam: Eyes darting and hands fidgeting, we chatter nervously. Committed to the cover-up, we scheme and squirm, changing the topic and changing direction. We don't want anyone to know the truth, especially God.

1. In what areas of life are many people tempted to shade the truth? Check all that apply.

   ❏ Integrity on the job
   ☒ Reporting on IRS forms
   ❏ Honesty in relationships
   ☒ Improving our image
   ☒ Avoiding blame

I pray that Christ will live in your hearts by faith and that your life will be strong in love and be built on love. And I pray that you and all God's holy people will have the power to understand the greatness of Christ's love—how wide and how long and how high and how deep that love is. Christ's love is greater than anyone can ever know, but I pray that you will be able to know that love. Then you can be filled with the fullness of God.

—Ephesians 3:17–19

2. Read Psalm 51:3–5 and fill in the blanks concerning David's confession.

God you are the one I have sinned against. I have _done_ what you say is _wrong_. You are _right_ when you speak and fair when you _judge_ _Right_

I know about my wrongs, and I can't forget my sin. You are the only one I have sinned against; I have done what you say is wrong. You are right when you speak and fair when you judge. I was brought into this world in sin. In sin my mother gave birth to me.

—Psalm 51:3–5

3. Based on what you just read in David's example, what is the biblical definition of what it means to "confess" one's sin?

We trust in the Lord to give up are sins Christ did on the cross for are sins. Is telling we wrong to trust leave us without sin

CONFESSION

Confession is a necessary part of our love relationship with God through Christ. We can't pretend with him to be someone we are not. He knows us through and through. Better yet, he loves us through and through. The act of confessing our sins to him ought to bring us closer to him—knowing we are deeply loved by the only One who can help us with our weaknesses.

Confession does for the soul what preparing the land does for the field. Before the farmer sows the seed he works the acreage, removing the rocks and pulling the stumps. He knows that seed grows better if the land is prepared. Confession is the act of inviting God to walk the acreage of our hearts. "There is a rock of greed over here, Father. I can't budge it. And that tree of guilt near the fence? Its roots are long and deep. And may I show you some dry soil, too crusty for seed?" God's seed grows better if the soil of the heart is cleared.

And so the Father and the Son walk the field together, digging and pulling, preparing the heart for fruit. Confession invites the Father to work the soil of the soul.

God's seed grows better if the soil of the heart is cleared.

4. Why is it necessary to "prepare our hearts" by confessing our sins?

by confessing are sin's bring us closer to him!

5. Based on what you have learned so far, what is the landscape like as Jesus scans across the acreage of your heart? Check all that apply.

- ☒ Rocky soil that stunts our growth by preventing our roots to go down deep.
- ❑ Hardened soil that is unyielding to God's touch—unteachable.
- ☒ Weeds of worry that choke out our ability to grow.
- ☒ Dry and barren places, thirsting for the water of the Word.
- ☒ Dark corners, so shaded by the past that the sun cannot reach the soil.
- ❑ Neglected patches, needing more frequent weeding and watering to bear fruit.
- ❑ Fertile ground, cleared and weeded and well-watered.

HONEST WORSHIP

Confession seeks pardon from God, not amnesty. Pardon presumes guilt; amnesty, derived from the same Greek word as amnesia, "forgets" the alleged offense without imputing guilt. Confession admits wrong and seeks forgiveness; amnesty denies wrong and claims innocence.

Many mouth a prayer for forgiveness while in reality claiming amnesty.

6. Read Psalm 51:7–12. Based on what you just read, which of the following statements are true concerning our need for forgiveness, and which ones are false? Mark your answers True (T) or False (F).

_T_ Sin soils our hearts.

_F_ God can only make us so clean from our sin—we cannot be completely cleansed.

We love because God first loved us.
—1 John 4:19

Take away my sin, and I will be clean. Wash me, and I will be whiter than snow.

—Psalm 51:7

Grace means you don't have to run anymore.

There's something inside us that longs to be back in fellowship with Jesus.

LOVE HUNG ON A CROSS

He looked around the hill and foresaw a scene. Three figures hung on three crosses. Arms spread. Heads fallen forward. They moaned with the wind.

Men clad in soldier's garb sat on the ground near the trio . . .

Women clad in sorrow huddled at the foot of the hill . . . faces tear-streaked.

All heaven stood to fight. All nature rose to rescue. All eternity poised to protect. But the Creator gave no command.

"It must be done . . ." he said, and withdrew.

The angel spoke again. "It would be less painful . . ."

The Creator interrupted softly. "But it wouldn't be love."

—*In the Eye of the Storm*

But God shows his great love for us in this way: Christ died for us while we were still sinners.

—Romans 5:8

___

God can restore our joy.

God cannot wipe out all guilt.

God can create a pure heart from an unclean one.

When we don't feel the need for forgiveness, our worship becomes cold (why thank God for a grace we don't need?) and our faith is weak (I'll handle my mistakes myself, thank you). We are better at keeping God out than we are at inviting God in. Sunday mornings are full of preparing the body for worship, preparing the hair for worship, preparing the clothes for worship, but preparing the soul?

Am I missing the mark when I say that many of us attend church on the run? Am I out of line when I say many of us spend life on the run?

Am I overstating the case when I announce, "Grace means you don't have to run anymore!"? It's the truth. Grace means it's finally safe to turn ourselves in.

A MODEL OF TRUTH

Let's take a look now at how true confession (and forgiveness) played out in the lives of one disciple. Remember Peter? "Flash the sword and deny the Lord" Peter? The apostle who boasted one minute and bolted the next? He snoozed when he should have prayed. He denied when he should have defended. He cursed when he should have comforted. He ran when he should have stayed. We remember Peter as the one who turned and fled, but do we remember Peter as the one who returned and confessed? We should.

I've got a question for you.

How did the New Testament writers know of his sin? Who told them of his betrayal? And, more importantly, how did they know the details? Who told them of the girl at the gate and the soldiers starting the fire? How did Matthew know it was Peter's accent that made him a suspect? How did Luke learn of the stare of Jesus? Who told all four of the crowing rooster and flowing tears?

The Holy Spirit? I suppose. Could be that each writer learned of the moment by divine inspiration. Or, more likely, each learned of the betrayal by an honest confession. Peter turned himself in. Like the bank robber, he bungled it and ran. Unlike the robber, Peter stopped and thought. Somewhere in the Jerusalem shadows he quit running, fell to his knees, buried his face in his hands, and gave up.

But not only did he give up, he opened up. He went back to the room where Jesus had broken the bread and shared the wine. (It says a lot about the disciples that they let Peter back in the door.)

There he is, every burly bit of him filling the doorframe. "Fellows, I've got something to get off my chest." And that's when they learn of the fire and the girl and the look from Jesus. That's when they hear of the cursing mouth and the crowing rooster. That's how they heard the story. He turned himself in.

If you have experienced Jesus, you know one thing is true: you just can't turn away from him. Deep down you really don't even want to despite your pretense to the contrary. There's something inside that longs to be back in fellowship with him again.

7. Based on Romans 2:4, which of the following are true? Check all that apply.

❑ God shames us into confessing our sins.
❑ God tricks us into confession.
☒ God's kindness "loves" us into confessing our sins.

8. How would you complete the following phrase?:

"To me, Jesus' 'love' is like . . ."
  a. Understanding the planetary system—I just don't get it.
  b. A childhood memory of a nursery song I used to sing.
  c. Something withheld from me unless I am perfect.
  d. The air I breathe—can't live without it.

Once there were a couple of farmers who couldn't get along with each other. A wide ravine separated their two farms, but as a sign of their mutual distaste for each other, each constructed a fence on his side of the chasm to keep the other out.

In time, however, the daughter of one met the son of the other, and the couple fell in love. Determined not to be kept apart by the folly of their fathers, they tore down the fence and used the wood to build a bridge across the ravine.

Confession does that. Confessed sin becomes the bridge over which we can walk back into the presence of God.

9. Based on Isaiah 1:18–19, match the statements on the right with the truths on the left.

_C_ Though our sins are deep red . . .   a. He will bless us.
_b_ Though our sins are like scarlet . . .   b. He will make us white as snow.
_A_ If we become willing and obey God . . .   c. He will make us white as wool.

10. What does this imagery say to you about God's ability to restore us completely?

We don't have to go throu life perma stain with sin. Gods word assured us if we belive and fo ullow christ will forgive our sin of past

Like the two lovers in this story, God calls us to tear down whatever separates our fellowship with him and "get on with it." There is love to be shared! "If we confess our sins, he will forgive our sins, because we can trust God to do what is right. He will cleanse us from all the wrongs we have done" (1 John 1:19).

May I ask a frank question? Are you keeping any secrets from God? Any parts of your life off limits? Any cellars boarded up or attics locked? Any part of your past or present that you hope you and God never discuss?

Learn a lesson from the robber: The longer you run, the worse it gets. Learn a lesson from Peter: The sooner you speak to Jesus, the more you'll speak for Jesus.

Once you're in the grip of grace, you're free to be honest. Turn yourself in before things get worse. You'll be glad you did.

THE HEART OF THE MATTER

- God's seed grows better if the soil of the heart is cleared through confession.
- Grace means you don't have to run anymore.
- There's something inside us that longs to be back in fellowship with Jesus.
- Confession builds a bridge over which we can walk back into God's presence.
- Don't try to hide your sins from God. Confess them so he can forgive them.

Now for a little review. Your memory verse for the week is Ephesians 3:18–19. Take a few moments to write it out on the lines below.

you may have power, together with all the saints to grasp how wide and long and high and deep is the love of christ and to know this love that surpasses knowledge- that you may be filled with the measure of all the fullness of God.

The Heart of Jesus

She looked annoyed to find him in her path. Obviously she'd hoped to be alone for a few minutes. When he asked her for water, she'd been polite enough, but he'd seen her back stiffen. Was she upset at having to do more work, surprised that he would ask her for a drink, or afraid of a Jewish man who ignored society's conventions. Her eyes were shadowed by disappointment, dissatisfaction, and distrust. She seemed tired of life, as if she'd given up caring anymore. She'd been brave enough to bluff though—dodging his words and posing intelligent-sounding questions. Until he'd cut to the heart of the

He has been very kind and patient, waiting for you to change, but you think nothing of his kindness. Perhaps you do not understand that God is kind to you so you will change your hearts and lives.
—Romans 2:4

Confession builds a bridge over which we can walk back into God's presence.

The Lord says, "Come, let us talk about these things. Though your sins are like scarlet, they can be as white as snow. Though your sins are deep red, they can be white like wool. If you become willing and obey me, you will eat good crops from the land.
—Isaiah 1:18–19

Don't try to hide your sins from God. Confess them so he can forgive them.

He saves my life from the grave and loads me with love and mercy.
—Psalm 103:4

matter. He knew her past, her present circumstance, and her greatest need. He had seen the deep longing inside—had know it was there. And so Jesus had gone out of his way, taken the scenic route south, and passed through unfriendly territories just for her. He'd rearranged his life to be at that well on that day at that time, because he loved the woman who would be there. She'd needed to experience the love of Jesus. And she did.

DAY THREE—THE HEAVINESS OF HATRED

SETTLING THE SCORE

Each week Kevin Tunell was required to mail a dollar to a family he'd rather forget. They sued him for $1.5 million but settled for $936, to be paid a dollar at a time. The family expected the payment each Friday so Tunell would not forget what happened on the first Friday of 1982.

That's the day their daughter was killed. Tunell was convicted of manslaughter and drunken driving. He was seventeen. She was eighteen. Tunell served a court sentence. He also spent seven years campaigning against drunk driving, six years more than his sentence required. But he kept forgetting to send the dollar.

The weekly restitution was to last until the year 2000. Eighteen years. Tunell made the check out to the victim, mailed it to her family, and the money was deposited in a scholarship fund.

The family took him to court four times for failure to comply. After one appearance, Tunell spent thirty days in jail. He insisted that he was not defying the order but rather was haunted by the girl's death and tormented by the reminders. He offered the family two boxes of checks covering the payments until the year 2001, one year more than required. They refused. It was not money they sought, but penance.

Quoting the mother, "We wanted to receive the check every week on time. He needed to remember what he did to our daughter every week for the 18 short years she lived." [1]

1. Why do we often require a sort of "payment" when it comes to issuing forgiveness to those who deeply hurt us?

   So they can hurt with remembering liked.

2. Look up the following verses and write down what you learn about how sin links to the idea of payment.

   Leviticus 26:15–16 – "If you turn away from my rules and hate my laws, refusing to obey all my commands, you have broken our agreement. As a result, I will do this to you: I will cause terrible things to happen to you."

   by breaking Gods laws.

   Psalm 49:8 – "Because the price of a life is high. No payment is ever enough."

   Gods ways are good. sometimes Hard to follow, but he is always right.

   Romans 6:23 – "When people sin, they earn what sin pays—death."

   wages of sin is death But the gift of God is enternal life in christ Jesus our Lord.

But the servant fell on his knees and begged, "Be patient with me, and I will pay you everything I owe." The master felt sorry for his servant and told him he did not have to pay it back. Then he let the servant go free.

—Matthew 18:26–27

Praise the Lord! Thank the Lord because he is good. His love continues forever.

—Psalm 106:1

HIS LOVE ENABLES US

It's human nature to want to settle the score. However, God calls us to be super-natural. God's grace toward us requires and actually enables us to be gracious toward others. If we experience his love through Christ, he requires us to act lovingly toward others—however undeserving they may appear to be.

"But what about the father who abandoned me as a kid?"

"And my wife who dumped me for a newer model?"

"And the boss who laid me off even though my child was sick?"

The Master silences them with a raised hand and the story of the forgetful servant.

3. Read Matthew 18:23–35. Jesus is the generous master in this parable, setting us free from a massive debt we could never repay. However, the man in this parable is more like us than we care to realize. Although he has been set free, he goes out and lives like someone still under the threat of eviction.

How did the servant respond to his predicament? (v. 26)

Not to Believe it,

How did the master respond? (v. 27)

lighting that come from the east is visable from the west so will be the coming of the sun of man

How did the unforgiving servant respond to those who owed him money? (vv. 28–31)

His decision make no sense But hatred never dos,

Something is wrong with this picture. Are these the actions of a man forgiven millions? Choking a person who owes him a few bucks? Are these the words of a man who has been set free? "Pay me the money you owe me!"

The decision makes no sense.

But hatred never does.

THE 7:47 PRINCIPLE

Hatred is so out of place in the Christian life. After we have been forgiven so much, how could we not forgive others? Hatred makes no sense. But the 7:47 Principle does. What's the 7:47 Principle?

Read verse 47 of Luke chapter 7: "A person who is forgiven little shows only little love." Just like the jumbo jet, the 7:47 Principle has wide wings. Just like the aircraft, this truth can lift you to another level. Read it one more time. "A person who is forgiven little shows only little love." In other words, we can't give what we've never received. If we've never received love, how can we love others?

But, oh, how we try! As if we can conjure up love by the sheer force of will. As if there is within us a distillery of affection that lacks only a piece of wood or a hotter fire. We poke it and stoke it with resolve. What's our typical strategy for treating a troubled relationship? Try harder.

"My spouse needs my forgiveness? I don't know how, but I'm going to give it."

"I don't care how much it hurts, I'm going to be nice to that bum."

"I'm supposed to love my neighbor? Okay. By golly, I will."

So we try. Teeth clinched. Jaw firm. We're going to love if it kills us! And it may do just that.

4. Put the 7:47 Principle into your own words:

love forgiven little Love Little Many who are forgiven for all love much

---

Hatred never makes sense.

LOVE IS ALL YOU'LL FIND

Water must be wet. A fire must be hot. You can't take the wet out of water and still have water. You can't take the heat out of fire and still have fire.

In the same way, you can't take the love out of [God] . . . and still have him exist. For he was . . . and is . . . Love.

Probe deep within him. Explore every corner. Search every angle. Love is all you find. Go to the beginning of every decision he has made and you'll find it. Go to the end of every story he has told and you'll see it.

Love.

No bitterness. No evil. No cruelty. Just love. Flawless love. Passionate love. Vast and pure love. He is love.

—*In the Eye of the Storm*

We have been forgiven so much. How could we not forgive others?

The Lord doesn't become angry quickly, but he has great love.

—Numbers 14:18a

Could it be we are missing a step? Could it be that the first step of love is not toward them but toward him? Could it be that the secret to loving is receiving?

You are rich in everything—in faith, in speaking, in knowledge, in truly wanting to help, and in the love you learned from us. In the same way, be strong also in the grace of giving.

—2 Corinthians 8:7

5. Read the following questions on the left. Then match it with the truth on the right that illustrates this 7:47 Principle in action.

 A Long to be more loving?   a. Philippians 2:6–7
 d Want to learn to forgive?   b. Ephesians 5:1–2
 a Want to put others first?   c. 2 Peter 3:9
 c Need more patience?   d. Ephesians 4:32
 f Need generosity?   e. Luke 6:35
 b Need tolerance?   f. 2 Corinthians 8:7

6. When it comes to what you need most in your life, which of these virtues—love, forgiveness, unselfishness, patience—is at the top of your list? And how do you think the 7:47 Principle might help in that specific area of your life?

Love, love and passion need to put others in front of me, and be truthfull

CHRIST'S LOVE—THE CURE FOR HATRED

As we grow to relish and experience the love of Christ, one of the results is a growing love for other people. An irrational, inexplicable desire to love and forgive them replaces time-worn bitterness. The Bible says when we experience great forgiveness ourselves, we are able to love others all the more (Luke 7:47). However, if we have yet to realize the weight of our own indebtedness to God, we will be stingy with our love.

To believe we are totally and eternally debt free is seldom easy. Even if we've stood before the throne and heard it from the king himself, we still doubt.

Apparently that was the problem of the servant. He still felt in debt. How else can we explain his behavior? Rather than forgive his transgressor, he chokes him! "I'll squeeze it out of you." He hates the very sight of the man. Why? Because the man owes him so much? I don't think so. He hates the man because the man reminds him of his debt to the Master.

"I will forgive them for the wicked things they did, and I will not remember their sins anymore."

—Jeremiah 31:34

In order to love as God loves, we must first receive God's love.

7. Read Jeremiah 31:34. Based on what you just read, fill in the blanks concerning God's memory when it comes to our sins.

God will *forgive* us for our sins—even the most wicked things we've done. In fact, once he has forgiven us, he says he will *take away* our sins *forever*.

The problem is if we haven't received love first, how can we give love to others? Apart from God, "the heart is deceitful above all things" (Jer. 17:9 NIV). A marriage-saving love is not within us. A friendship-preserving devotion cannot be found in our hearts. We need help from an outside source. A transfusion. Would we love as God loves? Then we start by receiving God's love.

We preachers have been guilty of skipping the first step. "Love each other!" we tell our churches. "Be patient, kind, forgiving," we urge. But instructing people to love without telling them they are loved is like telling them to write a check without our making a deposit in their accounts. No wonder so many relationships are overdrawn. Hearts have insufficient love. The apostle John models the right sequence. He makes a deposit before he tells us to write the check. First, the deposit: "God showed how much he loved us by sending his only Son into the world so that we might have eternal life through him. This is real love. It is not that we loved God, but that he loved us and sent his Son as a sacrifice to take away our sins" (1 John 4:9–10 NLT).

I trust in your love. My heart is happy because you saved me.
—Psalm 13:5

And then, having made such an outrageous, eye-opening deposit, John calls on you and me to pull out the checkbook: "Dear friends, since God loved us that much, we surely ought to love each other" (v. 11 NLT).

The secret to loving is living loved. This is the forgotten first step in relationships.

8. It isn't easy to always be patient, kind, and forgiving towards one another. What is the "secret" to showing love in this way?

practice, patient, kind, & forgiving to one another

Your friend broke his promises? Your boss didn't keep her word? I'm sorry, but before you take action, answer this question: How did God react when you broke your promises to him? *He still loves us.*

You've been lied to? It hurts to be deceived. But before you double your fists, think: How did God respond when you lied to him? *Still loves us*

You've been neglected? Forgotten? Left behind? Rejection hurts. But before you get even, get honest with yourself. Have you ever neglected God? *yes* Have you always been attentive to his will? *no* None of us have. How did he react when you neglected him? *love us*

The key to forgiving others is to quit focusing on what they did to you and start focusing on what God did for you.

But, Max, that's not fair! Somebody has to pay for what he did.

I agree. Someone must pay, and Someone already has.

Jesus' love is love in action. It effects change. It promotes healing. It gives the debtor the freedom to forgive other debtors.

9. Which of the following statements are true concerning what God did for us and why? Check all that apply. Use the Bible verses below to help you answer.

- ☑ His forgiveness is final. (Hebrews 10:18)
- ☑ Jesus' sacrifice takes away our sins. (1 John 2:2)
- ☑ Jesus' sacrifice demonstrated real love. (1 John 4:10)

THE HEART OF THE MATTER

- ❀ **Hatred never makes sense.**
- ❀ **We have been forgiven so much. How could we not forgive others?**
- ❀ **In order to love as God loves, we must first receive God's love.**
- ❀ **When you want someone to pay for what has been done to you, remember—Someone already has.**

Let's review your verse today by doing a little fill in the blank.

"And may you have the ___power___ to ___gether___, as all God's people should, how ___wide___, how ___long___, how ___high___, and how ___deep___ his ___love___ really is. May you ___know___ the ___love___ of Christ, though it is so ___surpass knowledge___ you will never fully ___understand___ it. Then you will be ___filled___ with the ___measure___ of live and the ___fullness___ that comes from ___God___." —Ephesians 3:18–19

The Heart of Jesus

Jesus had the chance to surround himself with the best and the brightest the world had to offer. When he started ministry, he could have created the ultimate Dream Team of service-minded men and women. He could have taken applications to find the most energetic, dedicated, and—team players. He could have made teachable hearts and the ability to follow through definite job requirements. A quick peek into hearts could have revealed those with the natural gifts of preaching, teaching, evangelism, and missions. He could have signed on a youth leader, a children's ministry coordinator, and even an administrative pastor for good measure. But he didn't. Take a look at the men and women who surrounded Jesus. They kept missing the point. They couldn't seem to trust their leader. They were always blowing it. And finally, they all bailed on him. Hardly what we'd expect in a ministry team. So why did Jesus pick this bunch of people for his closest companions? Because he loved them. And he knew how his love would change them into the kind of people God could use mightily.

DAY FOUR—A LOVE WORTH GIVING

THE POWER TO LOVE

Many people tell us to love. Only God gives us the power to do so.

1 Corinthians 13 describes the measureless love of Christ.

We know what God wants us to do. "This is what God commands: . . . that we love each other" (1 John 3:23). But how can we? How can we be kind to the vow breakers? To those who are unkind to us? How can we be patient with people who have the warmth of a vulture and the tenderness of a porcupine? How can we forgive the moneygrubbers and backstabbers we meet, love, and marry? How can we love as God loves? We want to. We long to. But how can we?

By living loved. By following the 7:47 Principle that we just reviewed in Day Three: Receive first, love second.

1. Why are forgiveness and love contrary to human nature?

_____

_____

Love is patient and kind. Love is not jealous, it does not brag, and it is not proud. Love is not rude, is not selfish, and does not get upset with others. Love does not count up wrongs that have been done. Love is not happy with evil but is happy with the truth. Love patiently accepts all things. It always trusts, always hopes, and always remains strong. Love never ends.

—1 Corinthians 13:4–7

Let's carry this principle up the Mount Everest of love writings. More than one person has hailed 1 Corinthians 13 as the finest chapter in the Bible. No words get to the heart of loving people like these verses. And no verses get to the heart of the chapter like verses 4 through 8.

2. Read 1 Corinthians 13:4–8 and fill in the blanks concerning love's qualities.

    Love is _patient_ and _kind_. Love is not _envy_, it does not _boast_, and it is not _proud~~angry~~_. Love is not _rude_, is not _self-seeking_, and does not get _easy angry_ with others. Love does not _bring_ up wrongs that have been done. Love is not _delight_ with evil but is happy with the _truth_. Love _~~refaul~~_ accepts all things. It always _faith_, always _hope_, and always remains _love_.

Several years ago someone challenged me to replace the word *love* in this passage with my name. I did and became a liar. "Max is patient, Max is kind. Max does not envy, he does not boast, he is not proud . . ." That's enough! Stop right there! Those words are false. Max is not patient. Max is not kind. Ask my wife and kids. Max can be an out-and-out clod! That's my problem.

And for years that was my problem with this paragraph. It set a standard I could not meet. No one can meet it. No one, that is, except Christ. Does this passage not describe the measureless love of God? Let's insert Christ's name in place of the word *love,* and see if it rings true.

The mountains may disappear, and the hills may come to an end, but my love will never disappear; my promise of peace will not come to an end," says the Lord who shows mercy to you.

—Isaiah 54:10

Jesus is patient, Jesus is kind. Jesus does not envy, he does not boast, he is not proud. Jesus is not rude, he is not self-seeking, he is not easily angered, he keeps no record of wrongs. Jesus does not delight in evil but rejoices with the truth. Jesus always protects, always trusts, always hopes, always perseveres. Jesus never fails.

3. Based on 1 Corinthians 13, which of the following attributes do you most consistently exercise with others? Check all that apply.

- ☒ Kindness
- ☒ Patience
- ☐ Humility
- ☒ Trust
- ☐ Forgiveness

4. Which of these attributes describing Jesus' love stands out most to you? Is it an area of God's love that you long to show?

Trusting, Kindness and Patience

THAT'S WHY JESUS CAME

He loves you. That's why he came.

That's why he endured the distance between us. "Love . . . endures *all things*."

That's why he endured the resistance from us. "Love . . . endures *all things*."

That's why he went the final step of the Incarnation: "God made him who had no sin to be sin for us, so that in him we might become the righteousness of God" (2 Cor. 5:21 NIV).

Why did Jesus do that? There is only one answer. And that answer has one word. Love. And the love of Christ "bears all things, believes all things, hopes all things, endures all things" (1 Cor. 13:7).

Think about that for a moment. Drink from that for a moment. Drink deeply. Don't just sip or nip. It's time to gulp. It's time to let his love cover all things in your life. All secrets. All hurts. All hours of evil, minutes of worry.

The mornings you awoke in the bed of a stranger? His love will cover that. The years you peddled prejudice and pride? His love will cover that. Every promise broken, drug taken, penny stolen. Every cross word, cuss word, and harsh word. His love covers all things.

Let it. Discover along with the psalmist: "He . . . loads me with love and mercy" (Ps. 103:4). Picture a giant dump truck full of love. There you are behind it. God lifts the bed until the love starts to slide. Slowly at first, then down, down, down until you are hidden, buried, covered in his love.

"Hey, where are you?" someone asks.

"In here, covered in love."

Let his love cover all things.

Do it for his sake. To the glory of his name.

Do it for your sake. For the peace of your heart.

And do it for their sake. For the people in your life. Let his love fall on you so yours can fall on them.

5. Look up the following verses and write down what you learn about the all-consuming effect God's love has on our lives regarding our sin.

1 Corinthians 6:11 – "You were washed clean. You were made holy, and you were made right with God in the name of the Lord Jesus Christ and in the Spirit of our God."

He gave his followers in any age _____ to high moral standard.

THE STRENGTH OF GOD'S LOVE

"Can anything make me stop loving you?" God asks. "Watch me speak your language, sleep on your earth, and feel your hurts. Behold the maker of sight and sound as he sneezes, coughs, and blows his nose. You wonder if I understand how you feel? Look into the dancing eyes of the kid in Nazareth; that's God walking to school. Ponder the toddler at Mary's table; that's God spilling his milk.

"You wonder how long my love will last? Find your answer on a splintered cross, on a craggy hill. That's me you see up there, your maker, your God, nail-stabbed and bleeding. Covered in spit and sin-soaked.

"That's your sin I'm feeling. That's your death I'm dying. That's your resurrection I'm living. That's how much I love you."

—*In the Grip of Grace*

Let Jesus' love cover all things in your life.

I showed them what you are like, and I will show them again. Then they will have the same love that you have for me, and I will live in them.

—John 17:26

1 Thessalonians 5:23 – "Now may God himself, the God of peace, make you pure, belonging only to him. May your whole self—spirit, soul, and body—be kept safe and without fault when our Lord Jesus Christ comes." *Yes.*

God can controll all of us not just our religous part.

Hebrews 9:13–14 – "The blood of goats and bulls and the ashes of a cow are sprinkled on the people who are unclean, and this makes their bodies clean again. How much more is done by the blood of Christ. He offered himself through the eternal Spirit as a perfect sacrifice to God. His blood will make our consciences pure from useless acts so we may serve the living God."

God can heal my conscience and deliver me from the frustration of trying to earn Gods favor

LOVING OUR ENEMIES

During World War I, a German soldier plunged into an out-of-the-way shell hole. There he found a wounded enemy. The fallen soldier was soaked with blood and only minutes from death. Touched by the plight of the man, the German soldier offered him water. Through this small kindness a bond was developed. The dying man pointed to his shirt pocket; the German soldier took from it a wallet and removed some family pictures. He held them so the wounded man could gaze at his loved ones one final time. With bullets raging over them and war all around them, these two enemies were, but for a few moments, friends.

What happened in that shell hole? Did all evil cease? Were all wrongs made right? No. What happened was simply this: Two enemies saw each other as humans in need of help. This is forgiveness. Forgiveness begins by rising above the war, looking beyond the uniform, and choosing to see the other, not as a foe or even as a friend, but simply as a fellow fighter longing to make it home safely.

6. Read Ephesians 4:32 and fill in the blanks regarding our response to those who hurt us.

   Be ___*Kind*___ and ___*compassionate*___ to each other just as ___*christ God*___ forgave ___*me*___ in ___*Christ God Jesus.*___

Call it a bad addiction. We start the habit innocently enough, indulging our hurts with doses of anger. Not much, just a needle or two of rancor. The rush numbs the hurt, so we come back for more and up the dosage; we despise not only what he did, but who he is. Insult him. Shame him. Ridicule him. The surge energizes. Drugged on malice, the roles are reversed; we aren't the victim, we're the victor. It feels good. Soon we hate him and anyone like him. ("All men are jerks." "Every preacher is a huckster." "You can't trust a woman.") The progression is predictable. Hurt becomes hate, and hate becomes rage as we become junkies unable to make it through the day without mainlining on bigotry and bitterness.

7. Read the following verses. Then match the verse with what you learn about the consequences of indulging our hurts.

   b Proverbs 10:12   a. Makes others weaker.
   d Romans 3:14–17   ~~b.~~ Fools us into wanting to do evil.
   A Ephesians 4:22   c. Stirs up trouble.
   c Ephesians 4:29   ~~d.~~ Causes ruin and misery.

Be kind and loving to each other, and forgive each other just as God forgave you in Christ.

—Ephesians 4:32

Many people tell us to love. Only God gives us the power to do so.

When you talk, do not say harmful things, but say what people need—words that will help others become stronger. Then what you say will do good to those who listen to you.

—Ephesians 4:29

So these three things continue forever: faith, hope, and love. And the greatest of these is love.

—1 Corinthians 13:13

Rather than letting 1 Corinthians 13 remind us of a love we cannot produce, let it remind us of a love we cannot resist—God's love.

Some of you are so thirsty for this type of love. Those who should have loved you didn't. Those who could have loved you didn't. You were left at the hospital. Left at the altar. Left with an empty bed. Left with a broken heart. Left with your question "Does anybody love me?"

Please listen to heaven's answer. God loves you. Personally. Powerfully. Passionately. Others have promised and failed. But God has promised and succeeded. He loves you with an unfailing love. And his love—if you will let it—can fill you and leave you with a love worth giving.

> *You are God's children whom he loves, so try to be like him. Live a life of love just as Christ loved us and gave himself for us as a sweet-smelling offering and sacrifice to God.*
>
> *—Ephesians 5:1–2*

8. Read Ephesians 5:1–2. Based on what you just read, which of the following statements are true, and which ones are false? Mark your answers True (T) or False (F).

   __F__ It's impossible for us to act like God's children.
   __T__ We must live a life of love.
   __T__ Jesus can help us love others like he loved us.
   __T__ Loving others the way we should is sometimes a sacrifice.

LIVING IN THE OVERFLOW

Am I living in the overflow of God's love? How well do I love the people in my life? Does the way I treat people reflect the way God has treated me?

Jesus invites us to live in the overflow of God's love.

Loving people isn't always easy. In fact, this has been a challenge for some of you. You've been forced to think again about some of the people in your life whom you find hard to love. This is serious business. It's not easy to love those who have been the source of heartache, abuse, rejection, or loneliness. Some of you wonder how you could ever love the people who have caused you such pain. So what can you do?

Conventional wisdom says that a lack of love implies a lack of effort, so we try harder, dig deeper, strain more.

But could a lack of love imply something else? Could we be skipping a step? An essential step? Could it be that we are trying to give what we don't have? Are we forgetting to receive first?

Hatred and bitterness are heavy burdens to bear.

The woman in Capernaum didn't forget. Remember her from the beginning of the week? Remember how she lavished love on Christ? Bathing his feet with tears. Drying his feet with her hair. If love were a waterfall, she'd be a Niagara.

And Simon, well, Simon was a Sahara. Dry. Parched. Hard. His arid heart surprises us. He was the churchgoer, the pastor, the seminarian. She, on the other hand, was the town slut. He'd forgotten more Bible than she ever knew. But she'd discovered one truth Simon had somehow missed: God's love has no limits.

> *"Master, how many times do I forgive a brother or sister who hurts me? Seven?"*
>
> *—Matt. 18:21 MSG*

HOW DO WE BREAK THE HABIT?

Peter is worried about over-forgiving an offender. The Jewish law stipulated that the wounded forgive three times. Peter is willing to double that and throw in one more for good measure. No doubt he thinks Jesus will be impressed. Jesus isn't. The Master's answer still stuns us. "Seven! Hardly. Try seventy times seven" (v. 22 MSG).

If you're pausing to multiply seventy times seven, you're missing the point. Keeping tabs on your mercy, Jesus is saying, is not being merciful. If you're calibrating your grace, you're not being gracious. There should never be a point when our grace is exhausted.

Let me be very clear. Hatred will sour your outlook and break your back. The load of bitterness is simply too heavy. Your knees will buckle under the strain, and your heart will break beneath the weight. The mountain before you is steep enough with-

> *Do all these things; but most important, love each other. Love is what holds you all together in perfect unity.*
>
> *—Colossians 3:14*

out the heaviness of hatred on your back. The wisest choice—the only choice—is for you to drop the anger. You will never be called upon to give anyone more grace than God has already given you.

9. Which of the following statements are true about anger? Check all that apply. Use the Bible verses below to help you answer.

❏ Jesus does not take our anger seriously. (Matthew 5:22)
❏ It's possible to be angry yet not sin. (Ephesians 4:26)
❏ Moderate anger helps us live the right kind of life God wants. (James 1:20)
☒ Anger gives the devil an opportunity to defeat us. (Ephesians 4:27)

"Love," Paul says, "never fails" (1 Cor. 13:8 NIV).

The verb Paul uses for the word *fail* is used elsewhere to describe the demise of a flower as it falls to the ground, withers, and decays. It carries the meaning of death and abolishment. God's love, says the apostle, will never fall to the ground, wither, and decay. By its nature, it is permanent. It is never abolished.

Love "will last forever" (NLT).
It "never dies" (MSG).
It "never ends" (RSV).
Love "is eternal" (TEV).
God's love "will never come to an end" (NEB).
Love never fails.

Governments will fail, but God's love will last. Crowns are temporary, but love is eternal. Your money will run out, but his love never will.

THE HEART OF THE MATTER

❧ **1 Corinthians 13 describes the measureless love of Christ.**
❧ **Let Jesus' love cover all things in your life.**
❧ **Many people tell us to love. Only God gives us the power to do so.**
❧ **Jesus invites us to live in the overflow of God's love.**
❧ **Hatred and bitterness are heavy burdens to bear.**
❧ **Love will last forever.**

Here we go again. Do you know it by heart yet? Write out Ephesians 3:18–19 here to test your memory.

may have power together with all the saints, to grasp how wide, & long & high & deep is the love of Christ [19] to know this love surpasses knowledge - that you may be filled to the measure of all fullness of God.

The Heart of Jesus

Jesus welcomed them with open arms. Sure they sometimes clung too close. Sure they asked the most outlandish questions. Then there were the stinky diapers, the sticky fingers, the spilled milk. Jesus had time for children. He listened to them. He took their wonderings seriously. He gave great bear hugs. Kids couldn't understand why they had to share Jesus with their parents. They didn't care if the adults wanted to discuss other things. All they wanted was one more piggy-back ride. Just one more story. Wide-eyed, energetic, trusting children—Jesus loves them too!

Anger will not help you live the right kind of life God wants.
—James 1:20

Love will last forever.

But if someone obeys God's teaching, then in that person God's love has truly reached its goal. This is how we can be sure we are living in God.
—1 John 2:5

DAY FIVE—WHAT WE REALLY WANT TO KNOW

HOW GREAT HIS LOVE

Human relationships teach us something about God's love.

It was her singing that did it. At first I didn't notice. Had no reason to. The circumstances were commonplace. A daddy picking up his six-year-old from a Brownie troop meeting.

I'd turned onto the road, turned on her favorite music, and turned my attention to more sophisticated matters of schedules and obligations.

But only steps into the maze of thought I stepped back out. Sara was singing. Singing about God. Singing to God. Head back, chin up, and lungs full, she filled the car with music. Heaven's harps paused to listen.

Is that my daughter? She sounds older. She looks older, taller, even prettier. Did I sleep through something? What happened to the chubby cheeks? What happened to the little face and pudgy fingers? She is becoming a young lady. Blonde hair down to her shoulders. Feet dangling over the seat. Somewhere in the night a page had turned and, well, look at her!

If you're a parent you know what I mean. Just yesterday diapers, today the car keys? Suddenly your child is halfway to the dormitory, and you're running out of chances to show your love, so you speak.

That's what I did. The song stopped and Sara stopped, and I ejected the tape and put my hand on her shoulder and said, "Sara, you're something special." She turned and smiled tolerantly. "Someday some hairy-legged boy is going to steal your heart and sweep you into the next century. But right now, you belong to me."

She tilted her head, looked away for a minute, then looked back and asked, "Daddy, why are you acting so weird?"

I suppose such words would sound strange to a six-year-old. The love of a parent falls awkwardly on the ears of a child. My burst of emotion was beyond her. But that didn't keep me from speaking.

There is no way our little minds can comprehend the love of God. But that didn't keep him from coming.

Although human love, even at its best, is faulty by comparison to God's love, we can't help but compare the two so we can get a handle on it. Perhaps we've been privileged to experience unconditional love from our parents or the sacrificial love of a mate. Perhaps we've only seen examples from afar. Either way, human relationships teach us something about God's love.

So what should we say about this? If God is with us, no one can defeat us. He did not spare his own Son but gave him for us all. So with Jesus, God will surely give us all things. Who can accuse the people God has chosen? No one, because God is the One who makes them right. Who can say God's people are guilty? No one, because Christ Jesus died, but he was also raised from the dead, and now he is on God's right side, begging God for us. Can anything separate us from the love Christ has for us? Can troubles or problems or sufferings or hunger or nakedness or danger or violent death? As it is written in the Scriptures: 'For we are in danger of death all the time. People think we are worth no more than sheep to be killed.' But in all these things we have full victory through God who showed his love for us. Yes, I am sure that neither death, nor life, nor angels, nor ruling spirits, nothing now, nothing in the future, no powers, nothing above us, nothing below us, nor anything else in the whole world will ever be able to separate us from the love of God that is in Christ Jesus our Lord.

—Romans 8:31–39

1. In what ways are human love relationships, although wonderful, still a pale comparison to the love relationship we have with God?

   Gods love will always be with us well never be alone

2. Read Psalm 22:1–8. Based on what you just read, what questions did the psalmist ask concerning God's love? Check all that apply.

   ❑ If you love me, why does it feel like you've rejected me?
   ❑ If you love me, why do you seem so far away?
   ❑ If you love me, won't you answer me?
   ❑ If you love me, won't you come to my rescue?

Paul's letter to the Romans tells us what he has learned about God's love. Only Paul poses his knowledge in the form of rhetorical questions. Five questions to be exact.

This is my prayer for you: that your love will grow more and more; that you will have knowledge and understanding with your love.

—Philippians 1:9

These questions are not new to you. You've asked them. In the night you've asked them; in anger you've asked them. The doctor's diagnosis brought them to the surface, as did the court's decision and the phone call from the bank. The questions are probes of pain and problem and circumstance. No, the questions are not new, but maybe the answers are.

THE QUESTION OF PROTECTION

The question is not simply, "Who can be against us?" You could answer that one. Who is against you? Disease, inflation, corruption, exhaustion. Calamities confront, and fears imprison. Were Paul's question, "Who can be against us?" we could list our foes much easier than we could fight them. But that is not the question. The question is, If GOD IS FOR US, who can be against us? Indulge me for a moment. Four words in this verse deserve your attention. Read slowly the phrase, "God is for us." Please pause for a minute before you continue. Read it again, aloud. (My apologies to the person next to you.) God is for us. Repeat the phrase four times, this time emphasizing each word. (Come on, you're not in that big of a hurry.)

GOD IS FOR US.

GOD IS FOR US.

GOD IS FOR US.

GOD IS FOR US.

God is for you. Your parents may have forgotten you, your teachers may have neglected you, your siblings may be ashamed of you; but within reach of your prayers is the maker of the oceans. God!

> 3. Look up the following verses below and write down what you learn about the benefits of having God on your side.
>
> **Genesis 18:14** – "Is anything too hard for the Lord? No!"
>
> _____
>
> _____
>
> **Deuteronomy 4:34** – "No other god has ever taken for himself one nation out of another. But the Lord your God did this for you in Egypt, right before your own eyes. He did it with tests, signs, miracles, war, and great sights, by his great power and strength."
>
> _____
>
> _____
>
> **Psalm 44:3** – "It wasn't their swords that took the land. It wasn't their power that gave them victory. But it was your great power and strength. You were with them because you loved them."
>
> _____
>
> _____

God is for you. Not "may be," not "has been," not "was," not "would be," but "God is!" He is for you. Today. At this hour. At this minute. As you read this sentence. No need to wait in line or come back tomorrow. He is with you. He could not be closer than he is at this second. His loyalty won't increase if you are better nor lessen if you are worse. He is for you.

God is for you. Turn to the sidelines; that's God cheering your run. Look past the finish line; that's God applauding your steps. Listen for him in the bleachers, shouting your name. Too tired to continue? He'll carry you. Too discouraged to fight? He's picking you up. God is for you.

God is for you. Had he a calendar, your birthday would be circled. If he drove a car, your name would be on his bumper. If there's a tree in heaven, he's carved your name in the bark. We know he has a tattoo, and we know what it says. "I have written your name on my hand," he declares (Is. 49:16).

God is for us.

Jesus answered, "If people love me, they will obey my teaching. My Father will love them, and we will come to them and make our home with them.
—**John 14:23**

THE QUESTION OF PROVISION

He who did not spare his own Son, but gave him up for us all—how will he not also, along with him, graciously give us all things? –Romans 8:32 NIV

Would he who gave his Son not meet our needs? But still we worry. We worry about the IRS and the SAT and the FBI. We worry about education, recreation, and constipation. We worry that we won't have enough money, and when we have money we worry that we won't manage it well. We worry that the world will end before the parking meter expires. We worry what the dog thinks if he sees us step out of the shower. We worry that someday we'll learn that fat-free yogurt was fattening.

Honestly, now. Did God save you so you could fret? Would he teach you to walk just to watch you fall? Would he be nailed to the Cross for your sins and then disregard your prayers? Come on. Is Scripture teasing us when it reads, "He has put his angels in charge of you to watch over you wherever you go"? (Ps. 91:11).

I don't think so either.

4. Read the following verses. Then match the verse with what you learn about God as our Provider.

   ___ Psalm 111:5   a. He gives us things to enjoy.
   ___ 1 Timothy 6:17   b. He cares for our basic needs.
   ___ 1 Peter 4:11   c. He gives us personal strength.

5. Read Matthew 7:11. Based on what you just read, which of the following statements are true, and which ones are false? Mark your answers True (T) or False (F).

   ___ God's primary concern is for our needs.
   ___ God is too busy to take care of all our needs.
   ___ He is often preoccupied trying to decide whose needs are legitimate and whose are not.
   ___ He enjoys providing good things for his children.

TWO QUESTIONS ABOUT GUILT AND GRACE

Who can accuse the people God has chosen? No one, because God is the One who makes them right. Who can say God's people are guilty? No one, because Christ Jesus died, but he was also raised from the dead, and now he is on God's right side, begging God for us. —Romans 8:33–34

Every moment of your life, your accuser is filing charges against you. He has noticed every error and marked each slip. Neglect your priorities, and he will jot it down. Abandon your promises, and he will make a note. Try to forget your past; he'll remind you. Try to undo your mistakes; he will thwart you.

This expert witness has no higher goal than to take you to court and press charges. Even his name, Diabolos, means "slanderer." Who is he? The devil.

6. Based on Revelation 12:10–12, why is accusation such an effective tool in our spiritual enemy's arsenal?

   _____

   _____

7. Read Hebrews 10:22. Summarize below what this verse teaches us about lingering guilt.

   _____

   _____

He is "the accuser of our brothers and sisters, who accused them day and night before our God" (Rev. 12:10). Can't you see him? Pacing back and forth before God's bench. Can't you hear him? Calling your name, listing your faults.

God did not save you so that you could fret.

Even though you are bad, you know how to give good gifts to your children. How much more your heavenly Father will give good things to those who ask him!
—Matthew 7:11

Let us come near to God with a sincere heart and a sure faith, because we have been made free from a guilty conscience, and our bodies have been washed with pure water.
—Hebrews 10:22

We do not need to feel guilty, because we have been forgiven.

Live a life of love just as Christ loved us and gave himself for us as a sweet-smelling offering and sacrifice to God.
—Ephesians 5:2

The Lord God helps me, so I will not be ashamed. I will be determined, and I know I will not be disgraced. He shows that I am innocent, and he is close to me. So who can accuse me? If there is someone, let us go to court together. If someone wants to prove I have done wrong, he should come and tell me.

—Isaiah 50:7–8

.

YOU HAVE CAPTURED GOD'S HEART

Have you ever noticed the way a groom looks at his bride during the wedding? I have. Perhaps it's my vantage point. As the minister of the wedding, I'm positioned next to the groom . . .

If the light is just so and the angle just right, I can see a tiny reflection in his eyes. Her reflection. And the sight of her reminds me why he is here. His jaw relaxes and his forced smile softens. He forgets he's wearing a tux. He forgets his sweat-soaked shirt . . . When he sees her, any thought of escape becomes a joke again. For it's written all over his face, "Who could bear to live without this bride?"

And such are precisely the feelings of Jesus. Look long enough into the eyes of our Savior and, there, too, you will see a bride. Dressed in fine linen. Clothed in pure grace . . . She is the bride . . . walking toward him . . .

And who is this bride for whom Jesus longs? . . . You are. You have captured the heart of God.

—*When Christ Comes*

Can anything separate us from the love Christ has for us? Can troubles or problems or sufferings or hunger or nakedness or danger or violent death?

—Romans 8:35

Nothing can change God's love for us.

Do everything in love.
—1 Corinthians 16:14

He rails: "This one you call your child, God. He is not worthy. Greed lingers within. When he speaks, he thinks often of himself. He'll go days without an honest prayer. Why, even this morning he chose to sleep rather than spend time with you. I accuse him of laziness, egotism, worry, distrust."

As he speaks, you hang your head. You have no defense. His charges are fair. "I plead guilty, your honor," you mumble.

"The sentence?" Satan asks.

"The wages of sin is death," explains the judge, "but in this case the death has already occurred. For this one died with Christ."

Satan is suddenly silent. And you are suddenly jubilant. You realize that Satan cannot accuse you. No one can accuse you! Fingers may point and voices may demand, but the charges glance off like arrows hitting a shield. Once the judge has released you, you need not fear the court.

8. Read Isaiah 50:7–8 and fill in the blanks concerning what Jesus has done with our guilt.

The Lord God _____ me, so I will not be _____. I will be _____, and I know I will not be _____. He shows that I am _____, and he is close to me. So who can _____ me?

THE QUESTION OF ENDURANCE

There it is. This is the question. Here is what we want to know. We want to know how long God's love will endure. Paul could have begun with this one. Does God really love us forever? Not just on Easter Sunday when our shoes are shined and our hair is fixed. We want to know (deep within, don't we really want to know?), how does God feel about me when I'm a jerk? Not when I'm peppy and positive and ready to tackle world hunger. Not then. I know how he feels about me then. Even I like me then.

I want to know how he feels about me when I snap at anything that moves, when my thoughts are gutter-level, when my tongue is sharp enough to slice a rock. How does he feel about me then?

That's the question. That's the concern. Oh, you don't say it; you may not even know it. But I can see it on your faces. I can hear it in your words. Did I cross the line this week? Last Tuesday when I drank vodka until I couldn't walk . . . last Thursday when my business took me where I had no business being . . . last summer when I cursed the God who made me as I stood near the grave of the child he gave me?

Did I drift too far? Wait too long? Slip too much?

That's what we want to know.

Can anything separate us from the love Christ has for us?

9. Based on Deuteronomy 33:27, which of the following statements are true? Check all that apply.

❑ God is everlasting.
❑ He is our place of safety.
❑ His arms hold us up.
❑ His protection and presence last forever.

"Can anything make me stop loving you?" God asks. "Watch me speak your language, sleep on your earth, and feel your hurts. Behold the maker of sight and sound as he sneezes, coughs, and blows his nose. You wonder if I understand how you feel? Look into the dancing eyes of the kid in Nazareth; that's God walking to school. Ponder the toddler at Mary's table; that's God spilling his milk.

"You wonder how long my love will last? Find your answer on a splintered cross, on a craggy hill. That's me you see up there, your maker, your God, nail-stabbed and bleeding. Covered in spit and sin-soaked. That's your sin I'm feeling. That's your death I'm dying. That's your resurrection I'm living. That's how much I love you."

That's what we really want to know. Will his love last forever? When we really believe the answer is yes, our lives open up to the potential for significant change.

10. According to 1 Corinthians 15:10, what happened as a result of Paul's encounter with God's love? Check your response.

❑ He stayed the same person.
❑ God's love changed him and made him who he was meant to be.

THE HEART OF THE MATTER

❧ **Human relationships teach us something about God's love.**
❧ **God is for us.**
❧ **God did not save you so that you could fret.**
❧ **We do not need to feel guilty, because we have been forgiven.**
❧ **Nothing can change God's love for us.**

Let's review that Bible verse one last time. Write out Ephesians 3:18–19 here.

_____

_____

The Heart of Jesus

His humiliation had been complete. One of his closest friends had betrayed him. All of his other friends had abandoned him. He'd been bullied and beaten. They'd mocked him, then mauled him. Their cruelty had been unspeakable. The pain was so great he could hardly stand. When his time in court came, he'd watched the witnesses lie and the judge turn a blind eye to obvious inconsistencies. He'd watched his oppressors' triumph over his demise, wicked glee dancing in their eyes. Whips had cracked over his head and back, and the blood loss had made him dizzy. The thorns in his scalp were hard to ignore whenever the cross on his back had bumped them. How much more could he endure? Then they'd stripped him, forcing him to stand before the city in complete nakedness. Then the nails had pierced him and the cross had been raised. Every breath was agony. Every muscle and nerve protested. The end was near. And with his last breaths he flung words out over the crowds. Not a backlash of curses. Not regrets. Not a promise of revenge. Jesus gasped out words of forgiveness. Though they had done their worst, Jesus still loved them—loved them enough to say "Father forgive them."

FOR FURTHER READING

Selections throughout this lesson were taken from *A Love Worth Giving*.

The everlasting God is your place of safety, and his arms will hold you up forever. He will force your enemy out ahead of you, saying, "Destroy the enemy!"
—Deuteronomy 33:27

Nothing can change God's love for us.

My children, we should love people not only with words and talk, but by our actions and true caring.
—1 John 3:18

¹ "Drunken Driver Skips $1 Weekly Payments to Victim's Parents," *San Antonio Light*, 31 March 1990.

LESSON 7
Experiencing the Power of Jesus

Imagine it's a Saturday afternoon in October. What you needed to get done today, you've already done. Your afternoon lies before you with no obligations. Free afternoons don't come as often as they once did, so you consider your options for the day. You pick up a paper to get some ideas. A movie? Nothing good is showing. Television? You can do that any time. Wait. What's this? An ad catches your eye.

Special Art Exhibit
"Bruised Reeds and Smoldering Wicks"
2:00 to 4:00 Saturday Afternoon
Lincoln Library

Hmm . . . It's been a while since you've seen some good art. Bruised Reeds and Smoldering Wicks? Probably some nature stuff. Besides, the walk would be nice. You'll do it. You lay down the paper, put on a coat, and grab some gloves.

You're greeted by the musty odor of books as you walk through the library doors.

It's an intimate room—no larger than a nice den. Bookshelves cover the walls, and books line the shelves. A fire crackles in a fireplace, and a couple of high wingback chairs invite you to spend the afternoon with a good book. Maybe later, you think. First, the art.

Placed around the room are the paintings. All framed. All in vivid color. All set on easels, in pairs, and always back to back. You put your gloves in your coat pocket, hang your coat on a hook, and move toward the first painting.

It's a portrait of a leper, the center figure on the canvas. He stoops like a hunchback. His fingerless hand, draped in rags, extends toward you, pleading. A tattered wrap hides all of his face except two pain-filled eyes. The crowd around the leper is chaotic. A father is grabbing a curious child. A woman trips over her own feet as she scrambles to get away. A man glares over his shoulder as he runs. The painting is entitled with the leper's plea, "If you will, you can . . ."

The next painting portrays the same leper, but the scene has changed dramatically. The title has only two words, "I will." In this sketch the leper is standing erect and tall. He is looking at his own outstretched hand—it has fingers! The veil is gone from his face and he is smiling. There is no crowd; only one other person is standing beside the leper. You can't see his face, but you can see his hand on the shoulder of the healed man.

"This is no nature exhibit," you whisper to yourself as you turn to the next painting.

The next portrait is surrealistic. A man's contorted face dominates the canvas. Orange hair twists against a purple background. The face stretches downward and swells at the bottom like a pear. The eyes are perpendicular slits in which a thousand tiny pupils bounce. The mouth is frozen open in a scream. You notice something odd—it's inhabited! Hundreds of spider-like creatures claw over each other. Their desperate voices are captured by the caption, "Swear to God you won't torture me!"

Fascinated, you step to the next painting. It is the same man, but now his features are composed. His eyes, no longer wild, are round and soft. The mouth is closed, and the caption explains the sudden peace: "Released." The man is leaning forward as if listening intently. His hand strokes his chin. And dangling from his wrist is a shackle and a chain—a broken chain.

Throughout the gallery the sequence repeats itself. Always two paintings, one of a person in trauma and one of a person in peace. "Before" and "after" testimonials to a

God says, "Be quiet and know that I am God. I will be supreme over all the nations; I will be supreme in the earth."
—Psalm 46:10

life-changing encounter. Scene after scene of serenity eclipsing sorrow. Purpose defeating pain. Hope outshining hurt.

Throughout this week, let's stroll through the gallery together. Let's ponder the moments when Christ met people at their points of pain. We'll see the prophecy proven true. We'll see bruised reeds straightened and smoldering wicks ignited.

A bruised reed he will not break, and a smoldering wick he will not snuff out.
—Matthew 12:20 NIV

EXPERIENCING THE POWER OF JESUS THIS WEEK

Before you read any further, spend some time in prayer now.

Dear Father, Your power is greater than my every need, than my every fear. Your power has conquered sin and death. Teach me to rest confidently in your strong hands. Help me to rely on your power, even when I do not understand why things are happening. Show me how Jesus can meet me at the point of my greatest weakness with his perfect power.

This week, memorize 2 Corinthians 12:9—Paul's secret source of strength:

But he said to me, "My grace is enough for you. When you are weak, my power is made perfect in you." So I am very happy to brag about my weaknesses. Then Christ's power can live in me.

DAY ONE—EVERYONE NEEDS A MIRACLE

POINT OF DESPERATION

She was a bruised reed: "bleeding for twelve years," "suffered very much," "spent all the money she had," and "getting worse."

A chronic menstrual disorder. A perpetual issue of blood. Such a condition would be difficult for any woman of any era. But for a Jewess, nothing could be worse. No part of her life was left unaffected.

Sexually . . . she could not touch her husband.

Maternally . . . she could not bear children.

Domestically . . . anything she touched was considered unclean. No washing dishes. No sweeping floors.

Spiritually . . . she was not allowed to enter the temple.

She was physically exhausted and socially ostracized.

She had sought help "under the care of many doctors" (v. 26 NIV). The Talmud gives no fewer than eleven cures for such a condition. No doubt she had tried them all. Some were legitimate treatments. Others, such as carrying the ashes of an ostrich egg in a linen cloth, were hollow superstitions.

She "had spent all she had" (v. 26 NIV). To dump financial strain on top of the physical strain is to add insult to injury. A friend battling cancer told me that the hounding of the creditors who demand payments for ongoing medical treatment is just as devastating as the pain.

"Instead of getting better she grew worse" (v. 26 NIV). She was a bruised reed. She awoke daily in a body that no one wanted. She is down to her last prayer. And on the day we encounter her, she's about to pray it.

1. Sometimes the point of total desperation is our turning point—where God steps in to perform a miracle. What does it mean to be "at the point of total desperation"?

is when God comes with power his

healing power,

You have the power and strength to make anyone great and strong.
—1 Chronicles 29:12b

When we reach the point of total desperation, God steps in.

2. Look up the following verses and write down what you learn about others who hit bottom and turned to God for help.

2 Samuel 12:16–17

David begged God to spare the child. He went without food and lay on the bare ground.

2 Kings 20:2–3

~~Then~~ He turned to the Lord in pray, reminded the Lord he had always ~~done~~ been faithful to the Lord

2 Corinthians 4:8–9

the were crushed by not driven to despair, they are not destroyed as the Lord was with them always.

JESUS RESPONDS TO FAITH

By the time she gets to Jesus, he is surrounded by people. He's on his way to help the daughter of Jairus, the most important man in the community. What are the odds that he will interrupt an urgent mission with a high official to help the likes of her? Very few. But what are the odds that she will survive if she doesn't take a chance? Fewer still. So she takes a chance.

"If I can just touch his clothes," she thinks, "I will be healed" (v. 28).

Risky decision. To touch him, she will have to touch the people. If one of them recognizes her . . . hello rebuke, good-bye cure. But what choice does she have? She has no money, no clout, no friends, no solutions. All she has is a crazy hunch that Jesus can help and a high hope that he will.

Maybe that's all you have: a crazy hunch and a high hope. You have nothing to give. But you are hurting. And all you have to offer him is your hurt.

But Jesus continued looking around to see who had touched him. The woman, knowing that she was healed, came and fell at Jesus' feet. Shaking with fear, she told him the whole truth. Jesus said to her, "Dear woman, you are made well because you believed. Go in peace; be healed of your disease."

—Mark 5:32–34

3. When we hit bottom, we can continue to linger there or turn to God in hopes of making our way back up. Choose your typical response when you find yourself in a difficult situation. Check all that apply.

   ☑ I tend to worry about my situation, thinking and rethinking my choices and options.

   ☑ I try to avoid thinking about my troubles by distracting myself with other things.

   ❑ I look for someone to blame for my desperate situation.

   ❑ I complain loudly about my circumstances to anyone who will listen.

   ❑ I begin an inevitable descent into sadness and depression.

   ☑ I find my faith is shaken, and I begin to wonder if God will ever rescue me.

   ☑ I never really lose faith, and can depend on Jesus to carry me through.

God did not give us a spirit that makes us afraid but a spirit of power and love and self-control.

—2 Timothy 1:7

4. The woman could have been afraid of what others would think of her desperate attempt to reach for Jesus. She could have let her fear stop her. Read the following verses. Then match the verse with what you learn about overcoming fear.

   _c_ 2 Timothy 1:7   a. God wants us to be very sure of our hope in him.

   _a_ Hebrews 3:6   b. God's love drives out fear.

   _b_ 1 John 4:18   c. God did not create us to be afraid.

Maybe that has kept you from coming to God. Oh, you've taken a step or two in his direction. But then you saw the other people around him. They seemed so clean, so neat, so trim and fit in their faith. And when you saw them, they blocked your view of him. So you stepped back.

God's power protects you through your faith until salvation is shown to you at the end of time.

—1 Peter 1:5

If that describes you, note carefully, only one person was commended that day for having faith. It wasn't a wealthy giver. It wasn't a loyal follower. It wasn't an acclaimed teacher. It was a shame-struck, penniless outcast who clutched onto her hunch that he could and her hope that he would.

Which, by the way, isn't a bad definition of faith: A conviction that he can and a hope that he will. Sounds similar to the definition of faith given by the Bible. "Without faith no one can please God. Anyone who comes to God must believe that he is real and that he rewards those who truly want to find him" (Heb. 11:6).

Not too complicated is it? Faith is the belief that God is real and that God is good. Faith is not a mystical experience or a midnight vision or a voice in the forest . . . it is a choice to believe that the one who made it all hasn't left it all and that he still sends light into shadows and responds to gestures of faith.

> **Faith is a conviction that Jesus can, and a hope that he will.**

> **Faith is the belief that God is real and that God is good.**

5. Which of the following phrases are true concerning faith, and which ones are false? Mark your answers True (T) or False (F). Use the Bible verses below to help you answer.

    _T_ If we believe God is strong enough to rescue us, we will trust in him. (Hebrews 11:6)

    _T_ If we doubt his power, we are not expressing true faith. (James 1:6–7)

    _F_ God is not powerful enough to help us with all of our problems. (Psalm 89:8)

> *Lord God All-Powerful, who is like you? Lord, you are powerful and completely trustworthy.*
>
> —Psalm 89:9

6. "A conviction that he can and a hope that he will." Read Hebrews 11:1 and fill in the blanks below about what you learn from this verse about faith.

    Faith means being _confidence_ of the things we _Hope_ for and knowing in our hearts that something is _happen_ even though we do not _see_ it with our eyes.

> *Faith means being sure of the things we hope for and knowing that something is real even if we do not see it.*
>
> —Hebrews 11:1

FAITH IN GOD'S POWER

There was no guarantee, of course. She hoped he'd respond . . . she longed for it . . . but she didn't know if he would. All she knew was that he was there and that he was good. That's faith.

Faith is not the belief that God will do what you want. Faith is the belief that God will do what is right.

"Blessed are the dirt-poor, nothing-to-give, trapped-in-a-corner, destitute, diseased," Jesus said, "for theirs is the kingdom of heaven" (Matt. 5:6, my translation).

God's economy is upside down (or right-side up and ours is upside down!). God says that the more hopeless your circumstance, the more likely your salvation. The greater your cares, the more genuine your prayers.

A healthy lady never would have appreciated the power of a touch of the hem of his robe. But this woman was sick, and when her dilemma met his dedication, a miracle occurred.

Her part in the healing was very small. All she did was extend her arm through the crowd.

"If only I can touch him."

> **God says that the more hopeless your circumstance, the more likely your salvation.**

7. Which of the following statements expresses faith in God's ability to act on our behalf? Check one.

    ❑ "If God does what I want, then I'll know he is a good God."

    ☑ "I don't know what might happen, but I know God is there, and I know he is good."

> *God moves mountains without anyone knowing it and turns them over when he is angry.*
>
> —Job 9:5

You get impatient with your own life, trying to master a habit or control a sin—and in your frustration begin to wonder where the power of God is. Be patient. God is using today's difficulties to strengthen you for tomorrow. He is equipping you. The God who makes things grow will help you bear fruit.

Dwell on the fact that God lives within you. Think about the power that gives you life. The realization that God is dwelling within you may change the places you want to go and the things you want to do today.
—*Walking with the Savior*

God's help is near and always available to those who seek it.

8. "The greater your cares, the more genuine your prayers." When was a time you experienced the truth of this statement?

Death of my son

Revisit the library gallery for a moment to see how the artist creatively portrays this story in the same pattern of a two-part series.

The artist's brush has captured a woman in midair, jumping from one side of a canyon to another. Her clothes are ragged. Her body is frail, and her skin is pale. She looks anemic. Her eyes are desperate as she reaches for the canyon wall with both hands. On the ledge is a man. All you see are his legs, sandals, and the hem of a robe. Beneath the painting are the woman's words, "If only . . ."

You step quickly to see the next scene. She is standing now. The ground beneath her bare feet is solid. Her face flushes with life. Her cautious eyes look up at the half-moon of people that surround her. Standing beside her is the one she sought to touch. The caption? His words. "Take heart . . ."

God's help is near and always available, but it is only given to those who seek it. Nothing results from apathy. The great work in this story is the mighty healing that occurred. But the great truth is that the healing began with her touch. And with that small, courageous gesture, she experienced Jesus' tender power.

9. How is Jesus both tender and powerful—all at the same time?

By our Faith. He's everything all at the same time. He is good. And I love him so much.

THE HEART OF THE MATTER

- When we reach the point of total desperation, God steps in.
- Faith is a conviction that Jesus can, and a hope that he will.
- Faith is the belief that God is real and that God is good.
- God says that the more hopeless your circumstance, the more likely your salvation.
- God's help is near and always available to those who seek it.

Take a couple of minutes to review your new memory verse for the week. Write out 2 Corinthians 12:9 on the lines below.

Each time he said, My grace is all you need, My power works best in weakness. So now I am Glad to boast about my weakness so that the power of christ can work through me

The Heart of Jesus

The rumors had been flying for months now. Some people said that this Jesus was a prophet. Some said he was a political reformer. But the greatest interest was roused by the rumors that this man could heal. The blind, the lame, the deaf, the diseased—all claimed to have been made whole by his touch. There were wilder stories of demons being cast out and the dead coming to life again. It was surely too good to be true, but the glimmer of hope was too much for the hurting ones to ignore. So wherever Jesus went, the seekers followed. They brought him all their sick. They begged him to let them touch just the edge of his coat. The weak and the needy longed to experience the power of Jesus.

—Matthew 14:34–36

God is in the highest part of heaven. See how high the highest stars are!
—Job 22:12

DAY TWO—THE POWER OF A TIMID PRAYER

POWER IN PRAYER

If you struggle with prayer, I've got just the guy for you. Don't worry, he's not a monastic saint. He's not a calloused-kneed apostle. Nor is he a prophet whose middle name is Meditation. He's not a too-holy-to-be-you reminder of how far you need to go in prayer. He's just the opposite. A fellow crop duster. A parent with a sick son in need of a miracle. The father's prayer isn't much, but the answer is and the result reminds us: The power is not in the prayer; it's in the one who hears it.

1. Which of the following statements are true concerning the power of prayer, and which ones are false? Mark your answers True (T) or False (F).

    __F__ We must pray just the right prayer to get Jesus to help us.
    __F__ Jesus only answers the prayers of the super-spiritual.
    __T__ The power we need is in Jesus not in our prayers.

2. Read the following verses. Then match the verse with what you learn about how God's power stacks up against our own.

    __c__ Psalm 20:7   a. He holds everything together in his power.
    __d__ Psalm 29:4   b. God created the earth by his power.
    __b__ Jeremiah 10:12   c. Trusting in God is better than trusting in others.
    __e__ Mark 1:7   d. The Lord's voice alone is powerful.
    __a__ Hebrews 1:3   e. Jesus is greater than the most "spiritual" person.

The Son . . . sustains the universe by the mighty power of his command.
—Hebrews 1:3 NLT

> *Jesus asked the boy's father, "How long has this been happening?" The father answered, "Since he was very young. The spirit often throws him into a fire or into water to kill him. If you can do anything for him, please have pity on us and help us." Jesus said to the father, "You said, 'If you can!' All things are possible for the one who believes." Immediately the father cried out, "I do believe! Help me to believe more!"* —Mark 9:21–24

The power we need is in Jesus, not in our prayers.

He prayed out of desperation. His son, his only son, was demon-possessed. Not only was he a deaf-mute and an epileptic, he was also possessed by an evil spirit. Ever since the boy was young, the demon had thrown him into fires and water.

Imagine the pain of the father. Other dads could watch their children grow and mature; he could only watch his suffer. While others were teaching their sons an occupation, he was just trying to keep his son alive.

What a challenge! He couldn't leave his son alone for a minute. Who knew when the next attack would come? The father had to remain on call, on alert twenty-four hours a day. He was desperate and tired, and his prayer reflects both.

"If you can do anything for him, please have pity on us and help us."

Listen to that prayer. Does it sound courageous? Confident? Strong? Hardly.

One word would have made a lot of difference. Instead of if, what if he'd said since? "Since you can do anything for him, please have pity on us and help us."

But that's not what he said. He said if. The Greek is even more emphatic. The tense implies doubt. It's as if the man were saying, "This one's probably out of your league, but if you can . . ."

God is supreme over the skies; his majesty covers the earth.
—Psalm 57:5

A classic crop duster appeal. More meek than mighty. More timid than towering. More like a crippled lamb coming to a shepherd than a proud lion roaring in the jungle. If his prayer sounds like yours, then don't be discouraged, for that's where prayer begins.

3. Despite our inconsistencies on a daily basis, a crisis often drives our prayers to the height of sincerity and honesty. We know we need help! Look up the following verses below and write down what you learn about acknowledging our neediness.

1 Samuel 1:10–11

We shouldn't Barter with prayers but God ans. anyway, be careful make sure you keep your promise.

Psalm 17:1

Strong Wording from a pray.

Romans 7:24

Have strong faith

IN OUR WEAKNESS

It begins as a yearning. An honest appeal. Ordinary people staring at Mount Everest. No pretense. No boasting. No posturing. Just prayer. Feeble prayer, but prayer nonetheless.

We are tempted to wait to pray until we know how to pray. We've heard the prayers of the spiritually mature. We've read of the rigors of the disciplined. And we are convinced we've a long way to traverse.

And since we'd rather not pray than pray poorly, we don't pray. Or we pray infrequently. We are waiting to pray until we learn how to pray.

Good thing this man didn't make the same mistake. He wasn't much of a pray-er. And his wasn't much of a prayer. He even admits it! "I do believe," he implored. "Help me to believe more" (Mark 9:24).

This prayer isn't destined for a worship manual. No Psalm will result from his utterance. His was simple—no incantation or chant. But Jesus responded. He responded, not to the eloquence of the man, but to the pain of the man.

Jesus had many reasons to disregard this man's request.

Jesus responds to our honesty, not to the eloquence of our prayers.

4. "I do believe. Help me to believe more." Why is this an appropriate prayer in times of crisis?

He has faith and believes but needs help to believe more. This is nice

5. Read the following verses and write down what you learn about how Jesus stressed the connection between belief and power.

Matthew 17:20 – "I tell you the truth, if your faith is as big as a mustard seed, you can say to this mountain, 'Move from here to there,' and it will move. All things will be possible for you.'" *just believe*

Mark 5:36 – "But Jesus paid no attention to what they said. He told the synagogue leader, 'Don't be afraid; just believe.'"

John 9:35, 38 – "Jesus found him and said, 'Do you believe in the Son of Man?' He said, 'Lord, I believe!' Then the man worshiped Jesus."

Believe in your heart not the prayer.

The Lord does what he pleases, in heaven and on earth, in the seas and the deep oceans.
—Psalm 135:6

Never has the arena of prayer been so poor. Where is the faith in this picture? The disciples have failed, the scribes are amused, the demon is victorious, and the father is desperate. You'd be hard-pressed to find a needle of belief in that haystack.

You may even be hard-pressed to find one in your own. Perhaps your life is a long way from heaven, too. Noisy household—screaming kids instead of singing angels. Divisive religion—your leaders squabble more than they minister. Overwhelming problems. You can't remember when you didn't wake up to this demon.

And yet out of the din of doubt comes your timid voice. "If you can do anything for me . . ."

Does such a prayer make a difference?

Let Mark answer that question.

> When Jesus saw that a crowd was quickly gathering, he ordered the evil spirit, saying, "You spirit that makes people unable to hear or speak, I command you to come out of this boy and never enter him again." The evil spirit screamed and caused the boy to fall on the ground again. Then the spirit came out. The boy looked as if he were dead, and many people said, "He is dead!" But Jesus took hold of the boy's hand and helped him to stand up. —Mark 9:25–27

He takes care of his people like a shepherd. He gathers them like lambs in his arms and carries them close to him. He gently leads the mothers of the lambs.

—Isaiah 40:11

This troubled the disciples. As soon as they got away from the crowds they asked Jesus, "Why couldn't we force that evil spirit out?"

His answer? "That kind of spirit can only be forced out by prayer."

What prayer? What prayer made the difference? Was it the prayer of the apostles? No, they didn't pray. Must have been the prayers of the scribes. Maybe they went to the temple and interceded. No. The scribes didn't pray either. Then it must have been the people. Perhaps they had a vigil for the boy. Nope. The people didn't pray. They never bent a knee. Then what prayer led Jesus to deliver the demon?

There is only one prayer in the story. It's the honest prayer of a hurting man. And since God is more moved by our hurt than our eloquence, he responded. That's what fathers do.

6. Our need puts Jesus' power into action. It sounds the alarm. It catches his ear. Why? Because he loves us. Read Isaiah 40:11 and respond to the following.

Our prayers make a difference.

What imagery is used to describe God's tender strength?

He feed and cares for those like a shepherd
the Lord has no Equal

How does he respond to weakness?

The Lord Has Know equal

That's exactly what Jim Redmond did.

His son, Derek, a twenty-six-year-old Briton, was favored to win the four-hundred-meter race in the 1992 Barcelona Olympics. Halfway into his semifinal heat, a fiery pain seared through his right leg. He crumpled to the track with a torn hamstring.

As the medical attendants were approaching, Redmond fought to his feet. "It was animal instinct," he would later say. He set out hopping, pushing away the coaches in a crazed attempt to finish the race.

When he reached the stretch, a big man pushed through the crowd. He was wearing a t-shirt that read "Have you hugged your child today?" and a hat that challenged, "Just Do It." The man was Jim Redmond, Derek's father.

So, trust the Lord always, because he is our Rock forever.

—Isaiah 26:4

"You don't have to do this," he told his weeping son.

"Yes, I do," Derek declared.

"Well, then," said Jim, "we're going to finish this together."

And they did. Jim wrapped Derek's arm around his shoulder and helped him hobble to the finish line. Fighting off security men, the son's head sometimes buried in the father's shoulder, they stayed in Derek's lane to the end.

The crowd clapped, then stood, then cheered, and then wept as the father and son finished the race.

What made the father do it? What made the father leave the stands to meet his son on the track? Was it the strength of his child? No, it was the pain of his child. His son was hurt and fighting to complete the race. So the father came to help him finish.

God does the same. Our prayers may be awkward. Our attempts may be feeble. But since the power of prayer is in the one who hears it and not the one who says it, our prayers do make a difference.

THE HEART OF THE MATTER

- **The power we need is in Jesus, not in our prayers.**
- **Jesus responds to our honesty, not to the eloquence of our prayers.**
- **Our prayers make a difference.**

A little review time. Take a few moments to write out your memory verse below—2 Corinthians 12:9.

each time said my grace is all you need my powers work best in weakness so Im glad to boast about my weakness so that the power of Christ can work though me

The Heart of Jesus

They were praying to God, but probably never realized that they were being overheard by God's Son. The first man—a Pharisee—was busy commending himself to God. "I tithe. I fast. I like me!" If that wasn't bad enough, this first man began to elaborate. "I like me. I am glad you made me me. The me that I am is so much better than anyone else." This little rant may have boosted the Pharisee's self esteem, but it never reached God. The second man—a tax collector—had come to the temple with a very different attitude. He lingered near the entrance, not daring to come further. His eyes were downcast, and the slope of his shoulders communicated sadness, regret, surrender. In humility, he acknowledged his sin. "God, have mercy on me, a sinner." His words were few, but his heart was sincere. Jesus announced that this second man's prayers had made all the difference in the world. He went home a forgiven man.

—Luke 18:9–14

Who has measured the oceans in the palm of his hand? Who has used his hand to measure the sky? Who has used a bowl to measure all the dust of the earth and scales to weigh the mountains and hills?

—Isaiah 40:12

DAY THREE—WHEN WE ARE OUT OF CHOICES

> *Now there is in Jerusalem by the Sheep Gate a pool, which is called in Hebrew, Bethesda, having five porches. In these lay a great multitude of sick people, blind, lame, paralyzed, waiting for the moving of the water. For an angel went down at a certain time into the pool and stirred up the water; then whoever stepped in first, after the stirring of the water, was made well of whatever disease he had. Now a certain man was there who had an infirmity thirty-eight years. When Jesus saw him lying there, and knew that he already had been in that condition a long time, He said to him, "Do you want to be made well?" The sick man answered Him, "Sir, I have no man to put me into the pool when the water is stirred up; but while I am coming, another steps down before me." Jesus said to him, "Rise, take up your bed and walk." And immediately the man was made well, took up his bed, and walked. And that day was the Sabbath.* —John 5:2–9 NKJV

For the longest time this story didn't make any sense to me. I couldn't figure it out. It's about a man who has barely enough faith to stand on, but Jesus treats him as if he'd laid his son on the altar for God. Martyrs and apostles deserve such honor, but not some pauper who doesn't know Jesus when he sees him. Or so I thought.

For the longest time I thought Jesus was too kind. I thought the story was too bizarre. I thought the story was too good to be true. Then I realized something. This story isn't about an invalid in Jerusalem. This story is about you. It's about me. The fellow isn't nameless. He has a name—yours. He has a face—mine. He has a problem—just like ours.

Jesus encounters the man near a large pool north of the temple in Jerusalem. It's 360 feet long, 130 feet wide, and 75 feet deep. A colonnade with five porches overlooks the body of water. It's a monument of wealth and prosperity, but its residents are people of sickness and disease.

It's called Bethesda. It could be called Central Park, Metropolitan Hospital, or even Joe's Bar and Grill. It could be the homeless huddled beneath a downtown overpass. It could be Calvary Baptist. It could be any collection of hurting people.

An underwater spring caused the pool to bubble occasionally. The people believed the bubbles were caused by the dipping of angels' wings. They also believed that the first person to touch the water after the angel did would be healed. Did healing occur? I don't know. But I do know crowds of invalids came to give it a try.

OUT OF OPTIONS

Remember, I told you this story was about us? Remember, I said I found our faces in the Bible? Well, here we are, filling the white space between the letters of verse 5: "A man was lying there who had been sick for thirty-eight years."

Maybe you don't like being described like that. Perhaps you'd rather find yourself in the courage of David or the devotion of Mary. We all would. But before you or I can be like them, we must admit we are like the paralytic. Invalids out of options. Can't walk. Can't work. Can't care for ourselves. Can't even roll down the bank to the pool to cash in on the angel water.

You may be holding this book with healthy hands and reading with strong eyes, and you can't imagine what you and this four-decade invalid have in common. How could he be you? What do we have in common with him?

We are all in the same predicament: only the holy will see God.

Surely you know. Surely you have heard. The Lord is the God who lives forever, who created all the world. He does not become tired or need to rest. No one can understand how great his wisdom is.

—Isaiah 40:28

Our goal is to be like Jesus; anything less is inadequate.

Simple. Our predicament and our hope. What predicament? It is described in Hebrews 12:14: "Anyone whose life is not holy will never see the Lord."

That's our predicament: Only the holy will see God. Holiness is a prerequisite to heaven. Perfection is a requirement for eternity.

1. Read the following verses and write down what you learn about our predicament.

   Leviticus 11:45 – "I am the Lord who brought you out of Egypt to be your God; you must be holy because I am holy."

   senful worshing him alone.
   leading a moral lives

   Matthew 5:48 – "So you must be perfect, just as your Father in heaven is perfect."

   we cannot be flawless, but we can
   aspire to be as much alike christ as possible

   1 Peter 1:15 – "But be holy in all you do, just as God, the One who called you, is holy."

   Our focus and priorities must
   be his. we cant be holy on our
   own. God gives us his Holy sprit

JESUS MEETS OUR NEED

We wish it weren't so. We act like it isn't so. We act like those who are "decent" will see God. We suggest that those who try hard will see God. We act as if we're good if we never do anything too bad. And that goodness is enough to qualify us for heaven.

Sounds right to us, but it doesn't sound right to God. And he sets the standard. And the standard is high. "You must be perfect, just as your Father in heaven is perfect" (Matt. 5:48).

You see, in God's plan, God is the standard for perfection. We don't compare ourselves to others; they are just as fouled up as we are. The goal is to be like him; anything less is inadequate.

That's why I say the invalid is you and me. We, like the invalid, are paralyzed. We, like the invalid, are trapped. We, like the invalid, are stuck; we have no solution for our predicament.

That's you and me lying on the ground. That's us wounded and weary. When it comes to healing our spiritual condition, we don't have a chance. We might as well be told to pole-vault the moon. We don't have what it takes to be healed. Our only hope is that God will do for us what he did for the man at Bethesda—that he will step out of the temple and step into our ward of hurt and helplessness.

Which is exactly what he has done.

We know that the law is spiritual, but I am not spiritual since sin rules me as if I were its slave. I do not understand the things I do. I do not do what I want to do, and I do the things I hate. And if I do not want to do the hated things I do, that means I agree that the law is good. But I am not really the one who is doing these hated things; it is sin living in me that does them. Yes, I know that nothing good lives in me—I mean nothing good lives in the part of me that is earthly and sinful. I want to do the things that are good, but I do not do them. I do not do the good things I want to do, but I do the bad things I do not want to do. So if I do things I do not want to do, then I am not the one doing them. It is sin living in me that does those things. So I have learned this rule: When I want to do good, evil is there with me. In my mind, I am happy with God's law. But I see another law working in my body, which makes war against the law that my mind accepts. That other law working in my body is the law of sin, and it makes me its prisoner. What a miserable man I am! Who will save me from this body that brings me death? I thank God for saving me through Jesus Christ our Lord! So in my mind I am a slave to God's law, but in my sinful self I am a slave to the law of sin.

—Romans 7:14–25

2. Read Romans 7: 14–25 on the left and fill in the blanks about what this passage says about the futility of living in our own strength.

   Sin rules in us as if we were its ___slave___ We do ___not___ do what we want to do (like obey Jesus), and instead we ___do___ the very things we hate (disobey him). This is how we know nothing ___good___ lives inside of the part of us that is earthly and sinful. It's like another law is working inside of us—the law of ___sin___. It makes us its ___SLAVE___. Who will save us from this body that brings us ___back___? Thank God for saving me through ___Jesus___ Christ our Lord!

WHAT GOD CAN DO

God is our protection and our strength. He always helps in times of trouble.
—**Psalm 46:1**

Read slowly and carefully Paul's description of what God has done for you: "When you were spiritually dead because of your sins and because you were not free from the power of your sinful self, God made you alive with Christ, and he forgave all our sins. He canceled the debt, which listed all the rules we failed to follow. He took away that record with its rules and nailed it to the Cross. God stripped the spiritual rulers and powers of their authority. With the Cross, he won the victory and showed the world that they were powerless" (Col. 2:13–15).

Let's isolate some phrases and see. First, look at your condition. "When you were spiritually dead . . . and . . . you were not free."

The invalid was better off than we are. At least he was alive. Paul says that if you and I are outside of Christ, then we are dead. Spiritually dead. Corpses. Lifeless. Cadavers. Dead. What can a dead person do? Not much.

But look what God can do with the dead.

3. Based upon what you have just read in Colossians, which of the following statements are true about what God has done. Check all that apply.

- ☑ God made you alive.
- ☑ God forgave.
- ☑ He canceled the debt.
- ☑ He took away that record.
- ☑ God stripped the spiritual rulers.
- ☑ He won the victory.
- ☑ He showed the world.

4. As you look at the words above, answer this question. Who is doing the work? You or God? Who is active? You or God? Who is doing the saving? You or God? Who is the one with strength? And who is the one paralyzed?

__God__   __Polly__

5. Read 1 Corinthians 1:18. Fill in the blanks about what this verse says about God's power expressed in the Cross of Jesus.

The teaching about the __cross__ is foolishness to those who are __lost__. They just don't get it. However, to those of us who are being __save__, the Cross of Jesus is the __power__ of God.

TAKING JESUS AT HIS WORD

Go back to Bethesda for a moment. I want you to look at the brief but revealing dialogue between the paralytic and the Savior. Before Jesus heals him, he asks him a question: "Do you want to be well?"

"Sir, there is no one to help me get into the pool when the water starts moving. While I am coming to the water, someone else always gets in before me" (v. 7).

Is the fellow complaining? Is he feeling sorry for himself? Or is he just stating the facts? Who knows. But before we think about it too much, look what happens next.

"'Stand up. Pick up your mat and walk.'"

"And immediately the man was well; he picked up his mat and began to walk."

I wish we would do that; I wish we would take Jesus at his word. I wish that we would learn that when he says something, it happens. What is this peculiar paralysis that confines us? What is this stubborn unwillingness to be healed? When Jesus tells us to stand, let's stand.

Is this your story? It can be. All the elements are the same. A gentle stranger has stepped into your hurting world and offered you a hand.

Now it's up to you to take it.

The power of God has made us alive.

The teaching about the cross is foolishness to those who are being lost, but to us who are being saved it is the power of God.
—1 Corinthians 1:18

Jesus has stepped into our hurting world and offered us a hand. Now it's up to us to take it.

GOD'S MIGHTY HAND

Through his power all things were made—things in heaven and on earth, things seen and unseen (Col. 1:16).

With one decision history began. Existence became measurable.

Out of nothing came light.

Out of light came day.

Then came sky . . . and earth.

And on this earth? A mighty hand went to work.

Canyons were carved. Oceans were dug. Mountains erupted out of flatlands. Stars were flung. A universe sparkled.

Look to the canyons to see the Creator's splendor. Touch the flowers and see his delicacy. Listen to the thunder and hear his power . . .

Today you will encounter God's creation. When you see the beauty around you, let each detail remind you to lift your head in praise. Express your appreciation for God's creation. Encourage others to see the beauty of his creation.

—In the Eye of the Storm

Where were you when I made the earth's foundation? Tell me, if you understand.
—Job 38:4

THE HEART OF THE MATTER

- ❦ **We are all in the same predicament: only the holy will see God.**
- ❦ **Our goal is to be like Jesus; anything less is inadequate.**
- ❦ **The power of God has made us alive.**
- ❦ **Jesus has stepped into our hurting world and offered us a hand. Now it's up to us to take it.**

Midweek memory verse review! Let's do some fill-in-the-blanks.

But he said to me, "My _grace_ is _all you need_ for you. When you are _weak_, my _power_ is made _w-ta-w-ate weak_ in you." So I am very _glad_ to brag about my _weakness_. Then Christ's _power_ can _work_ in me. —2 Corinthians 12:9

The Heart of Jesus

He was at his usual station, near a clump of shrubbery that gave him some relief from the heat of the sun. His mat was spread, and he sat cross-legged. Small, weak, hungry—he listened for the sound of hooves, the shuffle of feet, the plodding of camels. And then he would beg. Most folks never really saw him. He was just one of the many beggars on the road coming into Jericho. He was part of the scenery, a bit of local color. Just another blind beggar. Others had turned their head at his voice and were moved by compassion. They would drop a few coins into his bowl, or offer him a bit of food or drink before moving along. Then one morning, he heard the clamor of many voices. There seemed to be a parade going by—so many feet, so many voices. "What is this? What's going one?" he asked those nearest him. "I can see," commented another beggar nearby, "It is Jesus of Nazareth and his followers. They are passing by." The blind beggar paused for only a moment, then began to shout loudly, "Jesus, Son of David, have mercy on me!" Over and over he called, as loudly as he could. Some of the others began to reprimand him. "Hush!" "Be still!" "Don't bother him!" But the beggar did not stop, and Jesus turned his head. "Bring him to me," Jesus asked. And so the blind beggar found himself trembling in the presence of the Son of God. "What do you want me to do for you?" he asked. Should he ask for bread? Should he ask for wine? Should he ask for a few coins? No. This was not some passing merchant. He faced the one who had the power to give even more. "I want to see," the beggar pleaded. Touched by the man's faith, Jesus touched him with power. Sight was restored, and God received the praise.

—Luke 18:35–43

DAY FOUR—JESUS' POWER OVER DEATH

THE GRAVE FACT

You are leaving the church building. The funeral is over. The burial is next. Ahead of you walk six men who carry the coffin that carries the body of your son. Your only son.

You're numb from the sorrow. Stunned. You lost your husband, and now you've lost your son. Now you have no family. If you had any more tears, you'd weep. If you had any more faith, you'd pray. But both are in short supply, so you do neither. You just stare at the back of the wooden box.

The Lamb who was killed is worthy to receive power, wealth, wisdom, and strength, honor, glory, and praise!
—**Revelation 5:12**

Suddenly it stops. The pallbearers have stopped. You stop.

A man has stepped in front of the casket. You don't know him. You've never seen him. He wasn't at the funeral. He's dressed in a corduroy coat and jeans. You have no idea what he is doing. But before you can object, he steps up to you and says, "Don't cry."

Don't cry? Don't cry! This is a funeral. My son is dead. Don't cry? Who are you to tell me not to cry? Those are your thoughts, but they never become your words. Because before you can speak, he acts.

He turns back to the coffin, places his hand on it, and says in a loud voice, "Young man, I tell you, get up!"

"Now just a minute," one of the pallbearers objects. But the sentence is interrupted by a sudden movement in the casket. The men look at one another and lower it quickly to the ground. It's a good thing they do, because as soon as it touches the sidewalk the lid slowly opens . . .

Sound like something out of a science fiction novel? It's not. It's right out of the Gospel of Luke. "He went up and touched the coffin, and the people who were carrying it stopped. Jesus said, 'Young man, I tell you, get up!' And the son sat up and began to talk" (Luke 7:14–15).

Be careful now. Don't read that last line too fast. Try it again. Slowly.

"The son sat up and began to talk."

Incredible sentence, don't you think? At the risk of overdoing it, let's read it one more time. This time say each word aloud. "The son sat up and began to talk."

Good job. (Did everyone around you look up?) Can we do it again? This time read it aloud again, but very s-l-o-w-l-y. Pause between each word.

"The . . . son . . . sat . . . up . . . and . . . began . . . to . . . talk."

Now the question. What's odd about that verse?

You got it. Dead people don't sit up! Dead people don't talk! Dead people don't leave their coffins!

Unless Jesus shows up. Because when Jesus shows up, you never know what might happen.

1. Based upon what you have just read, which of the following statements are true concerning Jesus' power? Check your response.

   ❑ Everything can change at a word from Jesus.
   ☑ Jesus can reach us in the midst of our deepest sorrow.
   ❑ When Jesus shows up, anything might happen.
   ☑ Jesus' power is no match for realities like death.
   ☑ Nothing is beyond the power of Jesus.

WHEN JESUS SHOWS UP

Jairus can tell you. His daughter was already dead. The mourners were already in the house. The funeral had begun. The people thought the best Jesus could do was offer some kind words about Jairus's girl. Jesus had some words all right. Not about the girl, but for the girl.

"My child, stand up!" (Luke 8:54).

The next thing the father knew, she was eating, Jesus was laughing, and the hired mourners were sent home early.

2. Jesus merely spoke the words and the girl's lifeless body responded. Look up the following verses and write down what you learn about the power contained in God's words and his voice.

   Deuteronomy 8:3 – "People need more than bread for their life; real life comes by feeding on every word of the Lord." NLT

   Real life comes from the Lord Jesus
   Christ

Nothing is beyond the power of Jesus.

Death, where is your victory?
—1 Corinthians 15:55

VICTORY OVER DEATH

The fire that lit the boiler of the New Testament church was an unquenchable belief that if Jesus had only been a man, he would have stayed in the tomb. The earliest Christians couldn't stay silent about the fact that the one they saw hung on the cross walked again on the earth and appeared to five hundred people.

Let us ask our Father humbly, yet confidently in the name of Jesus, to remind us of the open tomb. Let us see the victorious Jesus: the conqueror of the tomb, the one who defied death. And let us be reminded that we, too, will be granted that same victory.
—*Walking with the Savior*

The Lord made the earth by his power. He used his wisdom to build the world and his understanding to stretch out the skies.

—**Jeremiah 51:15**

Psalm 29:3 – "The Lord's voice is heard over the sea. The glorious God thunders; the Lord thunders over the ocean."

The voice of the Lord is so powerfull and he will never leave us.

Isaiah 30:21 – "If you go the wrong way—to the right or to the left—you will hear a voice behind you saying, 'This is the right way. You should go this way.'"

The Lord will always lead you.

Joel 3:16 – "The Lord will roar like a lion from Jerusalem; his loud voice will thunder from that city, and the sky and the earth will shake. But the Lord will be a safe place for his people, a strong place of safety for the people of Israel."

And when he speacks the hold world will hear, but we never all left alone

John 5:28 – "Indeed, the time is coming when all the dead in their graves will hear the voice of God's Son." NLT

The power that God has all we have raise up out of the grave

Martha can tell you. She'd hoped Jesus would show up to heal Lazarus. He didn't. Then she'd hoped he'd show up to bury Lazarus. He didn't. By the time he made it to Bethany, Lazarus was four-days buried and Martha was wondering what kind of friend Jesus was.

She hears he's at the edge of town so she storms out to meet him. "Lord, if you had been here," she confronts, "my brother would not have died" (John 11:21).

There is hurt in those words. Hurt and disappointment. The one Man who could have made a difference didn't, and Martha wants to know why.

Maybe you do, too. Maybe you've done what Martha did. Someone you love ventures near the edge of life, and you turn to Jesus for help. You, like Martha, turn to the only one who can pull a person from the ledge of death. You ask Jesus to give a hand.

Martha must have thought, Surely he will come. Didn't he aid the paralytic? Didn't he help the leper? Didn't he give sight to the blind? And they hardly knew Jesus. Lazarus is his friend. We're like family. Doesn't Jesus come for the weekend? Doesn't he eat at our table? When he hears that Lazarus is sick, he'll be here in a heartbeat.

But he didn't come. Lazarus got worse. She watched out the window. Jesus didn't show. Her brother drifted in and out of consciousness. "He'll be here soon, Lazarus," she promised. "Hang on."

But the knock at the door never came. Jesus never appeared. Not to help. Not to heal. Not to bury. And now, four days later, he finally shows up. The funeral is over. The body is buried, and the grave is sealed.

And Martha is hurt.

Her words have been echoed in a thousand cemeteries. "If you had been here, my brother would not have died."

If you were doing your part, God, my husband would have survived. If you'd done what was right, Lord, my baby would have lived.

If only you'd have heard my prayer, God, my arms wouldn't be empty.

The grave unearths our view of God.

3. How does the reality of death sometimes cause us to doubt God's power?

No it better are than liven on earth. Jesus so we can see him all the people we love well be by us.

Facing the death of a loved one reveals our view of God.

Before the mountains were born and before you created the earth and the world, you are God. You have always been, and you will always be.
—Psalm 90:2

4. Death is a good example of God's power delayed. We know we will see our loved ones again someday, but we have to wait on the day God will raise all of us from the dead. And waiting is hard. Read the following verses. Then match the verse with what you learn about waiting on God.

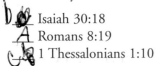 Isaiah 30:18   a. We wait, believing Jesus will come back.

Romans 8:19   b. If we wait on God, we will be happy.

1 Thessalonians 1:10   c. The whole earth waits for God to reveal his power.

DEFEATING DEATH

When we face death, our definition of God is challenged. Which, in turn, challenges our faith. Which leads me to ask a grave question. Why is it that we interpret the presence of death as the absence of God? Why do we think that if the body is not healed then God is not near? Is healing the only way God demonstrates his presence?

Sometimes we think so. And as a result, when God doesn't answer our prayers for healing, we get angry. Resentful. Blame replaces belief. "If you had been here, doing your part, God, then this death would not have happened."

It's distressing that this view of God has no place for death.

5. Scripture addresses the reality of death. It's as if God knew it would be the one thing that might still make us doubt him. Which of the following statements are true concerning death? Check all that apply. Use the Bible verses below to help you answer.

God will someday destroy death forever. (Isaiah 25:8)

If we believe in Jesus, we will never die spiritually. (John 10:27–28)

Jesus gives us life that cannot be destroyed. (2 Timothy 1:10)

God holds the keys to death. (Revelation 1:18)

Some time ago a visitor to our house showed my daughters some tricks. Magic acts. Simple sleight-of-hand stuff. I stood to the side and watched the girls' responses. They were amazed. When the coin disappeared, they gasped. When it reappeared, they were stunned. At first I was humored by their bewilderment.

But with time, my bewilderment became concern. Part of me didn't like what was happening. My kids were being duped. He was tricking them. They, the innocent, were being buffaloed by him, the sneak. I didn't like that. I didn't like seeing my children fooled.

So I whispered to my daughters. "It's in his sleeve." Sure enough it was. "It's behind his ear." And what do you know, I was right! Maybe I was rude to interfere with the show, but I don't enjoy watching a trickster pull one over on my children.

Neither does God.

Jesus couldn't bear to sit and watch the bereaved be fooled.

Please understand, he didn't raise the dead for the sake of the dead. He raised the dead for the sake of the living.

JESUS DOES THE IMPOSSIBLE

"Lazarus, come out!" (v. 43).

Martha was silent as Jesus commanded. The mourners were quiet. No one stirred as Jesus stood face to face with the rock-hewn tomb and demanded that it release his friend.

No one stirred, that is, except for Lazarus. Deep within the tomb, he moved. His stilled heart began to beat again. Wrapped eyes popped open. Wooden fingers lifted. And a mummified man in a tomb sat up. And want to know what happened next?

Let John tell you. "The dead man came out, his hands and feet wrapped with pieces of cloth, and a cloth around his face" (v. 44).

The Lord wants to show his mercy to you. He wants to rise and comfort you. The Lord is a fair God, and everyone who waits for his help will be happy.

—Isaiah 30:18

God holds the keys to life and death.

THE SHEPHERD'S VOICE

A day is coming when everyone will hear [Jesus'] voice. A day is coming when all other voices will be silenced; his voice—and his voice only—will be heard.

Some will hear his voice for the very first time. It's not that he never spoke, it's just that they never listened. For these, God's voice will be the voice of a stranger. They will hear it once—and never hear it again. They will spend eternity fending off the voices they followed on earth.

But others will be called from their graves by a familiar voice. For they are sheep who know their shepherd. They are servants who opened the door when Jesus knocked.

Now the door will open again. Only this time, it won't be Jesus who walks into our house; it will be we, who walk into his.

—*In the Eye of the Storm*

The Lord All-Powerful is with us; the God of Jacob is our defender.

—**Psalm 46:7**

There it is again. Did you see it? Read the first five words of the verse again.
"The dead man came out."
Again. Slower this time.
"The dead man came out."
One more time. This time out loud and very slowly. (I know you think I'm crazy, but I really want you to get the point.)
"The . . . dead . . . man . . . came . . . out."
Can I ask the same questions? (Of course I can; I'm writing the book!)
Question: What's wrong with this picture?
Answer: Dead men don't walk out of tombs.
Question: What kind of God is this?
Answer: The God who holds the keys to life and death.
The kind of God who rolls back the sleeve of the trickster and reveals death for the parlor trick it is.
The kind of God you want present at your funeral.

God raised Jesus from the dead and set him free from the pain of death, because death could not hold him.

—Acts 2:24

6. Jesus has power over death because he conquered it. He has personal experience with death—he knows it can be and one day will be defeated. Read Acts 2:24 and fill in the blanks of this verse about Jesus' power over death.

God raised ~~all Jesus~~ from the ~~dead grave~~ *Dead* and set him ~~dead~~ *free* from the ~~Pain~~ *Pain* of death. ~~Death~~ simply could not ~~hurt hold~~ *hold* Jesus in his grave.

He'll do it again, you know. He's promised he would. And he's shown that he can.
"The Lord himself will come down from heaven with a loud command" (1 Thess. 4:16).

When Jesus comes again, death will be no more.

The same voice that awoke the boy near Nain, that stirred the still daughter of Jairus, that awakened the corpse of Lazarus—the same voice will speak again. The earth and the sea will give up their dead. There will be no more death.
Jesus made sure of that.

THE HEART OF THE MATTER

- **Facing the death of a loved one reveals our view of God.**
- **Nothing is beyond the power of Jesus.**
- **Facing the death of a loved one reveals our view of God.**
- **God holds the keys to life and death.**
- **When Jesus comes again, death will be no more.**

How is your Bible memorization coming along? Take a few minutes here and review this week's verse. It's 2 Corinthians 12:9.

each time he said my grace is you need, my power works best in weakness to now I am glad to boast about my weakness so The Heart of Jesus *that the power of christ can to work through me*

They had sat there, side by side, clutching each other's hands even as fear clutched their hearts. Finally, her husband had left her alone—gone to find another doctor she supposed. And so she had clung to her daughter's hand instead, holding her breath until the girl drew another. She prayed, desperately and incoherently. "Please let Jairus bring help. Please don't let my baby die." Family members stirred in the lower level of the house, occasionally coming up to check on mother and daughter. So when the anguished cry reached their ears, they ran to her. Arms were ready to enfold the bereaved mother. Shoulders were offered to cry on. And quiet voices gave the orders that the funeral preparations should begin. By the time Jairus reached home with Jesus at his heels, mourners were gathered and sad music filled the house. Numbed and dismayed,

Be strong and brave. Don't be afraid of them and don't be frightened, because the Lord your God will go with you. He will not leave you or forget you.

—Deuteronomy 31:6

Jairus gathered his wife into his arms. Jesus' command that the mourners be sent away barely registered. The couple moved woodenly as Jesus and a few of his disciples guided them towards the stairs and into their daughter's room. Jairus had hoped that Jesus would have the power to heal his daughter. Imagine his astonishment when Jesus' power proved enough to raise her from the dead! Sorrow was whisked away. Only joy and rejoicing remained.

—Luke 8:41–56

DAY FIVE—THE STONE MOVER'S GALLERY

THE GALLERY OF WEAKNESS

The Bruised Reed
> *It stood with assurance.*
> *Head held high on strong stalk.*
> *But that was before the careless bump, the harsh rain.*
> *Now it's bruised, bent. Weakened.*
> *It seeks gentle fingers to straighten and not break.*
> *It needs a firm touch to heal and not to hurt.*
> *Tender power.*
> *Soft strength.*
> *Is there such a hand?*

Let's revisit the gallery we entered at the start of this study—the Exhibit on Bruised Reeds and Smoldering Wicks.

Alone in the center of the hall is a single painting. It is different from the others. There are no faces. No people. The artist has dipped his brush into ancient prophecy and sketched two simple objects—a reed and a wick.

A bruised reed he will not break, and a smoldering wick he will not snuff out. (Matt. 12:20 NIV)

Is there anything more frail than a bruised reed? Look at the bruised reed at the water's edge. A once slender and tall stalk of sturdy river grass, it is now bowed and bent.

Are you a bruised reed? Was it so long ago that you stood so tall, so proud? You were upright and sturdy, nourished by the waters and rooted in the riverbed of confidence.

Then something happened. You were bruised . . .
by harsh words
by a friend's anger
by a spouse's betrayal
by your own failure
by religion's rigidity.

And you were wounded, bent ever so slightly. Your hollow reed, once erect, now stooped, and hidden in the bulrush.

My Father gave my sheep to me. He is greater than all, and no person can steal my sheep out of my Father's hand.
—John 10:29

1. Look up the following verses below and write down what you learn about Jesus' familiarity with life's bruises.

Matthew 6:34 – "So don't worry about tomorrow, because tomorrow will have its own worries. Each day has enough trouble of its own."

do not Judge other and you will not be Judge

John 15:18 – "If the world hates you, remember that it hated me first."

the world would love you as one of its own if you belonged to it and I going to bye through Jesus Christ my Lord

John 16:33 – "I told you these things so that you can have peace in me. In this world you will have trouble, but be brave! I have defeated the world."

Jesus have peace in them, as the world is a mean world,

And the smoldering wick on the candle. Is there anything closer to death than a smoldering wick? Once aflame, now flickering and failing. Still warm from yesterday's passion, but no fire. Not yet cold but far from hot. Was it that long ago you blazed with faith? Remember how you illuminated the path?

Then came the wind . . . the cold wind, the harsh wind. They said your ideas were foolish. They told you your dreams were too lofty. They scolded you for challenging the time-tested.

The constant wind wore down upon you. Oh, you stood strong for a moment (or maybe a lifetime), but the endless blast whipped your flickering flame, leaving you one pinch away from darkness.

But I have this complaint against you. You don't love me or each other as you did at first! Look how far you have fallen from your first love! Turn back to me again and work as you did at first.
—Revelation 2:4–5 NLT

2. Read Revelation 2:4–5 on the left and write down what you learn about Jesus' concern for the fading passion of a smoldering wick.

you must listen to the Spirit and understand what God is saying

The bruised reed and the smoldering wick. Society knows what to do with you. The world has a place for the beaten. The world will break you off; the world will snuff you out.

But the artists of Scripture proclaim that God won't. Painted on canvas after canvas is the tender touch of a Creator who has a special place for the bruised and weary of the world. A God who is the friend of the wounded heart. A God who is the keeper of your dreams. That's the theme of the New Testament.

And that's the theme of the gallery.

God treats the wounded and weary with tenderness.

3. With the power of the universe at his command, he could obliterate us with a word. Yet Jesus approaches us with tender strength instead. He refuses to give up on us. Which of the following statements are true concerning Jesus' commitment to us? Use the Bible verses below to help you answer. Check all that apply.

- ☑ He will never leave us He will never forget us. (Hebrews 13:5)
- ☑ The Holy Spirit will be with us forever. (John 14:16)
- ☑ We can remain in God's love. (John 15:10)
- ☐ When we experience hard times it means he has abandoned us. (2 Corinthians 4:9)

WHAT JESUS DOES

Quite a gallery, don't you think? A room of pain-to-peace portraits. A ward of renewed strength. A forest of restored vigor.

Now Jesus has gone into heaven and is at God's right side ruling over angels, authorities, and powers.
—1 Peter 3:22

An exhibition of second chances.

Wouldn't it be incredible to visit a real one? Wouldn't it be great to walk through an actual collection of "Bruised Reeds and Smoldering Wicks"? What if you could see portrayal after portrayal of God meeting people at their points of pain? Not just biblical characters, but contemporary folks just like you? People from your generation and your world!

And what if this gallery contained not only their story, but yours and mine as well? What if there were a place where we could display our "before" and "after" experiences? Well, there might be one. I have an idea for such a gallery. It may sound far-fetched, but it's worth sharing.

Before I do, we need to discuss one final question. A crucial question. You've just read one story after another of God meeting people where they hurt. Tell me, why are these stories in the Bible? Why are the Gospels full of such people? Such hopeless people? Though their situations vary, their conditions don't. They are trapped. Estranged. Rejected. They have nowhere to turn. On their lips, a desperate prayer. In their hearts, desolate dreams. And in their hands, a broken rope. But before their eyes a never-say-die Galilean who majors in stepping in when everyone else steps out.

Surprisingly simple, the actions of this man. Just words of mercy or touches of kindness. Fingers on sightless eyes. A hand on a weary shoulder. Words for sad hearts . . . all fulfilling the prophecy: "A bruised reed he will not break, and a smoldering wick he will not snuff out."

Again I ask. Why are these portraits in the Bible? Why does this gallery exist? Why did God leave us one tale after another of wounded lives being restored? So we could be grateful for the past? So we could look back with amazement at what Jesus did?

No. No. No. A thousand times no. The purpose of these stories is not to tell us what Jesus did. Their purpose is to tell us what Jesus does.

> **Jesus is still healing hearts and restoring lives.**

4. We can count on Jesus' strength in the past to be there for us in the present and future. Read the following verses. Then match the verse with what you learn about the consistency of what Jesus does.

   b ____ Matthew 28:20   a. Jesus lives forever.
   d ____ 1 Corinthians 13:7   b. He will be with us always.
   a ____ Hebrews 7:24   c. He is the same yesterday, today and forever.
   c ____ Hebrews 13:8   d. His love always remains strong.

> **The Bible records moments when a real God met real pain.**

> *"Everything that was written in the past was written to teach us," Paul penned. "The Scriptures give us patience and encouragement so that we can have hope"* —(Romans 15:4).

These are not just Sunday school stories. Not romantic fables. Not somewhere-over-the-rainbow illusions. They are historic moments in which a real God met real pain so we could answer the question, "Where is God when I hurt?"

5. How would you answer the question, "Where is God when I hurt?"

   He is carrying me. We have to
   listen for him

CELEBRATING HIS STRENGTH

Now that you've read their stories, reflect on yours. Stand in front of the canvases that bear your name and draw your portraits.

It doesn't have to be on a canvas with paint. It could be on a paper with pencil, on a computer with words, in a sculpture with clay, in a song with lyrics. It doesn't matter how you do it, but I urge you to do it. Record your drama. Retell your saga. Plot your journey.

> *The Lord said, "If your faith were the size of a mustard seed, you could say to this mulberry tree, 'Dig yourself up and plant yourself in the sea,' and it would obey you."*
> —Luke 17:6

Begin with "before." What was it like before you knew him? Do you remember? Could be decades ago. Perhaps it was yesterday. Maybe you know him well. Maybe you've just met him. Again, that doesn't matter. What matters is that you never forget what life is like without him. *give me peace and a warm heart*

But don't just portray the past, depict the present. Describe his touch. Display the difference he has made in your life. This task has its challenges, too. Whereas painting the "before" can be painful, painting the "present" can be unclear. He's not finished with you yet!

Ah, but look how far you've come! I don't even know you, but I know you've come a long way. God has begun a work in your heart. And what God begins, God completes. "God began doing a good work in you, and I am sure he will continue it until it is finished when Jesus Christ comes again" (Phil. 1:6). *praise God*

So chronicle what Christ has done. If he has brought peace, sketch a dove. If joy, splash a rainbow on a wall. If courage, sing a song about mountain-movers. And when you're finished, don't hide it away. Put it where you can see it. Put it where you can be reminded, daily, of the Father's tender power.

6. Where do you long to see Jesus working his tender power in your life?

to help me remember his words of peace, love, joy, want him to grab if I start fading.

HE STILL MOVES STONES

That's my idea. I know it's crazy, but what if, when we all get home, we make a gallery? I don't know if they allow this kind of stuff in heaven. But something tells me the Father won't mind. After all, there's plenty of space and lots of time.

And somewhere in the midst of this arena of hope is your story. Person after person comes. They listen as if they have all the time in the world. (And they do!) They treat you as if you are royalty. (For you are!) Solomon asks you questions. Job compliments your stamina. Joshua lauds your courage. And when they all applaud, you applaud too. For in heaven, everyone knows that all praise goes to one Source.

And speaking of the Source, he's represented in the heavenly gallery as well. Turn and look. High above the others. In the most prominent place. Exactly in the middle. There is one display elevated high on a platform above the others. Visible from any point in the gallery is a boulder. It's round. It's heavy. It used to seal the opening of a tomb.

But not anymore. Ask Mary and Martha. Ask Peter. Ask Lazarus. Ask anyone in the gallery. They'll tell you. Stones were never a match for God.

Will there be such a gallery in heaven? Who knows? But I do know there used to be a stone in front of a tomb. And I do know it was moved. And I also know that there are stones in your path. Stones that trip and stones that trap. Stones too big for you.

7. Read Colossians 1:11. Fill in the blanks below about what you learn concerning God's ability to strengthen you with his power.

God will *strengthen* you with his own *glorious* power. He does this so we will not *give* up when *storms* come our way. He wants us to be *strong*.

Please remember, the goal of these stories is not to help us look back with amazement, but forward with faith. The God who spoke still speaks. The God who forgave still forgives. The God who came still comes. He comes into our world. He comes into your world. He comes to do what you can't. He comes to move the stones you can't budge.

Stones are no match for God. Not then and not now. He still moves stones.

We also pray that you will be strengthened with his glorious power so that you will have all the patience and endurance you need. May you be filled with joy.
—Colossians 1:11

The goal of Bible stories is to help us look forward with faith.

If you remain in me and follow my teachings, you can ask anything you want, and it will be given to you.
—John 15:7

THE HEART OF THE MATTER

❧ **God treats the wounded and weary with tenderness.**
❧ **The Bible records moments when a real God met real pain.**
❧ **The goal of Bible stories is to help us look forward with faith.**

The Heart of Jesus

Thomas had seen it all. For three years he had watched Jesus feed the hungry, heal the sick, even raise the dead. The miracles had been amazing. Jesus had seemed to possess the very power of heaven. So then why had he died? Jesus had been able to slip away from his pursuers before. What made him vulnerable now? Where had the power been when Judas betrayed him? Where had the power been when the soldiers beat him? Where had the power been when Pilate condemned him? Where had the power been when the cross was thrust onto his shoulders? Where had the power been when they nailed him to that cross? Where had the power been when Jesus died? Now Jesus was dead, and the power was gone. That was that. Thomas felt duped, disappointed, and doubtful. He would be more careful about what he trusted in the future. So when the disciples came to him with the astonishing news that Jesus had returned, Thomas put his foot down. "No way. Unless I get a good look myself, I won't believe it. In fact, I want to touch the man, look into his eyes, see the scars." And so Jesus came. The power had never been gone, and Thomas was welcomed to experience it anew.

FOR FURTHER READING

Selections throughout this lesson were taken from *He Still Moves Stones.*

He who guards Israel never rests or sleeps.

—Psalm 121:4

Experiencing the Forgiveness of Jesus

NOT PERFECTION, BUT FORGIVENESS

It wasn't the Romans who nailed Jesus to the cross. It wasn't spikes that held Jesus to the cross. What held him to that cross was his conviction that it was necessary that he become sin—that he who is pure become sin and that the wrath of God be poured down, not upon the creation, but upon the Creator.

When the one who knew no sin became sin for us, when the sinless one was covered with all the sins of the world, God didn't call his army of angels to save him. He didn't, because he knew he would rather give up his Son than give up on us.

Regardless of what you've done, it's not too late. Regardless of how far you've fallen, it's not too late. It doesn't matter how low the mistake is, it's not too late to dig down, pull out that mistake, and then let it go—and be free.

What makes a Christian a Christian is not perfection but forgiveness.

—*Walking with the Savior*

If we—speckled with foibles and greed—love to give gifts, how much more does God, pure and perfect God, enjoy giving gifts to us? Jesus asked, "If you hardhearted, sinful men know how to give good gifts to your children, won't your Father in heaven even more certainly give good gifts to those who ask him for them?" (Matt. 7:11 TLB).

God's gifts shed light on God's heart, God's good and generous heart. Jesus' brother James tells us: "Every desirable and beneficial gift comes out of heaven. The gifts are rivers of light cascading down from the Father of Light" (James 1:17 MSG). Every gift reveals God's love . . . but no gift reveals his love more than the gifts of the Cross. They came, not wrapped in paper, but in passion. Not placed around a tree, but a cross. And not covered with ribbons, but sprinkled with blood.

The gifts of the Cross.

Much has been said about the gift of the Cross itself, but what of the other gifts? What of the nails, the crown of thorns? The garments taken by the soldiers. The garments given for the burial. Have you taken time to open these gifts?

He didn't have to give them, you know. The only act, the only required act for our salvation was the shedding of blood, yet he did much more. So much more.

Could it be that the hill of the Cross is rich with God's gifts? Let's examine them throughout this week, shall we? Let's unwrap these gifts of grace as if—or perhaps, indeed—for the first time. And as you touch them—as you feel the timber of the cross and trace the braid of the crown and finger the point of the spike—pause and listen. Perchance you will hear him whisper:

"I did it just for you."

EXPERIENCING THE FORGIVENESS OF JESUS THIS WEEK

Before you read any further, spend some time in prayer.

Dear Lord, take me to the Cross this week. Help me see this precious gift of forgiveness with new eyes. Give me a glimpse of your fathomless love, the enormous price, and your perfect plan. Help me appreciate the cost of my forgiveness. And as I experience the forgiveness of Jesus this week, show me how to extend that same forgiveness to those around me. Amen.

This week, memorize Colossians 1:13–14—a testimony to Jesus' forgiveness.

God has freed us from the power of darkness, and he brought us into the kingdom of his dear Son. The Son paid for our sins, and in him we have forgiveness. —*Colossians 1:13–14*

God gave him as a way to forgive sin through faith in the blood of Jesus' death. This showed that God always does what is right and fair, as in the past when he was patient and did not punish people for their sins.
—Romans 3:25

DAY ONE—CONSIDER THE COST

TIME'S UP

> So the Word became human and lived here on earth among us. He was full of un-
> failing love and faithfulness. And we have seen his glory, the glory of the only Son
> of the Father." –John 1:14 NLT

Scripture says that the number of God's years is unsearchable (Job 36:26). We may search out the moment the first wave slapped on a shore or the first star burst in the sky, but we'll never find the first moment when God was God, for there is no moment when God was not God. He has never not been, for he is eternal. God is not bound by time.

But when Jesus came to the earth, all this changed. He heard for the first time a phrase never used in heaven: "Your time is up." As a child, he had to leave the temple because his time was up. As a man, he had to leave Nazareth because his time was up. And as a Savior, he had to die because his time was up. For thirty-three years, the stallion of heaven lived in the corral of time.

1. Based on Matthew 1:18–21, which of the following statements apply to the significance of Jesus' birth? Check all that apply.

   ☑ Jesus was fully human and fully God—conceived by the Spirit and born of a woman.

   ☐ Jesus' birth was controversial from the start.

   ☑ Jesus' humanity was as essential to God's plan as his divinity.

BOUND BY TIME

When God entered time and became a man, he who was boundless became bound. Imprisoned in flesh. Restricted by weary-prone muscles and eyelids. For more than three decades, his once limitless reach would be limited to the stretch of an arm, his speed checked to the pace of human feet.

Do you ever wonder, as I do, was he ever tempted to reclaim his boundlessness? In the middle of a long trip, did he ever consider transporting himself to the next city? When the rain chilled his bones, was he tempted to change the weather? When the heat parched his lips, did he give thought to popping over to the Caribbean for some refreshment?

If ever he entertained such thoughts, he never gave in to them. Not once. Stop and think about this. Not once did Christ use his supernatural powers for personal comfort. With one word he could've transformed the hard earth into a soft bed, but he didn't. With a wave of his hand, he could've boomeranged the spit of his accusers back into their faces, but he didn't. With an arch of his brow, he could've paralyzed the hand of the soldier as he braided the crown of thorns. But he didn't.

2. Read the following verses and write down what you learn about how Scripture uses the imagery of a sacrificial lamb to demonstrate Jesus' willingness to sacrifice in order to secure our forgiveness.

   Isaiah 53:7–8 – "He was beaten down and punished, but he didn't say a word. He was like a lamb being led to be killed. He was quiet, as a sheep is quiet while its wool is being cut; he never opened his mouth. Men took him away roughly and unfairly. He died without children to continue his family. He was put to death; he was punished for the sins of my people."

I feel in my heart him so rich to have

> *You know that in the past you were living in a worthless way, a way passed down from the people who lived before you. But you were saved from that useless life. You were bought, not with something that ruins like gold or silver, but with the precious blood of Christ, who was like a pure and perfect lamb. Christ was chosen before the world was made, but he was shown to the world in these last times for your sake.*
> —1 Peter 1:18–20

Jesus as my savior

> **In Christ we are set free by the blood of his death, and so we have forgiveness of sins. How rich is God's grace.**
> —Ephesians 1:7

Forgiveness could come only at a great price.

THE MESSAGE OF GOD TO MAN

"It is finished."

Stop and listen a moment. Let the words wind through your heart. Imagine the cry from the cross. The sky is dark. The other two victims are moaning. Jeering mouths of the crowd are silent. Perhaps there is thunder. Perhaps there is weeping. Perhaps there is silence. Then Jesus draws in a deep breath, pushes his feet down on that Roman nail, and cries, "It is finished!"

What is finished?

The history-long plan of redeeming man was finished. The message of God to man was finished. The works done by Jesus as a man on earth were finished . . . The sting of death had been removed. It was over.

—No Wonder They Call Him the Savior

Jesus experienced the fruits of sin for our sake—fear, shame, disgrace, guilt, discouragement.

Christ had no sin, but God made him become sin so that in Christ we could become right with God.

—2 Corinthians 5:21

Though your sins are like scarlet, they can be as white as snow. Though your sins are deep red, they can be white like wool.

—Isaiah 1:18

John 1:29 – "The next day John saw Jesus coming toward him. John said, "Look, the Lamb of God, who takes away the sin of the world!"

1 Peter 1:18–19 – "You know that in the past you were living in a worthless way, a way passed down from the people who lived before you. But you were saved from that useless life. You were bought, not with something that ruins like gold or silver, but with the precious blood of Christ, who was like a pure and perfect lamb."

Revelation 5:12 – "The Lamb who was killed is worthy to receive power, wealth, wisdom, and strength, honor, glory, and praise!"

when a church faces persecution remember Christ love internal strife conflict remember Christ concern for purity and his intolerance of sin

THE MESSAGE OF THE THORNS

Jesus' gift of forgiveness is costly. It cost him to become bound by time. It cost him to become bound in a human body. However, most remarkable of all, he surrendered his sinless lips to taste the bitter fruit of our sinfulness. "Using thorny branches, they made a crown, put it on his head, and put a stick in his right hand. Then the soldiers bowed before Jesus and made fun of him, saying, 'Hail, King of the Jews!'" (Matt. 27:29).

Isn't this the message of the crown of thorns?

An unnamed soldier took branches—mature enough to bear thorns, nimble enough to bend—and wove them into a crown of mockery, a crown of thorns.

The fruit of sin is thorns—spiny, prickly, cutting thorns.

What exactly is the fruit of sin? Step into the briar patch of humanity and feel a few thistles. Shame. Fear. Disgrace. Discouragement. Anxiety. Haven't our hearts been caught in these brambles?

The heart of Jesus, however, had not. He had never been cut by the thorns of sin. What you and I face daily, he never knew. Anxiety? He never worried! Guilt? He was never guilty! Fear? He never left the presence of God! Jesus never knew the fruits of sin until he became sin for us.

And when he did, all the emotions of sin tumbled in on him like shadows in a forest. He felt anxious, guilty, and alone. Can't you hear the emotion in his prayer? "My God, my God, why have you rejected me?" (Matt. 27:46). These are not the words of a saint. This is the cry of a sinner.

3. Read 2 Corinthians 5:21 and fill in the blanks about Jesus' experience.
   Christ had *no* sin, but God made him *become* sin so that in *Christ* we could become *right* with God.

4. The message of the crown of thorns is that forgiveness is costly. Read Psalm 49:7–9. Based on what you just read, which of the following statements are true regarding our salvation? Check all that apply.

   ☑ Salvation is costly.
   ☐ People can pay God for their own lives.
   ☑ Only Jesus' sacrifice qualifies as payment.

JUST FOR YOU

Want to know the coolest thing about the coming?

Not that the One who played marbles with the stars gave it up to play marbles with marbles. Or that the One who hung the galaxies gave it up to hang doorjambs to the displeasure of a cranky client who wanted everything yesterday but couldn't pay for anything until tomorrow.

Not that he refused to defend himself when blamed for every sin of every slut and sailor since Adam. Or that he stood silent as a million guilty verdicts echoed in the tribunal of heaven and the giver of light was left in the chill of a sinner's night.

Not even that after three days in a dark hole he stepped into the Easter sunrise with a smile and a swagger and a question for lowly Lucifer—"Is that your best punch?"

That was cool, incredibly cool.

But want to know the coolest thing about the One who gave up the crown of heaven for a crown of thorns?

He did it for you. Just for you.

> *No one can buy back the life of another. No one can pay God for his own life, because the price of a life is high. No payment is ever enough. Do people live forever? Don't they all face death?*
> —Psalm 49:7–9

5. How would you "rate" your understanding of Jesus' forgiveness on a scale of 1 to 5? (Place an "X" where you consider yourself to be.)

5   4   3   2   1

____ "I am confident Jesus has forgiven and forgotten all my sins—past, present, and future."

____ "I am haunted by my past and wonder how Jesus could forgive."

He forgives everything

Jesus was blamed for every sin that would ever be committed.

6. A gift is valuable because the giver has invested time, money, or thought into it. Realizing its price increases our appreciation of the gift. Jesus' gift, the gift of the crown of thorns, cost him everything. Based on 2 Corinthians 8:9, which of the following statements are true, and which ones are false? Mark your answers True (T) or False (F).

F Jesus' sacrifice didn't cost him much.

T Jesus' sacrifice cost him everything.

T Jesus became poor for our sake.

T His poverty made us rich.

THE HEART OF THE MATTER

- ❦ **Forgiveness could only come at a great price.**
- ❦ **Jesus experienced the fruits of sin for our sake—fear, shame, disgrace, guilt, and discouragement.**
- ❦ **Jesus was blamed for every sin that would ever be committed.**

Take a few moments to practice your new Bible memory verse for this week. It is Colossians 1:13–14.

13 For He (God) has rescued us from the Kingdom of darkness and transferred us into the Kingdom of his dear Son, 14 who purchased our freedom and forgave our sins.

The Heart of Jesus

People brought him the sick. Jesus had touched and healed people with every conceivable disease. He did not shrink from the outcasts and the unlovely. Blind eyes, shriveled limbs, pocked cheeks, decaying skin, twitching muscles, deaf ears. He had seen it all. But the outward ailments were only part of it. Jesus also knew what lay in the hearts of people. He could see it in their eyes—liars, cheaters, backstabbers, murderers, bigots, adulterers, gossips. He could heal their bodies, but he longed for the chance to heal their sin-sick souls. That's why he came—for every selfish, angry, competitive, self-righteous, manipulative, cheating, stingy, ungrateful one who would come to him for forgiveness.

> *He forgives all my sins and heals all my diseases.*
> —**Psalm 103:3**

DAY TWO—HIS CHOICE

KEEPING A LIST

When you were spiritually dead because of your sins and because you were not free from the power of your sinful self, God made you alive with Christ, and he forgave all our sins. He canceled the debt, which listed all the rules we failed to follow. He took away that record with its rules and nailed it to the cross.

—Colossians 2:13–14

The list of our failures and shortcomings is a long one.

He never should have asked me to keep the list. I dread showing it to him. He's a skilled builder, a fine friend. And he has built us a great house. But the house has a few mistakes.

Until this week I didn't see them. But, then again, until this week I didn't live in the house. Once you take up residence in a place, you see every flaw.

"Make a list of them," he told me.

"If you say so," I thought.

A bedroom door won't lock. The storage room window is cracked. Someone forgot to install towel racks in the girls' bathroom. Someone else forgot the knobs to the den door. As I said, the house is nice, but the list is growing.

Looking at the list of the builder's mistakes caused me to think about God making a list of mine. After all, hasn't he taken up residence in my heart? And if I see flaws in my house, imagine what he sees in me. Oh, dare we think of the list he could compile?

The door hinges to the prayer room have grown rusty from underuse.

The stove called jealousy is overheating.

The attic floor is weighted with too many regrets.

The cellar is cluttered with too many secrets.

And won't someone raise the shutter and chase the pessimism out of this heart?

The list of our weaknesses. Would you like anyone to see yours? Would you like them made public? How would you feel if they were posted high so that everyone, including Christ himself, could see? *awful indeed*

May I take you to the moment it was? Yes, there is a list of your failures. Christ has chronicled your shortcomings. And, yes, that list has been made public. But you've never seen it. Neither have I.

Come with me to the hill of Calvary, and I'll tell you why.

1. Look up the following verses and write down what you learn regarding accountability for sin.

   Psalm 130:3–4 – "Lord, if you punished people for all their sins, no one would be left, Lord. But you forgive us, so you are respected."

   Oh how I love you Lord, all the pain Sue every caused you is all in the past and forgotten

   Romans 3:19 – "We know that the law's commands are for those who have the law. This stops all excuses and brings the whole world under God's judgment."

   Praise God always for all things all forgiven and the love shines your love

   Romans 14:12 – "So each of us will have to answer to God."

   my own body make me sick, when we die we will not be a spirit without a body we will have new body that will be perfect for our everlasting life

   Hebrews 4:13 – "Nothing in all the world can be hidden from God. Everything is clear and lies open before him, and to him we must explain the way we have lived."

   Nothing we say or do is kept form God. and he is the one we accountable to.

There is no God like you. You forgive those who are guilty of sin.
—Micah 7:18a *praise God!*

THE HAND OF GOD

Watch as the soldiers shove the Carpenter to the ground and stretch his arms against the beams. One presses a knee against a forearm and a spike against a hand. Jesus turns his face toward the nail just as the soldier lifts the hammer to strike it.

Couldn't Jesus have stopped him? With a flex of the biceps, with a clench of the fist, he could have resisted. Is this not the same hand that stilled the sea? Cleansed the temple? Summoned the dead?

But the fist doesn't clench . . . and the moment isn't aborted.

The mallet rings and the skin rips and the blood begins to drip, then rush. Then the questions follow. Why? Why didn't Jesus resist?

"Because he loved us," we reply. That is true, wonderfully true, but—forgive me—only partially true. There is more to his reason. He saw something that made him stay. As the soldier pressed his arm, Jesus rolled his head to the side, and with his cheek resting on the wood he saw:

A mallet? Yes.

A nail? Yes.

The soldier's hand? Yes.

But he saw something else. He saw the hand of God.

With a wave, this hand toppled Babel's tower and split the Red Sea.

From this hand flew the locusts that plagued Egypt and the raven that fed Elijah.

Is it any wonder the psalmist celebrated liberation by declaring: "You drove out the nations with Your hand . . . It was Your right hand, Your arm, and the light of Your countenance" (Ps. 44:2–3 NKJV).

The hand of God is a mighty hand.

The crowd at the Cross concluded that the purpose of the pounding was to skewer the hands of Christ to a beam. But they were only half-right. We can't fault them for missing the other half. They couldn't see it. But Jesus could. And heaven could. And we can.

> *The cross of our Lord Jesus Christ is my only reason for bragging. Through the cross of Jesus my world was crucified, and I died to the world.*
>
> —Galatians 6:14

2. Read the following verses. Then match the verse with what you learn about the Cross of Jesus. Use the Bible verses below to help you answer.

A	1 Corinthians 1:17	a.	Some people live like enemies of the Cross.
c	1 Corinthians 1:18	b.	We can boast only in the Cross.
b	Galatians 6:14	c.	The Cross has power.
d	Philippians 3:18	d.	Many see the Cross as foolishness.

3. God was not a spectator at the Cross of Jesus. He was intimately involved in accomplishing our salvation. Read Isaiah 53:10 and fill in the blanks concerning God's decision at the Cross.

But it was the ___Lord Jesus___ who decided to ___crush___ him and make Jesus suffer. The ___Lord___ made his life a ___penalty offering___

> *But it was the Lord who decided to crush him and make him suffer. The Lord made his life a penalty offering, but he will still see his descendants and live a long life. He will complete the things the Lord wants him to do.*
>
> —Isaiah 53:10

THE MESSAGE OF THE NAILS

Through the eyes of Scripture we see what others missed but what Jesus saw. "He canceled the record that contained the charges against us. He took it and destroyed it by nailing it to Christ's cross" (Col. 2:14 NLT).

Between his hand and the wood there was a list. A long list. A list of our mistakes: our lusts and lies and greedy moments and prodigal years. A list of our sins.

God has done with us what I am doing with our house. He has penned a list of our faults. The list God has made, however, cannot be read. The words can't be deciphered. The mistakes are covered. The sins are hidden. Those at the top are hidden by his hand; those down the list are covered by his blood. Your sins are "blotted out" by Jesus (KJV). "He has forgiven you all your sins: he has utterly wiped out the written evidence

The blood of Jesus has blotted out the list of our sins.

> *Get along with each other, and forgive each other. If someone does wrong to you, forgive that person because the Lord forgave you.*
>
> —Colossians 3:13

of broken commandments which always hung over our heads, and has completely annulled it by nailing it to the cross" (Col. 2:14 PHILLIPS).

The record of our sins has been erased.

Amen
Amen
Amen

4. What does it mean that our list of sins is completely unreadable?

unreadable to us not Jesus

5. Which of the following statements are true, and which ones are false? Mark your answers True (T) or False (F). Use the Bible verses below to help you answer.

F Jesus holds our sins against us. (2 Corinthians 5:19)
T Jesus took away the record of our sins. (Colossians 2:14)
T Jesus satisfied the penalty for sin—death. (2 Timothy 1:10)

This is why he refused to close his fist. He saw the list! What kept him from resisting? This warrant, this tabulation of your failures. He knew the price of those sins was death. He knew the source of those sins was you, and since he couldn't bear the thought of eternity without you, he chose the nails.

THE DEBT IS PAID

When Jesus told us to pray for forgiveness of our debts as we forgive our own debtors, he knew who would be the one to pay the debt. As he would hang on the cross he would say, "It is finished" . . . the debt is paid!

There are some facts that will never change. One fact is that you are forgiven. If you are in Christ, when he sees you, your sins are covered—he doesn't see them. He sees you better than you see yourself. And that is a glorious fact of your life.

—Walking with the Savior

6. Read Colossians 2:14 and fill in the blanks concerning this blow-by-blow account of why Jesus chose the nails.

Jesus *canceled* our debt that listed all the *rules* we failed to *follow*. He took away that *record* with its rules and *nailed* it to the *cross*.

7. Based on what you have learned so far, why did God require Jesus' death to cover for our sins? Check all that apply. Use the Bible verses below to help you answer.

☑ The price for sin is death. (Romans 6:23)
☑ Sins cannot be forgiven apart from Jesus' blood. (Hebrews 9:22)
☑ Jesus' blood "bought people for God." (Romans 5:9)

He canceled the debt, which listed all the rules we failed to follow. He took away that record with its rules and nailed it to the cross.

—Colossians 2:14

Even as we progress to more of a paperless society—a one where one wonders how we ever existed without online bill-paying and the convenience of fax and email—we still have not lost our esteem for record-keeping. In the business world, we may no longer jot our lists of creditors and debtors on paper, but we are still scrupulous when it comes to data entry. This leads us to the question: Based on what you have learned so far concerning the enormous charge Jesus paid, why didn't God keep our record of sin "on file"?

He has taken our sins away from us as far as the east is from west.

—Psalm 103:12

8. Read Psalm 103:12. Based on what you just read, which of the following are true? Check all that apply.

❏ God keeps our sins before us to chide us.
☑ God takes away our sins.
☑ Our sins are as far as the east is from the west.

JESUS FORGIVES YOU

The hand squeezing the handle was not a Roman infantryman.
The force behind the hammer was not an angry mob.
The verdict behind the death was not decided by jealous Jews.
Jesus himself chose the nails.

So the hands of Jesus opened up. Had the soldier hesitated, Jesus himself would have swung the mallet. He knew how; he was no stranger to the driving of nails. As a carpenter he knew what it took. And as a Savior he knew what it meant. He knew that the purpose of the nail was to place your sins where they could be hidden by his sacrifice and covered by his blood.

Peter said to them, "Change your hearts and lives and be baptized, each one of you, in the name of Jesus Christ for the forgiveness of your sins. And you will receive the gift of the Holy Spirit."
—Acts 2:38

9. Read Matthew 26:42 and summarize how it demonstrates Jesus' willingness to sacrifice himself for our sake.

My Father if this cup cannot be taken away unless I drink it, "your will be done,"

THE HEART OF THE MATTER

- **The list of our failures and shortcomings is a long one.**
- **The blood of Jesus has blotted out the list of our sins.**
- **The record of our sins has been erased.**

Practice your memory verse for this week by writing it out here. It is Colossians 1:13–14.

13 for He has rescued us from the Kingdom of darkness and transferred us into the Kingdom of His dear Son 14 who purchased our freedom and forgave our sins,

Then Jesus went away a second time and prayed, "My Father, if it is not possible for this painful thing to be taken from me, and if I must do it, I pray that what you want will be done."

—Matthew 26:42

The Heart of Jesus

The trap had been set, and the ambush planned. While Jesus and his disciples had spent the evening in prayer, soldiers had been sharpening their swords and lighting their torches. Gethsemane was quiet, except for the murmured prayers of Jesus and the snoring of his friends. Then suddenly, noise. Tramping feet, crackling firebrands, shouted orders. They were surrounded. The disciples leapt to their feet, momentarily dazed by the light. A surge of men entered their circle, and then Peter, James and John stand before Jesus in order to protect him. Peter draws out a sword, and in one clumsy slash, cuts off the ear of Malchus. A full-blown brawl is imminent. But Jesus defuses the situation, even now offering mercy to one of the very men who will carry him off—to beat him, to taunt him, to bloody his face, and to nail him to a cross. This man is just obeying orders. He is part of a mob, and cannot realize what he is doing, nor to whom it is being done. Jesus forgives him, reaches out a hand, and heals Malchus' ear.

—John 18:10

DAY THREE—OUR CHOICE

DETERMINING YOUR DESTINY

Meet Edwin Thomas, a master of the stage. During the latter half of the 1800s, this small man with the huge voice had few rivals. Debuting in Richard III at the age of fifteen, he quickly established himself as a premier Shakespearean actor. In New York he performed Hamlet for one hundred consecutive nights. In London he won the approval of the tough British critics. When it came to tragedy on the stage, Edwin Thomas was in a select group.

When it came to tragedy in life, the same could be said as well.

Edwin had two brothers, John and Junius. Both were actors, although neither rose to his stature. In 1863, the three siblings united their talents to perform Julius Caesar. The fact that Edwin's brother John took the role of Brutus was an eerie harbinger of what awaited the brothers—and the nation—two years hence.

For this John who played the assassin in Julius Caesar is the same John who took the role of assassin in Ford's Theatre. On a crisp April night in 1865, he stole quietly into the rear of a box in the Washington theater and fired a bullet at the head of

But if we confess our sins, he will forgive our sins, because we can trust God to do what is right. He will cleanse us from all the wrongs we have done.

—1 John 1:9

Abraham Lincoln. Yes, the last name of the brothers was Booth—Edwin Thomas Booth and John Wilkes Booth.

Edwin was never the same after that night. Shame from his brother's crime drove him into retirement. He might never have returned to the stage had it not been for a twist of fate at a New Jersey train station. Edwin was awaiting his coach when a well-dressed young man, pressed by the crowd, lost his footing and fell between the platform and a moving train. Without hesitation, Edwin locked a leg around a railing, grabbed the man, and pulled him to safety. After the sighs of relief, the young man recognized the famous Edwin Booth.

Edwin, however, didn't recognize the young man he'd rescued. That knowledge came weeks later in a letter, a letter he carried in his pocket to the grave. A letter from General Adams Budeau, chief secretary to General Ulysses S. Grant. A letter thanking Edwin Booth for saving the life of the child of an American hero, Abraham Lincoln. How ironic that while one brother killed the president, the other brother saved the president's son. The boy Edwin Booth yanked to safety? Robert Todd Lincoln.[1]

Edwin and John Booth. Same father, mother, profession, and passion—yet one chooses life, the other, death. How could it happen? I don't know, but it does. Though their story is dramatic, it's not unique.

Abel and Cain, both sons of Adam. Abel chooses God. Cain chooses murder. And God lets him.

Abraham and Lot, both pilgrims in Canaan. Abraham chooses God. Lot chooses Sodom. And God lets him.

David and Saul, both kings of Israel. David chooses God. Saul chooses power. And God lets him.

Peter and Judas, both deny their Lord. Peter seeks mercy. Judas seeks death. And God lets him.

In every age of history, on every page of Scripture, the truth is revealed: God allows us to make our own choices.

God allows us to make our own choices.

1. Based on Jesus we have choices to make. What are our options according to Matthew 6:24?

   No one can serve 2 masters hate one + love the other you will be ingrolled to one + despise the other cannot serve Both God + money

2. God gives eternal choices, and these choices have eternal consequences. "Then they [those who rejected God] will go away to eternal punishment, but the righteous to eternal life" (Matt. 25:46 NIV). So why doesn't God just make all of our decisions, small and large, for us?

   When Jesus warns against unbelief, he is trying to save us from agonizing eternal punishment

While God is omniscient, meaning he is all-powerful, he has limited his power in one area of his creation. Our human will. He will not force himself or his ways upon us. He gave his creation the dignity of choice—choosing whether or not we will accept his offer of forgiveness, repent of our sin, and turn to him.

3. Read Genesis 2:15–17; 3:6 and answer the following.

   What choices did God give Adam?

   to not eat off the tree of knowledge

   What was Adam's ultimate choice? (3:6)

   because his wife the tree was beautiful and the fruit looked delicious + she wanted wisdom it would give her she ate some gave some to adam and he ate some.

THE MESSAGE OF THE TWO CROSSES

Jesus' forgiveness is a done deal, accomplished at Calvary. However, "Calvary's trio" of crosses reminds us we must personally accept and embrace this gift in our lives.

Ever wonder why there were two crosses next to Christ? Why not six or ten? Ever wonder why Jesus was in the center? Why not on the far right or far left? Could it be that the two crosses on the hill symbolize one of God's greatest gifts? The gift of choice.

The two criminals have so much in common. Convicted by the same system. Condemned to the same death. Surrounded by the same crowd. Equally close to the same Jesus. In fact, they begin with the same sarcasm: "The two criminals also said cruel things to Jesus" (Matt. 27:44 CEV).

But one changed.

One of the criminals on a cross began to shout insults at Jesus: "Aren't you the Christ? Then save yourself and us." But the other criminal stopped him and said, "You should fear God! You are getting the same punishment he is. We are punished justly, getting what we deserve for what we did. But this man has done nothing wrong." Then he said, "Jesus, remember me when you come into your kingdom." Jesus said to him, "I tell you the truth, today you will be with me in paradise." (Luke 23:39–43).

Much has been said about the prayer of the penitent thief, and it certainly warrants our admiration. But while we rejoice at the thief who changed, dare we forget the one who didn't? What about him, Jesus? Wouldn't a personal invitation be appropriate? Wouldn't a word of persuasion be timely?

There are times when God sends thunder to stir us. There are times when God sends blessings to lure us. But then there are times when God sends nothing but silence as he honors us with the freedom to choose where we spend eternity.

4. Jesus places another choice before his followers in Matthew 7:13–14. What are the options?

The narrow gate
The high way to hell gate is wide for the many that go a road that way

5. God voluntarily restricts his all-powerful nature when it comes to our privilege to choose or reject him. What choice have you made in regard to accepting or rejecting Jesus' offer of forgiveness?

Try to make my right choose, if I don't know I trust Jesus he will led me

THE CHOICE IS OURS

Have we been given any greater privilege than that of choice? Not only does this privilege offset any injustice, the gift of free will can offset any mistakes.

Think about the thief who repented. Though we know little about him, we know this: He made some bad mistakes in life. He chose the wrong crowd, the wrong morals, the wrong behavior. But would you consider his life a waste? Is he spending eternity reaping the fruit of all the bad choices he made? No, just the opposite. He is enjoying the fruit of the one good choice he made. In the end all his bad choices were redeemed by a solitary good one.

6. Read Deuteronomy 30:19. Based on what you have learned so far, which of the following are true and which are false regarding our choices? Check all that apply.

- ☑ God does not allow choice.
- ☐ God sets options before us.
- ☐ He makes the choices obvious—death or life.
- ☐ He is indifferent about our choice.
- ☑ He wants us to choose life.

Enter through the narrow gate. The gate is wide and the road is wide that leads to hell, and many people enter through that gate. But the gate is small and the road is narrow that leads to true life. Only a few people find that road.

—Matthew 7:13–14

No matter how many bad choices we have made in the past, they are redeemed by one good choice—to follow Jesus.

THE BIG CHOICE

[God's] invitation is clear and nonnegotiable. He gives all and we give him all. Simple and absolute. He is clear in what he asks and clear in what he offers. The choice is up to us. Isn't it incredible that God leaves the choice to us? Think about it. There are many things in life we can't choose. We can't, for example, choose the weather. We can't control the economy.

We can't choose whether or not we are born with a big nose or blue eyes or a lot of hair. We can't even choose how people respond to us. But we can choose where we spend eternity. The big choice, God leaves to us. The critical decision is ours.

That is the only decision which really matters.

—*And the Angels Were Silent*

He has taken our sins away from us as far as the east is from west.

—**Psalm 103:12**

Today I ask heaven and earth to be witnesses. I am offering you life or death, blessings or curses. Now, choose life! Then you and your children may live.

—Deuteronomy 30:19

We know we have left death and have come into life because we love each other. Whoever does not love is still dead.

—1 John 3:14

Jesus loves you enough to let you choose.

If you use your mouth to say, "Jesus is Lord," and if you believe in your heart that God raised Jesus from the dead, you will be saved. We believe with our hearts, and so we are made right with God. And we use our mouths to say that we believe, and so we are saved.

—Romans 10:9–10

Happy is the person whose sins are forgiven, whose wrongs are pardoned.
—Psalm 32:1

7. What does 1 John 3:14 say about the choice to accept Jesus? Check all that apply.

T ❏ Once we accept Jesus, we now come into life from death.
F ❏ No one can be sure whether he or she has left death and come into life.
T ❏ If you do not love, you have no life.

8. Jesus presents us with another important choice in Matthew 7:24–27. What decision are you confronted with?

a. Choose a place to live on solid ground.

YOUR CHOICE

How can two brothers be born of the same mother, grow up in the same home, and one choose life and the other choose death? I don't know, but they do.

How could two men see the same Jesus and one choose to mock him and the other choose to pray to him? I don't know, but they did.

And when one prayed, Jesus loved him enough to save him. And when the other mocked, Jesus loved him enough to let him.

He allowed him the choice.

He does the same for you.

9. The message of the two crosses is that forgiveness requires a choice. Jesus freely offers it, but we must choose to accept it. Read Romans 10:9–10 then fill in the blanks about how this passage outlines how we can accept Jesus' offer.

We use our mouth to say, "*Jesus* *is* *Lord*" We believe in our hearts that God *raised* *Jesus* from the dead.

THE HEART OF THE MATTER

- **God allows us to make our own choices.**
- **Because God gives us choices, we must realize that all choices have consequences, both good and bad.**
- **No matter how many bad choices we have made in the past, they are redeemed by one good choice—to follow Jesus.**
- **Jesus loves you enough to let you choose.**

The Heart of Jesus

Forgiveness was not a foreign concept to the Pharisees. After all, they obeyed the Law, attended the feasts, brought their sacrifices. In the heart of their city, the temple was a hubbub of priestly activity. The savory smoke of grilled meat filled the air as it rose towards heaven. Morning sacrifices, evening sacrifices, offerings brought for firstborn babies, for the new harvests, for thanksgiving, as a tithe. Animal after animal took their place on the altar so that God would not be angry with them. The prayers, the worship, the sacrifices—they were a familiar backdrop to every Jew's life in Jerusalem. But when the perfect sacrifice came through town, they missed him completely. In fact, their plotting brought about his capture, his trial, his sentence, and his sacrifice. But Jesus didn't hold it against them. He offered them the same choice he offers to everyone—forgiveness.

Praise God

DAY FOUR—CLOTHED IN CHRIST

SPIRITUALLY UNDERDRESSED

The maître d' wouldn't change his mind. He didn't care that this was our honeymoon. It didn't matter that the evening at the classy country club restaurant was a wedding gift. He couldn't have cared less that Denalyn and I had gone without lunch to save room for dinner. All of this was immaterial in comparison to the looming problem.

I wasn't wearing a jacket.

Didn't know I needed one. I thought a sport shirt was sufficient. It was clean and tucked in. But Mr. Black-Tie with the French accent was unimpressed. He seated everyone else. Mr. and Mrs. Debonair were given a table. Mr. and Mrs. Classier-Than-You were seated. But Mr. and Mrs. Didn't-Wear-a-Jacket?

If I'd had another option, I wouldn't have begged. But I didn't. The hour was late. Other restaurants were closed or booked, and we were hungry. "There's got to be something you can do," I pleaded. He looked at me, then at Denalyn, and let out a long sigh that puffed his cheeks.

"All right, let me see."

He disappeared into the cloakroom and emerged with a jacket. "Put this on." I did. The sleeves were too short. The shoulders were too tight. And the color was lime green. But I didn't complain. I had a jacket, and we were taken to a table. (Don't tell anyone, but I took it off when the food came.)

I needed a jacket, but all I had was a prayer. The fellow was too kind to turn me away but too loyal to lower the standard. So the very one who required a jacket gave me a jacket, and we were given a table.

Isn't this what happened at the cross? Seats at God's table are not available to the sloppy. But who among us is anything but? Unkempt morality. Untidy with truth. Careless with people. Our moral clothing is in disarray. Yes, the standard for sitting at God's table is high, but the love of God for his children is higher. So he offers a gift.

Not a lime-colored jacket but a robe. A seamless robe. Not a garment pulled out of a cloakroom but a robe worn by his Son, Jesus.

1. Imagine sharing the robe of God himself! Look up the following verses and write down what you learn about God's appearance.

   Job 40:9–10 – "Are you as strong as God? Can your voice thunder like his? If so, then decorate yourself with glory and beauty; dress in honor and greatness, as if they were clothing." *Put on, Glory in splendor honor majesty your*

   Psalm 93:1 – "The Lord is king. He is clothed in majesty. The Lord is clothed in majesty and armed with strength."

   Psalm 104:1–2 – "Lord my God, you are very great. You are clothed with glory and majesty; you wear light like a robe. You stretch out the skies like a tent."

   dressed in honor and Greatness, majesty and armed with strength you clothed with glory and majesty

THE MESSAGE IN THE GARMENT

Scripture says little about the clothes Jesus wore. We know what his cousin John the Baptist wore. We know what the religious leaders wore. But the clothing of Christ is nondescript: neither so humble as to touch hearts nor so glamorous as to turn heads.

One reference to Jesus' garments is noteworthy. "They divided his clothes among the four of them. They also took his robe, but it was seamless, woven in one piece from the top. So they said, 'Let's not tear it but throw dice to see who gets it'" (John 19:23–24 NLT).

"This is the mystery of the riches of divine grace for sinners; for by a wonderful exchange our sins are now not ours but Christ's, and Christ's righteousness is not Christ's but ours."

—Martin Luther

For Christ died for sins once for all, the righteous for the unrighteous, to bring you to God.

—1 Peter 3:18 NIV

THE BASIN OF GOD'S GRACE

John tells us, "We are *being cleansed* from every sin by the blood of Jesus." In other words, we are *always being cleansed.* The cleansing is not a promise for the future but a reality in the present. Let a speck of dust fall on the soul of a saint, and it is washed away. Let a spot of filth land on the heart of God's child, and the filth is wiped away . . .

Our Savior kneels down and gazes upon the darkest acts of our lives. But rather than recoil in horror, he reaches out in kindness and says, "I can clean that if you want." And from the basin of his grace, he scoops a palm full of mercy and washes away our sin.

But that's not all he does. Because he lives in us, you and I can do the same. Because he has forgiven us, we can forgive others.

—*Just Like Jesus*

Then I confessed my sins to you and didn't hide my guilt. I said, "I will confess my sins to the Lord," and you forgave my guilt.

—Psalm 32:5

Jesus was robed in humility and righteousness.

You changed my sorrow into dancing. You took away my clothes of sadness, and clothed me in happiness.

—Psalm 30:11

I put on right living as if it were clothing; I wore fairness like a robe and a turban.

—Job 29:14

But Jesus said, "I tell you the truth, the Son can do nothing alone. The Son does only what he sees the Father doing, because the Son does whatever the Father does."

—John 5:19

I can do nothing alone. I judge only the way I am told, so my judgment is fair. I don't try to please myself, but I try to please the One who sent me.

—John 5:30

Jesus wore our sin and shame to the cross.

I, I am the One who forgives all your sins, for my sake; I will not remember your sins.

—Isaiah 43:25

It must have been Jesus' finest possession. Jewish tradition called for a mother to make such a robe and present it to her son as a departure gift when he left home. Had Mary done this for Jesus? We don't know. But we do know the tunic was without seam, woven from top to bottom.

Scripture often describes our behavior as the clothes we wear. Peter urges us to be "clothed with humility" (1 Pet. 5:5 NKJV). David speaks of evil people who clothe themselves "with cursing" (Ps. 109:18 NKJV). Garments can symbolize character, and like his garment, Jesus' character was seamless. Coordinated. Unified. He was like his robe: uninterrupted perfection.

2. Read the following verses. Then match the verse with what you learn about our spiritual clothing.

   _C_ Job 29:14   a. We "wear" happiness instead of sadness.
   _A_ Psalm 30:11   b. We clothe ourselves with Jesus.
   _d_ Isaiah 61:10   c. We wear our right living like clothing.
   _b_ Romans 13:14   d. God dresses us as for a wedding.

3. Have you ever met a well-dressed man or woman, spiritually speaking? What was it about them that caught your eye?

The shine of their face the well fitting dress for Jesus.

The character of Jesus was a seamless fabric woven from heaven to earth, from God's thoughts to Jesus' actions. From God's tears to Jesus' compassion. From God's word to Jesus' response. All one piece. All a picture of the character of Jesus.

4. Read John 5:19 and 5:30 and fill in the blanks about the seamless transition from God's thoughts to Jesus' actions.

John 5:19
But Jesus said, "I tell you the _truth_, the _Son_ can do _nothing_ alone. The Son does _only_ what he sees the _Father_ doing, because the _Son_ does whatever the Father does.

John 5:30
Jesus can do _nothing_ alone. He judges only the way he is _fair_. He doesn't try to _please_ himself, but he tries to please the _One_ who sent him.

TAKE HIS ROBE

But when Christ was nailed to the Cross, he took off his robe of seamless perfection and assumed a different wardrobe, the wardrobe of indignity.

The clothing of Christ on the Cross? Sin—yours and mine. The sins of all humanity.

While on the Cross, Jesus felt the indignity and disgrace of a criminal. No, he was not guilty. No, he had not committed a sin. And, no, he did not deserve to be sentenced. But you and I were, we had, and we did. We were left in the same position I was with the maître d'—having nothing to offer but a prayer.

Jesus willingly lifted our shame from our shoulders so he could don the burden on his way to the Cross. Our shame is gone. Over. Finished. So why do we still insist on walking around our Father's world as if we are underdressed? Cowering in shame as if we had not been forgiven of each and every sin?

5. Based on 1 Peter 2:24, why did Christ "carry our sins in his body"? Check all that apply.

   ☑ So we would stop living for sin.
   ☑ So we would continue to wear our old clothes of sin.
   ☑ So we would start living for what is right.
   ☐ So we would continue to be spiritually underdressed.

Christ carried our sins in his body on the cross so we would stop living for sin and start living for what is right. And you are healed because of his wounds.
—1 Peter 2:24

6. Why shouldn't Christians dig out their "old clothes" and slip into all-too-comfortable habits of low self-esteem, self-criticism, shame, and guilt?

   if we are please fill good & are keeping are morells Jesus. if we have old clothes As long as their clean we should't matter

7. How would you complete the following phrase?

   "When I think about Jesus' 'forgiveness', I think . . ." *what an lesson*
   a. Why me? I don't deserve it. *none of us deserve to go to God. Jesus has for us.*
   b. I'd like to believe I'm forgiven . . . but I'm just not sure. *I'm so happy I know I'm not*
   c. I grew up in church—I already know all there is to know about that. *I always forgot I can learn more*
   d. Sure he forgives. But does he forget? *NO*
   e. Because of Jesus', forgiveness, I will live forever. *Praise God from Who all Blessing fall*

Jesus offers us his own robe of seamless purity.

If anyone belongs to Christ, there is a new creation. The old things have gone; everything is made new!
—2 Corinthians 5:17

Jesus, however, goes further than the maître d'. Can you imagine the restaurant host removing his tuxedo coat and offering it to me? *No way I don't like Big shot places*

Jesus does. We're not talking about an ill-fitting, leftover jacket. He offers a robe of seamless purity and dons my patchwork coat of pride, greed, and selfishness.

8. Read the following verses. Then draw a line between the verse on the left side to the corresponding truth on the right concerning what Jesus did.

   Isaiah 11:5   We wear the "strong coat of his love."
   Isaiah 59:17   We wear "clothes of salvation."
   Isaiah 61:10   We wear Christ himself.
   Galatians 3:13   He girds us with a belt of "goodness and fairness."
   Galatians 3:27   He changed places, taking our sin so we could wear his righteousness.

9. Considering your current spiritual wardrobe, which of the above images do you most need right now?   *Isaiah 11:5*

Jesus' forgiveness has clothed us in salvation.

It wasn't enough for him to prepare you a feast.

It wasn't enough for him to reserve you a seat.

It wasn't enough for him to cover the cost and provide the transportation to the banquet.

He did something more. He let you wear his own clothes so that you would be properly dressed.

He did that . . . just for you.

10. The message of the garment is that forgiveness restores us to like-new condition. Read 2 Corinthians 5:17. Which of the following statements are true, and which ones are false? Mark your answers True (T) or False (F).

   _T_ Forgiveness in Christ makes us new creations.
   _F_ Some old things, like a guilty conscience, never go away.
   _F_ Some old habits, past failures, and mistakes haunt us forever.
   _T_ Everything is made new in Christ.

Lord, you are kind and forgiving and have great love for those who call to you.
—Psalm 86:5

THE HEART OF THE MATTER

❦ **Jesus was robed in humility and righteousness.**
❦ **Jesus wore our sin and shame to the Cross.**
❦ **Jesus offers us his own robe of seamless purity.**
❦ **Jesus' forgiveness has clothed us in salvation.**

The Heart of Jesus

Peter was feeling pretty disgruntled. He'd been taken advantage of—let down again by someone he knew better than he'd like to. Head down, feet hitting the dust a little harder than necessary, he stomped back into camp. He'd almost run into Jesus before coming to a quick halt. Then with one look into his Teacher's compassionate eyes, he'd blurted out his question without even thinking it through. "How many times do we have to forgive someone who sins against us—seven times?" Peter seemed to be attempting generosity, but lingering frustration tinged his question. He was obviously tired of forgiving. Seven times was more than fair. Jesus' answer was startling. "No. Not seven times, but seventy times seven." Some of the other disciples' jaws dropped. Matthew, the tax collector, made a quick calculation. But they got the point. There was no limit to God's ability to forgive the sins of people, and the followers of Christ were likewise to forgive and forgive and forgive.

—Matthew 18:22

DAY FIVE—WHAT WILL YOU LEAVE AT THE CROSS?

Cast all your anxiety on him because he cares for you.

—1 Peter 5:7 NIV

Absurdities and ironies. The hill of Calvary is nothing if not both.

We would have scripted the moment differently. Ask us how a God should redeem his world, and we will show you! White horses, flashing swords. Evil flat on his back. God on his throne.

But God on a cross?

A split-lipped, puffy-eyed, blood-masked God on a cross?

Sponge thrust in his face?

Spear plunged in his side?

Dice tossed at his feet?

No, we wouldn't have written the drama of redemption this way. But, then again, we weren't asked to. These players and props were heaven-picked and God-ordained. We were not asked to design the hour.

But we have been asked to respond to it. In order for the Cross of Christ to be the cross of your life, you and I need to bring something to the hill.

We have seen what Jesus brought. With scarred hands he offered forgiveness. Through torn skin he promised acceptance. He took the path to take us home. He wore our garment to give us his own. We have seen the gifts he brought.

Now we ask, what will we bring?

We aren't asked to paint the sign or carry the nails. We aren't asked to wear the spit or bear the crown. But we are asked to walk the path and leave something at the Cross.

This is my blood which is the new agreement that God makes with his people. This blood is poured out for many to forgive their sins.

—Matthew 26:28

1. Look up the following verses and write down what you learn about our responsibility to follow Jesus and his example.

Matthew 16:24 – "Then Jesus said to his followers, "If people want to follow me, they must give up the things they want. They must be willing even to give up their lives to follow me."

The best way to enjoy life is to loosen our greedy grasp on earthly rewards so that we can be free to follow Christ

John 10:4 – "When he brings all his sheep out, he goes ahead of them, and they follow him because they know his voice."

We know his voice and we know by following Jesus, he will watch over us always

1 Peter 2:21 – "This is what you were called to do, because Christ suffered for you and gave you an example to follow. So you should do as he did."

Give him my soul.

> **Jesus invites you to leave your sins and your worries at the Cross.**

May I urge you to leave something at the Cross? You can observe the Cross and analyze the Cross. You can read about it, even pray to it. But until you leave something there, you haven't embraced the Cross.

You've seen what Christ left. Won't you leave something as well?

2. Using your imagination, survey the scene of Calvary after Jesus' death on the Cross. The nails in a bin. The shadows of the three now empty crosses on the ground. Jesus' blood still fresh in the soil by your feet. It seems an impossible task, but what comes to mind as an appropriate gift in response to the act of forgiveness these things represent?

Give my heart to Jesus. Help me to think before I talk.

> *I will forgive them for the wicked things they did, and I will not remember their sins anymore.*
> —Hebrews 8:12

BAD MOMENTS

Why don't you start with your bad moments?

Those bad habits? Leave them at the Cross. Your selfish moods and white lies? Give them to God. Your binges and bigotries? God wants them all. Every flop, every failure. He wants every single one. Why? Because he knows we can't live with them.

Listen to his promise: "This is my commitment to my people: removal of their sins" (Romans 11:27 MSG).

God does more than forgive our mistakes; he removes them! We simply have to take them to him.

> **Once Jesus forgives the sin we confess, we need never bring it up again.**

3. Read the following verses. Then match the verse with what you learn about how God removes our sin.

   b Psalm 103:12   a. He removes our stubborn hearts.
   a Ezekiel 36:26   b. He takes our sin far away.
   c 1 John 1:9   c. He cleanses us from all wrongs.

4. Read Hebrews 8:12 and fill in the blanks.

   God will _forgive_ us for the wicked things we do. He will _not_ _remember_ their sins anymore.

Sometimes we want to remind Jesus of our past mistakes, even after we have confessed them and received his forgiveness. Their memory begins to bother us, and we feel the need to bring them up in conversation. We say, "Jesus, remember the time I . . . " as

> *The Son paid for our sins, and in him we have forgiveness.*
> —Colossians 1:14

FORGIVENESS FREES THE SOUL

Is there any emotion that imprisons the soul more than the unwillingness to forgive? What do you do when people mistreat you or those you love? Does the fire of anger boil within you, with leaping flames consuming your emotions? Or do you reach somewhere, to some source of cool water and pull out a bucket of mercy—to free yourself?

Don't get on the roller coaster of resentment and anger. You be the one who says, "Yes, he mistreated me, but I am going to be like Christ. I'll be the one who says, 'Forgive them, Father, they don't know what they're doing.'"
—*Walking with the Savior*

Get along with each other, and forgive each other. If someone does wrong to you, forgive that person because the Lord forgave you.

—Colossians 3:13

We are commanded to forgive, just as we have been forgiven.

Be kind and loving to each other, and forgive each other just as God forgave you in Christ.
—Ephesians 4:32

we go into the horrid details. Jesus patiently interrupts us mid-sentence and says, "No, child. I don't remember that at all." When Jesus forgives us, he truly forgets. The past is just that—it has passed.

MAD MOMENTS

What can you leave at the Cross? Start with your bad moments. And while you are there, give God your mad moments.

God wants your list. He inspired one servant to write, "Love does not keep a record of wrongs" (1 Cor. 13:5 TEV). He wants us to leave the list at the Cross.

"Just look what they did to me!" we defy and point to our hurts.

"Just look what I did for you," he reminds and points to the Cross.

5. Based on Colossians 3:13, which of the following are true concerning our responsibility to forgive others. Check all that apply.

❏ If someone wrongs us, we must pay them back.
❏ If certain people wrong us, we may legitimately hold a grudge.
☒ If someone wrongs us, we must forgive because Jesus forgave us.

You and I are commanded—not urged, commanded—to keep no list of wrongs.

Besides, do you really want to keep one? Do you really want to catalog all your mistreatments? Do you really want to growl and snap your way through life? God doesn't want you to either.

6. When it comes to describing your ability to forgive those who have hurt you, which of the following phrases would apply?

❏ "It comes naturally to me—I wouldn't dream of holding a grudge against someone."
❏ "I struggle at first, but eventually forgive—once I've had a chance to cool down."
❏ "People should never cross me—I always find a way to get even."
☒ "Forgive? Yes. Forget? I don't think so." *I want to forget*

ANXIOUS MOMENTS

Take your anxieties to the Cross—literally. Next time you're worried about your health or house or finances or flights, take a mental trip up the hill. Spend a few moments looking again at the pieces of passion.

Run your thumb over the tip of the spear. Balance a spike in the palm of your hand. Read the wooden sign written in your own language. And as you do, touch the velvet dirt, moist with the blood of God.

Blood he bled for you.
The spear he took for you.
The nails he felt for you.

He did all of this for you. Knowing this, knowing all he did for you there, don't you think he'll look out for you here?

7. That last question deserves an honest answer. Knowing about all he did for you, *do* you trust Jesus to take care of you now?

Yes I do. and I pray more this in his word, my soul will rejoice

If we don't believe he can provide a little thing like rent money, for example, how will we ever believe he can accomplish our salvation? However, forgiveness makes a bold statement. It is Jesus' way of asking, "If I can accomplish this, is there anything I can't do for you?" *NO*

8. Read Mark 2:1–12. What is remarkable about Jesus' statement in verse 10? Check all that apply.

- ☒ Jesus could care for both the body and the soul.
- ☐ Jesus was the first prophet who claimed to forgive sins.
- ☒ Jesus' powers proved unlimited—he could even forgive sin.
- ☒ The people had never seen anyone do anything like this before.

YOUR FINAL MOMENT

And may I suggest one more? Your final moment.

Barring the return of Christ first, you and I will have one. A final moment. A final breath. A final widening of the eyes and beating of the heart. In a split second you'll leave what you know and enter what you don't.

God promises to come at an unexpected hour and take us from the gray world we know to a golden world we don't. But since we don't, we aren't sure we want to go. We even get upset at the thought of his coming.

Listen to his promise: "Don't let your hearts be troubled," he urged. "I will come back and take you to be with me so that you may be where I am" (John 14:1, 3).

FREE IN CHRIST

We may not "feel" any more forgiven than we did when we started this study. The truth is, forgiveness is not a feeling; it is a fact, regardless of our finicky feelings. However, the closer you are to the person of Jesus, the more you will feel the effects of his forgiveness in your life. When we experience him, we experience the fullness of what it feels like to be free.

9. Read John 8:36 and fill in the blanks concerning our freedom through our forgiveness.

If the _Son_ makes you _Free_, you will be _truly_ _Free_.

THE HEART OF THE MATTER

- ❦ **Jesus invites you to leave your sins and your worries at the Cross.**
- ❦ **Once Jesus forgives the sin we confess, we need never bring it up again.**
- ❦ **We are commanded to forgive, just as we have been forgiven.**
- ❦ **Even if we don't *feel* forgiven, it is a fact of our salvation.**

The Heart of Jesus

The disciples were gathered around a fire, and the topic of the evening's conversation had turned to the importance of forgiveness. They were trying to pull together what they remembered from their Master's teaching over the last several months. It seemed to be a frequent topic of his teaching—forgiveness was important to Jesus. "We are to forgive one another, as well as our enemies," (Luke 23:34) started one. "And if we don't forgive, God won't forgive us!" reminded another (Matt. 6:15). "God won't even listen to our prayers if we are harboring a grudge against someone" (Mark 11:25). "Our forgiveness must have no limits," supplied a wry Peter (Matt. 18:21). With a nod of approval, Jesus stated, "Forgive because you are forgiven."

FOR FURTHER READING

Selections throughout this lesson were taken from *He Chose the Nails*.

---

[1] Paul Aurandt, *Paul Harvey's the Rest of the Story* (New York: Bantam Press, 1977), 47.

When Jesus saw the faith of these people, he said to the paralyzed man, "Young man, your sins are forgiven." Some of the teachers of the law were sitting there, thinking to themselves, "Why does this man say things like that? He is speaking as if he were God. Only God can forgive sins."

—Mark 2:5–7

Even if we don't feel forgiven, it is a fact of our salvation.

So if the Son makes you free, you will be truly free.

—John 8:36

I have swept away your sins like a big cloud; I have removed your sins like a cloud that disappears into the air. Come back to me because I saved you.

—Isaiah 44:22

Experiencing the Prayer of Jesus

I'd like to talk with you this week about your house. Let's step through the front door and walk around a bit. Every so often it's wise to do a home inspection, you know—check the roof for leaks and examine the walls for bows and the foundation for cracks. We'll see if your kitchen cupboards are full and glance at the books on the shelves in your study.

I'm not talking about your visible house of stone or sticks, wood or straw, but your invisible one of thoughts and truths and convictions and hopes. I'm talking about your spiritual house.

You have one, you know. And it's no typical house. Conjure up your fondest notions and this house exceeds them all. A grand castle has been built for your heart. Just as a physical house exists to care for the body, so the spiritual house exists to care for your soul.

You've never seen a house more solid:
the roof never leaks,
the walls never crack,
and the foundation never trembles.
You've never seen a castle more splendid:
the observatory will stretch you,
the chapel will humble you,
the study will direct you,
and the kitchen will nourish you.

Ever lived in a house like this? Chances are you haven't. Chances are you've given little thought to housing your soul. We create elaborate houses for our bodies, but our souls are relegated to a hillside shanty where the night winds chill us and the rain soaks us. Is it any wonder the world is so full of cold hearts?

Doesn't have to be this way. We don't have to live outside. It's not God's plan for your heart to roam as a Bedouin. God wants you to move in out of the cold and live with him. Under his roof there is space available. At his table a plate is set. In his living room a wingback chair is reserved just for you. And he'd like you to take up residence in his house.

Remember, this is no house of stone. You won't find it on a map. You won't find it described in a realtor journal.

But you will find it in your Bible. You've seen the blueprint before. You've read the names of the rooms and recited the layout. You're familiar with the design. But chances are you never considered it to be a house plan. You viewed the verses as a prayer.

Indeed they are. The Lord's Prayer. It would be difficult to find someone who hasn't quoted the prayer or read the words:

Our Father who art in heaven,
Hallowed be thy name.
Thy kingdom come,
Thy will be done,
On earth as it is in heaven.
Give us this day our daily bread;
And forgive us our debts,
As we have forgiven our debtors;

The Lord has heard my cry for help; the Lord will answer my prayer.
—Psalm 6:9

And lead us not into temptation,
But deliver us from evil.
For thine is the kingdom and the power and the glory forever. Amen. (Matt. 6:9–13 RSV)

Children memorize it. Parishioners recite it. Students study it . . . but I want to challenge us to do something different throughout this week's lessons. I want us to live in it . . . to view it as the floor plan to our spiritual house. In these verses Christ has provided more than a model for prayer, he has provided a model for living. These words do more than tell us what to say to God; they tell us how to exist with God. These words describe a grand house in which God's children were intended to live . . . with him, forever.

EXPERIENCING THE PRAYER OF JESUS THIS WEEK

Before you read any further, spend some time in prayer.

Dear Father, thank you for providing a home for my heart through prayer and fellowship with you. I am struck with awe at your greatness, and humbled that my words of praise are precious to you. I trust that you hear me, and I depend on you to answer. Amen.

This week, memorize Ephesians 6:18.
Pray at all times and on every occasion in the power of the Holy Spirit. Stay alert and be persistent in your prayers for all Christians everywhere. NLT

JUST PRAY

Do you want to know how to deepen your prayer life? Pray. Don't prepare to pray. Just pray. Don't read about prayer. Just pray. Don't attend a lecture on prayer or engage in discussion about prayer. Just pray.

Posture, tone, and place are personal matters. Select the form that works for you. But don't think about it too much. Don't be so concerned about wrapping the gift that you never give it. Better to pray awkwardly than not at all.

And if you feel you should only pray when inspired, that's okay. Just see to it that you are inspired every day.
—*When God Whispers Your Name*

DAY ONE—THE OBSERVATORY —A HEAVENLY AFFECTION

FROM HEAVEN'S PERSPECTIVE

No telescope is needed in this room. The glass ceiling magnifies the universe until you feel all of the sky is falling around you. Elevated instantly through the atmosphere, you are encircled by the heavens. Stars cascade past until you are dizzy with their number. Had you the ability to spend a minute on each planet and star, one lifetime would scarcely be enough to begin.

Jesus waits until you are caught up in the splendor of it all, and then he reminds you softly, "Your Father is in heaven."

I can remember as a youngster knowing some kids whose fathers were quite successful. One was a judge. The other a prominent physician. I attended church with the son of the mayor. In Andrews, Texas, that's not much to boast about. Nevertheless the kid had clout that most of us didn't. "My father has an office at the courthouse," he could claim.

Guess what you can claim? "My Father rules the universe."

"The heavens tell the glory of God and the skies announce what his hands have made. Day after day they tell the story; night after night they tell it again. They have no speech or words; they have no voice to be heard. But their message goes out through all the world; their words go everywhere on earth" (Ps. 19:1–5).

Nature is God's workshop. The sky is his resume. The universe is his calling card. You want to know who God is? See what he has done. You want to know his power? Take a look at his creation. Curious about his strength? Pay a visit to his home address: 1 Billion Starry Sky Avenue. Want to know his size? Step out into the night and stare at starlight emitted one million years ago and then read 2 Chronicles 2:6, "But no one can really build a house for our God. Not even the highest of heavens can hold him."

The Lord sees the good people and listens to their prayers.
—1 Peter 3:12

Your Father is in heaven.

He is untainted by the atmosphere of sin,
unbridled by the time line of history,
unhindered by the weariness of the body.

1. Often prayer begins with praise. Read the following verses. What can you learn from these scriptures about God and the greatness of his power?

   What reasons does David give for people to praise God in 1 Chronicles 29:11–12?

   Every thing about Jesus, what he does for us praise his name eweays

   What does God give Job a glimpse of in Job 38:4–11?

   God himself is the hightest of standers. Our only option is to subnit to his authority and rest in his care

   How can parents pass on God's habit of praise according to Psalm 145:1–6?

   tell all Gods children, tell each generation the greatness of our God the power in whow he has over us

Lord, you are great and powerful. You have glory, victory, and honor. Everything in heaven and on earth belongs to you. The kingdom belongs to you, Lord; you are the ruler over everything. Riches and honor come from you. You rule everything. You have the power and strength to make anyone great and strong.

—1 Chronicles 29:11–12

2. Based on what you have just learned about who God is, why is prayer such an incredible privilege?

   through are prayer during all praises we can pray to Jesus he is always with us.

The resources of heaven belong to God to deal with our problems.

EARTHLY CONCERNS

What controls you doesn't control him. What troubles you doesn't trouble him. What fatigues you doesn't fatigue him. Is an eagle disturbed by traffic? No, he rises above it. Is the whale perturbed by a hurricane? Of course not, he plunges beneath it. Is the lion flustered by the mouse standing directly in his way? No, he steps over it.

How much more is God able to soar above, plunge beneath, and step over the troubles of the earth! "With man this is impossible, but with God all things are possible" (Matt.. 19:26, NIV). Our questions betray our lack of understanding:

How can God be everywhere at one time? (Who says God is bound by a body?)

How can God hear all the prayers which come to him? (Perhaps his ears are different from yours.)

How can God be the Father, the Son, and the Holy Spirit? (Could it be that heaven has a different set of physics than earth?)

How vital that we pray, armed with the knowledge that God is in heaven. Pray with any lesser conviction and your prayers are timid, shallow, and hollow. But spend some time walking in the workshop of the heavens, seeing what God has done, and watch how your prayers are energized.

PRAYER REMINDS US

Prayer is the recognition that if God had not engaged himself in our problems, we would still be lost in the blackness. It is by his mercy that we have been lifted up. Prayer is the process that reminds us of who God is and who we are.

I believe there's great power in prayer. But I don't believe we tell God what to do and when to do it.

God knows that we, with our limited vision, don't even know that for which we should pray. When we entrust our requests to him, we trust him to honor our prayers with holy judgment.

—*Walking with the Savior*

3. "What controls you doesn't control him. What troubles you doesn't trouble him. What fatigues you doesn't fatigue him." What earthly concerns currently control, trouble, or fatigue you? Check all that apply.

   ☑ Relationship struggles
   ❑ Stock market
   ❑ Monthly bills
   ☑ Illness
   ☑ Crime and violence in the world
   ☑ Work

Pray continually.
—1 Thessalonians 5:17

4. Which of the following statements are true about God's perspective on our problems, and which ones are false? Mark your answers True (T) or False (F). Use the Bible verses below to help you answer.

_T_ The resources of heaven belong to God to deal with our problems. (Psalm 115:16)

_T_ Our heavenly Father knows exactly what we need. (Matthew 6:32)

_F_ God is not interested in listening to our concerns. (Psalm 65:2)

_T_ What limitations control us on earth do not control him in heaven. (Psalm 103:11)

Your heavenly Father already knows all your needs.

—Matthew 6:32 NLT

HIS WAYS ARE HIGHER

God dwells in a different realm. "The foolishness of God is wiser than human wisdom, and the weakness of God is stronger than human strength" (1 Cor. 1:25). He occupies another dimension. "My thoughts are not like your thoughts. Your ways are not like my ways. Just as the heavens are higher than the earth, so are my ways higher than your ways and my thoughts higher than your thoughts" (Is. 55:8–9).

Make special note of the word *like*. God's thoughts are not our thoughts, nor are they even *like* ours. We aren't even in the same neighborhood. We're thinking, *Preserve the body;* he's thinking, *Save the soul.* We dream of a pay raise. He dreams of raising the dead. We avoid pain and seek peace. God uses pain to bring peace. "I'm going to live before I die," we resolve. "Die, so you can live," he instructs. We love what rusts. He loves what endures. We rejoice at our successes. He rejoices at our confessions. We show our children the Nike star with the million-dollar smile and say, "Be like Mike." God points to the crucified carpenter with bloody lips and a torn side and says, "Be like Christ."

Our thoughts are not like God's thoughts. Our ways are not like his ways. He has a different agenda. He dwells in a different dimension. He lives on another plane. And that plane is named in the first phrase of the Lord's prayer, *"Our Father who is in heaven."*

The disciples asked Jesus to teach them how to pray. Yet he gave them a revelation—not just information. Before he could give them the practicalities of prayer, he first revealed the Father. He is unlike anything or anyone we've ever known.

5. Which of the following statements are true regarding the difference between human activity and God's ways? Check all that apply.

❑ Human potential has a limit.
☑ God has unlimited power and resources.
☑ Only God knows what is best for us.
❑ We know what is best for us.

6. Let's consider a recent concern you have brought to God in prayer. Are you expecting God to work along human lines (what you think should be done) or are you asking for his higher ways?

I just ask God his way and if it not for me I just forget it

Now as you stand in the observatory viewing God's workshop, let me pose a few questions. If he is able to place the stars in their sockets and suspend the sky like a curtain, do you think it remotely possible that God is able to guide your life? If your God is mighty enough to ignite the sun, could it be that he is mighty enough to light your path? If he cares enough about the planet Saturn to give it rings or Venus to make it sparkle, is there an outside chance that he cares enough about you to meet your needs? Or, as Jesus says, _yes_

When a believing person prays, great things happen.

—James 5:16b

With God's power working in us, God can do much, much more than anything we can ask or imagine.

—Ephesians 3:20

> "Look at the birds in the air. They don't plant or harvest or store into barns, but your heavenly Father feeds them. And you know you are worth much more than the birds . . . Why do you worry about clothes? Look at how the lilies in the field grow. They don't work or make clothes for themselves. But I tell you that even Solomon with his riches was not dressed as beautifully as one of these flowers. God clothes the grass in the field, which is alive today but tomorrow is thrown into the fire. So you can even be sure that God will clothe you. Don't have so little faith!"
> —Matthew 6:26–30

The God who created the heavens is able to answer our prayers.

7. Read Ephesians 3:20. Fill in the blanks below about what you learn concerning God meeting your needs.

With _God_ power working in _us_, God can do much *March* ~~not more~~ than anything we can _ask_ or _imagine_.

8. Despite all the evidence to the contrary, why do we still fear God will not meet our needs?

Turely when we believe we know when we pray ~~somthing~~ will happen w have to be patcen

LIVING IN HIM

Why would he want you to share his home?

Simple, he's your Father.

You were intended to live in your Father's house. Any place less than his is insufficient. Any place far from his is dangerous. Only the home built for your heart can protect your heart. And your Father wants you to dwell *in* him.

No, you didn't misread the sentence and I didn't miswrite it. Your Father doesn't just ask you to live *with* him, he asks you to live *in* him. As Paul wrote, "For in him we live and move and have our being" (Acts 17:28 NIV).

Don't think you are separated from God, he at the top end of a great ladder, you at the other. Dismiss any thought that God is on Venus while you are on earth. Since God is Spirit (John 4:23), he is next to you: God himself is our roof. God himself is our wall. And God himself is our foundation.

Remain in me, and I will remain in you . . . I loved you as the Father loved me. Now remain in my love.

—John 15:4, 9

God wants to be your dwelling place—your home.

7. Read the following verses. Then match the verse with what you learn about living in God through Christ.

b John 15:4   a. In Christ, we are no longer judged guilty.
a John 15:9   b. If we remain in Christ, he will remain in us.
f Romans 8:1   c. We remain in Christ's love.
_ 1 Corinthians 1:30   d. God makes us strong in Christ.
d 2 Corinthians 1:21   e. God gives us every spiritual blessing in Christ.
e Ephesians 1:3   f. In Christ, we are put right with God.

God *wants* to be your dwelling place. He has no interest in being a weekend getaway or a Sunday bungalow or a summer cottage. Don't consider using God as a vacation cabin or an eventual retirement home. He wants you under his roof now and always. He wants to be your mailing address, your point of reference; he wants to be your home. Listen to the promise of his Son, "If people love me, they will obey my teaching. My Father will love them, and we will come to them and make our home with them" (John 14:23).

For many this is a new thought. We think of God as a deity to discuss, not a place to dwell. We think of God as a mysterious miracle worker, not a house to live in. We think of God as a creator to call on, not a home to reside in. But our Father wants to

If you believe, you will get anything you ask for in prayer.
—Matthew 21:22

be much more. He wants to be the one in whom "we live and move and have our being" (Acts 17:28 NIV).

THE HEART OF THE MATTER

- 🐦 **Your Father is in heaven.**
- 🐦 **The resources of heaven belong to God to deal with our problems.**
- 🐦 **The God who created the heavens is able to answer our prayers.**
- 🐦 **God wants to be your dwelling place—your home.**

Let's review your Bible memory verse this week. Write out Ephesians 6:18 here

Pray in the Spirit at all time on an ever Occasion, stay alert and be persistent in your prayer for all believers everyone

The Heart of Jesus

Together. They were always together. Walking, talking, eating, sleeping. They had watched him do the impossible. They had seen him change lives. They knew the sound of his step, the tone of his voice, they rhythm of his snoring, the echo of his laughter. The twelve knew Jesus like no one else could. He was their companion, their leader, their teacher. But then there were times when he'd be gone. Jesus would simply withdraw from the group, slipping away to be alone. Sometimes for a few hours at a time, sometimes for the whole night. Where did he go? What could he be doing? A couple of them were curious enough to follow Jesus cautiously. Even from a distance, they could see him—first sitting quietly, then pacing back and forth—and the sound of his voice drifting through the night. When they asked him about it in the morning, his answer astonished them. Prayer. He was talking with his Father. They exchanged startled glances, then grew quiet. They had watched him do the impossible. They had seen him change lives. They knew him better than anyone, and they wanted to be like him. Their plea rose up from the longing in their hearts. "Please, Jesus, teach *us* to pray."

—Luke 11:1

DAY TWO—THE THRONE— TOUCHING THE KING'S HEART

PRAYER TOUCHES HIS HEART

Our family went desk hunting recently. I needed a new one for the office, and we'd promised Andrea and Sara desks for their rooms. Sara was especially enthused. When she comes home from school, guess what she does? She plays school! I never did that as a kid. I tried to forget the classroom activities, not rehearse them. Denalyn assures me not to worry, that this is one of those attention-span differences between genders. So off to the furniture store we went.

When Denalyn buys furniture she prefers one of two extremes—so antique it's fragile or so new it's unpainted. This time we opted for the latter and entered a store of in-the-buff furniture.

Andrea and Sara succeeded quickly in making their selections, and I set out to do the same. Somewhere in the process Sara learned we weren't taking the desks home

Continue praying, keeping alert, and always thanking God.

—Colossians 4:2

God is moved by the sincerity of our prayers.

Your prayers are honored in heaven as precious jewels. Purified and empowered, the words rise in a delightful fragrance to our Lord . . . Your words do not stop until they reach the very throne of God.
—*The Great House of God*

We really are God's children.

Yes, it is through Christ we all have the right to come to the Father in one Spirit.
—**Ephesians 2:18**

that day, and this news disturbed her deeply. I explained that the piece had to be painted and they would deliver the desk in about four weeks. I might as well have said four millennia.

Her eyes filled with tears, "But, Daddy, I wanted to take it home today."

Much to her credit she didn't stomp her feet and demand her way. She did, however, set out on an urgent course to change her father's mind. Every time I turned a corner she was waiting on me.

"Daddy, don't you think we could paint it ourselves?"

"Daddy, I just want to draw some pictures on my new desk."

"Daddy, please let's take it home today."

After a bit she disappeared, only to return, arms open wide and bubbling with a discovery. "Guess what, Daddy. It'll fit in the back of the car!"

You and I know that a seven-year-old has no clue what will or won't fit in a vehicle, but the fact that she had measured the trunk with her arms softened my heart. The clincher, though, was the name she called me: "Daddy, can't we please take it home?"

The Lucado family took a desk home that day.

I heard Sara's request for the same reason God hears ours. Her desire was for her own good. What dad wouldn't want his child to spend more time writing and drawing? Sara wanted what I wanted for her, she only wanted it sooner. When we agree with what God wants, he hears us, as well (1 John 5:14).

Sara's request was heartfelt. God, too, is moved by our sincerity. The "earnest prayer of a righteous man has great power" (James 5:16 TLB).

But most of all, I was moved to respond because Sara called me "Daddy." Because she is my child, I heard her request. Because we are his children, God hears ours. The king of creation gives special heed to the voice of his family. He is not only willing to hear us, he loves to hear us. He even tells us what to ask him.

"Thy kingdom come."

1. Based on what you just read, what moves an earthly father's heart regarding a request a child makes? Check all that apply.

    ☒ When the request aligns with the father's desires for his child.
    ☒ When the request is sincere and heartfelt.
    ☐ Simply because the child belongs to him.

2. Read the following verses and summarize what you learn about our new relationship with God.

    John 1:12–13 – *But to all who did accept him and believe in him he gave the right to become children of God. They did not become his children in any human way—by any human parents or human desire. They were born of God.*

    Romans 8:16 – *And the Spirit himself joins with our spirits to say we are God's children.*

    Ephesians 2:19 – *Now you who are not Jewish are not foreigners or strangers any longer, but are citizens together with God's holy people. You belong to God's family.*

    1 John 3:1 – *The Father has loved us so much that we are called children of God. And we really are his children.*

AT THE THRONE

There are times when to speak is to violate the moment . . . when silence represents the highest respect. The word for such times is reverence. The prayer for such times is "Hallowed be thy name." And the place for this prayer is the chapel.

If there are walls, you won't notice them. If there is a pew, you won't need it. Your eyes will be fixed on God, and your knees will be on the floor. In the center of the room is a throne, and before the throne is a bench on which to kneel. Only you and God are here, and you can surmise who occupies the throne.

3. God's throne is not a place as much as it is something to be experienced. Read the following verses. Then match the verse with what you learn about the throne of God.

<u>c</u> Psalm 45:6   a. Jesus is seated at the right side of his throne.
<u>b</u> Isaiah 66:1   b. Heaven is his throne.
<u>d</u> Daniel 7:9   c. His throne will last forever.
<u>e</u> Hebrews 4:16   d. His throne is made from fire.
<u>a</u> Hebrews 12:2   e. We can boldly approach God's throne in prayer.

THY KINGDOM COME

We entered the throne room of God with a satchel full of requests—promotions desired, pay raises wanted, transmission repairs needed, and tuitions due. We'd typically say our prayers as casually as we'd order a burger at the drive-through: "I'll have one solved problem and two blessings, cut the hassles, please."

But such complacency seems inappropriate in the chapel of worship. Here we are before the King of kings. We've just covered our mouths out of reverence for his holiness, now do we open them with the topic of transmissions? Not that our needs don't matter to him, mind you. It's just that what seemed so urgent outside the house seems less significant in here. The pay raise is still needed and the promotion is still desired, but is that where we start?

4. What is the typical starting point for your prayers?

I just talk to him, every time is different

Jesus tells how to begin. "When you pray, pray like this. 'Our Father who is in heaven, hallowed be thy name. Thy kingdom come.'"

When you say, "Thy kingdom come," you are inviting the Messiah himself to walk into your world. "Come, my King! Take your throne in our land. Be present in my heart. Be present in my office. Come into my marriage. Be Lord of my family, my fears, and my doubts." This is no feeble request; it's a bold appeal for God to occupy every corner of your life. _I'm hopping he will do that in time_

5. In the passage above, underline the areas of our lives in which we should ask for God's complete authority. What others would you add to the list?

not to talk so much, let him help you be at peace with him.

6. Read Luke 12:29–31. Fill in the blanks about what you learn concerning Jesus' priority on seeking the kingdom of God.

We should not always _think_ about our needs—what we are going to eat or what we will _drink_. Jesus says to stop _____. All the people in the _world_ are trying to get these things. And our heavenly _Father_ knows what we need. If we first seek his _Kingdom_ then he will give us _all_ the other things we _need_ as well.

BE BOLD IN PRAYER

Who are you to ask such a thing? Who are you to ask God to take control of your world? You are his child, for heaven's sake! And so you ask boldly. "So let us come

Pray for God to occupy every corner of your life.

PRAYERS MAKE A DIFFERENCE

Most of our prayer lives could use a tune-up.

Some prayer lives lack consistency. They're either a desert or an oasis. Long, arid, dry spells interrupted by brief plunges into the waters of communion . . .

Others of us need sincerity. Our prayers are a bit hollow, memorized, and rigid. More liturgy than life. And though they are daily, they are dull.

Still others lack, well, honesty. We honestly wonder if prayer makes a difference. Why on earth would God in heaven want to talk to me? If God knows all, who am I to tell him anything? If God controls all, who am I to do anything? . . .

Our prayers may be awkward. Our attempts may be feeble. But since the power of prayer is in the one who hears it and not the one who says it, our prayers do make a difference.

—*He Still Moves Stones*

Don't always think about what you will eat or what you will drink, and don't keep worrying. All the people in the world are trying to get these things, and your Father knows you need them. But seek God's kingdom, and all the other things you need will be given to you.

—Luke 12:29–31

I call to you, God, and you answer me. Listen to me now, and hear what I say.

—Psalm 17:6

We have access to God's throne.

(boldly) to the very throne of God and stay there to receive his mercy and to find grace to help us in our times of need" (Heb. 4:16 TLB).

A wonderful illustration of this kind of boldness is in the story of Hadassah. Though her language and culture are an atlas apart from ours, she can tell you about the power of a prayer to a king. There are a couple of differences, though. Her request was not to her father, but to her husband, the king. Her prayer was for the delivery of her people. And because she entered the throne room, because she opened her heart to the king, he changed his plans and millions of people in 127 different countries were saved.

Oh, how I'd love for you to meet Hadassah. But since she lived in the fifth century B.C., such an encounter is not likely. We'll have to be content with reading about her in the book which bears her name—her other name—the Book of Esther.

7. Read the following accounts in the Book of Esther, and then reflect on the following questions.

   Why do you think coming into the presence of King Xerxes would have been an intimidating experience? (1:1–22)
   effective prayer 1 praise 2 thanksgiving
   3 repentance 4 spectic request
   5 commit end

   What role did Mordecai play in encouraging Esther to make her request known to the king? (2:1–18 and 4:1–17)
   effort vanzew the wall aroun
   Jerusalmen

Esther, Mordecai's adopted daughter, became queen by winning a Miss Persia contest. In one day she went from obscurity to royalty, and in more ways than one she reminds you of you. Both of you are residents of the palace: Esther, the bride of Xerxes, and you, the bride of Christ. Both of you have access to the throne of the king, and you both have a counselor to guide and teach you. Your counselor is the Holy Spirit. Esther's counselor was Mordecai.

8. Choose the responses below that summarize the similarities between Esther and us. Check all that apply.

   ☒ We are residents of a mighty kingdom.
   ☐ We are both brides of an influential ruler.
   ☒ We have access to the throne.
   ☒ We have a counselor to guide us in the king's presence.

THE REQUEST

It was Mordecai who urged Esther to keep her Jewish nationality a secret. It was also Mordecai who persuaded Esther to talk to Xerxes about the impending massacre. You may wonder why she would need any encouragement. Mordecai must have wondered the same thing. Listen to the message he got from Esther: "No man or woman may go to the king in the inner courtyard without being called. There is only one law about this: Anyone who enters must be put to death unless the king holds out his gold scepter. Then that person may live. And I have not been called to go to the king for thirty days" (Esth. 4:11).

As strange as it may sound to us, not even the queen could approach the king without an invitation. To enter his throne room uninvited was to risk a visit to the gallows. But Mordecai convinces her to take the risk.

Watch how Esther responds. "Esther put on her royal robes and stood in the inner courtyard of the king's palace, facing the king's hall" (Esth. 5:1).

Lord, every morning you hear my voice. Every morning, I tell you what I need, and I wait for your answer.
—**Psalm 5:3**

9. In what ways did Esther demonstrate boldness in approaching the king? Check all that apply.

❏ She hadn't been called into the king's presence recently.
❏ She risked her life for violating this rule.
❏ Her urgency regarding her request motivated her past the practicalities.
❏ She acted immediately despite the odds against her.

THE RESPONSE

"When the king saw Queen Esther standing in the courtyard, he was pleased" (5:2). Let me give you my translation of that verse: "When the king saw Queen Esther standing in the courtyard he said, 'a-hubba-hubba-hubba.'" "He held out to her the gold scepter that was in his hand, so Esther went forward and touched the end of it" (5:2).

10. Based on what you have learned about Jesus' prayer so far, how do we know God is pleased whenever we come into his presence?

_____

_____

And how does the story end?

Haman gets Mordecai's rope. Mordecai gets Haman's job. Esther gets a good night's sleep. The Jews live to see another day. And we get a dramatic reminder of what happens when we approach our King.

Like Esther, we have been plucked out of obscurity and given a place in the palace.

Like Esther, we have royal robes; she was dressed in cloth, we are dressed in righteousness.

Like Esther, we have the privilege of making our request.

We have the privilege of making our requests to God.

THE HEART OF THE MATTER

- ❦ **God is moved by the sincerity of our prayers.**
- ❦ **We are really God's children.**
- ❦ **Pray for God to occupy every corner of your life.**
- ❦ **We have access to God's throne.**
- ❦ **We have the privilege of making our requests to God.**

Here's another chance to review your memory verse for the week. Let's hide it in your heart! Practice it by writing it out below.

_____

_____

_____

The Heart of Jesus

Jesus was a prayer warrior if there ever was one. He fasted and prayed for forty days. He found time for hours of solitude in the midst of a busy ministry schedule. He sometimes prayed through the night while those around him slept. When Jesus prayed, people were changed—healed, released, made whole. When he spoke to his Father, God answered. Such an impressive prayer resume is a little intimidating. How can we possibly emulate our Savior in this way? But Jesus didn't just pray about big stuff

He will answer the prayers of the needy; he will not reject their prayers.
—Psalm 102:17

in big ways. There were the same kinds of everyday prayers that we still lift up today. Did you know that Jesus thanked the Father for his food, and blessed it before eating (Matt. 14:19)? Anytime we pause in our days to whisper a few words to our Father, we are being just like Jesus.

DAY THREE—THE FURNACE— BECAUSE SOMEONE PRAYED

Prayer is essential in this ongoing warfare. Pray long and hard. Pray for your brothers and your sisters.

—Ephesians 6:18 MSG

Do not worry about anything, but pray and ask God for everything you need, always giving thanks.

—Philippians 4:6

A PARENT'S PRECIOUS PRAYERS

Never underestimate the ponderings of a Christian parent. Never underestimate the power that comes when a parent pleads with God on behalf of a child. Who knows how many prayers are being answered right now because of the faithful ponderings of a parent ten or twenty years ago? God listens to thoughtful parents.

Praying for our children is a noble task. If what we are doing, in this fast-paced society, is taking us away from prayer time for our children, we're doing too much. There is nothing more special, more precious than time that a parent spends struggling and pondering with God on behalf of a child.

—*Walking with the Savior*

Ask, and God will give to you. Search, and you will find. Knock, and the door will open for you. Yes, everyone who asks will receive. Everyone who searches will find. And everyone who knocks will have the door opened.

—Matthew 7:7–8

1. Why does prayer affect every area of your life?

_____

_____

I'd like you to think about someone. His name is not important. His looks are immaterial. His gender is of no concern. His title is irrelevant. He is important not because of who he is, but because of what he did.

He went to Jesus on behalf of a friend. His friend was sick, and Jesus could help, and someone needed to go to Jesus, so someone went. Others cared for the sick man in other ways. Some brought food, others provided treatment, still others comforted the family. Each role was crucial. Each person was helpful, but none was more vital than the one who went to Jesus.

2. Why is asking heaven to touch our earthly concerns such a "vital" role in prayer? Check all that apply. Use the Bible verses below to help you answer.

❏ Jesus expects us to ask God for everything we need. (Philippians 4:6)
❏ Jesus prioritized intercession by including it in the Lord's Prayer. (Matthew 6:10)
❏ Jesus himself asks God to help us. (Hebrews 7:25)
❏ The Bible instructs us to pray for others. (Ephesians 6:18)

THE ONE WHO PRAYS

He went because he was asked to go. An earnest appeal came from the family of the afflicted. "We need someone who will tell Jesus that my brother is sick. We need someone to ask him to come. Will you go?"

The question came from two sisters. They would have gone themselves, but they couldn't leave their brother's bedside. They needed someone else to go for them. Not just anyone, mind you, for not just anyone could. Some were too busy, others didn't know the way. Some fatigued too quickly, others were inexperienced on the path. Not everyone could go.

And not everyone would go. This was no small request the sisters were making. They needed a diligent ambassador, someone who knew how to find Jesus. Someone who wouldn't quit mid-journey. Someone who would make sure the message was delivered. Someone who was as convinced as they were that Jesus *must* know what had happened.

They knew of a trustworthy person, and to that person they went. They entrusted their needs to someone, and that someone took those needs to Christ.

"So Mary and Martha sent *someone* to tell Jesus, 'Lord, the one you love is sick'" (John 11:3, emphasis mine).

Someone carried the request. Someone walked the trail. Someone went to Jesus on behalf of Lazarus. And because someone went, Jesus responded.

3. For whom are you regularly interceding—friends, family, church members? List them by name below.

_____

_____

God responds to the requests we bring him.

4. How is your role similar to the anonymous friend who went to Jesus on Mary and Martha's behalf?

_____

_____

Prayer doesn't hold a secondary role—it is essential.

Let me ask you, how important was this person in the healing of Lazarus? How essential was his role? Some might regard it as secondary. After all, didn't Jesus know everything? Certainly he knew that Lazarus was sick. Granted, but he didn't respond to the need until someone came to him with the message. "When Jesus heard this, he said, 'This sickness will not end in death. It is for the glory of God to bring glory to the son of God'" (v. 4).

5. Which of the following statements are true concerning how our prayers invoke God's response, and which are false? Mark your answers True (T) and False (F).

____ God is indifferent toward our prayers. (1 Peter 3:12)
____ God answers us in our times of trouble. (Psalm 86:7)
____ God sometimes responds to prayer before we even finish praying. (Genesis 24:45)

For the eyes of the Lord are on the righteous, And His ears are open to their prayers.
—1 Peter 3:12 NKJV

When was Lazarus healed? After *someone* made the request. Oh, I know the healing wouldn't unfold for several days, but the timer was set when the appeal was made. All that was needed was the passage of time.

Would Jesus have responded if the messenger had not spoken? Perhaps, but we have no guarantee. We do, however, have an example: The power of God was triggered by prayer. Jesus looked down the very throat of death's cavern and called Lazarus back to life . . . all because someone prayed.

Pray in the Spirit at all times with all kinds of prayers, asking for everything you need. To do this you must always be ready and never give up. Always pray for all God's people.
—Ephesians 6:18

6. Read Ephesians 6:18. Fill in the blanks below about what you learn from this verse concerning prayer.

We ought to _____ in the Spirit at _____ times with _____ kinds of prayers. We can ask God for _____ we need. We ought to always be _____ to pray and never give up praying for _____ people.

The power of God is triggered by prayer.

7. Read the following passage in John concerning the request, and underline where the Bible pinpoints the outcome of Lazarus' story—before Jesus even went to see him.

"So Mary and Martha sent someone to tell Jesus, 'Lord the one you love is sick.' When Jesus heard this, he said, 'This sickness will not end in death. It is for the glory of God, to bring glory to the Son of God.'" —John 11:3–4

In the economy of heaven, the prayers of saints are a valued commodity. John, the apostle, would agree. He wrote the story of Lazarus and was careful to show the sequence: The healing began when the request was made.

While Jesus lived on earth, he prayed to God and asked God for help. He prayed with loud cries and tears to the One who could save him from death, and his prayer was heard because he trusted God.
—Hebrews 5:7

THE ONE WHO HEARS

You can talk to God because God listens.

I will provide for their needs before they ask, and I will help them while they are still asking for help.

—Isaiah 65:24

WITHIN REACH
OF YOUR PRAYERS

If God is for us, who can be against us? (Rom. 8:31 NIV). The question is not simply, "Who can be against us?" You could answer that one. Who is against you? Disease, inflation, corruption, exhaustion. Calamities confront, and fears imprison. Were Paul's question, "Who can be against us?" we could list our foes much easier than we could fight them. But that is not the question. The question is, If GOD IS FOR US, *who can be against us?*

God is for you. Your parents may have forgotten you, your teachers may have neglected you, your siblings may be ashamed of you; but within reach of your prayers is the maker of the oceans. God!

—*In the Grip of Grace*

Listen to my cry for help, my King and my God, because I pray to you.
—Psalm 5:2

The phrase the friend of Lazarus used is worth noting. When he told Jesus of the illness he said, "Lord, the one you love is sick." He doesn't base his appeal on the imperfect love of the one in need, but on the perfect love of the Savior. He doesn't say, "The one *who loves you* is sick." He says, "The one *you love* is sick." The power of the prayer, in other words, does not depend on the one who makes the prayer, but on the one who hears the prayer.

Although we may love our friends and family more than anyone on earth, Jesus wants us to know he loves them more than anyone in heaven and earth. If we are concerned for our loved ones, how much more is he!

8. Read the following verses and write down what you learn about God's love for us.

Psalm 36:5 – Your unfailing love, O LORD, is as vast as the heavens; your faithfulness reaches beyond the clouds. NLT

_____

_____

John 14:21 – Those who accept my commandments and obey them are the ones who love me. My Father will love those who love me; I too will love them and reveal myself to them. TEV

_____

_____

Romans 5:5 – God has poured out his love to fill our hearts. He gave us his love through the Holy Spirit, whom God has given to us. NCV

_____

_____

We can and must repeat the phrase in manifold ways. "The one you love is tired, sad, hungry, lonely, fearful, depressed." The words of the prayer vary, but the response never changes. The Savior hears the prayer. He silences heaven, so he won't miss a word. He hears the prayer. Remember the phrase from John's Gospel? "When Jesus *heard* this, he said, 'This sickness will not end in death'" (John 10:4 emphasis mine).

The Master heard the request. Jesus stopped whatever he was doing and took note of the man's words. This anonymous courier was heard by God.

You and I live in a loud world. To get someone's attention is no easy task. He must be willing to set everything aside to listen: turn down the radio, turn away from the monitor, turn the corner of the page and set down the book. When someone is willing to silence everything else so he can hear us clearly, it is a privilege. A rare privilege, indeed.

9. Read the following verses. Then match the verse with what you learn about examples of God's promise to hear his people's prayers.

___ Exodus 2:24　　　　a. God heard the Hebrews' cry in Egypt.
___ 2 Chronicles 7:14　　b. God promised to answer before we call.
___ Isaiah 65:24　　　　c. God promised Solomon he would hear his people.

You can talk to God because God listens. Your voice matters in heaven. He takes you very seriously. When you enter his presence, the attendants turn to you to hear your voice. No need to fear that you will be ignored. Even if you stammer or stumble, even if what you have to say impresses no one, it impresses God—and he listens. He listens to the painful plea of the elderly in the rest home. He listens to the gruff confession of the death-row inmate. When the alcoholic begs for mercy, when the spouse seeks guidance, when the businessman steps off the street into the chapel, God listens.

PRAYERS MAKE A DIFFERENCE

You are the someone of God's kingdom. You have access to God's furnace. Your prayers move God to change the world. You may not understand the mystery of prayer. You don't need to. But this much is clear: Actions in heaven begin when someone prays on earth. What an amazing thought!

When you speak, Jesus hears.

And when Jesus hears, thunder falls.

And when thunder falls, the world is changed.

All because someone prayed.

Your prayers move God to change the world.

THE HEART OF THE MATTER

- **God responds to the requests we bring him.**
- **Prayer doesn't hold a secondary role—it is essential.**
- **The power of God is triggered by prayer.**
- **You can talk to God because God listens.**
- **Your prayers move God to change the world.**

For your verse review today, fill in the blanks below

_____ at all _____ and on every _____ in the _____ of the _____ _____. Stay _____ and be _____ in your prayers for all _____ everywhere. —Ephesians 6:18 NLT

The Heart of Jesus

Jesus didn't *have* to pray out loud. God knew his thoughts. The Son didn't have to share his private conversations with his Father. According to the Gospels, Jesus slipped away from the rest and spent most of his prayer time in solitude. No eavesdroppers allowed! His inner musings and urgent entreaties to God might never have reached the pages of our Bibles. But Jesus welcomes us into these intimate moments. He offers us a peek at his prayers. He guided his disciples through a primer of petition. He led the way to the throne of God. Jesus prayed out loud for our benefit.

DAY FOUR—THE KITCHEN— GOD'S ABUNDANT TABLE

COMING TO GOD'S HOUSE HUNGRY

Everybody has a kitchen story because everybody has a history in the kitchen. Whether yours was a campfire in the jungle or a culinary castle in Manhattan, you learned early that in this room your basic needs were supplied. A garage is optional. A living room is negotiable. An office is a luxury. But a kitchen? Absolutely essential. Every house has one. Even the Great House of God.

Or perhaps we should say *especially* the Great House of God. For who is more concerned with your basic needs than your Father in heaven? God is not a mountain guru only involved in the mystical and spiritual. The same hand that guides your soul gives food for your body. The one who clothes you in goodness is the same one who clothes you in cloth. In the school of life, God is both the Teacher and the Cook. He provides

And if you ask for anything in my name, I will do it for you so that the Father's glory will be shown through the Son. If you ask me for anything in my name, I will do it.

—**John 14:13–14**

Don't be afraid to ask.

The Lord is close to everyone who prays to him, to all who truly pray to him.

—Psalm 145:18

LIVING IN GOD'S PRESENCE

How do I live in God's presence? How do I detect his unseen hand on my shoulder and his inaudible voice in my ear?. . . How can you and I grow familiar with the voice of God? Hear are a few ideas:

Give God your waking thoughts. Before you face the day, face the Father. Before you step out of bed, step into his presence.

Give God your waiting thoughts. Spend time with him in silence.

Give God your whispering thoughts. Imagine considering every moment as a potential time of communion with God.

Give God your waning thoughts. At the end of the day, let your mind settle on him. Conclude the day as you began it: talking to God.

—*Just Like Jesus*

Also, the Spirit helps us with our weakness. We do not know how to pray as we should. But the Spirit himself speaks to God for us, even begs God for us with deep feelings that words cannot explain.
—Romans 8:26

fire for the heart and food for the stomach. Your eternal salvation and your evening meal come from the same hand. There is a kitchen in God's Great House; let's journey downstairs and enjoy its warmth.

God doesn't leave us out in the cold—he sees our needs and longs to invite us in and serve us at his abundant table.

1. Read the following verses and write down what you learn about God's concern for the needy.

   Psalm 72:12 – He will help the poor when they cry out and will save the needy when no one else will help. NCV

   _____

   _____

   Isaiah 58:11 – The Lord will always lead you. He will satisfy your needs in dry lands and give strength to your bones. You will be like a garden that has much water, like a spring that never runs dry. NCV

   _____

   _____

   Hebrews 4:16 – Let us have confidence, then, and approach God's throne, where there is grace. There we will receive mercy and find grace to help us just when we need it. TEV

   _____

   _____

DON'T BE SHY, ASK

The table is long. The chairs are many and the food ample. On the wall hangs a simple prayer: "*Give us this day our daily bread.*"

Beneath the prayer, "Give us this day our daily bread," I can envision two statements. You might call them rules of the kitchen. You've seen such rules before. "No singing at the table." "Wash before you eat." "Carry your plate to the sink." "Max gets double portions of dessert." (I wish!)

God's kitchen has a couple of rules as well. The first is a rule of dependence:
Rule #1: Don't be shy, ask.

2. Jesus' prayer reminds us that God wants us to call on him. Read the following verses. Then match the verse with what you learn about calling on God.

   ____ Psalm 145:18   a. He gives us pure speech so we can speak his name.
   ____ Jeremiah 33:3   b. He saves those who call on him.
   ____ Zephaniah 3:9   c. He will answer and tell us what we need to know.
   ____ Romans 10:13   d. God is close to everyone who prays to him.

The first word in the phrase, "Give us this day our daily bread," seems abrupt. Sounds terse, doesn't it? Too demanding. Wouldn't an "If you don't mind" be more appropriate? Perhaps a "Pardon me, but could I ask you to give . . . " would be better? Am I not being irreverent if I simply say, "Give us this day our daily bread"? Well, you are if this is where you begin. But it isn't. If you have followed Christ's model for prayer, your preoccupation has been his wonder rather than your stomach. The first three petitions are God-centered, not self-centered. "Hallowed be your name . . . your kingdom come . . . your will be done."

Proper prayer follows such a path, revealing God to us before revealing our needs to God. (You might reread that one.) The purpose of prayer is not to change God, but to change us, and by the time we reach God's kitchen, we are changed people. Wasn't our heart warmed when we called him Father? Weren't our fears stilled when we contemplated his constancy? Weren't we amazed as we stared at the heavens?

3. Which of the following statements are true and which are false? Mark your answer True (T) or False (F). Use the Bible verses below to help you answer.

___ Understanding who God is changes our perspective on our needs. (Job 42:5–6)

___ Jesus says we should begin our prayers by reciting our needs. (Matthew 6:9)

___ Jesus says we should begin our prayers by focusing on what God wants. (Matthew 6:10)

___ It is impossible to truly understand and know God. (Romans 1:19–20)

4. "The purpose of prayer is not to change God, but to change us." How does the process of prayer change us? Check all that apply.

❑ We realize how much God loves us.
❑ We realize if he loves us, we can trust him.
❑ We realize if we trust him, he will provide us with all good things.
❑ We realize he is more than willing to provide us with what he already wants for us.

Seeing his holiness caused us to confess our sin. Inviting his kingdom to come reminded us to stop building our own. Asking God for his will to be done placed our will in second place to his. And realizing that heaven pauses when we pray left us breathless in his presence.

By the time we step into the kitchen, we're renewed people! We've been comforted by our father, conformed by his nature, consumed by our creator, convicted by his character, constrained by his power, commissioned by our teacher, and compelled by his attention to our prayers.

5. Underline all the changes outlined in the passage above that result from the process of coming to God in prayer. Then, choose from the statements below concerning what it means to be a changed person as a result of prayer. Check all that apply.

❑ We are forgiven.
❑ We reject self-sufficiency.
❑ We are confident he can meet our needs.

OUR DAILY CONCERNS

First he addresses our need for bread. The term means all of a person's physical needs. Martin Luther defined bread as "Everything necessary for the preservation of this life, including food, a healthy body, house, home, wife, and children." This verse urges us to talk to God about the necessities of life. He may also give us the luxuries of life, but he certainly will grant the necessities.

Any fear that God wouldn't meet our needs was left in the observatory that we walked through earlier in the week. Would he give the stars their glitter and not give us our food? Of course not. He has committed to care for us. We aren't wrestling crumbs out of a reluctant hand, but rather confessing the bounty of a generous hand. The essence of the prayer is really an affirmation of the Father's care. Our provision is his priority.

Turn your attention to Psalm 37.

> *Trust in the Lord and do good. Live in the land and feed on truth. Enjoy serving the Lord and he will give you what you want. Depend on the Lord; trust him and he will take care of you.* (vv. 3–4)

Proper prayer reveals God to us.

Pray in the Spirit at all times with all kinds of prayers, asking for everything you need. To do this you must always be ready and never give up. Always pray for all God's people.

—Ephesians 6:18

God is committed to caring for our needs. Paul tells us that a man who won't feed his own family is worse than an unbeliever (1 Tim. 5:8). How much more will a holy God care for his children? After all, how can we fulfill his mission unless our needs are met? How can we teach or minister or influence unless we have our basic needs satisfied? Will God enlist us in his army and not provide a commissary? Of course not.

6. Which of the following statements are true concerning our dependence on God? Check all that apply.

❏ God is committed to caring for our needs.
❏ He knows he must meet our needs in order for us to fulfill his mission for us.
❏ He has enlisted us in his army and we are under his charge.

We pray, only to find our prayer already answered! We are like the high school senior who decides to go to college and then learns the cost of tuition. He runs to his father and pleads, "I'm sorry to ask so much, Dad, but I have nowhere else to go. I want to go to college and I don't have a penny." The father puts his arms around the son and smiles and says, "Don't worry, son. The day you were born I began saving for your education. I've already provided for your tuition."

The boy made the request only to find the father had already met it. The same happens to you. At some point in your life it occurs to you that someone is providing for your needs. You take a giant step in maturity when you agree with David's words in 1 Chronicles 29:14: "Everything we have has come from you, and we only give you what is yours already" (TLB). You may be writing a check and stirring the soup, but there's more to putting food on the table than that. What about the ancient symbiosis of the seed and the soil and the sun and the rain? Who created animals for food and minerals for metal? Long before you knew you needed someone to provide for your needs, God already had.

TRUST THE COOK

So the first rule in the kitchen is one of dependence. Ask God for whatever you need. He is committed to you. God lives with the self-assigned task of providing for his own, and so far, you've got to admit, he's done pretty well at the job.

The second rule is one of trust.

Rule #2: trust the cook.

The kitchen in God's house is no restaurant. It's not owned by a stranger, it's run by your Father. It's not a place you visit and leave; it's a place to linger and chat. It's not open one hour and closed the next; the kitchen is ever available. You don't eat and then pay; you eat and say thanks. But perhaps the most important difference between a kitchen and a restaurant is the menu. A kitchen doesn't have one.

God's kitchen doesn't need one. Things may be different in your house, but in the house of God, the one who provides the food is the one who prepares the meal. We don't swagger into his presence and demand delicacies. Nor do we sit outside the door and hope for crumbs. We simply take our place at the table and gladly trust him to "Give us this day our daily bread."

7. Why is it significant that God's kitchen has no "menu"?

_____

_____

8. What is difficult about "gladly trusting" the cook—our Father?

_____

_____

We are urged to talk to God about the necessities of life.

These things did not really come from me and my people. Everything comes from you; we have given you back what you gave us.

—1 Chronicles 29:14

DON'T MISS GOD'S ANSWER

The God of surprises strikes again . . . God does that for the faithful. Just when the womb gets too old for babies, Sarai gets pregnant. Just when the failure is too great for grace, David is pardoned . . .

The lesson? Three words. Don't give up . . .

Is the road long? Don't stop.

Is the night black? Don't quit.

God is watching. For all you know right at this moment . . . the check may be in the mail.

The apology may be in the making.

The job contract may be on the desk.

Don't quit. For if you do, you might miss the answer to your prayers.

—*He Still Moves Stones*

If you believe, you will get anything you ask for in prayer.

—**Matthew 21:22**

What a statement of trust! Whatever you want me to have is all I want. In his book *Victorious Praying,* Alan Redpath translates the phrase, "Give us this day bread suited to our need." Some days the plate runs over. God keeps bringing out more food and we keep loosening our belt. A promotion. A privilege. A friendship. A gift. A lifetime of grace. An eternity of joy.

And then there are those days when, well, when we have to eat our broccoli. Our daily bread could be tears or sorrow or discipline. Our portion may include adversity as well as opportunity.

"We know that in everything God works for the good of those who love him" (Rom. 8:28). We, like Paul, must learn the "secret of being happy at anytime in everything that happens, when I have enough to eat and when I go hungry, when I have more than I need and when I do not have enough. I can do all things through Christ, because he gives me strength" (Phil. 4:12).

THE HEART OF THE MATTER

- ❦ **Don't be afraid to ask—God is committed to caring for our needs.**
- ❦ **Proper prayer reveals God to us.**
- ❦ **We are urged to talk to God about the necessities of life.**
- ❦ **There is no menu in life. We must accept what comes with trust and thanks.**

Another day, another chance to review your verse. How are you doing with memorizing Ephesians 6:18? Test yourself by writing the verse out below.

_____

_____

_____

The Heart of Jesus

There had been urgency in his eyes, intensity in his tone. "Come with me tonight. Pray with me." The disciples were by now accustomed to Jesus slipping away into the night to pray alone. He often had these little interludes with his Father. But he had never asked for company before. Tonight was different—there was tension in the air, a sense of imminence. Something was about to happen, and their Master had invited them to join him in the garden to pray. Peter, James, and John were delighted, but drowsy. Their good intentions would have ended in a good night's sleep had Jesus not shaken their shoulders to rouse them. Seeing the sorrow in the Savior's eyes, they renewed their efforts to intercede. On a night when distress threatened to overwhelm Jesus, he asked his closest friends to do the one thing that could help. Jesus asked the men to pray for him, and through their prayers, he experienced encouragement, peace, and strength for the day ahead of him.

—Matthew 26:36–39

There is no menu in life. We must accept what comes with trust and thanks.

I call to you in times of trouble, because you will answer me.
—Psalm 86:7

DAY FIVE—THE CHAPEL— RELYING ON GOD'S POWER

For thine is the kingdom and the power and the glory forever. Amen.

—Matthew 6:13 KJV

When it comes to the kingdom, power, and glory, the pronoun is *thine*, not *mine*.

And this is the boldness we have in God's presence: that if we ask God for anything that agrees with what he wants, he hears us.

—1 John 5:14

I came across an article of a lady who reminds me of us. She went up a mountain she should have avoided. No one would have blamed her had she stayed behind. At twelve below zero, even Frosty the Snowman would have opted for the warm fire. Hardly a day for snow skiing, but her husband insisted and she went.

While waiting in the lift line she realized she was in need of a restroom, dire need of a restroom. Assured there would be one at the top of the lift, she and her bladder endured the bouncy ride, only to find there was no facility. She began to panic. Her husband had an idea: Why not go into the woods? Since she was wearing an all-white outfit, she'd blend in with the snow. And what better powder room than a piney grove?

What choice did she have? She skied past the tree line and arranged her ski suit at half-mast. Fortunately, no one could see her. Unfortunately, her husband hadn't told her to remove her skis. Before you could say, "Shine on harvest moon," she was streaking backwards across the slope, revealing more about herself than she ever intended. (After all, hindsight is 20/20.) With arms flailing and skis sailing, she sped under the very lift she'd just ridden and collided with a pylon.

As she scrambled to cover the essentials, she discovered her arm was broken. Fortunately her husband raced to her rescue. He summoned the ski patrol, who transported her to the hospital.

While being treated in the emergency room, a man with a broken leg was carried in and placed next to her. By now she'd regained her composure enough to make small talk. "So, how'd you break your leg?" she asked.

"It was the darndest thing you ever saw," he explained. "I was riding up the ski lift and suddenly I couldn't believe my eyes. There was this crazy woman skiing backwards, at top speed. I leaned over to get a better look and I guess I didn't realize how far I'd moved. I fell out of the lift."

Then he turned to her and asked, "So how'd you break your arm?"

Don't we make the same mistake? We climb mountains we were never intended to climb. We try to go up when we should have stayed down, and as a result, we've taken some nasty spills in full view of a watching world. The tale of the lady (sorry, I couldn't resist) echoes our own story. There are certain mountains we were never made to climb. Ascend them and you'll end up bruised and embarrassed. Stay away from them and you'll sidestep a lot of stress. These mountains are described in the final phrase of the Lord's prayer, "Thine is the kingdom and the power and the glory forever. Amen."

Read the following verses below and write down what you learn about God's kingdom, power and glory.

1. What does Psalm 47:7 say about God's kingdom?

_____

_____

2. What does Job 37:23 say about God's power?

_____

_____

3. What does Psalm 19:1 say about God's glory?

_____

_____

MOUNTAINS ONLY GOD CAN CLIMB

There are certain mountains only God can climb. The names of these mountains? You'll see them as you look from the window of the chapel in the Great House of God. "Thine is the kingdom, and the power and the glory forever." A trio of peaks mantled by the clouds. Admire them, applaud them, but don't climb them.

It's not that you aren't welcome to try, it's just that you aren't able. The pronoun is *thine*, not *mine; thine* is the kingdom, not *mine* is the kingdom. If the word Savior is in your job description, it's because you put it there. Your role is to help the world, not save it. Mount Messiah is one mountain you weren't made to climb.

If Jesus' prayer teaches us anything, it teaches us to depend on God. No wonder Jesus concludes his prayer with this God's exultation.

4. Why are people sometimes tempted to bypass God and help themselves? What is usually the result of that strategy?

_____

_____

Nor is Mount Self-Sufficient. You aren't able to run the world, nor are you able to sustain it. Some of you think you can. You are self-made. You don't bow your knees, you just roll up your sleeves and put in another twelve-hour day . . . which may be enough when it comes to making a living or building a business. But when you face your own grave or your own guilt, your power will not do the trick.

5. Our dependence upon God is an important, recurring theme of Jesus' prayer. Read the following verses. Then match the verse with its promise.

___ Psalm 34:19   a. He saves us from the wicked—he is our protection.
___ Psalm 37:40   b. His name is "Savior."
___ Psalm 116:8   c. God will solve all our problems.
___ Romans 11:26   d. God will dry our tears and keep us from defeat.

You were not made to run a kingdom, nor are you expected to be all-powerful. And you certainly can't handle all the glory. Mount Applause is the most seductive of the three peaks. The higher you climb the more people applaud, but the thinner the air becomes. More than one person has stood at the top and shouted, "Mine is the glory!" only to lose their balance and fall.

"Thine is the kingdom and the power and the glory forever." What protection this final phrase affords. As you confess that God is in charge, you admit that you aren't. As you proclaim that God has power, you admit that you don't. And as you give God all the applause, there is none left to dizzy your brain.

Let's let the lady on the slope teach us a lesson: There are certain mountains we weren't meant to climb. Stay below where you were made to be, so you won't end up exposing yourself to trouble.

6. How do we get in trouble when we change the "thine" to "mine" when it comes to kingdoms, power and glory? Check all that apply.

❑ We can only climb so high on these mountains before we will fall.
❑ We challenge God in our arrogance.
❑ We assume a role we are unsuited to fulfill.
❑ We steal God's glory.

7. Read Isaiah 42:8. Fill in the blanks in this verse regarding God's glory.

God will not _____ his glory to any other person. He will not let _____ take the praise that belongs to him.

Prayer teaches us to depend on God.

People who do what is right may have many problems, but the Lord will solve them all.

—Psalm 34:19

HEAVEN'S SOLUTION

What Jesus dreamed of doing and what he seemed able to do were separated by an impossible gulf. So Jesus prayed.

We don't know what he prayed about. But I have my guesses. . . . He prayed for the impossible to happen.

Or maybe I'm wrong. Maybe he didn't ask for anything. Maybe he just stood quietly in the presence of Presence and basked in the Majesty. Perhaps he placed his war-weary self before the throne and rested.

Maybe he lifted his head out of the confusion of earth long enough to hear the solution of heaven. Perhaps he was reminded that hard hearts don't faze the Father. That problem people don't perturb the Eternal One.

—*In the Eye of the Storm*

I am the Lord. That is my name. I will not give my glory to another; I will not let idols take the praise that should be mine.

—Isaiah 42:8

The Lord is close to everyone who prays to him, to all who truly pray to him.

—Psalm 145:18

A RETURN TO THE CHAPEL

God wants us to begin and end our prayers thinking of Him.

Our Lord's prayer has given us a blueprint for the Great House of God. From the living room of our Father to the family room with our friends, we are learning why David longed to "live in the house of the Lord forever" (Ps. 23:6). In God's house we have everything we need: a solid foundation, an abundant table, a steady furnace. And now, having seen every room and explored each corner, we have one final stop. Not to a new room, but to one we have visited earlier. We return to the chapel. We return to the room of worship.

The chapel is the only room in the house of God we visit twice. It's not hard to see why. It does us twice as much good to think about God as it does to think about anyone or anything else. God wants us to begin and end our prayers thinking of him. Jesus is urging us to look at the peak more than we look at the trail. The more we focus up there, the more inspired we are down here.

Some years ago a sociologist accompanied a group of mountain climbers on an expedition. Among other things, he observed a distinct correlation between cloud cover and contentment. When there was no cloud cover and the peak was in view, the climbers were energetic and cooperative. When the gray clouds eclipsed the view of the mountaintop, though, the climbers were sullen and selfish.

The same thing happens to us. As long as our eyes are on his majesty there is a bounce in our step. But let our eyes focus on the dirt beneath us and we will grumble about every rock and crevice we have to cross. For this reason Paul urged, "Don't shuffle along, eyes to the ground, absorbed with the things right in front of you. Look up, and be alert to the things going on around Christ—that's where the action is. See things from his perspective" (Col. 3:2 MSG).

LISTENING FOR GOD

Equipped with the right tools, we can learn to listen to God. What are those tools? Here are the ones I have found helpful.

A regular time and place. Select a slot on your schedule and a corner of your world, and claim it for God. For some it may be the best to do this in the morning . . . Others prefer the evening . . .

A second tool you need [is] *an open Bible.* God speaks to us through his Word. The first step in reading the Bible is to ask God to help you understand it . . . Don't go to Scripture looking for your own ideas; go searching for God's . . .

There is a third tool . . . Not only do we need a regular time and an open Bible, we also need *a listening heart* . . . If you want to be just like Jesus, let God have you. Spend time listening for him until you receive your lesson for the day—then apply it.

—Just Like Jesus

8. Jesus' prayer encourages us to trade our earthly perspective for his heavenly one. Which of the following statements are true regarding God's point of view and which ones are false? Mark your answers True (T) or False (F).

____ Our most disconcerting earthly problems intimidate God.
____ Our concerns overwhelm God sometimes.
____ Nothing is impossible for God.

PRAYER MAGNIFIES JESUS

In worship, we take our mind off ourselves and set it on God.

Paul challenges you to "be alert to the things going on around Christ." (Col. 3:2 MSG). The psalmist reminds you to do the same, only he uses a different phrase. "O magnify the Lord with me and let us exalt his name together" (Ps. 34:3 NRSV).

Magnify. What a wonderful verb to describe what we do in the chapel. When you magnify an object, you enlarge it so that you can understand it. When we magnify God, we do the same. We enlarge our awareness of him so we can understand him more. This is exactly what happens in the chapel of worship—we take our mind off ourselves and set it on God. The emphasis is on him. "Thine is the kingdom and the power and the glory forever."

And this is exactly the purpose of this final phrase in the Lord's prayer. These words magnify the character of God. I love the way this phrase is translated in *The Message:*

You're in charge!
You can do anything you want!
You're ablaze in beauty!
Yes! Yes! Yes![41]

God, listen to my prayer and do not ignore my cry for help.
—Psalm 55:1

9. What areas of your life would you need to adjust in order to confess this conclusion to Jesus' prayer truthfully? Check all that apply.

❏ Finances
❏ Family
❏ Career
❏ Future
❏ Friendships
❏ Entertainment
❏ Hobbies
❏ Time

10. Now read Luke 6:46. Fill in the blanks below about what it means to give Jesus control over our lives.

If we call Jesus _____ we must be willing to _____ what he says.

Why do you call me, 'Lord, Lord,' but do not do what I say?

—Luke 6:46

Could it be any simpler? God is in charge! This concept is not foreign to us. When the restaurant waiter brings you a cold hamburger and a hot soda, you want to know who is in charge. When a young fellow wants to impress his girlfriend, he takes her down to the convenience store where he works and boasts, "Every night from five to ten o'clock, I'm in charge." We know what it means to be in charge of a restaurant or a store, but to be in charge of the universe? This is the claim of Jesus.

God raised him from the dead and set him on a throne in deep heaven, *in charge* of running the universe, everything from galaxies to governments, no name and no power is exempt from his rule. And not just for the time being but forever. "He is *in charge* of it all, has the final word on everything. At the center of all this Christ rules the church." (Eph. 1:22–23 MSG, emphasis mine)

Doesn't he deserve to hear us proclaim his authority? Isn't it right for us to shout from the bottom of our hearts and at the top of our voice, "Thine is the kingdom and the power and the glory forever!" Isn't it right for us to stare at these mountain peaks of God and worship him?

Of course it is. Not only does God deserve to hear our praise, we need to give it.

THE HEART OF THE MATTER

- **When it comes to the kingdom, power, and glory, the pronoun is *thine*, not *mine*.**
- **Prayer teaches us to depend on God.**
- **God wants us to begin and end our prayers thinking of Him.**
- **In worship, we take our mind off ourselves and set it on God.**

Have you gotten that verse down pat yet? Write out Ephesians 6:18 again here for good measure.

_____
_____
_____

The Heart of Jesus

It was as if Jesus knew how difficult the next days would be for the disciples. He would have to leave them soon. They would be plunged into fear, confusion, disbelief, pain, grief, desolation. They didn't really understand what lay ahead, even though Jesus tried to prepare them. So, Jesus prayed for them. He gathered his followers together, and he

I will provide for their needs before they ask, and I will help them while they are still asking for help.

—Isaiah 65:24

prayed aloud for each of them. "These men are mine. I have kept them safe. Protect them when I am gone. Give them my joy." He could not change what was coming, and he could not make things any easier for them, but Jesus could pray for them. And his prayers would carry them through. —John 17

FOR FURTHER READING

Selections throughout this lesson were taken from *The Great House of God.*

Then you will call my name. You will come to me and pray to me, and I will listen to you.

—Jeremiah 29:12

LESSON 10

Experiencing the Hope of Jesus

―――――――◎―――――――

THIS ISN'T HOME

All of us know what it is like to be in a house that is not our own. Perhaps you've spent time in a dorm room or army barrack. Maybe you've slept in your share of hotels or bunked in a few hostels. They have beds. They have tables. They may have food and they may be warm, but they are a far cry from being "your father's house."

Your father's house is where your father is . . .

We don't always feel welcome here on earth. We wonder if there is a place here for us. People can make us feel unwanted. Tragedy leaves us feeling like intruders. Strangers. Interlopers in a land not ours. We don't always feel welcome here.

We shouldn't. This isn't our home. To feel unwelcome is no tragedy. Indeed it is healthy. We are not home here. This language we speak, it's not ours. This body we wear, it isn't us. And the world we live in, this isn't home.

—*A Gentle Thunder*

You are in your car driving home. Thoughts wander to the game you want to see or meal you want to eat, when suddenly a sound unlike any you've ever heard fills the air. The sound is high above you. A trumpet? A choir? A choir of trumpets? You don't know, but you want to know. So you pull over, get out of your car, and look up. As you do, you see you aren't the only curious one. The roadside has become a parking lot. Car doors are open, and people are staring at the sky. Shoppers are racing out of the grocery store. The Little League baseball game across the street has come to a halt. Players and parents are searching the clouds.

And what they see, and what you see, has never before been seen.

As if the sky were a curtain, the drapes of the atmosphere part. A brilliant light spills onto the earth. There are no shadows. None. From whence came the light begins to tumble a river of color—spiking crystals of every hue ever seen and a million more never seen. Riding on the flow is an endless fleet of angels. They pass through the curtains one myriad at a time, until they occupy every square inch of the sky. North. South. East. West. Thousands of silvery wings rise and fall in unison, and over the sound of the trumpets, you can hear the cherubim and seraphim chanting, "Holy, holy, holy."

The final flank of angels is followed by twenty-four silver-bearded elders and a multitude of souls who join the angels in worship. Presently the movement stops and the trumpets are silent, leaving only the triumphant triplet: "Holy, holy, holy." Between each word is a pause. With each word, a profound reverence. You hear your voice join in the chorus. You don't know why you say the words, but you know you must.

Suddenly, the heavens are quiet. All is quiet. The angels turn, you turn, the entire world turns—and there he is. Jesus. Through waves of light you see the silhouetted figure of Christ the King. He is atop a great stallion, and the stallion is atop a billowing cloud. He opens his mouth, and you are surrounded by his declaration: "I am the Alpha and the Omega."

The angels bow their heads. The elders remove their crowns. And before you is a figure so consuming that you know, instantly you know: Nothing else matters. Forget stock markets and school reports. Sales meetings and football games. Nothing is newsworthy. All that mattered, matters no more, for Christ has come.

Would you like to discuss the end of time and feel better because of it? Could you use some comforting words regarding the return of Christ? If so, I think I've found some to share with you throughout this week's lessons.

EXPERIENCING THE HOPE OF JESUS THIS WEEK

Before you read any further, spend some time in prayer now.

Dear Father, thank you for giving me hope through your promise—Jesus is coming quickly. Stir up anticipation in my heart for that long-awaited moment. When I begin to feel hopeless amid life's worries and burdens, open my eyes to what really matters. Teach me to wait forwardly, to be watchful, because any day now Jesus will return. Give me a glimpse of eternity this week. Encourage me by ever increasing my hope in your return. Amen.

This week, memorize Romans 8:25:

We are hoping for something we do not have yet, and we are waiting for it patiently.
—*Romans 8:25*

Lord, you are my hope. Lord, I have trusted you since I was young.
—**Psalm 71:5**

DAY ONE—THE BEGINNING OF THE VERY BEST

WHEN WILL HE COME?

In a comprehensive survey conducted by Lucado and Friends (I interviewed a couple of people in the hallway), I determined the most dreaded question in parentdom. What is the single query hated most by moms and dads? It's the one posed by the five-year-old on the trip, "How much farther?"

Give us the dilemmas of geometry and sexuality, just don't make a parent answer the question, "How much farther?"

It's an impossible question. How do you speak of time and distance to someone who doesn't understand time and distance? The world of a youngster is delightfully free of mile markers and alarm clocks. You can speak of minutes and kilometers, but a child has no hooks for those hats. So what do you do? Most parents get creative. When our girls were toddlers, they loved to watch *The Little Mermaid*. So Denalyn and I used the movie as an economy of scale. "About as long as it takes you to watch *The Little Mermaid* three times."

And for a few minutes that seemed to help. But sooner or later, they ask again. And sooner or later, we say what all parents eventually say, "Just trust me. You enjoy the trip and don't worry about the details. I'll make sure we get home OK."

And we mean it. We don't want our kids to sweat the details. So we make a deal with them, "We'll do the taking. You do the trusting."

Sound familiar? It might. Jesus has said the same to us. Just prior to his Crucifixion, he told his disciples that he would be leaving them. "Where I am going you cannot follow now, but you will follow later" (John 13:36).

Such a statement was bound to stir some questions. Peter spoke for the others and asked, "Lord, why can't I follow you now?" (v. 37).

See if Jesus' reply doesn't reflect the tenderness of a parent to a child: "Don't let your hearts be troubled. Trust in God, and trust in me. There are many rooms in my Father's house; I would not tell you this if it were not true. I am going there to prepare a place for you . . . I will come back and take you to be with me so that you may be where I am going" (John 14:1–3).

> **We need to trust God to take us where we are going.**

1. Reminding ourselves of our role as children helps put hope in perspective. We have hope in our Father—he knows what he is doing so we don't have to know everything! Look up the following verses below and write down what you learn about the parent-child relationship we have with the Father.

   Deuteronomy 14:1 – "You are the children of the Lord your God."

   John 1:12 – "To all who did accept him and believe in him he gave the right to become children of God."

   1 John 3:1 – "The Father has loved us so much that we are called children of God. And we really are his children."

   _____

   _____

TRUSTING HIM

Reduce the paragraph to a sentence and it might read: "You do the trusting and I'll do the taking." A healthy reminder when it comes to anticipating the return of Christ. For many, the verb trust is not easily associated with his coming.

> *Why am I so sad? Why am I so upset? I should put my hope in God and keep praising him.*
>
> **—Psalm 42:5**

Those who know the Lord trust him, because he will not leave those who come to him.

—Psalm 9:10

I trust in your love. My heart is happy because you saved me.

—Psalm 13:5

We cannot understand eternity, so Jesus asks us to trust him to handle the details.

Then he said, "I tell you the truth, you must change and become like little children. Otherwise, you will never enter the kingdom of heaven."

—Matthew 18:3

I say this because I know what I am planning for you," says the Lord. "I have good plans for you, not plans to hurt you. I will give you hope and a good future.

—Jeremiah 29:11

2. Match all the following phrases below with the appropriate verse on trusting God.

____ Trust in his love.	a. Psalm 9:10
____ Trust in his holy name.	b. Psalm 119:42
____ Trust God with your problems.	c. Psalm 13:5
____ Trust that God will never leave us.	d. Psalm 33:21
____ Trust what he says.	e. Psalm 62:8

Our pre-K minds are ill-equipped to handle the thoughts of eternity. When it comes to a world with no boundaries of space and time, we don't have the hooks for those hats. Beyond the exact nature and sequence of events regarding Christ's return, the very fact that he is returning some day so we can live eternally with him is mind boggling!

Consequently, our Lord takes the posture of a parent, "You do the trusting and I'll do the taking." This is precisely his message in these warm words of John 14. Let's ponder them for a bit.

All of his words can be reduced to two: Trust me. "Don't let your hearts be troubled. Trust in God, and trust in me" (v. 1).

Don't be troubled by the return of Christ. Don't be anxious about things you cannot comprehend. Issues like the millennium and the Antichrist are intended to challenge and stretch us, but not overwhelm and certainly not divide us. For the Christian, the return of Christ is not a riddle to be solved or a code to be broken, but rather a day to be anticipated.

In its purest form, hope comes from childlike trust—not from scratching our heads trying to figure out everything (as if we could!).

3. Read Matthew 18:3 and fill in the blanks about what Jesus teaches in this passage regarding childlike trust versus our grown-up tendencies to trust only what we understand.

Jesus says we must _____ and become like little _____. Otherwise, we will never _____ the kingdom of _____.

4. Why does Jesus want you to trust him?

_____

_____

ROOM FOR US

Jesus wants us to trust him. He doesn't want us to be troubled, so he reassures us with these truths.

I have ample space for you. "There are many rooms in my Father's house" (v. 2). Why does Jesus refer to "many rooms"? Why does our Master make a point of mentioning the size of the house? You can answer that question as you think of the many times in life you've heard the opposite. Haven't there been occasions when you've been told: "We have no room for you here"?

Have you heard it in the workplace? "Sorry, I don't have room for you in my business."

Have you heard it in sports? "We don't have room for you on this team."

From someone you love? "I don't have room for you in my heart."

From a bigot? "We don't have room for your type in here."

Most sadly, have you heard it from a church? "You've made too many mistakes. We don't have room for you here."

Some of the saddest words on earth are: "We don't have room for you."

Jesus knew the sound of those words. He was still in Mary's womb when the innkeeper said, "We don't have room for you."

When the residents of his hometown tried to stone him, were they not saying the same? "We don't have room for prophets in this town."

When the religious leaders accused him of blasphemy, weren't they shunning him? "We don't have room for a self-proclaimed Messiah in this country."

And when he was hung on the Cross, wasn't the message one of utter rejection? "We don't have room for you in this world."

4. Those who have no room for Jesus have little capacity for hope. Based on Revelation 3:20, which of the following statements are true, and which ones are false? Mark your answers True (T) or False (F).

____ Jesus stands at the door of our hearts and knocks.
____ He will make his way inside us whether we respond to him or not.
____ Jesus only comes inside when we hear his voice and invite him in.
____ We have hope because he is inside us.

Even today Jesus is given the same treatment. He goes from heart to heart, asking if he might enter. But more often than not, he hears the words of the Bethlehem innkeeper: "Sorry. Too crowded. I don't have room for you here."

But every so often, he is welcomed. Someone throws open the door of his or her heart and invites him to stay. And to that person Jesus gives this great promise: "Do not let your heart be troubled. Trust in God. And trust in me. In my Father's house are many rooms."

"I have ample space for you," he says. What a delightful promise he makes us! We make room for him in our hearts, and he makes room for us in his house. His house has ample space.

5. Read the following verses. Then match the verse with what you learn about our confidence concerning his return.

____ 2 Corinthians 5:8   a. We must keep our confidence until the end.
____ 1 Thessalonians 1:3   b. He will reward our confidence in him.
____ Hebrews 3:14   c. Hope makes us strong.
____ Hebrews 10:35   d. His return gives us courage for today.

PREPARED FOR US

I have a prepared place for you. "I am going there to prepare a place for you" (v. 2). A few years back I spent a week speaking at a church in California. The members of the congregation were incredible hosts and hostesses. All my meals were lined up, each at a different house, each house with a full table and at each table wonderful conversation. But after a few meals, I noticed something strange. All we ate was salad. I like salad as much as the next guy, but I prefer it as a warm-up to the main act. But everywhere I went, it was the main act. No meat. No dessert. Just salads.

At first I thought it was a California thing. But finally I had to ask. The answer confused me. "We were told that you eat nothing but salads." Well, I quickly corrected them, and wondered how they had heard such a preposterous distortion. As we traced the trail back, we determined that a miscommunication had occurred between our office and theirs.

The hosts meant well, but their information was bad. I'm happy to say that we corrected the problem and enjoyed some good meat. I'm even happier to say Jesus won't make the same mistake with you.

He is doing for you what my California friends did for me. He is preparing a place. There is a difference, however. He knows exactly what you need. You needn't worry about getting bored or tired or weary with seeing the same people or singing the same songs. And you certainly needn't worry about sitting down to meal after meal of salad.

He is preparing the perfect place for you. I love John MacArthur's definition of eternal life, "Heaven is the perfect place for people made perfect."

Here I am! I stand at the door and knock. If you hear my voice and open the door, I will come in and eat with you, and you will eat with me.

—Revelation 3:20

Jesus has made a place for you.

GOD'S MAGNUM OPUS
When you arrive [in heaven] . . . something wonderful will happen. A final transformation will occur. You will be just like Jesus . . .

Of all the blessings of heaven, one of the greatest will be you! You will be God's magnum opus, his work of art. The angels will gasp. God's work will be completed. At last, you will have a heart like his.

You will love with a perfect love.

You will worship with a radiant face.

You'll hear each word God speaks.

Your heart will be pure, your words will be like jewels, your thoughts will be like treasures.

You will be just like Jesus. You will, at long last, have a heart like his.

—*Just Like Jesus*

I say to myself, "The LORD is mine, so I hope in him."

—Lamentations 3:24

Jesus knows exactly what you need and is making preparations accordingly.

A thief comes to steal and kill and destroy, but I came to give life—life in all its fullness.

—John 10:10

Don't be like them, because your Father knows the things you need before you ask him.

—Matthew 6:8

We also have joy with our troubles, because we know that these troubles produce patience. And patience produces character, and character produces hope. And this hope will never disappoint us, because God has poured out his love to fill our hearts. He gave us his love through the Holy Spirit, whom God has given to us.

—Romans 5:3–5

Trust the promises of Christ. "I have ample space for you; I have a prepared place for you."

6. While we don't exactly know what heaven will be like—we do know we will be with Jesus. Imagine just being with him—our best Friend, our Creator, our Lover. Read John 10:10 and fill in the blanks about how being with Jesus means really living for the first time.

Jesus came to earth to give every person _____. Not only that, he will give us _____ in all its _____.

7. Read Matthew 6:8. Based on what you have learned so far, check all the statements below that apply to what this verse says we can anticipate with God.

❑ God doesn't really know what will make us happy.
❑ We can anticipate periodic boredom in heaven.
❑ God knows our needs before we ask.

And one last commitment from Jesus:

I'm not kidding. "I will come back and take you to be with me so that you may be where I am going" (v. 3). Can you detect a slight shift of tone in the last verse? The first sentences are couched in warmth. "Don't be troubled." "Trust God." "There are many rooms." There is kindness in these words. But then the tone changes. Just slightly. The kindness continues but is now spiked with conviction. "I will come back."

George Tulloch displayed similar determination. In 1996 he led an expedition to the spot where the Titanic sank in 1912. He and his crew recovered numerous artifacts, everything from eyeglasses to jewelry to dishware. In his search, Tulloch realized that a large piece of the hull had broken from the ship and was resting not far from the vessel. Tulloch immediately saw the opportunity at hand. Here was a chance to rescue part of the ship itself.

The team set out to raise the twenty-ton piece of iron and place it onto the boat. They were successful in lifting it to the surface, but a storm blew in and the ropes broke and the Atlantic reclaimed her treasure. Tulloch was forced to retreat and regroup. But before he left, he did something curious. He descended into the deep and, with the robotic arm of his submarine, attached a strip of metal to a section of the hull. On the metal he'd written these words, "I will come back, George Tulloch."

At first glance, his action is humorous. I mean, it's not like he has to worry about a lot of people stealing his piece of iron. For one thing, it's two and one-half miles below the surface of the Atlantic. For another, well, it's a piece of junk. We wonder why anyone would be so attracted to it.

Of course one might say the same about you and me. Why would God go to such efforts to reclaim us? What good are we to him? He must have his reasons because two thousand years ago, he entered the murky waters of our world in search of his children. And on all who will allow him to do so, he lays his claim and tags his name. "I will come back," he says.

George Tulloch did. Two years later he returned and rescued the piece of iron.

8. We have hope because we are God's own. Look up the following verses and write down what you learn about how those who believe in Christ belong to God.

Luke 6:35 – "But love your enemies, do good to them, and lend to them without hoping to get anything back. Then you will have a great reward, and you will be children of the Most High God, because he is kind even to people who are ungrateful and full of sin."

_____

_____

Romans 8:17 – "If we are God's children, we will receive blessings from God together with Christ. But we must suffer as Christ suffered so that we will have glory as Christ has glory."

_____

_____

Romans 14:8 – "If we live, we are living for the Lord, and if we die, we are dying for the Lord. So living or dying, we belong to the Lord."

_____

_____

1 Corinthians 15:23 – "But everyone will be raised to life in the right order. Christ was first to be raised. When Christ comes again, those who belong to him will be raised to life."

_____

_____

THE HEART OF THE MATTER

- **We need to trust God to take us where we are going.**
- **We cannot understand eternity, so Jesus asks us to trust him to handle the details.**
- **Jesus has made a place for you.**
- **Jesus knows exactly what you need and is making preparations accordingly.**

This week's memory verse is Romans 8:25. Take a few moments to write it out on the lines provided here.

_____

_____

_____

The Heart of Jesus

A whole life of sin—bad friends, poor choices, wrong paths. He'd spent most of his life in dark corners and back alleys. All of his dreams had been replaced by schemes. He'd stolen from shops, from market vendors, from homes. He'd picked his share of pockets and nabbed his share of purses. He'd done shameful things, wicked things, things he'd never tell about. And now it was too late to change. As the soldier's pinned his hands and feet to the beams of a cross, the thief writhed from both pain and regret. He couldn't go back and change what he'd done. He couldn't escape back into the dark corners and back alleys he knew so well. He was caught, and the hopelessness of death was only hours away. His eyes shifted to the other two crosses on the hill, and watched the other criminal taunting the silent man in the middle. It was as if he wanted to rile the man, Jesus. After a while, the first criminal told the mocker to shut his mouth. They were only getting what they deserved. Let Jesus die in peace. At that, Jesus' eyes turned to his. It was as if all the regret and despair were laid open to him. And when Jesus spoke to him, it was with words of forgiveness, and hope. "You will be with me today in paradise." Even a dying man can experience the hope of Jesus for the very first time.

So, Lord, what hope do I have? You are my hope.

—**Psalm 39:7**

DAY TWO—WAITING FORWARDLY

A DAY TO ANTICIPATE

Funny how Scripture remembers different people. Abraham is remembered trusting. Envision Moses, and you envision a person leading. Paul's place in Scripture was carved by his writing and John is known for his loving. But Simeon is remembered, interestingly enough, not for leading nor preaching nor loving, but rather for looking.

"Now in Jerusalem there was a man named Simeon. He was an upright and devout man; he *looked forward* to Israel's comforting and the Holy Spirit rested on him" (Luke 2:25 TJB, emphasis mine).

Let's take a look at Simeon, the man who knew how to wait for the arrival of Christ. The way he waited for the first coming is a model for how we should wait for the Second Coming.

1. Read Simeon's story in Luke 2:25–35 and answer the following.

   How does the Bible describe Simeon? (v. 25)

   _____

   _____

   What had the Holy Spirit promised Simeon? (v. 26)

   _____

   _____

   What did Simeon say about Jesus? (vv. 34–35)

   _____

   _____

Our brief encounter with Simeon occurs eight days after the birth of Jesus. Joseph and Mary have brought their son to the temple. It's the day of a sacrifice, the day of circumcision, the day of dedication. But for Simeon, it's the day of celebration.

Let's imagine a white-headed, wizened fellow working his way down the streets of Jerusalem. People in the market call his name and he waves but doesn't stop. Neighbors greet him and he returns the greeting but doesn't pause. Friends chat on the corner and he smiles but doesn't stop. He has a place to be and he hasn't time to lose.

Verse 27 contains this curious statement: "Prompted by the Spirit he came to the Temple" (NJB). Simeon apparently had no plans to go to the temple. God, however, thought otherwise. We don't know how the prompting came—a call from a neighbor, an invitation from his wife, a nudging within the heart—we don't know. But somehow Simeon knew to clear his calendar and put away his golf clubs. "I think I'll go to church," he announced.

On this side of the event, we understand the prompting. Whether Simeon understood or not, we don't know. We do know, however, that this wasn't the first time God tapped him on the shoulder. At least one other time in his life, he had received a message from God.

"The Holy Spirit had revealed to him that he would not die until he had seen him—God's anointed King" (v. 26 TLB).

You've got to wonder what a message like that would do to a person. What does it do to you if you know you will someday see God? We know what it did to Simeon.

He was "constantly expecting the Messiah" (v. 25 TLB).

He was "living in expectation of the salvation of Israel" (v. 25 PHILLIPS).

He "watched and waited for the restoration of Israel" (v. 25 NEB).

Simeon is a man on tiptoe, wide-eyed and watching for the one who will come to save Israel.

So what kind of people should you be? You should live holy lives and serve God, as you wait for and look forward to the coming of the day of God.

—2 Peter 3:11–12

Through Christ you believe in God, who raised Christ from the dead and gave him glory. So your faith and your hope are in God.

—1 Peter 1:21

2. Read the following verses. Then match the verse with what you learn about waiting on God's timing.

___ Acts 1:4   a. Our bodies must wait to be redeemed.
___ Romans 8:22   b. Creation waits for Jesus' return.
___ Romans 8:23   c. The disciples had to wait for the Holy Spirit.

CONFIDENT WAITING

Maybe you know what it's like to look for someone who has come for you. I do. When I travel somewhere to speak, I often don't know who will pick me up at the airport. Someone has been sent, but I don't know the person. Hence, I exit the plane searching the faces for a face I've never seen. But though I've never seen the person, I know I'll find him. He may have my name on a sign, or my book in his hand, or just a puzzled expression on his face. Were you to ask me how I will recognize the one who has come for me, I would say, "I don't know, I just know I will."

I bet Simeon would have said the same. "How will you know the King, Simeon?" "I don't know. I just know I will." And so he searches. Like Colombo after clues, he searches. Studying each passing face. Staring into the eyes of strangers. He's looking for someone.

The Greek language, rich as it is with terms, has a stable full of verbs which mean "to look." One means to "look up," another "look away;" one is used to "look upon" and another "looking in." To "look at something intently" requires one word and to "look over someone carefully" mandates another.

Of all the forms of look, the one which best captures what it means to "look for the coming" is the term used to describe the action of Simeon: *prosdechomai*. *Dechomai* meaning "to wait." *Pros* meaning "forward." Combine them and you have the graphic picture of one "waiting forwardly." The grammar is poor, but the image is great. Simeon was waiting; not demanding, not hurrying, he was waiting.

3. Some are tempted to lose hope, wondering why God doesn't hurry up and come for us. Read 2 Peter 3:8–9. Which of the following statements are true concerning God's timing as we wait for Christ's return?

❏ God operates according to a human timetable.
❏ God's timing is vastly different from ours.
❏ God is not slow in doing what he promises.
❏ God has a good reason for his seeming delay.

At the same time, Simeon was waiting forwardly. Patiently vigilant. Calmly expectant. Eyes open. Arms extended. Searching the crowd for the right face, and hoping the face appears today.

Such was the lifestyle of Simeon, and such can be ours. Haven't we, like Simeon, been told of the coming Christ? Aren't we, like Simeon, heirs of a promise? Are we not prompted by the same Spirit? Are we not longing to see the same face?

Absolutely. In fact, the very same verb is used later in Luke to describe the posture of the waiting servant:

Be dressed, ready for service, and have your lamps shining. Be like servants who are waiting [prosdechomai] for their master to come home from a wedding party. When he comes and knocks, the servants immediately open the door for him. They will be blessed when their master comes home, because he sees that they were watching for him. I tell you the truth, the master will dress himself to serve and tell the servants to sit at the table, and he will serve them. (Luke 12:35–37)

But do not forget this one thing, dear friends: To the Lord one day is as a thousand years, and a thousand years is as one day. The Lord is not slow in doing what he promised—the way some people understand slowness. But God is being patient with you. He does not want anyone to be lost, but he wants all people to change their hearts and lives.
—2 Peter 3:8–9

We should be vigilant, expectant, patiently awaiting Christ's coming.

But we have the true hope that comes from being made right with God, and by the Spirit we wait eagerly for this hope.
—Galatians 5:5

4. Underline the words in the passage above that describe the servants' urgent expectation. Based on what you have just read, how then should we prepare for Jesus' return?

_____

_____

If our hope in Christ is for this life only, we should be pitied more than anyone else in the world.

—1 Corinthians 15:19

THE KEY OF OUR FAITH

For . . . any follower of Christ, the promise is simply this: The resurrection of Jesus is proof and preview of our own.

But can we trust the promise? Is the resurrection a reality? Are the claims of the empty tomb true? This is not only a good question. It is *the* question. For as Paul wrote, "If Christ has not been raised, then your faith has nothing to it; you are still guilty of your sins" (1 Cor. 15:17). In other words, if Christ has been raised, then his followers will join him; but if not, then his followers are fools. The resurrection, then, is the keystone in the arch of the Christian faith.

—*When Christ Comes*

While we wait, we are to live holy lives.

We should live like that while we wait for our great hope and the coming of the glory of our great God and Savior Jesus Christ.

—**Titus 2:13**

Please note the posture of the servants: ready and waiting. Please note the action of the master. He is so thrilled that his attendants are watching for him that he takes the form of a servant and serves them! They sit at the feast and are cared for by the master! Why? Why are they honored in such a way? The master loves to find people looking for his return. The master rewards those who "wait forwardly."

5. Hope is the bridge between what we experience in this life and what we can anticipate in the next. Read 1 Corinthians 15:19. Fill in the blanks below about what you learn concerning Paul's argument that unless Jesus rewards us for hoping in him both now and in the life to come—our faith is in vain.

   If our _____ in Christ is for this _____ only, we are in bad shape. In fact, we should be _____ more than anyone else in the _____.

6. Why would Jesus reward those who have hope in him?

_____

_____

IN THE MEANTIME

First, we must wait. Paul says "we are hoping for something we do not have yet, and we are waiting for it patiently" (Rom. 8:25). Simeon is our model. He was not so consumed with the "not yet" that he ignored the "right now." Luke says Simeon was a "good man and godly" (2:25). Peter urges us to follow suit.

"The day of the Lord will come like a thief. The skies will disappear with a loud noise. Everything in them will be destroyed by fire, and the earth and everything in it will be burned up. In that way everything will be destroyed. So what kind of people should you be?" (2 Pet. 3:10–11).

Great question. What kind of people should we be? Peter tells us: "You should live holy lives and serve God, as you wait for and [here is that word again] look forward to the coming of the day of God" (vv. 11–12).

Hope of the future is not a license for irresponsibility in the present. Let us wait forwardly, but let us wait.

7. Which of the following statements are true concerning our responsibility to live holy lives, and which are false? Mark your answers True (T) or False (F). Use the Bible verses below to help you answer.

   ____ We are free to do what we want until Christ returns. (1 Corinthians 6:19–20)
   ____ Others watch how we live while we wait for Christ's return. (1 Corinthians 8:9)
   ____ We should be careful how we live while we wait. (Ephesians 5:15)

But for most of us, waiting is not our problem Or, maybe I should state, waiting is our problem. We are so good at waiting that we don't wait forwardly. We forget to look. We are so patient that we become complacent. We are too content. We seldom search the skies. We rarely run to the temple. We seldom, if ever, allow the Holy Spirit to interrupt our plans and lead us to worship so that we might see Jesus.

It is to those of us who are strong in waiting and weak in watching that our Lord was speaking when he said, "No one knows when that day or time will be, not the angels in heaven, not even the Son. Only the Father knows . . . So always be ready, because you don't know the day your Lord will come . . . The Son of Man will come at a time you don't expect him" (Matt. 24:36, 42, 44).

Simeon reminds us to "wait forwardly." Patiently vigilant. But not so patient that we lose our vigilance. Nor so vigilant that we lose our patience.

8. We can take our cues from creation when it comes to patient vigilance. Read Romans 8:19–21 and answer the following.

What is God's creation waiting for him to do? (v. 19)

_____

_____

How does the Bible describe creation waiting? (v. 19)

_____

_____

What is the ultimate hope? (v. 21)

_____

_____

In the end, the prayer of Simeon was answered. "Simeon took the baby in his arms and thanked God; 'Now, Lord, you can let me, your servant, die in peace, as you said'" (Luke 2:28–29).

One look into the face of Jesus, and Simeon knew it was time to go home. And one look into the face of our Savior, and we will know the same.

THE HEART OF THE MATTER

- We should be vigilant, expectant, patiently awaiting Christ's coming.
- While we wait, we are to be living holy lives.
- We must not become complacent in our waiting.

Time for a little review. Write out Romans 8:25.

_____

_____

_____

The Heart of Jesus

Saul was an enthusiast. He had deep convictions, and he lived by them. Self-assured. Confident. Driven. When he did something, he gave it one hundred percent. No holds barred. Full throttle. Relentless. Tireless. All very good qualities, of course. *Unless* you are hopelessly misguided. Saul was living his life for God and giving it his best shot, but he was out of the loop. You see, he knew his Bible forwards and backwards. He knew all the rules for righteous living like the back of his hand. But he didn't know Jesus. Enthusiasm, sincerity, and effort don't count for much if you're on the wrong path. So Jesus dazzled Saul's eyes and grabbed his attention. He set the man straight, and channeled all that go-getter attitude in the right direction. Saul, now called Paul, was introduced to the hope that only Jesus holds, and it changed his life forever.

We must not become complacent in our waiting.

Everything God made is waiting with excitement for God to show his children's glory completely. Everything God made was changed to become useless, not by its own wish but because God wanted it and because all along there was this hope: that everything God made would be set free from ruin to have the freedom and glory that belong to God's children.
—Romans 8:19–21

So prepare your minds for service and have self-control. All your hope should be for the gift of grace that will be yours when Jesus Christ is shown to you.
—1 Peter 1:13

DAY THREE—THE BRAND-NEW YOU

A DAY OF REJUVENATION

Suppose you were walking past my farm one day and saw me in the field crying. (I don't have a farm nor am I prone to sitting in fields, but play along with me.) There I sit, disconsolate at the head of a furrowed row. Concerned, you approach me and ask what is wrong. I look up from beneath my John Deere tractor hat and extend a palm full of seeds in your direction. "My heart breaks for the seeds," I weep. "My heart breaks for the seeds."

"What?"

Between sobs I explain, "The seeds will be placed in the ground and covered with dirt. They will decay, and we will never see them again."

As I weep, you are stunned. You look around for a turnip truck off which you are confident I tumbled. Finally, you explain to me a basic principle of farming: Out of the decay of the seed comes the birth of a plant.

You put a finger in my face and kindly remind me: "Do not bemoan the burial of the seed. Don't you know that you will soon witness a mighty miracle of God? Given time and tender care, this tiny kernel will break from its prison of soil and blossom into a plant far beyond its dreams."

Well, maybe you aren't that dramatic, but those are your thoughts. Any farmer who grieves over the burial of a seed needs a reminder: A time of planting is not a time of grief. Any person who anguishes over the burial of a body may need the same. We may need the reminder Paul gave the Corinthians. "There is an order to this resurrection: Christ was raised first; then, when Christ comes back, all his people will be raised" (1 Cor. 15:23 NLT).

1. We tend to lose hope when we don't understand his ways. And death tends to make us question his ways more than anything. Read the following verses and write down what you learn about God's ways.

    2 Samuel 22:31 – "The ways of God are without fault; the Lord's words are pure. He is a shield to those who trust him."

    _____

    _____

    Psalm 25:10 – "All the Lord's ways are loving and true for those who follow the demands of his agreement."

    _____

    _____

    Isaiah 55:8–9 – "The Lord says, "My thoughts are not like your thoughts. Your ways are not like my ways. Just as the heavens are higher than the earth, so are my ways higher than your ways and my thoughts higher than your thoughts."

    _____

    _____

Upon death, our souls will journey immediately to the presence of God while we await the resurrection of our bodies. And when will this resurrection occur? You guessed it. When Christ comes. "When Christ comes again, those who belong to him will be raised to life, and then the end will come" (1 Cor. 15:23–24).

This kind of verse stirs a classroom of questions: What does Paul mean, "those who belong to him will be raised to life"? What will be raised? My body? If so, why this body? I don't like my body. Why don't we start over on a new model?

Come with me back to the farm, and let's look for some answers.

There is an order to this resurrection: Christ was raised first; then, when Christ comes back, all his people will be raised.

—1 Corinthians 15:23 NLT

When Christ comes back, all his people will be raised.

God decided to let his people know this rich and glorious secret which he has for all people. This secret is Christ himself, who is in you. He is our only hope for glory.

—Colossians 1:27

THE TRANSFORMATION

If you were impressed with my seed allegory, I'd better be honest. I stole the idea from the apostle Paul. The fifteenth chapter of his letter to the Corinthians is the definitive essay on our resurrection. We won't study the entire chapter, but we will isolate a few verses and make a few points.

2. Read 1 Corinthians 15:35–38. Which of the following statements apply to Paul's illustration in this passage? Check all that apply.

❏ When you sow a seed, it must die in the ground before it can live and grow.
❏ The seed does not have the same "body" it will have later.
❏ What you sow is only a bare seed.
❏ God gives the seed a body he has planned for it.

But someone may ask, "How are the dead raised? What kind of body will they have?" Foolish person! When you sow a seed, it must die in the ground before it can live and grow. And when you sow it, it does not have the same "body" it will have later. What you sow is only a bare seed, maybe wheat or something else. But God gives it a body that he has planned for it, and God gives each kind of seed its own body.
—1 Corinthians 15:35–38

In other words: You can't have a new body without the death of the old body.[i] Or, as Paul says, "When you sow a seed, it must die in the ground before it can live and grow" (v. 35).

A friend told me that Paul's parallel between seeds sown and bodies buried reminded her of a remark made by her youngest son. He was a first grader, and his class was studying plants about the same time the family attended a funeral of a loved one. One day, as they were driving past a cemetery, the two events came together in one statement. "Hey, Mom," he volunteered, pointing toward the graveyard. "That's where they plant people."

The apostle Paul would have liked that. In fact, Paul would like us to change the way we think about the burial process. The graveside service is not a burial, but a planting. The grave is not a hole in the ground, but a fertile furrow. The cemetery is not the resting place, but rather the transformation place.

The seed (body) buried in the earth will blossom in heaven.

3. Jesus brings forth hope from death. In fact, we can be exceedingly hopeful. Read the following verses. Then match the verse with what you learn about our hope regarding death.

___ 1 Corinthians 15:26   a. Life in Jesus cannot be destroyed.
___ 2 Timothy 1:10   b. Heaven has no death.
___ Revelation 1:18   c. Jesus will destroy death last.
___ Revelation 21:4   d. Jesus holds the keys to death.

Jesus said to her, "I am the resurrection and the life. Those who believe in me will have life even if they die."
—John 11:25

4. To find out what Jesus says about hope and death, read John 11:25 and fill in the blanks.

_____ am the _____ and the _____. Those who _____ in me will have _____ even if they _____.

He destroyed death, and through the Good News he showed us the way to have life that cannot be destroyed.
—2 Timothy 1:10

Most assume that death has no purpose. It is to people what the black hole is to space—a mysterious, inexplicable, distasteful, all-consuming power. Avoid it at all costs. And so we do! We do all we can to live and not die. God, however, says we must die in order to live. When you sow a seed, it must die in the ground before it can grow (v. 35). What we see as the ultimate tragedy, he sees as the ultimate triumph.

And when a Christian dies, it's not a time to despair, but a time to trust.

When a Christian dies, it's not a time to despair, but a time to trust.

ALL THINGS NEW

Out of curiosity I made a list of the news I've heard in the last twenty-four hours concerning failing health. Here is what has come my way:

🌿 **A professor was diagnosed with Parkinson's disease.**
🌿 **A middle-aged man is concerned about his test results. We learn tomorrow if he has cancer.**
🌿 **A friend's father is scheduled for eye surgery.**
🌿 **Another friend had a stroke.**
🌿 **A minister died after four decades of preaching.**

But respect Christ as the holy Lord in your hearts. Always be ready to answer everyone who asks you to explain about the hope you have.
—1 Peter 3:15

YOUR DAY IS COMING

Some of you have never won a prize in your life. Oh, maybe you were quartermaster in your Boy Scout troop or in charge of sodas at the homeroom Christmas party, but that's about it. You've never won much. You've watched the Mark McGwires of this world carry home the trophies and walk away with the ribbons. All you have are "almosts" and "what ifs."

If that hits home, then you'll cherish this promise: "And when the Chief Shepherd appears, you will receive the crown of glory that will never fade away" (1 Pet. 5:4 NIV).

Your day is coming. What the world has overlooked, your Father has remembered, and sooner than you can imagine, you will be blessed by him.

—*When Christ Comes*

Your soul and body will reunite, and you will be like Jesus.

Happy are those who are helped by the God of Jacob. Their hope is in the Lord their God.
—Psalm 146:5

Can you relate? You probably can. In fact, I wonder if God wants to use the next few lines to speak directly to you. Your body is so tired, so worn. Joints ache and muscles fatigue. You understand why Paul described the body as a tent. "We groan in this tent," he wrote (2 Cor. 5:2).

5. Read the following translations of Philippians 3:21. Underline the descriptive words or phrases that pique your imagination or interest.

☙ **"He will take these dying bodies of ours and change them into glorious bodies like his own"** (TLB).

☙ **"He will transfigure these wretched bodies of ours into copies of his glorious body"** (TJB).

☙ **"He will transfigure the body belonging to our humble state, and give it a form like that of his own resplendent body"** (NEB).

☙ **"He will change our simple bodies and make them like his own glorious body."** (NCV)

☙ **"Who will transform our lowly body that it may be conformed to His glorious body."** (NKJV)

☙ **"He will take these weak mortal bodies of ours and change them into glorious bodies like his own."** (NLT)

Regardless of the wording, the promise is the same. Your body will be changed. You will not receive a different body; you will receive a renewed body. Just as God can make an oak out of a kernel or a tulip out of a bulb, he makes a "new" body out of the old one. A body without corruption. A body without weakness. A body without dishonor. A body identical to the body of Jesus.

My friend Joni Eareckson Tada makes this same point. Rendered a quadriplegic by a teenage diving accident, the last two decades have been spent in discomfort. She, more than most, knows the meaning of living in a lowly body. At the same time, she more than most, knows the hope of a resurrected body. Listen to her words:

"Somewhere in my broken, paralyzed body is the seed of what I shall become. The paralysis makes what I am to become all the more grand when you contrast atrophied, useless legs against splendorous resurrected legs. I'm convinced that if there are mirrors in heaven (and why not?), the image I'll see will be unmistakably "Joni," although a much better, brighter Joni. So much so, that it's not worth comparing . . . I will bear the likeness of Jesus, the man from heaven."

CERTAIN HOPE

Your pain will NOT last forever. Believe it.

Are your joints arthritic? They won't be in heaven.

Is your heart weak? It will be strong in heaven.

Has cancer corrupted your system? There is no cancer in heaven.

Are your thoughts disjointed? Your memory failing? Your new body will have a new mind.

Does this body seem closer to death than ever before? It should. It is. And unless Christ comes first, your body will be buried. Like a seed is placed in the ground, so your body will be placed in a tomb. And for a season, your soul will be in heaven while your body is in the grave. But the seed buried in the earth will blossom in heaven. Your soul and body will reunite, and you will be like Jesus.

6. What are you most looking forward to concerning this change?

_____

_____

THE HEART OF THE MATTER

❦ **When Christ comes back, all his people will be raised.**
❦ **The seed (body) buried in the earth will blossom in heaven.**
❦ **When a Christian dies, it's not a time to despair, but a time to trust.**
❦ **Your soul and body will reunite, and you will be like Jesus.**

Time for your midweek memory verse review. Fill in the blanks of Romans 8:25.

"We are _____ for _____ we do not _____ _____, and we are _____ for it _____."

The Heart of Jesus

Peter was stranded in a pretty hopeless situation. The authorities had cornered him. He'd been locked in a jail cell and threatened with his very life. They wanted him to turn his back on Jesus, but that was impossible. They'd wanted him to stop preaching, but how could he when the Spirit compelled him to speak? And so he sat in moldy straw and listened to scurrying mice. As he turned his heart towards his Savior in prayer, his friends were doing the very same across town. The other disciples had quietly gathered when news of Peter's arrest was heard. In the face of hopelessness, they too prayed. And God answered by doing the impossible. Shackles fell, doors opened, and that prisoner was set free. Nothing is too hard for God. With him, there is always hope.

DAY FOUR—SEEING JESUS

A DAY OF JOYFUL AMAZEMENT

Augustine once posed the following experiment. Imagine God saying to you, "I'll make a deal with you if you wish. I'll give you anything and everything you ask: pleasure, power, honor, wealth, freedom, even peace of mind, and a good conscience. Nothing will be a sin; nothing will be forbidden; and nothing will be impossible to you. You will never be bored and you will never die. Only . . . you will never see my face."[ii]

The first part of the proposition is appealing. Isn't there a part of us, a pleasure-loving part of us, that perks up at the thought of guiltless, endless delight? But then, just as we are about to raise our hands and volunteer, we hear the final phrase, "You will never see my face."

And we pause. Never? Never know the image of God? Never, ever behold the presence of Christ? At this point, tell me, doesn't the bargain begin to lose some of its appeal? Don't second thoughts begin to surface? And doesn't the test teach us something about our hearts? Doesn't the exercise reveal a deeper, better part of us that wants to see God?

For many it does.

1. As a saying goes, people can live without many things, but they cannot live without hope. There is no hope apart from God. Check out the following Bible verses and match the verse with the hope that we have in God.

   ___ Psalm 33:18   a. We hope in his word.
   ___ Psalm 42:11   b. Hope in him secures our future.
   ___ Psalm 62:5   c. Hope in him chases away our sadness.
   ___ Psalm 119:74   d. We have hope in his love.
   ___ Proverbs 23:18   e. We can rest in his hope.

We know that when Christ comes again, we will be like him, because we will see him as he really is.

—1 John 3:2

In our hearts, we long to see God.

But we belong to the day, so we should control ourselves. We should wear faith and love to protect us, and the hope of salvation should be our helmet.

—1 Thessalonians 5:8

For others, however, Augustine's exercise doesn't raise interest as much as it raises a question. An awkward question, one you may be hesitant to ask for fear of sounding naive or irreverent. Since you may feel that way, why don't I ask it for you? At the risk of putting words in your mouth, let me put words in your mouth. "Why the big deal?" you ask. "No disrespect intended. Of course I want to see Jesus. But to see him forever!? Will he be that amazing?"

According to Paul he will. "On the day when the Lord Jesus comes," he writes, "all the people who have believed will be amazed at Jesus" (2 Thess. 1:10).

Amazed at Jesus. Not amazed at angels or mansions or new bodies or new creations. Paul doesn't measure the joy of encountering the apostles or embracing our loved ones. If we will be amazed at these, which certainly we will, he does not say. What he does say is that we will be amazed at Jesus.

What we have only seen in our thoughts, we will see with our eyes. What we've struggled to imagine, we will be free to behold. What we've seen in a glimpse, we will then see in full view. And, according to Paul, we will be amazed.

What will be so amazing?

Of course I have no way of answering that question from personal experience. But I can lead you to someone who can. One Sunday morning many Sundays ago, a man named John saw Jesus. And what he saw, he recorded, and what he recorded has tantalized seekers of Christ for two thousand years.

I find rest in God; only he gives me hope.
—Psalm 62:5

SEEING JESUS

You and I only read about the hands that fed the thousands. Not John. He saw them—knuckled fingers, callused palms. He saw them. You and I only read about the feet that found a path through the waves. Not John. John saw them—sandaled, ten-toed, and dirty. You and I only read about his eyes—his flashing eyes, his fiery eyes, his weeping eyes. Not so with John. John saw them. Gazing on the crowds, dancing with laughter, searching for souls. John had seen Jesus.

When we see Jesus, we will be amazed.

For three years he'd followed Christ. But this encounter was far different from any in Galilee. The image was so vivid, the impression so powerful, John was knocked out cold. "When I saw him I fell in a dead faint at his feet" (Revelation 1:17 TJB).

1. Read Revelation 1:1–3 and answer the following.

   How did John receive this revelation? (v. 1)

   _____

   _____

   Whose message is this revelation? (v. 2)

   _____

   _____

   How does John describe what our reaction should be to this message? (v. 3)

   _____

   _____

This is the revelation of Jesus Christ, which God gave to him, to show his servants what must soon happen. And Jesus sent his angel to show it to his servant John, who has told everything he has seen. It is the word of God; it is the message from Jesus Christ. Happy is the one who reads the words of God's message, and happy are the people who hear this message and do what is written in it. The time is near when all of this will happen.
—Revelation 1:1–3

I told you these things so that you can have peace in me. In this world you will have trouble, but be brave! I have defeated the world.
—John 16:33

I turned to see who was talking to me. When I turned, I saw seven golden lampstands and someone among the lampstands who was "like a Son of Man." He was dressed in a long robe and had a gold band around his chest. His head and hair were white like wool, as white as snow, and his eyes were like flames of fire. His feet were like bronze that glows hot in a furnace, and his voice was like the noise of flooding water. He held seven stars in his right hand, and a sharp double-edged sword came out of his mouth. He looked like the sun shining at its brightest time. When I saw him, I fell down at his feet like a dead man. He put his right hand on me and said, "Do not be afraid. I am the First and the Last." —Revelation 1:12–17

2. Read Revelation 1:12–17 and fill in the blanks below about what John describes.

_____ golden lampstands

Someone standing among them who was _____ a _____ of Man

He was dressed in a long _____ with a _____ band around his chest

His hair and _____ were like _____, as white as _____

His eyes were like flames of _____

His feet were like _____ that glows hot in a furnace

His _____ was like the noise of flooding _____

He looked like the _____ shining at its _____ time

When we see Christ, we will see the perfect priest.

When we see Christ, what will we see?

We will see the perfect priest. "He was dressed in a long robe and had a gold band around his chest" (v. 13). The first readers of this message knew the significance of the robe and band. Jesus is wearing the clothing of a priest. A priest presents people to God and God to people.

You have known other priests. There have been others in your life, whether clergy or not, who sought to bring you to God. But they, too, needed a priest. Some needed a priest more than you did. They, like you, were sinful. Not so with Jesus. "Jesus is the kind of high priest we need. He is holy, sinless, pure, not influenced by sinners, and he is raised above the heavens" (Heb. 7:26).

Jesus is the perfect priest.

These two things cannot change: God cannot lie when he makes a promise, and he cannot lie when he makes an oath. These things encourage us who came to God for safety. They give us strength to hold on to the hope we have been given. We have this hope as an anchor for the soul, sure and strong. It enters behind the curtain in the Most Holy Place in heaven, where Jesus has gone ahead of us and for us. He has become the high priest forever, a priest like Melchizedek.

—Hebrews 6:18–20

3. Knowing Jesus will present us to God, and God to us, means we can be confident before God. With Jesus by our side, we don't have to worry on the day we appear before God. He promises to walk us through it. Read Hebrews 6:18–20. Which of the following statements are true, and which ones are false? Mark your answers True (T) or False (F).

____ We cannot take God at his word.

____ God encourages us through the hope we have in his word.

____ Jesus goes before us and for us into God's presence.

____ Jesus' role as priest is only temporary.

When we see Jesus, we will see sinless perfection.

4. Based on Hebrews 10:21–23, which of the following are true concerning God's trustworthy promise? Check all that apply.

❏ Because of our great priest (Jesus), we can come near to God.

❏ We can have sure faith in him.

❏ We can hold firmly to the hope that we have confessed.

❏ God will do what he promised.

He is also pure and purifying: "His head and hair were white like wool, as white as snow, and his eyes were like flames of fire" (Rev. 1:14).

What would a person look like if he had never sinned? If no worry wrinkled his brow and no anger shadowed his eyes? If no bitterness snarled his lips and no selfishness bowed his smile? If a person had never sinned, how would he appear? We'll know when we see Jesus. What John saw that Sunday on Patmos was absolutely spotless. He was reminded of the virgin wool of sheep and the untouched snow of winter.

And John was also reminded of fire. Others saw the burning bush, the burning altar, the fiery furnace, or the fiery chariots, but John saw the fiery eyes. And in those eyes he saw a purging blaze which will burn the bacteria of sin and purify the soul.

5. Jesus' purity gives us hope. Because he is pure, he was God's perfect sacrifice—there is nothing left undone regarding our sin. Jesus took care of it. Read Hebrews 10:14 and fill in the blanks about how Jesus makes us holy and perfect.

With _____ sacrifice, Jesus made us _____ _____.
Through Jesus, we are being made _____.

And if Christ has not been raised, then our preaching is worth nothing, and your faith is worth nothing.

—1 Corinthians 15:14

EVERYONE WILL SEE HIM

Someday, according to Christ, he will set us free. He will come back.

In the blink of an eye, as fast as the lightning flashes from the east to the west, he will come back. And everyone will see him—you will, I will. Bodies will push back the dirt and break the surface of the sea. The earth will tremble, the sky will roar, and those who do not know him will shudder. But in that hour you will not fear, because you know him.

—*When Christ Comes*

When we see Jesus we will see absolute strength.

And this hope will never disappoint us, because God has poured out his love to fill our hearts. He gave us his love through the Holy Spirit, whom God has given to us.
—Romans 5:5

The master answered, "You did well. You are a good and loyal servant. Because you were loyal with small things, I will let you care for much greater things. Come and share my joy with me."
—Matthew 25:21

Then the King will say to the people on his right, "Come, my Father has given you his blessing. Receive the kingdom God has prepared for you since the world was made."
—Matthew 25:34

We can be sure when we say, "I will not be afraid, because the Lord is my helper. People can't do anything to me."
—Hebrews 13:6

When we see Jesus we will see absolute strength. "His feet were like bronze that glows hot in a furnace" (v. 15).

John's audience knew the value of this metal. Eugene Peterson helps those of us who don't by explaining:

Bronze is a combination of iron and copper. Iron is strong but it rusts. Copper won't rust but it's pliable. Combine the two in bronze and the best quality of each is preserved, the strength of the iron and the endurance of the copper. The rule of Christ is set on this base: the foundation of his power is tested by fire.[iii]

Every power you have ever seen has decayed. The muscle men in the magazines, the automobiles on the racetrack, the armies in the history books. They had their strength and they had their day, but their day passed. But the strength of Jesus will never be surpassed. Never. When you see him, you will, for the first time, see true strength.

6. Jesus' strength gives us hope. At the moment we need him most, his grip will prove strong enough. He will not disappoint us. What is our assurance of this according to Romans 5:5?

_____

_____

HEARING JESUS

Ever wonder how you would feel if Jesus spoke to you? John felt like he was near a waterfall: "His voice was like the noise of flooding water" (v. 15).

The sound of a river rushing through a forest is not a timid one. It is the backdrop against all other sounds. Even when nature sleeps, the river speaks. The same is true of Christ. In heaven his voice is always heard—a steady, soothing, commanding presence.

7. Read the following verses and fill in the blanks about, according to Scripture, what Jesus will say when Christians arrive in heaven?

Matthew 25:21 – You did _____. You are a _____ and loyal _____. _____ and share my _____ with _____.

Matthew 25:34 – _____, my Father has given you his _____. Receive the _____ God has _____ for you since the _____ was made.

What are we to do with such a picture? How are we to assimilate these images? Are we to combine them on a canvas and consider it a portrait of Jesus? I don't think so. I don't think the goal of this vision is to tell us what Jesus looks like, but rather who Jesus is.

8. Which of the following statements describing who Jesus is means the most to you? Check all that apply.

❏ The Perfect Priest
❏ The Only Pure One
❏ The Source of Strength
❏ The Sound of Love

OUR GREATEST HOPE

And what will happen when you see Jesus?

You will see unblemished purity and unbending strength. You will feel his unending presence and know his unbridled protection. And—all that he is, you will be, for you will be like Jesus. Wasn't that the promise of John? "We know that when Christ comes again, we will be like him, because we will see him as he really is" (1 John 3:2).

9. Match the following statements on the left with the corresponding truth on the right by drawing a line to connect them. Use the Bible verses below to help you answer.

Since you'll be pure as light in heaven where there is no sin . . .

Since you will be upheld by his hand. . .

Since you'll dwell with Jesus in heaven . . .

Since the work of the priest will have been finished . . .

you will never feel lonely again. (John 14:3)

you will never doubt again. (John 19:30)

you will never sin again. (1 John 1:7)

you will never stumble in weakness again. (Isaiah 41:10)

All that he is, you will be, for you will be like Jesus.

THE HEART OF THE MATTER

- **In our hearts, we long to see God.**
- **When we see Jesus we will be amazed.**
- **When we see Christ, we will see the perfect priest.**
- **When we see Jesus, we will see sinless perfection.**
- **When we see Jesus, we will see absolute strength.**
- **All that he is, you will be, for you will be like Jesus.**

Give some thought to your Bible memorization verse for this week. Have you got it down yet? Write it out here for a little review—it's Romans 8:25.

_____

_____

_____

The Heart of Jesus

Sadness. Emptiness. Loneliness. Shock. Depression. Regret. Longing. When someone that we love is suddenly gone, it hurts. We miss them. We miss the way things were. We want them back. When Mary and Martha were faced with the death of their brother, they reacted differently. Mary hid herself away, not wanting to leave her room. Martha went on the warpath, looking for someone to blame. Jesus confronted Martha. With a sigh, she admitted that she knew, really knew, that she would see her brother again someday. Clinging to that hope, she returned home to comfort her sister. Jesus offers that same hope to every Christian—we will see our brothers and sisters in Christ again someday, at the resurrection. Though we all grieve differently, we all can cling to the same hope.

DAY FIVE—CROSSING THE THRESHOLD

A MATCH MADE IN HEAVEN

The story of the prince and his peasant bride. A more intriguing romance never occurred. His attraction to her is baffling. He, the stately prince. She, the common peasant. He, peerless. She, plain. Not ugly, but she can be. And often is. She tends to be sullen and sour, even cranky. Not the kind of soul you'd want to live with.

But according to the prince, she is the soul he can't live without. So he proposed to her. On the dusty floor of her peasant's cottage, he knelt, took her hand, and asked her to be his bride. Even the angels inclined an ear to hear her whisper, "Yes."

"I'll return for you soon," he promised.

So don't worry, because I am with you. Don't be afraid, because I am your God. I will make you strong and will help you; I will support you with my right hand that saves you.

—Isaiah 41:10

Jesus has chosen us for his bride.

I promised to give you to Christ, as your only husband. I want to give you as his pure bride.

—2 Corinthians 11:2

We live by what we believe, not by what we can see.

—2 Corinthians 5:7

Sometimes we forget that Jesus is coming back for us.

But our homeland is in heaven, and we are waiting for our Savior, the Lord Jesus Christ, to come from heaven.

—Philippians 3:20

"I will be waiting," she pledged.

No one thought it odd that the prince would leave. He is, after all, the son of the king. Surely he has some kingdom work to do. What's odd is not his departure, but her behavior during his absence. She forgets she's engaged!

You'd think the wedding would be ever on her mind, but it isn't. You'd think the day would be on the tip of her tongue. But it's not. Some of her friends have never heard her speak of the event. Days pass—even weeks—and his return isn't mentioned. Why, there have been times, perish the thought, when she has been seen cavorting with the village men. Flirting. Whispering. In the bright of day. Dare we wonder about her activities in the dark of night?

Is she rebellious? Maybe. But mostly, she is just forgetful. She keeps forgetting that she is engaged. That's no excuse, you say. Why, his return should be her every thought! How could a peasant forget her prince? How could a bride forget her groom?

That's a good question. How could we? You see, the story of the prince and his peasant bride is not an ancient fable. It's not a tale about them, but rather a portrayal of us. Are we not the bride of Christ? Have we not been set apart "as a pure bride to one husband" (2 Cor. 11:2 NLT)? Did God not say to us, "I will make you my promised bride forever" (Hos. 2:19)?

1. One of the reasons we may be remiss is the fact we cannot see our bridegroom in the flesh or with our eyes. Read the following verses. Then match what you learn about how Scripture confirms our hope in the unseen.

   ____ Romans 1:17
   ____ 2 Corinthians 4:18
   ____ 2 Corinthians 5:7
   ____ Hebrews 11:1

   a. What we see is temporary at best.
   b. Faith means believing something is real even if we don't see it.
   c. We should live by trusting him.
   d. We live by what we believe, not what we see.

WE HAVE CAPTURED GOD'S HEART

I first witnessed the power of a marriage proposal in college. I shared a class with a girl who got engaged. I don't remember much about the class, except that the hour was early and the teacher was dull. (Doctors used to send insomniacs to his class for treatment.) I don't even remember the name of the girl. I do remember that she was shy and unsure of herself. She didn't stand out in the crowd and seemed to like it that way. No makeup. No dress-up. She was ordinary.

One day, however, that all began to change. Her hair changed. Her dress changed. Even her voice changed. She spoke. She spoke with confidence. What made the difference?

Simple. She was chosen. A young man she loved looked her squarely in the eye and said, "Come and spend forever with me." And she was changed. Empowered by his proposal. Validated by his love. His love for her convinced her that she was worth loving.

God's love can do the same for us. We, like the girl, feel so common. Insecurities stalk us. Self-doubt plagues us. But the marriage proposal of the prince can change all that.

2. Look up the following verses and write down what you learn about God's keen interest in us.

   Jeremiah 1:5 – "Before I made you in your mother's womb, I chose you. Before you were born, I set you apart for a special work. I appointed you as a prophet to the nations."

   _____

   _____

Psalm 33:12 – "Happy is the nation whose God is the Lord, the people he chose for his very own."

_____

_____

Ephesians 1:4 – "That is, in Christ, he chose us before the world was made so that we would be his holy people—people without blame before him."

_____

_____

Want a cure for insecurity? An elixir for self-doubt? Then meditate on these words intended for you:

My sister, my bride, you have thrilled my heart; you have thrilled my heart with a glance of your eyes, with one sparkle from your necklace. Your love is so sweet, my sister, my bride. Your love is better than wine, and your perfume smells better than any spice . . . My sister, my bride, you are like a garden locked up, like a walled-in spring, a closed-up fountain. —Song of Solomon 4:9–12

Does such language strike you as strange? Do you find it odd to think of God as an enthralled lover? Do you feel awkward thinking of Jesus as a suitor intoxicated on love? If so, how else do you explain his actions? Did logic put God in a manger? Did common sense nail him to a cross? Did Jesus come to earth guided by a natural law of science? No, he came as a prince with his eye on the maiden, ready to battle even the dragon itself if that's what it took to win her hand.

> *And this hope will never disappoint us, because God has poured out his love to fill our hearts. He gave us his love through the Holy Spirit, whom God has given to us.*
> —Romans 5:5

3. Scripture ties our hope and God's love for us together. Read Romans 5:5. Then fill in the blanks concerning what you learn about God's love for us.

And this _____ will never disappoint us because _____ has poured out his _____ to fill our _____. He gave us his _____ through the _____ _____ whom _____ has given to us.

JESUS' LOVE FOR US

And that is exactly what it took. It took a battle with the dragon of hell. He has "loved you with an everlasting love; [he has] drawn you with loving-kindness" (Jer. 31:3 NIV).

Have you ever noticed the way a groom looks at his bride during the wedding? I have. Perhaps it's my vantage point. As the minister of the wedding, I'm positioned next to the groom. Side by side we stand, he about to enter the marriage, I about to perform it. By the time we reach the altar, I've been with him for some time backstage as he tugged his collar and mopped his brow. His buddies reminded him that it's not too late to escape, and there's always a half-serious look in his eyes that he might. As the minister, I'm the one to give him the signal when it's our turn to step out of the wings up to the altar. He follows me into the chapel like a criminal walking to the gallows. But all that changes when she appears. And the look on his face is my favorite scene in the wedding.

Most miss it. Most miss it because they are looking at her. But when other eyes are on the bride, I sneak a peek at the groom. When he sees her, any thought of escape becomes a joke again. For it's written all over his face, "Who could bear to live without this bride?"

And such are precisely the feelings of Jesus. Look long enough into the eyes of our Savior and, there, too, you will see a bride. Dressed in fine linen. Clothed in pure grace. From the wreath in her hair to the clouds at her feet, she is royal; she is the princess. She is the bride. His bride. Walking toward him, she is not yet with him. But he sees her, he awaits her, he longs for her.

"Who could bear to live without her?" you hear him whisper.

> **Our hope in Jesus' return is tied to our understanding of his great love for us.**

> *Remember that I commanded you to be strong and brave. Don't be afraid, because the Lord your God will be with you everywhere you go.*
> —Joshua 1:9

A PROMISE DELIVERED

The Holy City, John says, is like "a bride beautifully dressed for her husband."

What is more beautiful than a bride?

. . .

Maybe it is the aura of whiteness that clings to her as a dew clings to a rose. Or perhaps it is the diamonds that glisten in her eyes. Or maybe it's the blush of love that pinks her cheeks or the bouquet of promises she carries.

A bride. A commitment robed in elegance. "I'll be with you forever." Tomorrow bringing hope today. Promised purity faithfully delivered.

When you read that our heavenly home is similar to a bride, tell me, doesn't it make you want to go home?
—*The Applause of Heaven*

The Lord makes me very happy; all that I am rejoices in my God. He has covered me with clothes of salvation and wrapped me with a coat of goodness, like a bridegroom dressed for his wedding, like a bride dressed in jewels.

—Isaiah 61:10

From Paul, a servant of God and an apostle of Jesus Christ. I was sent to help the faith of God's chosen people and to help them know the truth that shows people how to serve God. That faith and that knowledge come from the hope for life forever, which God promised to us before time began. And God cannot lie.

—Titus 1:1–2

After I go and prepare a place for you, I will come back and take you to be with me so that you may be where I am.
—John 14:3

4. We don't have to wonder how Jesus feels about us. We don't need to fear dashing our hopes against disappointment. His love is real, lasting, and unconditional—of that we can be sure. Which of the following statements are true, and which ones are false regarding Jesus' feelings toward us? Mark your answers True (T) or False (F). Use the Bible verses below to help you answer.

___ He cannot love us in the same way the Father loves him. (John 15:9)
___ He loved us so much he willingly sacrificed himself for us. (Ephesians 5:2)
___ We loved him before he loved us. (1 John 4:19)

HOPE FOR OUR HEARTS

You have captured the heart of God. "As a man rejoices over his new wife, so your God will rejoice over you" (Is. 62:5).

The challenge is to remember that. To meditate on it. To focus on it. To allow his love to change the way you look at you.

Do you ever feel unnoticed? New clothes and styles may help for a while. But if you want permanent change, learn to see yourself as God sees you.

Does your self-esteem ever sag? When it does, remember what you are worth. "You were bought, not with something that ruins like gold or silver, but with the precious blood of Christ, who was like a pure and perfect lamb" (1 Pet. 1:18–19).

5. Read Isaiah 61:10. Based on what you just read, which of the following describe how Jesus sees us? Check all that apply.

❏ Covered with clothes of salvation
❏ Wrapped with a coat of goodness
❏ Like a bridegroom dressed for his wedding
❏ Like a bride dressed in jewels

Are you concerned whether the love will last? You needn't be. "It is not our love for God, it is God's love for us in sending his Son to be the way to take away our sins" (1 John 4:10).

6. Read Titus 1:1–2 and answer the following.

How long will our life be with God in heaven? (v. 2)

_____
_____

When did God promise us this "hope for life forever"? (v. 2)

_____
_____

Ever feel like you have nothing?

Just look at the gifts he has given you: He has sent his angels to care for you, his Holy Spirit to dwell in you, his church to encourage you, and his word to guide you. You have privileges only a fiancée could have. Anytime you speak, he listens; make a request and he responds. He will never let you be tempted too much or stumble too far. Let a tear appear on your cheek, and he is there to wipe it. Let a love sonnet appear on your lips, and he is there to hear it. As much as you want to see him, he wants to see you more.

7. Jesus overwhelms us with hope. We near burst with possibility. Read Romans 15:13 and fill in the blanks concerning Paul's prayer that our hope would overflow.

I pray that the _____ who gives _____ will fill you with much _____ and _____ while you trust in him. Then your _____ will overflow by the _____ of the _____ Spirit.

THE HOPE OF THE NOT YET

He is building a house for you. And with every swing of the hammer and cut of the saw, he's dreaming of the day he carries you over the threshold. "There are many rooms in my Father's house; I would not tell you this if it were not true. I am going there to prepare a place for you. After I go and prepare a place for you, I will come back and take you to be with me so that you may be where I am" (John 14:2–3).

You have been chosen by Christ. You are released from your old life in your old house, and he has claimed you as his beloved. "Then where is he?" you might ask. "Why hasn't he come?"

8. Like generations before us, we have to hold onto hope—a firm belief Jesus will return. Based on Hebrews 10:37, which of the following are true concerning Jesus' return? Check all that apply.

   ❏ Scripture says it will be a very long time before he returns.
   ❏ Scripture assures us it will be a very short time before his return.
   ❏ The One who is coming will come.
   ❏ He will not be delayed.

There is only one answer. His bride is not ready. She is still being prepared.

Engaged people are obsessed with preparation. The right dress. The right weight. The right hair and the right tux. They want everything to be right. Why? So their fiancée will marry them? No. Just the opposite. They want to look their best because their fiancée is marrying them.

The same is true for us. We want to look our best for Christ. We want our hearts to be pure and our thoughts to be clean. We want our faces to shine with grace and our eyes to sparkle with love. We want to be prepared.

9. Read Titus 2:11–13 and summarize what this passage says about the way we should live while we wait for Christ's return.

   That is the way we should live, because God's grace that can save everyone has come. It teaches us not to live against God nor to do the evil things the world wants us to do. Instead, that grace teaches us to live now in a wise and right way and in a way that shows we serve God. We should live like that while we wait for our great hope and the coming of the glory of our great God and Savior Jesus Christ. —Titus 2:11–13

   _____

   _____

Why do we want to be prepared? In hopes that he will love us? No. Just the opposite. Because he already does.

You are spoken for. You are engaged, set apart, called out, a holy bride. Forbidden waters hold nothing for you. You have been chosen for his castle. Don't settle for one-night stands in the arms of a stranger.

Be obsessed with your wedding date. Guard against forgetfulness. Be intolerant of memory lapses. Write yourself notes. Memorize verses. Do whatever you need to do to remember. "Aim at what is in heaven . . . Think only about the things in heaven" (Col. 3:1–2). You are engaged to royalty, and your Prince is coming to take you home.

THE HEART OF THE MATTER

- ☙ **Jesus has chosen us for his bride.**
- ☙ **Sometimes we forget that Jesus is coming back for us.**
- ☙ **Our hope in Jesus' return is tied to our understanding of his great love for us.**
- ☙ **Jesus' bride is not yet ready. She is still being prepared.**

I pray that the God who gives hope will fill you with much joy and peace while you trust in him. Then your hope will overflow by the power of the Holy Spirit.
—Romans 15:13

Jesus' bride is not yet ready. She is still being prepared.

For in a very short time, "The One who is coming will come and will not be delayed."
—Hebrews 10:37

And this hope will never disappoint us, because God has poured out his love to fill our hearts. He gave us his love through the Holy Spirit, whom God has given to us.
—Romans 5:5

Your memory verse for *hope* is Romans 8:25. Write it out one more time here.

_____

_____

_____

The Heart of Jesus

How did Jesus manage it all? He faced hunger, discomfort, tiredness, and pain. He reached out to thousands of individuals. He traveled with faithless disciples. He composed parables to teach God's truths. He spent sleepless nights in prayer. He endured the testing and word traps of religious rulers. He was forced to turn away people who thought he was some kind of circus act. He was driven out of synagogues and towns. His own family questioned his sanity. You'd think he'd just throw up his hands in frustration and say "What next?" What kept Jesus focused? Hope. He had the hope of returning to his Father one day, his task complete. He cherished the hope of returning for his followers, and carrying them back to heaven with him. He knew that eternity was waiting just beyond their sight, and he wanted to enter it triumphantly. For the sake of what was ahead of him, for the hope of what he knew was coming, Jesus endured everything that life could throw at him.

FOR FURTHER READING

Selections throughout this lesson were taken from *When Christ Comes.*

I know Jesus, the One in whom I have believed. And I am sure he is able to protect what he has trusted me with until that day.
—2 Timothy 1:12b

[i] Unless, of course, you are alive when Christ returns, and then you will also get a new body. Paul says this in 1 Corinthians 15:51.
[ii] Peter Kreeft, *Heaven: The Heart's Deepest Longing* (San Francisco: Ignatius Press, 1980), 49.
[iii] Eugene Peterson, *Reversed Thunder* (San Francisco: HarperSanFrancisco, 1988), 36–37.